Praise for *I Have Lived Here Since the World Began*

"*I Have Lived Here Since the World Began* provides the general reader with a useful introduction to many aspects of Aboriginal Canada's history ... The many well-chosen illustrations complement the text superbly."—*The Globe and Mail*

"... engaging ... a familiar story retold firmly from the original inhabitants' point of view. Chock full of hundreds of photos, drawings and maps, many in vivid colour, this handsome book in the ideal primer."—*The Toronto Star*

"... a sympathetic but clear-headed account."—*Ottawa Citizen*

"Written in clear language and comprehensively illustrated, *I Have Lived Here Since the World Began* is an excellent introduction to the history of the relationship between Canada's Native people and the various European governments they encountered."—*The Record* (Kitchener)

"... intriguing and provocative ... This is not the kind of book destined to gather dust on the shelf ... written with commitment and passion."—*The Beaver*

"[Arthur Ray's] sympathies are clear, but they do not lead him into mere propaganda; the facts speak eloquently for themselves, and our own sympathies are thus more strongly engaged."—*The Hamilton Spectator*

"Readers will marvel at the narrative prowess and vast knowledge of Arthur Ray, who has performed an invaluable service in producing this all-encompassing history. Filled with sumptuous, rarely seen illustrations of historical figures, documents, artworks, lifestyles and more, *I Have Lived Here Since the World Began* is a passionate, powerful and important book."—*Book of the Month Club News*

"Written in an easy-flowing, conversational manner, it is both eye-opening and controversial."—*The StarPhoenix* (Saskatoon)

"In keeping with Ray's standing as one of the leading historians of Canada, it is a resolutely materialist history which examines the labouring lives of Native people in the modern era as comprehensively as the pre-colonial life." —*University of Toronto Quarterly*

An Illustrated History of Canada's Native People

I Have Lived Here Since the World Began

FOURTH EDITION

Arthur J. Ray

MCGILL-QUEEN'S UNIVERSITY PRESS   Montreal & Kingston • London • Chicago

© 2016 McGill-Queen's University Press

ISBN 978-0-7735-4800-8 (paper)
ISBN 978-0-7735-9958-1 (ePDF)

Legal deposit third quarter 2016
Bibliothèque nationale du Québec

First published as *I Have Lived Here Since the World Began* by Lester Publishing and Key Porter Books in 1996.

McGill-Queen's University Press acknowledges the support of the Canada Council for the Arts for our publishing program. We also acknowledge the financial support of the Government of Canada through the Canada Book Fund for our publishing activities.

Library and Archives Canada Cataloguing in Publication

Ray, Arthur J., 1941–
[I have lived here since the world began]
An illustrated history of Canada's Native people: I have lived here since the world began/
Arthur J. Ray. – Fourth edition.

Revision of: Ray, Arthur J., 1941–. I have lived here since the world began.
Includes bibliographical references and index.
Issued in print and electronic formats.
ISBN 978-0-7735-4800-8 (pbk). –
ISBN 978-0-7735-9958-1 (ePDF)

1. Native peoples – Canada – History. I. Title. II. Title: I have lived here since the world began

E78.C2R39 2016	971.004'97	C2016-901877-6
		C2016-901878-4

Cartography: Stuart Daniel, Starshell Maps
Design: Jean Lightfoot Peters
Electronic Formatting: Heidi Palfrey

Printed in Canada on acid-free paper

Page ii: A line etching of Marie Muges de Tetactu, wife of Tetactu (c. 1800)
Page iv: Innu Indians at Pointe-Bleue, Quebec (c. 1800)
Page viii: An Inuit wearing goggles made from driftwood, Padlei, Northwest Territories (1949)
Page xviii: A Siksika couple, Weasel Calf and his wife

For Dianne

They came to a wigwam. It was a long wigwam with a door at each end. The man inside the wigwam said, "I have lived here since the world began. I have my grandmother, she was here when the world was made. . . ."
—Mi'kmaq folktale (1800s)

CONTENTS

PREFACE TO THE FOURTH EDITION

There was an air of optimism in Aboriginal communities across the country when I began preparing this preface for the fourth edition of *An Illustrated History of Canada's Native People*. The federal Liberal government led by Prime Minister Justin Trudeau had just been elected and sworn in and a centrepiece of his campaign was the promise to fundamentally change the relationship between Canada's federal government and Aboriginal peoples. Symbolic of the future and the potential for change, Aboriginal children were invited to perform at his swearing-in ceremony. Theland Kicknosway, a twelve-year-old Cree hand drummer, led the procession of government officials and dignitaries into Rideau Hall in Ottawa, the official home of the governor general of Canada, where the ceremonies took place. Following Kicknosway's performance, Governor General David Johnston acknowledged—for the first time at a swearing-in ceremony, it is believed—that the event was taking place on traditional Algonquin territory. As the event unfolded, two young girls of Inuit descent, Samantha Metcalfe and Cailyn Degrandpre, performed Inuit throat songs. To conclude the event, the young Métis dance troupe Prairie Fire Jiggers—Hunter, Riley, and Jacob McKenzie—led the exiting procession from Rideau Hall. In these and other ways, the art, heritage, and futures of the three Aboriginal groups recognized in Canada's constitution received acknowledgment—the First Nations, the Inuit, and the Métis.

The new government included eight Aboriginal MPs, the highest number in Canada's history. Prime Minister Trudeau appointed two of these MPs to key cabinet positions. One was the Honourable Hunter Tootoo, an Inuk businessman and former elected member of the Nunavut legislature. He was appointed minister of Fisheries, Oceans, and the Canadian Coast Guard. The Honourable Jody Wilson-Raybould was the other cabinet appointee—she became the chief law officer of the Crown as minister of Justice and attorney general of Canada. Minister Wilson-Raybould is a member of the We Wai Kai Nation/Cape Mudge Band of British

Columbia. She has, among other accomplishments, advanced First Nations rights in British Columbia by serving in a variety of capacities with the British Columbia Treaty Commission, including as a commissioner, and as a regional chief of the British Columbia Assembly of First Nations.

Prime Minister Trudeau's government's commitment to reconciliation, rather than confrontation, with Canada's Indigenous peoples was reflected in his letters of mandate to the new cabinet ministers. The prime minister emphasized to all ministers that "no relationship is more important to me and to Canada than the one with Indigenous Peoples. It is time for a renewed, nation-to-nation relationship with Indigenous Peoples, based on recognition of rights, respect, co-operation, and partnership." The new government was particularly committed to addressing the dark legacies of residential schools and missing and murdered Aboriginal women, as well as addressing needs for better education in Aboriginal communities, cultural preservation, and improving the adversarial nature of relationships between the Crown and Indigenous peoples concerning Aboriginal and treaty rights.

Never before have Canada's Indigenous peoples received so much attention by an incoming federal government. Unquestionably this attention reflected the increasing effectiveness of Indigenous people and their leaders in bringing their demands for justice and reconciliation to centre stage through political action and ongoing litigation that has garnered attention and support from all quarters across Canada and beyond. The power of Indigenous Canadians' calls for justice and reconciliation is perhaps best manifested in relation to the residential school issue. I noted in the first edition of *An Illustrated History of Canada's Native People* (1996) that Aboriginal leaders understood at the beginning of the nineteenth century that their children needed new forms of education. Leaders framed their requests in terms expressing that they wanted their children to be able to participate in the emerging economic order. In the latter part of the nineteenth century and into the twentieth century Indigenous people obtained promises for schools in the numbered treaties with Canada. They were betrayed.

The residential school system put in place by the federal government and various denominations of Christian churches enforced an assimilation agenda intended to wipe out all vestiges of Aboriginal cultures by isolating students from their parents and punishing them for speaking Indigenous languages. Residential schools were authoritarian institutions that made Aboriginal children vulnerable to widespread physical, psychological, and sexual abuse. Although the last of the federally run residential schools finally closed in 1996, the system's dreadful, divisive legacy continues to show its effects in Aboriginal communities' disproportionately higher rates of domestic abuse and violence against women and children, substance abuse, suicide rates, incarceration, and a disproportionate number of broken families. These problems created the erroneous impression that most First Nations families were dysfunctional and led to the practice of child welfare agencies placing large numbers of Aboriginal children from broken homes in the foster homes of non-Aboriginal families. This continued to cut off Aboriginal children from their cultural and kinship roots, a practice that had begun with residential schools.

In earlier editions, I noted that Indigenous peoples' insistence that the terrible legacy of residential schools be addressed led to the establishment of financial compensation for former students in 2006, the Truth and Reconciliation Commission of Canada in 2007, and apologies for residential school abuses by then Prime Minister Stephen Harper in 2008. On 15 December 2015, the TRC issued its seven-volume final report, six months after the release of the report's executive summary and calls to action. Before the final report's release, Justin Trudeau had committed his government, if elected, to implementing all of the TRC's recommendations. The commission's ninety-four calls to action cover a number of broad issues. These include: protecting the welfare of Indigenous children; promoting Aboriginal languages and culture; developing improved and culturally sensitive health care on and off reserve; reforming the justice system to address the over-representation of Aboriginal people in custody; undertaking reforms to legal education so that law graduates are familiar with the history of Aboriginal people, their traditional laws, and their constitutional, Aboriginal, and treaty rights; preparing a national action plan for reconciliation that is guided by the United Nations Declaration on the Rights of Indigenous Peoples (2007), which the Government of Canada refused to sign until November 2010; re-establishing the principle of nation-to-nation relations between Aboriginal people and the Crown; and encouraging the teaching of residential school history. The comprehensive and complex set of calls to action present a tall order for the newly elected Liberal government.

The success of Aboriginal peoples in their Aboriginal rights and title cases since the 1980s certainly has given federal and provincial governments the incentive and legal obligation to shift direction away from adversarial relationships to ones that seek reconciliation. A critical Supreme Court of Canada decision since the last edition of *An Illustrated History of Canada's Native People* (2011) was *Tsilhqot'in v. British Columbia* (2014). A historic land-title case, *Tsilhqot'in* asserts that it is the duty of governments to consult meaningfully whenever Aboriginal title is involved.

In previous rulings, beginning with *Taku River Tlingit First Nation v. British Columbia* (2004) and *Haida Nation v. British Columbia (Minister of Forests)* (2004), the Supreme Court established this duty as a procedural right, which meant that the Crown merely had to inform relevant First Nations of their intentions. The *Tsilhqot'in* ruling transformed this procedure into a substantive right that required the Crown to engage with First Nations who will be effected by a given development plan. This judgment also put to rest the long-held position of the Crown that native title is limited to scattered sites of intensive use. In declaring over 1,900 km² of the claim area for the Tsilhqot'in, the Supreme Court held that "Aboriginal title is not confined to specific sites of settlement but extends to tracts of land that were regularly used for hunting, fishing or otherwise exploiting resources and over which the group exercised effective control at the time of assertion of European sovereignty." In this way, the *Tsilhqot'in* decision acknowledged the spatial reality of the land-use practices of traditional Aboriginal peoples' economies, which were oriented to harvesting fish and wildlife resources.

In a second landmark judgment, the Métis, in *Manitoba Metis Federation Inc. v. Canada (Attorney General)* (2013), successfully demonstrated the Canadian government's failure to implement properly sections 31 and 35 of the Manitoba Act of 1870, which is defined by the Constitution Act (1982) as forming part of the Constitution of Canada. These sections of the Manitoba Act promised the allotment of 1.4 million acres of land to Métis children and the recognition of existing landholdings. Beginning in 1981, the Manitoba Métis Federation's case was unsuccessful in its attempts to convince the provincial courts of Manitoba, which held that these sections of the Manitoba Act neither promised fiduciary obligations on the part of the Crown toward the Métis, nor guaranteed an obligation that the Crown must act honourably towards Aboriginal people. Additionally, the Manitoba courts ruled that the claim was barred by the "doctrine of laches," which is the principle that too much time had elapsed from the time when the alleged injustice took place to the time when the MMF filed its claim. But the Supreme Court of Canada disagreed with the lower courts and ruled in favour of the MMF appeal. The court observed that the honour-of-the-Crown principle's ultimate purpose is to facilitate reconciliation between pre-existing Aboriginal societies and the assertion of Canadian sovereignty. The primary objective of the Manitoba Act was to reconcile the rights of the Manitoba Métis community with the sovereignty of the Crown and thereby facilitate the creation of the Province of Manitoba. Through its failure to act with due diligence with respect to sections 31 and 35 of the Manitoba Act, the federal government had not upheld the honour of the

Crown, and therefore, reconciliation with the Manitoba Métis was incomplete. The Supreme Court's ruling shows that when the honour of the Crown is engaged in this way and concerns the Constitution of Canada, the passage of time cannot be invoked to deny a claim.

After a sixteen-year legal battle, the Métis and non-status Indians achieved a major victory in *Harry Daniels v. Canada* (2016) when the Supreme Court of Canada determined that the use of the word "Indian" in section 91(24) of the Constitution Act of 1867 had been intended to include Métis and non-status Indians. The ruling ends a federal-provincial jurisdictional limbo that prevented some 600,000 Aboriginal Canadians from addressing deep-seated economic, political, and social issues, because neither level of government would assume responsibility. Métis National Council president Clément Chartier hailed the decision, saying that it removed "a major jurisdictional obstacle on the road to Métis Nation self-determination" and paved the way for "a true and lasting reconciliation between the Métis Nation and the government of Canada, including the right to a land base and self-government within the constitutional framework of Canada."

For the First Nations, Inuit, and Métis of Canada, justice and reconciliation with the Government of Canada remain unfinished projects, but the signs are hopeful. Canada seems poised to turn away from its record of tough confrontation in the legal and political arenas that have dominated relations between Indigenous peoples and the Crown for far too long, and turn toward a commitment to deploy human and financial resources toward reconciliation.

ADDITIONAL SOURCES

Chartier, Clément, personal communication with the author, 14 April 2016.

Daniels v. Canada (Indian Affairs and Northern Development), 2016 SCC 12.

Fournier, Suzanne, and Ernie Crey. *Stolen from Our Embrace: The Abduction of First Nations Children and the Restoration of Aboriginal Communities.* Madeira Park· Douglas and McIntyre Publishers, 1998.

Manitoba Metis Federation Inc. v. Canada (Attorney General), 2013 SCC 14.

Truth and Reconciliation Commission of Canada. *Canada's Residential Schools: The Final Report of the Truth and Reconciliation Commission of Canada*, 7 vols. Montreal: McGill-Queen's University Press, 2015.

Tsilhqot'in Nation v. British Columbia (Minister of Forests), 2014 SCC 44.

The Tsilhqot'in chiefs singing a drum song in celebration immediately after the *Tsilhqot'in v. British Columbia* (2014) decision. Since long before the gold rushes of the nineteenth century, the Tsilhqot'in of British Columbia have asserted their Aboriginal title and struggled to protect their traditional territory. The court's judgment put to rest the often-argued position of the Crown that Native title is limited to sites of intensive use. It also held that the duty to consult First Nations about developments in their territories is a substantive right where consent may be required. *Left to right*: Tl'esqox Chief Francis Laceese, Tsi Deldel Chief Percy Guichon, Tl'etinqox Chief Joe Alphonse (tribal chairman, Tsilhqot'in National Government), Xeni Gwet'in Chief Roger William (vice-chair, Tsilhqot'in National Government), and Yunesit'in Chief Russell Myers Ross. (Courtesy of the Tsilhqot'in National Government)

Métis political leaders celebrating the *Manitoba Metis Federation Inc. v. Canada (Attorney General)* (2013) decision at the gravesite of Louis Riel in St Boniface, Manitoba, the day after it was announced on 8 March 2013. The decision held that the federal government failed to act with due diligence in implementing provisions of the Manitoba Act (1870), guaranteed the Métis of Manitoba title to the lands they farmed, and allocated 1.4 million acres (5,700 km^2) of land to their children. The provisional government of Louis Riel had shaped the Manitoba Act through negotiations with the federal government. *Left to right*: Andrew Carrier, Manitoba Metis Federation (MMF) board member; John Morrisseau, former MMF president (he filed the claim in 1981); Denise Thomas, MMF board member; David Chartrand, MMF president; Clem Chartier, Métis Nation of Canada (MNC) president; Audrey Poitras, Métis Nation of Alberta President. (Photograph by Ke Ning, executive assistant, MNC)

PREFACE TO THE THIRD EDITION

I prepared the second edition of *I Have Lived Here Since the World Began* (2005) in the immediate aftermath of the landmark *Regina v. Powley* decision, which was the first Métis rights case to reach the Supreme Court of Canada. Although I had been involved at the trial level as an expert witness on behalf of the defendants, Steve and Rodney Powley, it was not yet clear to me in 2004 what the long-term impact of *Powley* would be for Canadian Aboriginal rights law generally and for the Métis in particular. Likewise, its implication for Native history was uncertain. In 2009, as we prepare the third edition, now titled *An Illustrated History of Canada's Native People*, it is clear that one immediate and continuing effect has been a flood of rights claims by communities of mixed Aboriginal and European ancestry, making Métis rights litigation one of the most active and innovative areas of Aboriginal law in Canada since 2002. Claimants are from the vast and loosely defined domain of the historic Métis Nation, which reached from the upper Great Lakes, across the Prairies, to the Mackenzie River Valley and the Rocky Mountains. Claimants also are from lands beyond that vast territory that are not normally associated with the historic Métis. Jean Teillet, who was lead council for the Powley defendants, has continued to play a leading role in this ongoing litigation. She also is a role model and mentor to Aboriginal and non-Aboriginal people who are involved in the field of Canadian Aboriginal rights.

While pushing the boundaries of Aboriginal law, *Powley* also has stimulated a massive research effort that is altering our understanding of Native history. This is because the ruling raised fundamental historical and contemporary questions that arise from coast to coast: who is Métis in the eyes of Canadian law? Where and how did Métis communities emerge? What were their varied cultural and economic characteristics? What were the spatial parameters of these communities? How did they interact with their First Nations relatives and neighbours? Have historic Métis communities survived to the present day? What implications does Métis rights litigation have for our understanding of First Nations history in the post-contact era?

XX   An Illustrated History of Canada's Native People

These questions have led the Federal and provincial governments, the Métis Nation of Canada and provincial Métis associations, especially the Manitoba Métis Federation and the Métis Nation of Alberta, to invest heavily in historical research. The result is that Métis history has become one of the most active areas of research in Canadian history. It has been the focus of my research since 2002, partly because of my ongoing involvement in Métis rights litigation. My engagement also arises from my participation in a multidisciplinary national historical research project initiated by the Métis Nation of Canada, which is directed by Professor Nicole St. Onge of Ottawa University and funded by the Department of Indian and Northern Affairs' Office of the Federal Interlocutor for Métis. These various developments have led me to add a closing chapter to *An Illustrated History of Canada's Native People* that focuses on the Métis. In this edition I have also addressed other important developments, such as the comprehensive agreement between the federal government and Aboriginal groups to address the sorry legacy of residential schools, which included the creation of the Truth and Reconciliation Commission and an apology by Prime Minister Stephen Harper, and new developments in the area of Aboriginal law.

I would also like to take this opportunity to again say a special thanks to my spouse, Dr. Dianne Newell, Director of the Peter Wall Institute, for her constant support, encouragement, critical advice and for sharing with me her path-breaking research on First Nations and the west-coast fisheries.

Preface to the Second Edition

I decided to write this book for a general readership in the midst of a lengthy cross-examination by attorneys representing the governments of Canada and British Columbia. The lawyers were challenging my testimony as an expert witness on behalf of the Gitxsan and Wet'suwet'en Tribal Council in *Delgamuukw v. Her Majesty the Queen*, the trial of their comprehensive claim for land and joint sovereignty of their traditional territory. My cross-examiners wanted to know why my interpretation of the early-post-contact economic history of Gitxsan and Wet'suwet'en of central British Columbia was so different from the one I had presented in my book *Indians in the Fur Trade* (1974), which focused on the Assiniboine, Cree, and Ojibwa people of the Canadian central Subarctic and Prairie West.

These concerns were understandable. Most of the literature dealing with Aboriginal people is oriented toward the study of particular groups or regions in specific eras. Little comparative work in Native history has been published in Canada for the general reader. None of it has emphasized the economic dimension that history, which is of central importance to First Nations' struggles for rights in the political and legal arenas. Consequently, the highly varied nature of the historical experiences of Canada's Aboriginal people is known only to a handful of ethnohistorical specialists. This meant that, in court, I had to devote a considerable portion of my testimony to explaining why the dissimilar physical and cultural environments of these regions led to the rise of very different fur-trading economies.

The extensive contemporary media coverage devoted to the continuing struggle by Native people for recognition of their Aboriginal rights, settlement of their outstanding land claims, and self-government reflects the public interest in these issues. Despite this, there is little understanding of the historical roots of these struggles, or of the contributions Aboriginal people have made to the development of Canada and their own distinct societies.

A NOTE ON TERMINOLOGY

In the first edition (1996) I noted that many First Nations today prefer to be identified by names they have traditionally used to describe themselves in place of the terms Europeans and Canadians applied to them. The problem was that for many groups the names and/or their spellings had not been standardized. Since then many of the "new" names have gained wide acceptance and are now commonly recognized. Accordingly, in this edition, I have adopted them. A few names and terms remain problematic, however. For example, the speakers of five dialects of the central Algonquian language known as Ojibwa or Anishnabe (also Anishinabe) have not adopted a single name for themselves or their language. For this reason, I have continued to use the general term Ojibwa for the following groups in the Great Lakes region, northwestern Ontario, and the Prairies: Algonquins, Anishinabek, Chippewas, Mississauga, and Ojibwa (also Ojibway).

In this edition I have again used standard anthropological terminology to describe cultural practices that were common to more then one group in a region, even though traditionally these terms may not have been used by any or all of the groups concerned. The most notable examples are "potlatch," which is a key ceremony to Pacific Coast First Nations, and the "sun" or "thirst" dance, which was central to the ceremonial life of the buffalo-hunting people and their descendants.

The following names, which First Nations use to identify themselves, have come into common usage and replaced those used in the traditional ethnographic literature and historical record:

Chiniki (Stoney)

Deh Cho (Decho)

Dene (Chipewyan)

Dunne-za (Beaver)

Gitxsan (Gitksan)

Innu (Montagnais and Naskapi)

Kainaiwa (Blood)

Kwakwaka'wakw (Kwakiutl)

Lakota (Dakota)

Mi'kmaq (Micmac)

Nisga'a (Nishga)

Nuu chah nulth (Nootka)

Nuxalk (Bella Coola)

Piikani (Piegan)

Sahtu (Sah'tu)

Siksika (Blackfoot)

Siksika Nation (Blackfoot Nation); it
    included the Tsuu T'ina and Piikani.

Stó:lö (Stalo)

Tlicho (Dogrib)

Tsek'ehne (Sekani)

Tsuu T'ina (Sarcee)

INTRODUCTION

Until the early 1970s, Canada's Aboriginal people were largely ignored by historians, who treated them as part of the background in their heroic stories about the great Euro-Canadian men who had built the country. This meant that Native history remained the domain of anthropology and archaeology. Before the Second World War, these scholars were primarily interested in the cultures of Aboriginal people as vestiges of earlier stages of cultural evolution that were about to be obliterated by the advance of Western civilization. These "salvage ethnologists" travelled to remote areas to study the fragments of Native culture that they deemed to be relics from pre-contact times. An erroneous but all too common underlying notion of this work was that to retreat "into the bush" away from major urban centres was equivalent to stepping back in time. These ethnologists focused their attention on material culture, religious beliefs, and social customs. The contemporary economic life of Native people was of little interest, so their ongoing participation in the modern Canadian economy was never written.

The highly influential late-nineteenth-century work of Franz Boas, one of the founders of American anthropology, is an example. Boas's extensive fieldwork among the Kwakwaka'wakw of the central coast of British Columbia scarcely mentions their intensive involvement in commercial fishing or industrial fish-canning plants. This early "salvage rescarch," which provided the foundation for the anthropology of Canadian Aboriginal people, created the general impression that these people were inherently conservative, able only to cling to old practices or assimilate into the mainstream of a society that others had created. Anthropologists subsequently helped to perpetuate that image by continuing to emphasize continuity and the recording of traditional practices in their studies of Native societies.

In 1932 the New Zealand–born and Oxford-trained anthropologist Diamond Jenness published *The Indians of Canada*, which remained the standard general historical reference until the late 1980s. Indeed, it is still in print and prominently displayed in the bookstores of Canadian museums of anthropology. Reflecting his time and the sources that were available to him—mostly archaeological and ethnographic studies—Jenness emphasized pre-contact and early contact periods; he cast Native people in passive and dependant roles vis-à-vis the Europeans; he downplayed the contributions they made to the development of Canada (apart from cultural objects, most notably the canoe); and he was pessimistic about their future, predicting their demise as a "race" within a generation. One of his underlying concerns was to explain why Canadian Aboriginal people had remained so "backward" compared to Europe.

After the Second World War a much more dynamic historical image of Native people began to emerge. A number of developments explain this shift, the most notable being Aboriginal people's struggle for their rights. In 1946 the United States congress established the Indian Claims Commission (ICC) to create a forum where Native people could air their historical grievances against the federal government. The commission operated for over thirty years, and the research undertaken in response to cases Indians brought before it was a major stimulus for the development of a new interdisciplinary and multi-source approach to the study of Aboriginal/non-Native relations in the United States and Canada known as ethnohistory. For the first time, the interests of Native communities drove research agendas in claims cases, and researchers' conclusions often challenged the conventional wisdom of anthropologists and historians. In Canada, claims research continues to have this destabilizing impact.

Beyond the classroom and the courtroom, Native scholars, most notably the late Métis historian and activist Howard Adams, raised a host of historical questions through film, in the media, and in a range of publications. One of the most memorable of these was the highly provocative film *The Other Side of the Ledger* (1972), which was co-sponsored by the National Indian Brotherhood and the National Film Board. Narrated by the Brotherhood's president, George Manuel, and featuring Adams, the film was a Native reply to the tricentennial celebration of the founding of the Hudson's Bay Company in 1670. It was a direct attack on heroic histories of Canada that emphasized non-Aboriginal perspectives. Challenges of this sort, and the highly effective political activism of a succession of Native leaders, such as Manuel, Frank Calder, Harold Cardinal, Georges Eramus, and more recently Ovide Mercredi, Ethel Blondin-Andrew, Mathew Coon Come, and Phil Fontaine, redefined the public perception of Native people as founding First Nations. Collectively they played major roles in moving Native people out of the backdrop of Canadian history and on to centre stage.

The St Lawrence River valley and southern Ontario has been the focus of intensive archaeological research since the late nineteenth century. In the early 1970s archaeologists and historical geographers drew on this work and documentary sources—particularly missionary records—to develop richly detailed ethnohistories of the Huron and their neighbours. Subsequently, they expanded on this work and explored the contributions various Aboriginal groups made to the development of New France. These new works also stressed the dynamic nature of Aboriginal people and the distinctiveness of their societies. These ideas influenced historians, and in the latter half of the 1970s and the early 1980s they began to look at various dimensions of Native/non-Native relations in the older settlements of northeastern North America. New topics included the ideological and religious aspects of Native people's interaction with French missionaries and settlers, Mi'kmaq relations with the colonial societies of Atlantic Canada, and the extensive Aboriginal participation in European and American colonial wars.

The fur trade of the Canadian North was one aspect of Native economic history that captured the interest of Canadian scholars in the early twentieth century. In his 1930 classic, *The Fur Trade in Canada*, the internationally renowned Canadian political economist Harold Innis looked at the roles of Aboriginal people in the fur industry; he pondered their motivations for taking part; and he considered the impact that the fur trade had on their cultures. Innis's pioneering work raised a number of questions that many of us are still attempting to answer. How different were Aboriginal people from Europeans in their economic motivations and practices? How quickly did various Aboriginal groups become economically interdependent with Europeans? How did specific Native groups carry the fur trade across Canada? And in what ways did the industry affect their location, relations with neighbouring groups, and cultural practices?

For most areas of northern and western Canada, it was not possible to address these questions in detail until the late 1960s, when the Hudson's Bay company opened its vast London-based archives to the public. Scholars, myself included, quickly took advantage of this opportunity, especially after the archives were moved to Winnipeg, Manitoba, in 1970, as a part of the province's centennial celebrations. Beginning in 1974 regional histories appeared that stressed all aspects of Aboriginal participation in the fur trade. Most of this new work elaborated the roles Native men played in the business, but by the late 1970s scholars wanted to know more about the involvement of Native women and the development of a multicultural and multiracial fur-trade society.

Prior to the 1980s, scholars had emphasized the pre-Confederation era.

Thereafter, they also included the post-Confederation period and considered new questions, most notably, the role the Canadian government played in all aspects of Aboriginal affairs. This generated a belated interest in the political history of Native people, which in turn shone light on various aspects of Native economic life during the late nineteenth and twentieth centuries, particularly Native engagement in the modern fur trade, agriculture in the prairie West, and resource industries in British Columbia, especially in the industrial salmon fishery. The Supreme Court of Canada's 1973 Calder decision made it clear for the first time that Native history was relevant to Aboriginal and treaty rights litigation. The decision also forced the Canadian government to establish an Aboriginal claims process and led Canadian First Nations to sponsor a massive amount of new research in support of their submissions and litigation. Likewise, Inuit and Métis claims have fostered a reconsideration of all aspects of their respective histories. In the 1990s, a growing number of scholarly publications began to appear that were based on claims research.

In recent years, Native voices have contributed to the recording of Canadian history. Aboriginal people have cultures in which the elders traditionally have had the primary responsibility for orally passing on histories and traditions to succeeding generations. The ravages of European diseases—which often had their most devastating impact on the elderly—government and missionary assimilation programs, and the near obliteration of a number of Native languages have made it extremely difficult for many First Nations to continue the custom. Capturing Aboriginal impressions of the early contact experience in central and eastern Canada is especially problematic. Europeans arrived in these regions thirteen to sixteen generations (four hundred to five hundred years) ago. This means that historians have relied heavily on archaeology and the account of European explorers, missionaries, traders, and government officials to generate images of Aboriginal societies at the time of initial contact. These are uncertain pictures, however, because the voices of Native people are filtered through the documentary records, overwhelmingly written by European men, mostly about Native men. Recent oral history research among the Mi'kmaq shows us that Aboriginal perspectives can still be obtained even from among the first groups to greet the European newcomers. Present-day historians register Native viewpoints in a variety of ways: orally in the field, by means of various types of archival records, and using a rapidly increasing number of published autobiographies, biographies, life histories, and memoirs of Native men and women. Very recently First Nations, such as the Cowichan and

Stó:lö of British Columbia, have begun to employ all of these lines of evidence to produce histories of their own.

The blossoming of the field of history by and about Native people over the past three decades has brought a new understanding that counters early-twentieth-century precepts. Yet, in keeping with the anthropological tradition, these new general histories continue to stress ideological, religious, social, and political themes; the economic history of Aboriginal people is still essentially overlooked outside of the courtroom. This is the history I present.

CHAPTER 1

THE LAND AS HISTORY BOOK

A long time ago all the world was water. Crow saw that Sea Lion owned the only island in the world. The rest was water. Sea Lion is the only one with land. The whole place was ocean.

Crow is resting on a piece of log. He's tired. He sees Sea Lion with that little island just for himself. He wants land too.

So he stole that Sea Lion's kid.

"Give me back that kid," said Sea Lion.

"Give me some beach, some sand," says Crow. So Sea Lion gave him sand. You know how sand in water floats? Crow threw that sand around the ocean.

"Be world!" he tells it. And it became the world.

—Origin myth told by Angela Sidney, of Tagish and Tlingit ancestry

Many of Canada's Indigenous people define themselves in terms of the homelands that sustained their ancestors. These are the places where their spiritual roots lie. Drawing from their natural surroundings, Native groups have developed powerful metaphors, symbols, and narrative traditions to express their religious and philosophical views. As the Tlingit-Tagish say, these narratives are true stories about how the land came to be. Some groups named the features of the landscape to recall important events in their individual and collective lives. In effect, the land was their history book.

CANADA'S FIRST EXPLORERS AND SETTLERS

According to many of the creation narratives, the ancestors of Canada's Native people appeared in the country at a time when the land was covered in water, and animals were the only living creatures. Painstakingly collected archaeological evidence in fact suggests that the first inhabitants emigrated from Eurasia by crossing the Bering Land Bridge connecting Siberia and Alaska sometime between forty thousand and twelve thousand years ago, a time when much of the land was blanketed in massive continental glaciers and vast meltwater lakes. The Ice Age migrants moved steadily southward, passing through an ice-free corridor lying between the massive northeastern Laurentide Ice Sheet, which buried two-thirds of the country, and the cordilleran glaciers that covered most of the coast ranges and large sections of the Rocky Mountains.

Today, the fluted stone points of their lances provide the most striking evidence for the presence of the hardy Ice Age hunters. Archaeologists have unearthed such artifacts in the prairies, in southern Ontario, and in the Maritimes. Unfortunately, we do not know much about these so-called fluted-point people who lived ten to twelve thousand years ago because few traces of them survive.

Carvings and paintings on stone known as petroglyphs are an ancient and widespread Native art-form. These petroglyphs are from Sproat Lake, Vancouver Island.

The organic remains that have been scientifically recovered from their ancient camping and hunting sites tell us that these folk, the country's original explorers and pioneers, were large-game hunters of mammoth, mastodon, bison, and caribou. Probably they lived in small hunting groups. Their lance points were made from carefully selected quartz, quartzite, and chert, a dark mineral resembling flint. The way they highlighted any banding or other natural patterns in the rock is a testament both to their skills as lithic toolmakers and to their aesthetic sense.

Between ten thousand and five thousand years ago, the climate moderated, causing the continental and cordilleran

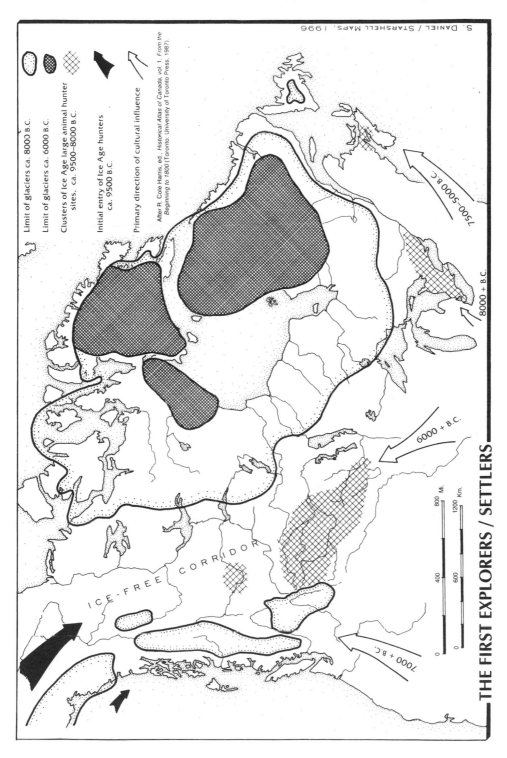

THE FIRST EXPLORERS / SETTLERS

Limit of glaciers ca. 8000 B.C.

Limit of glaciers ca. 6000 B.C.

Clusters of Ice Age large animal hunter sites, ca. 9500–8000 B.C.

Initial entry of Ice Age hunters ca. 9500 B.C.

Primary direction of cultural influence

After R. Cole Harris, ed., *Historical Atlas of Canada*, vol. 1, *From the Beginning to 1800* (Toronto: University of Toronto Press, 1987).

S. DANIEL / STARSHELL MAPS, 1996

ICE-FREE CORRIDOR

7500–5000 B.C.

8000 + B.C.

6000 + B.C.

7000 + B.C.

800 Mi.

400

0

1200 Km.

600

0

A romanticized depiction of Iroquoian women pounding corn from François du Creux's Historiae Canadensis, *1664. The corn that women planted, harvested, and stored was a mainstay of the diet and figured prominently in inter-nation exchange.*

glaciers to melt away. It was not until 1500 B.C. that the environment became very similar to that of present-day Canada. While these changes were taking place, the forebears of Canada's First Nations adjusted to their altered surroundings and, according to oral tradition and archaeological evidence, moved into lands formerly blanketed by ice or covered by glacial lakes.

Early inhabitants also responded to external cultural influences. Among the more revolutionary of the imported technologies were pottery making, the use of the bow and arrow, and horticulture. Shortly after 1000 B.C., for instance, groups living in the forested country between the middle Churchill River, in what is now Manitoba, and the St Maurice River, of present-day Quebec, learned to make pottery from groups living farther south. At approximately the same time, the local hunters began using bows and arrows, although it is unclear where this technological advance originated. The proto-Iroquoian-speaking people living in the lower Great Lakes area made one of the most revolutionary changes fifteen hundred years later when they took up corn cultivation. Corn, one of the many Native North American gifts to human civilization, became domesticated in Mexico about five thousand years ago, and the practice of cultivating it and other crops slowly spread northward from this region. Well before the arrival of Europeans, the Iroquoians were skilled horticulturists.

Far to the north, meanwhile, two comparatively late waves of migration from Eurasia led to the first peopling of the central and eastern Arctic. Before 4000 B.C., lingering ice sheets had barred settlement in this area. The initial occupation was about 2000 B.C. when paleo-Eskimo people from Alaska began pushing eastward. Their descendants reached coastal Newfoundland some fifteen hundred years later, but for unknown reasons they abandoned the island before A.D. 900. By this time another group, whom archaeologists call the "Thule people," were already migrating eastward from Alaska, displacing their predecessors along the way. On the eve of contact, their descendants, the Inuit, had reached eastern Labrador near the Strait of Belle Isle.

By then Canada's Native people spoke numerous languages and countless dialects that derived from eleven major language families. Some of these languages, most notably Algonquian, Athapaskan, and Inuktituk, were spoken over immense areas. Others, particularly those of the Pacific slope, were spoken by large numbers of people who lived in densely populated smaller territories. Linguistic divisions did not create insurmountable communication barriers: European accounts of early contact relate that most of the groups living near these boundaries had members who were bilingual as a consequence of centuries-old trading, warring, and diplomatic traditions. This ten-to-twelve-thousand-year history of settlement and cultural development in Native Canada meant that Europeans encountered very diverse and well-rooted peoples when they arrived on the scene.

IROQUOIAN FARMERS

Although all Native groups engaged in food collecting and hunting, and most of them also fished, these activities varied in importance from region to region according to cultural traditions, local environmental circumstances, and seasonal cycles. The ancestors of the Iroquoian-speakers of the eastern Great Lakes– St Lawrence valley developed a diverse economy featuring hunting, fishing, horticulture, and the collection of berries and a variety of other wild-plant foods. By the end of the fifteenth century, their descendants—the Stadaconans, Hochelagans, Huron, Petun, and Neutral—obtained most of their food from their fields, which were managed by the women. Using fire-hardened dibble sticks, hoes made of wood and deer hipbones, and brush rakes, they planted corn, beans, squash, sunflowers, and tobacco. The men assisted, mostly at the beginning of the field-rotation cycle, by clearing the fields with their stone axes. Because it was too troublesome to fell large trees with these tools, the men killed them by stripping away the bark around their bases. They also chopped down the underbrush, piled it on the field, and burned it. The ashes provided much-needed potash fertilizer.

Once a field was cleared, the women could cultivate it for about a decade before declining nutrient levels in the soil forced them to prepare new plots. After sowing the seeds they had gleaned from the previous year's harvest, the women weeded during the growing season and, helped by their children, kept a watchful eye on the fields to ward off birds and other pests. At harvest time, everyone helped. This slash-and-burn agriculture may seem primitive by modern standards, or even by those of fifteenth-century Europe, but it was highly productive nonetheless. In most years the women produced substantial surpluses, which they dried and stored in their houses or in storage pits. The produce of their labour provided from 50 to 75 per cent of the caloric intake of their families.

If the cultivated fields were largely the domain of women, the forests, lakes, and rivers were to a great extent the domain of men. Among the Huron, for instance, the men ventured to Lake Couchiching at the northern end of Lake Simcoe for sturgeon in the spring. In the early autumn and late winter, they mounted hunting expeditions to the south of their homeland for white-tailed deer, which they drove into brush enclosures. Huron hunting parties were thus able to kill large numbers of herd animals with ease. Late autumn was another fishing season, when whole families travelled to spawning sites on Georgian Bay, where they caught and processed whitefish and lake trout.

Other Iroquoian groups developed similar seasonal cycles. The Stadaconans, for example, fished and hunted for part of the year in the Gulf of St Lawrence. After planting their fields in the spring, entire villages often set out on lengthy canoe voyages as far away as the Gaspé to hunt marine mammals and catch mackerel and eel. They returned home in time to harvest their fields.

SUBARCTIC NOMADS

Many Canadians who live along the southern border of the country think of the Subarctic boreal forest as a harsh and grudging land. Native residents have a

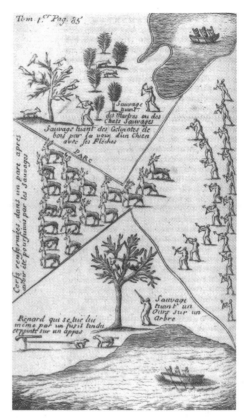

This stylized drawing of an Iroquoian communal deer hunt appeared in Baron de Lahontan's New Voyages to North America, *1703. Early European observers featured large-game hunting, a predominantly male activity, in their illustrations, even though the women's fields produced most of the food.*

different view. Job Bearskin of Chisasibi (Fort George), Quebec, recently said, "This whole place is like a garden, because many things grow here, and the Indians are one of the things that grow here." He added, "The animals were given to the Indians so they could feed their children and old people, and everyone has always shared the food from this garden."

Various groups of Algonquian-speakers occupied the central and eastern portions of the vast evergreen forest that stretches from interior Labrador into the Yukon. These people and their northwestern neighbours, the Athapaskan-speakers, were skilful nomadic hunters, fishers, and gatherers. Moose and woodland caribou

In most areas of Canada, Aboriginal people used a wide variety of ingenious animal traps and snares. This deadfall trap is baited with a fish.

were the most prized large-game animals living in the boreal forest. Small hunting parties stalked these creatures and killed them at close range with bows and arrows and lances. A moose provided up to 500 pounds of dressed meat, a caribou 100 to 150 pounds. Their hides were used to make clothing, footwear, and summer-lodge covers.

Herds of barren-ground caribou roamed along the forest-tundra boundary. During the winter, they browsed in the sheltering woods. In the summer, they moved out on the open tundra, migrating eastward from the Lower Nelson River region as far as Akimiski Island in James Bay to calve. The nations who depended on these animals developed a number of ingenious hunting techniques that took advantage of the predictability of herd movements. The Dene worked in large parties to build brush enclosures, called surrounds or pounds, in places where herds normally wintered. The hunters set snares inside the pounds to catch the caribou they drove in. The Dene and the Swampy Cree also built intricate barricades across the trails regularly used by caribou, placing snares in the gaps left in these "deer hedges." During the open-water season, Dene hunting parties herded caribou into rivers and lakes, where fellow hunters speared them with ease from canoes.

The Algonquian and Athapaskan groups employed various snares and dead-fall traps to kill fur-bearing animals. Beavers, muskrats, and hares were their most common prey. The beaver coat, which Native people wore with the hair against their bodies for warmth, was an essential article of winter clothing, as were hare blankets and coats. The meat of small animals, especially beavers, was a crucial food source as well. An adult beaver could provide a hunter and his family with up to forty pounds of meat.

At the end of winter, several hunting groups from adjacent territories would camp together at a fresh-water fishery for several weeks or more. They used hooks and lines, spears, dip nets, and fences (weirs), depending on the site and species sought. For many groups, freshly caught fish was the mainstay of their diet between late spring and early autumn. Women usually preserved a small surplus to carry their families into the winter. Ojibwa women, for example, dried and pounded sturgeon and mixed it with fish oil. This concentrated, protein-rich food had a storage life of several months, provided that the weather remained reasonably cool. Subarctic women also made a glue from the swim bladders of sturgeon, which they used to fix the colours in the paint that decorated everything from their bodies to their dwellings.

An Innu woman making snowshoes, Pointe Bleue, Quebec. Among most northern people, men made the frames and women did the stringing.

During the spring and autumn, when the Subarctic teemed with millions of waterfowl, the hunters took prodigious numbers of ducks and geese. Geese were a particularly treasured food for the Swampy and Eastmain Cree who lived along the shores of Hudson Bay and James Bay. In the fall, hunters preserved large numbers of birds simply by letting them freeze in the cold air, but protracted winter thaws sometimes spoiled their larders.

The people worked in teams. Men did most of the large-game hunting, made the stone tools and hunting weapons, fashioned snowshoe frames, and built canoes and sleds. Men, women, and children trapped fur-bearing animals. Women did most of the fishing; they collected various plant foods and fibres; gathered firewood and supplies for canoe building and repairing; processed and cooked the food; scraped and tanned hides and pelts; made the clothing and household equipment; and strung the snowshoes.

During the winter, women freighted most of the gear when the hunting parties trudged from camp to camp by snowshoe and sled. Pack and sled dogs often helped, but most families could not afford to feed many of these voracious creatures. Although some Dene groups fed their animals caribou meat, fish—particularly whitefish—was the ideal dog food, and often the productivity of the winter fishery determined the number of animals a group could sustain. In most areas, each family could support only one two-dog team. Obviously, summer movement by canoe was much less taxing for women. A typical canoe could hold a family with one or two children and several hundred pounds of cargo.

ATLANTIC MARITIME HUNTERS AND GATHERERS

In New Brunswick and Nova Scotia, the stumpy boreal forest yields to mixed evergreen and deciduous forests. Just before the first Europeans arrived, the Beothuk, Mi'kmaq, and Maliseet occupied this region. Their economies were similar to those of the Subarctic people during the winter when they stalked large game and trapped fur-bearing animals inland, deep in the woods. At other times, the Atlantic groups lived very differently, turning to the sea for food. On the beaches, they collected a variety of shellfish, and from their canoes they caught fish, especially mackerel and cod. They also hunted seal and other marine mammals.

Archaeological remains suggest that for several thousand years the ancestors of this region's First Nations spent the entire year on the Atlantic Coast. Apparently moving inland during the winter was a very late pre-contact development; it is possible it may even have been a response to trade with European fishermen and whalers who sought furs.

ARCTIC MARINE HUNTERS

The coastline and offshore islands between the Strait of Belle Isle and the Alaskan border are the homeland of the Inuit—the greatest marine hunters of North America. Among their treacherous quarry were ringed and bearded seals, walrus, narwhals, beluga whales, and polar bears. For many, seal was the basic raw material of life. Some Inuit groups, particularly those of the Ungava district and the central Arctic, also relied heavily

An Inuit man uses a bow drill. The Inuit have always been noted for their skill in working with bone and ivory using traditional and imported tools.

on barren-ground caribou. Like their woodland neighbours, the Inuit hunted various fur-bearing animals. They prized arctic hares and arctic foxes, but wolves and wolverines were significant, too. Groups living in the Mackenzie River delta took beavers and muskrats, which were absent in most other areas of the Arctic. All Inuit caught large quantities of fish; they particularly liked arctic char and lake trout.

To take this array of fish, large game, and marine mammals, the Inuit developed a remarkable sensitivity to even the subtlest variations in the land, sea, and ice landscape and used very effective hunting and transport technologies. Their seasonal migratory rounds took them from the offshore ice shelves in winter to the inland tundra in summer. For their pursuit of seals, walrus, and whales, Inuit men made toggling harpoons, driftwood-handled harpoons with detachable bone points attached to a line, and throwing boards (*atlatals*), which were used to propel spears. Like Native groups elsewhere, they fashioned spears, bows, and arrows. Because they lived beyond the tree line, the Inuit often made their bows from bone, and they invented a double-curved sinew-backed design to obtain more thrust. Their fishing gear included many of the same kinds of equipment found elsewhere, such as barbless bone fishing hooks, jigs, nets, and spears. They also built willow-brush and stone weirs in the rivers to trap the migratory arctic char.

An Inuit family travels in an umiak on Hudson Bay in the early 1900s. These large craft, which were twenty to thirty feet in length, were designed for whaling and moving families between hunting and fishing sites.

The wood-framed and skin-covered kayak is probably one of the best-known objects of traditional Inuit life. It was used by hunters to stalk and kill their prey along the edges of ice floes and to spear caribou swimming across lakes and rivers. Inuit also constructed the less familiar umiak. This flat-bottomed boat, with a puncture-resistant seal-, beluga-, or walrus-hide cover, could carry ten people and several tons of cargo. During July and August, hunters chased a variety of dangerous mammals, including whales and polar bears, from these boats. When bands headed upriver in the autumn to catch char and hunt caribou, they hauled their belongings in their umiaks.

Like their Subarctic neighbours, the Inuit used dog sleds made from drift-wood, bone, or antler. They also used their dogs as pack animals; a fully loaded pack dog could carry thirty to forty pounds. Again, shortages of dog food often placed severe constraints on the number of animals a group could support.

PEOPLE OF THE BUFFALO

The buffalo people of the prairies lived in what a European fur trader described as a vast "sea of grass and scattered islands of woods," which teemed with bison. Bison, or buffalo as they are usually called, North America's largest terrestrial animal, had been the main focus of the Plains people's economies since the great Ice Age. The adult male buffalo weighs up to two thousand pounds and could provide the hunter with as much as a thousand pounds of dressed meat. A female yielded much less, about four hundred pounds, but her meat's greater tenderness was preferred. Buffalo tongues and bosses (the fatty humps located between the shoulders) were considered delicacies. The Plains people also depended on buffalo for an array of essential raw materials. Their heavy winter coats served as warm robes for bedding and outer wear. The hides were ideal for making lodge coverings, *parflèches* (leather containers), clothing, *babiche* (leather cording), and war shields. Men worked bison bone into a variety of tools, and the women used the stomach as a cooking and storage container. In short, this one majestic animal provided the foundation for their way of life.

Buffalo hunts were all-consuming enterprises akin to military campaigns. When the summer rutting season approached, the buffalo gathered into enormous herds numbering in the tens of thousands; as the autumn winds grew chilly, they scattered into smaller herds and headed for the shelter of the aspen parklands to face the winter. Herd movements were highly predictable, and hunters devised strategies to take advantage of this. During the winter, they pitched camp in sheltered locations near places the buffalo frequented. Under the direction of the "poundmaker," or winter village chief, they constructed a circular brush enclosure with a fenced chute leading to the nearby prairie. When a herd approached, skilled hunters went out to meet it, disguised as buffalo or wolves. They lured the unsuspecting buffalo into the chute where their kinfolk, hidden behind the fence, helped drive the animals into the pound by spooking them. Once the buffalo were inside, men, women, and even children slaughtered them with lances and bows and arrows. The pounds, if well maintained, lasted for many years.

Before Spaniards introduced horses to North America, the cliff drive was the most productive summer buffalo-hunting technique. When everything worked according to plan, a carefully set fire, or men and women drovers working in a V-shaped formation, terrorized thousands of buffalo and sent them thundering over precipices to their deaths. The Plains people frequently built an enclosure at the base of the cliff to make it easier to dispatch any animals that did not die in the fall. Pre-contact "buffalo-jump" sites still dot the prairie landscape and testify to the effectiveness of this technique. Archaeologists have learned that Native people used some of these kill sites repeatedly over thousands of years. Excavations have exposed bone layers up to fifteen feet deep. Today, examples of these impressive ancient hunting

A Siksika woman pounds dried meat in the early 1920s. In Plains buffalo-hunting societies, women traditionally produced a variety of meat products—most notably pemmican—from dried buffalo meat, grease, and saskatoon berries.

locations may be visited at Old Woman Buffalo Jump and the world heritage sites of Head-Smashed-In Buffalo Jump in Alberta and Wanuskewin, Saskatchewan.

The "surround" was an impromptu hunting strategy. A group of hunters on foot approached and surrounded part of a herd. The brave hunters then drew themselves into an ever-smaller circle, killing as many animals as possible until the herd broke through and ran away. Clearly this practice demanded nerves of steel and required considerable experience.

As in other regions, after the hunt was over the women did most of the butchering and processed the hides and robes. They also made one of the most famous Aboriginal foods—pemmican. This highly nutritious product was a mixture of dried and pulverized buffalo meat and melted fat flavoured with berries—usually saskatoon berries. The women poured the pemmican mixture into *parflèches* to congeal. Each container held about ninety pounds, and its contents had an extremely long shelf life. Pemmican was the ideal travelling food because a single *parflèche* held the equivalent of nine hundred pounds of fresh meat, or that of two adult female buffalo. Every summer and autumn, Plains groups accumulated a stock of pemmican for their winter use and for trade.

Although these people were probably more focused on a single species of animal than any other Aboriginal hunters, they did pursue other prey. Wapiti (elk), which weighed up to eleven hundred pounds and lived in the bordering woods, was an important back-up food when the buffalo herds failed to leave the open grasslands, as happened during exceptionally mild winters. The Plains groups also took moose in the woods. Some of the Plains Cree and Ojibwa, who were recent immigrants from the woodlands, still relished moose meat. In addition, Plains hunters preyed on the packs of wolves that stalked the buffalo herds, and pursued a variety of other fur-bearing animals —notably beavers and muskrats—in the aspen woods bordering the rivers and countless lakes that dot the prairie land-scape. During the spring and autumn, migrating waterfowl provided another alter-native food source.

For some Plains groups, fishing was a very important food source in the spring and fall. The Assiniboine and Cree built weirs on the Assiniboine and Red rivers in the spring to catch sturgeon. In marked contrast, the Siksika people refused to eat fish.

FISHERS OF THE PACIFIC SLOPE

The Pacific-slope people were the premier fishers of Native Canada. They enjoyed eating and trading fish, particularly salmon. Of the five species of this fish, one or more made spawning runs through the territory of every nation living west of the Continental Divide. Most salmon species are found in abundance along the lower sections of the rivers near the coast, but only the crimson-fleshed sockeye swim great distances inland up the mighty Fraser and Skeena rivers and their tributaries. Coastal people, then, could almost always harvest salmon—and other seafood—but groups living far inland were at the mercy of the sockeye runs. Salmon have marked cyclical population fluctuations; the Fraser River sockeye, for example, has a four-year cycle. At the height of the cycle, the rivers teem with the fish, but at its low ebb the inland groups often could not catch enough for their needs. In narrow canyons, landslides added to the uncertainty of the upriver fishery by destroying fishing stations and spawning beds. For these reasons, inland groups relied more heavily on hunting.

The genius of the West Coast Native economies was the development of a sophisticated salmon-fishing technology; it included spear fishing, trolling with hook and line, and the use of an impressive array of stationary nets, fish weirs, and various traps, which were custom-made for each fishing site and often formed multi-purpose fishing facilities. Along and near the coast, and inland in narrow or shallow rivers and creeks, they relied heavily on hooks and lines, nets, stone and basket traps, and weirs; in the narrower canyons and at waterfalls, they used long-handled gaff hooks, dip nets, spears, and large basket-trap complexes. Even coastal groups took most of their salmon in rivers and creeks. Although fishing in the raging waters of narrow canyons was very risky, it was generally much less hazardous than fishing on the sea.

A few weeks of concerted effort usually enabled coastal groups to catch enough fish to satisfy most of their annual consumption and trade requirements. The processing and storage techniques they had developed to stockpile their harvests made this possible. Women, working in groups, filleted the salmon (mostly caught by the men), smoked or dried the fillets, then stored them in various containers and above-ground caches. They also processed the oil and made fish eggs into stew or dried cakes for local consumption and trade.

Eulachon, which runs in the spring, was another important fish to West Coast people. The Nass River became the unrivalled centre of this fishery. Native people prized the eulachon for its rich oil. Because the dried-salmon diet of the winter and spring was very low in fat, oil provided a much-needed dietary supplement. The Nisga'a developed what amounted to a processing industry for eulachon oil. They packaged the oil so that it could be carried long distances inland over an intricate network of trading routes, which came to be known as the "grease trails."

Halibut, shellfish, herring and salmon roe, sea-bird eggs, seaweed, and marine mammals—seals, sea otters, and whales—also figured prominently in the coastal economy. To harvest these and other resources of the ocean, groups like the Tsimshian, Haida, and Nuu chah nulth built impressive sea-going dugout canoes with decorated cedar-plank prows. Working with bone, stone, and hardwood axes, chisels, and wedges, the men built thirty-five- to seventy-five-foot-long canoes that could carry crews of up to fifty paddlers over great distances. They also custom-built smaller shallow-draft canoes for river travel. The Haida were particularly famous for their canoe construction skills.

Coastal groups did some hunting, but the dense rain forests of their lands offered poor prospects. Upriver people were better situated for this activity, and accordingly, they devoted more time to it. The Gitxsan hunted bears and mountain goats, which they prized for wool and horns. They also trapped a variety of

This fishing weir on the Cowichan River, Vancouver Island, was photographed about 1867. Aboriginal fishers across Canada tailored weirs and fishing gear for specific locations.

fur-bearing animals, particularly groundhogs. Their neighbours, the Wet'suwet'en and Babine, placed a premium on beavers, which they treasured as ceremonial food.

As in all other regions of Native Canada, women collected and processed an assortment of berries and other plants for food and fibre. Huckleberry cakes were a favourite food and an important article of commerce. Women made them by crushing the berries in a cedar box and boiling them over red-hot rocks. They spread the cooked huckleberries on a bed of skunk-cabbage leaves arranged over a drying rack. Using a low-burning fire located under the rack, the women dried the berry "cakes," rolled them into tubes, and hung them in a warm place to finish drying. Afterwards, they flattened and chopped the tubes and packed them into cedar boxes for storage or trade.

Coastal women also collected a variety of bark (especially cedar bark), spruce root, nettle, and sea grasses for making fishnets, baskets, and numerous other items. They were the only weavers in Native Canada. The Chilkat blanket, a patterned blanket that combined plant fibres and mountain-goat wool, was the finest example of their work. They also made waterproof basket hats, outer wear, and basket traps for fishing. As in other regions, the women tailored warm winter clothing from hides and fur pelts. The luxurious sea-otter cloak was the most valuable of these garments, worn only by people of high social rank.

In addition to building impressive dugout canoes, West Coast men constructed the largest houses in Native Canada. These dwellings, which were some-

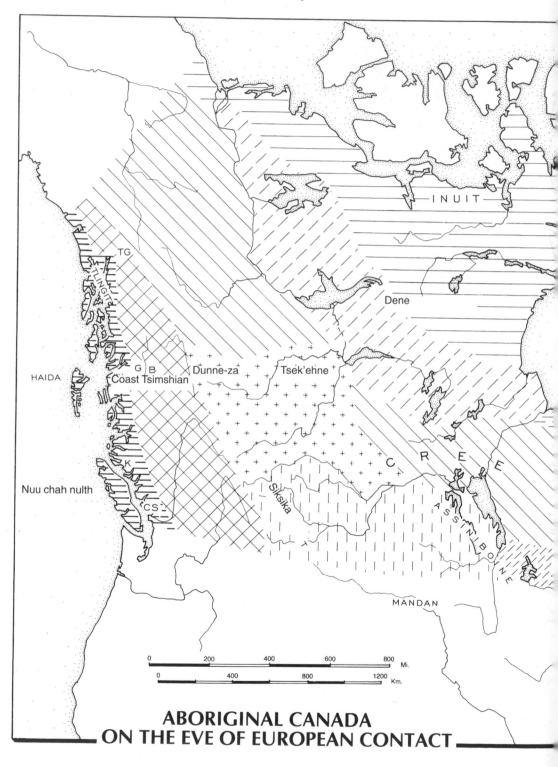

HAIDA

TG

TLINGIT

G B
Coast Tsimshian

Dunne-za

Tsek'ehne

Dene

INUIT

K

Nuu chah nulth

CS

CREE

Siksika

ASSINIBONE

MANDAN

| 0 | 200 | 400 | 600 | 800 | Mi. |

| 0 | 400 | 800 | 1200 | Km. |

ABORIGINAL CANADA
ON THE EVE OF EUROPEAN CONTACT

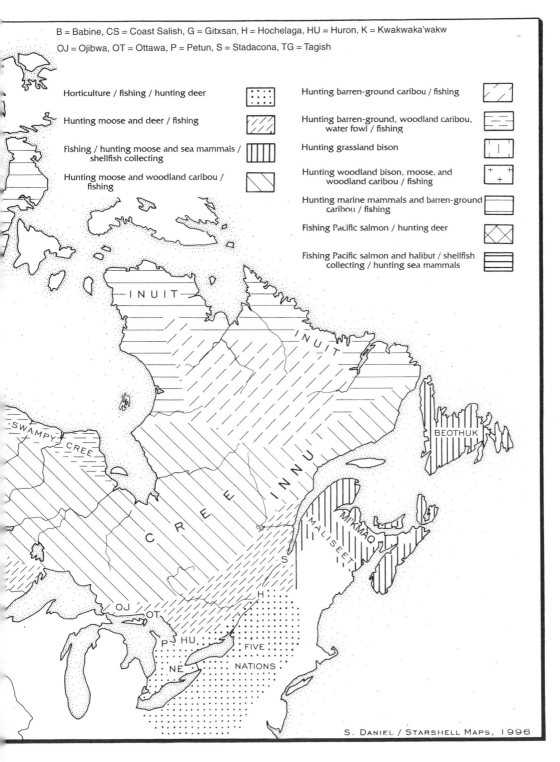

B = Babine, CS = Coast Salish, G = Gitxsan, H = Hochelaga, HU = Huron, K = Kwakwaka'wakw
OJ = Ojibwa, OT = Ottawa, P = Petun, S = Stadacona, TG = Tagish

Horticulture / fishing / hunting deer

Hunting moose and deer / fishing

Fishing / hunting moose and sea mammals / shellfish collecting

Hunting moose and woodland caribou / fishing

Hunting barren-ground caribou / fishing

Hunting barren-ground, woodland caribou, water fowl / fishing

Hunting grassland bison

Hunting woodland bison, moose, and woodland caribou / fishing

Hunting marine mammals and barren-ground caribou / fishing

Fishing Pacific salmon / hunting deer

Fishing Pacific salmon and halibut / shellfish collecting / hunting sea mammals

INUIT

INUIT

SWAMPY

CREE

BEOTHUK

CREE

INNU

MI'KMAQ

MALISEET

S

OJ

OT

H

P

HU

FIVE

NE

NATIONS

S. DANIEL / STARSHELL MAPS, 1996

times highly decorated, featured massive cedar supports covered by cedar planks. The planks were often detachable because most families maintained several fishing, hunting, and berrying camps as well as a principal winter residence. When they moved from one settlement to another, they often transported the planks to place over the permanent ridge poles left in each camp.

The carved bentwood cedar box was the most important piece of household furniture made by the men. The sides were fashioned from a single cedar board, which was steamed, bent into a rectangular shape, and joined at one corner. These boxes served as chairs and as storage for possessions. Other versions, often with dividers inside, were used as food-storage and shipping containers.

THE POPULATION QUESTION

Today there is no scholarly consensus on how many people the regional economies supported in Native Canada, or elsewhere in the Americas, for that matter, before diseases introduced by Europeans swept the land with devastating effect—often preceding the newcomers' arrival in a particular locale. Early in this century, most anthropologists, including Diamond Jenness, who wrote the 1932 classic, *The Indians of Canada*, concluded that pre-contact population-growth rates must have been very low in most areas because Aboriginal groups lived a precarious migratory existence, with accidents, frequent famines, and conflicts within and between nations causing high mortality and low fertility rates. Jenness speculated that pre-contact infant mortality rates had always been high "partly through ignorance of some of the most elementary principles in child welfare." These assumptions were plainly wrong, having been made at a time when the surviving Native cultures led a marginalized existence, which was itself largely responsible for the living conditions Jenness described. Also, it was a time when cultural-evolution models were popular among anthropologists. These schemes placed the hunters and gatherers of the world on the low end of the cultural-evolutionary scale and postulated that the people exist- ed on the edge of starvation.

We now know that fishers, hunters, and gatherers in general, and many Native Canadian societies in particular, obtained stable supplies of food with far less effort and much more ingenuity than was previously supposed. In fact, some anthropologists suggest that these were the original affluent societies because peo- ple spent remarkably little time working to meet basic requirements. This new per- spective does not deny that starvation occurred but suggests that famines were probably no more frequent among hunters, fishers, and gatherers than among farmers. There is no reason to infer that the economic orientation of Indigenous societies severely limited population growth or that warfare caused a chronic drain on population numbers.

More recently, it has become clear that the low population densities of many of the Aboriginal hunters and gatherers in Canada, and elsewhere around the world at the beginning of this century, were the result of repeated epidemics and protracted neglect at the hands of colonial societies. Earlier historical demographic projections based on these groups are now considered suspect by many scholars. Today, the tendency is to revise pre-contact population estimates for the whole of the Americas upwards from those made at the turn of the twentieth century. Scholars are deeply divided among themselves, however, about the extent of the revisions that ought to be made. The so-called high counters suggest an increase of twelve-fold or more is in order, which would indicate a Canadian pre-contact population of well over one million people. Other scholars reject these new estimates. In spite of the debate, many scholars do agree that on the eve of contact Canada's Native people were concentrated, in order of density, in the Pacific slope (150,000–200,000), the eastern Great Lakes and St Lawrence valley (100,000–150,000), and the grassland-parkland areas of the Western Interior (50,000–100,000). Perhaps fewer than 100,000 lived elsewhere. This suggests that, at most, slightly more than 500,000 people occupied the land when Europeans arrived at the end of the fifteenth century to transform their lives.

CHAPTER 2

THE CULTURAL MOSAIC

I have listened to many wonderful stories that were told by the older men. At times, these storytellings went on for several days.... No one went to sleep until the wee hours of the morning, and everyone awoke by sunrise to resume the storytelling.

—Percy Bullchild, Siksika

Before European contact, most commerce, diplomacy, and warfare took place between neighbouring groups. Nevertheless, people occasionally travelled great distances and brought back stories about other nations and places that lay far beyond their homelands. Travellers would have learned about strangers who ate exotic foods, dressed in unusual clothes, had very distinctive social customs, held different spiritual beliefs, and participated in unfamiliar ceremonies.

A LIVELY COMMERCE

Archaeological findings and the written accounts of the first European intruders indicate that trading was extensive in at least three regions—Iroquoia and its borderlands, the prairie parklands and grasslands, and the Pacific slope.

The surplus corn grown by Huron women was the mainstay of a lively commerce with northern Algonquian neighbours, who often ran short of food in late winter and early spring. In addition to providing an important safety net for these forest dwellers, Huron dried corn was an excellent travel food. The Algonquians also valued Huron tobacco and fishnets. In exchange, the Huron accepted hides, furs, small numbers of buffalo robes, and winter clothing, particularly beaver coats. From other Iroquoian-speakers living to the south, the Huron obtained luxury goods, such as black squirrel coats.

In the prairie region, the Plains nations participated in a trading network that

A fanciful etching of an Iroquoian village by a European artist. Archaeology reveals that longhouses were never arranged in neat rows, and villages were usually enclosed by palisades made of timber and brush, not neat picket fences.

was even larger than the one in Iroquoia. At its centre were the northern Missouri River valley villages of the Arikara and Mandan, who had mixed horticultural and buffalo-hunting economies. Like the Iroquoians, the women produced large surpluses of corn that figured prominently in external trade. The men and women of the villages were the artisans of the northern plains: they excelled at feather craft and painting buffalo hides. Groups from the south and west as well as from the Canadian prairies flocked every summer to the trade fairs at the Missouri villages to buy handicrafts and stocks of dried corn. It is not clear what the northern Plains nations took south to exchange during the pre-contact era, but very likely northern furs were leading items, because the Mandan and Arikara lived beyond the prime fur-producing regions. The northern buffalo people probably obtained some of these furs from their woodland neighbours and relatives in exchange for prairie products, which could explain how buffalo robes entered barter networks reaching as far east as Huronia.

Without doubt the Pacific-slope groups were the most fervent traders among the Native people. They bartered an astonishing array of raw materials, processed

A Siksika woman wrapped in a buffalo robe, 1907. Some Plains artists excelled in decorating hides and robes.

foods, and crafts. The different natural environments and economies of the region provided the basis for exchange networks that extended along the coast and deep into the interior. Traders hauled upriver products from the ocean and seashore, including dried seaweed, eulachon oil, dried and smoked shellfish, dried cod and halibut, dried and smoked salmon, herring and salmon roe, dried seal and sea-lion meat, dentalium and abalone shell, hinged scallop-shell bracelets, copper, sea-lion teeth and whiskers, and killer-whale-jaw clubs. Their canoes returned laden with dried berries, mountain-goat dried meat and fat, dried caribou meat, moose hides, furs, obsidian and amber, mountain sheep and goat horns (for spoons), stone clubs, jade adze blades, goat-wool and groundhog blankets, and wooden arrow shafts. Groups processed many resources in special ways to make them more appealing to their trading partners. For instance, most West Coast people ate salmon roe, but some produced roe cakes with flavourings as a kind of gourmet delicacy.

Beyond the lands of the salmon people, the buffalo hunters, and the Iroquoian horticulturists, trade was more limited. Over most of the Subarctic and Arctic, only a few rare raw materials or finished goods circulated. Copper found in the native state was probably the most notable trade item. Most of it came from the vicinity of Lake Superior and moved in a trading network that extended as far east as Lac St Jean on the upper Saguenay River. Copper from another deposit located on the lower Coppermine River in the western Arctic was passed between groups occupying the vast territory between the lower Mackenzie River and the western shores of Hudson Bay. Although most groups had nothing out of the ordinary to offer others, here as elsewhere they had social and political reasons to establish trading contacts.

KINSHIP CONNECTIONS

The ancestors of Canada's First Nations all lived in "small scale" societies, in the sense that day-to-day contacts of individual members were usually limited to close relatives. Kinship connections strongly influenced patterns of social and economic interaction, and they frequently determined a person's position in a society. As well, all groups esteemed co-operation and sharing among kinfolk. This important feature of Native life found expression in numerous ways, but without exception leaders were expected to be generous. Even in those nations where individuals or families were highly status conscious, gift giving, rather than the hoarding of wealth or private ownership, was the key to enhanced social position, even among the most affluent of the Pacific slope.

Nations differed in the sizes of the kinship groupings, the manner in which people traced descent, and the degree to which heritage determined a person's social and political position. Generalizing very broadly, there were two kinds of societies. One featured clans, or large kinship groups claiming a mythical ancestor, and the other emphasized small groups of closely related families.

The nations of Iroquoia and the Pacific slope were organized into clans. Typically, clan members were identified by a symbol. The Huron, for example, recognized eight clans—Turtle, Wolf, Bear, Beaver, Deer, Hawk, Porcupine, and Snake; and four clans—Fireweed, Wolf, Eagle, and Raven—dominated the Tsimshian society on the West Coast. A lineage, consisting of a number of closely related "fireside" (nuclear) families living under one roof, was the building block of the clan. In Iroquoia, the lineage typically occupied an elm-bark-covered longhouse. Its members traced their descent along the female line, with the senior woman acting as matriarch of the house. In larger villages, lineages belonging to the same clan lived in adjacent longhouses. As in the East, lineages on the Pacific Coast resided in large dwellings; however, the way groups traced their ancestry varied considerably in this region. Along the north coast, families traced their lineage through the female line; on the south coast, they followed the male line; and along the central coast, they recognized both lines.

In these societies, lineages, or "houses," held the rights to the resources of specific tracts of land. Among the Iroquois, members of a longhouse cultivated particular fields and controlled certain trading routes. On the Pacific slope, house territories were well defined and, along the coast, often extended to offshore fishing and collecting grounds. The head of the house regulated fishing and collecting

These fish-drying houses on the Bulkley River in British Columbia belonged to different lineages. The totem poles indicate the ownership of each smokehouse.

sites, hunting grounds, and trading trails. Families considered it a hostile act when outsiders travelled through their lands without first obtaining the permission of the head of the house.

The winter village, ranging in size from fewer than one hundred residents to more than a thousand, was the principal settlement of the Iroquoians. Several clans usually resided in a village. A council presided over village affairs. Its members included clan chiefs, the peace chiefs (known as *sachems*) of the various lineages, and wise men.

Superficially, politics seemed to be male dominated, but in reality men held their positions based on the ancestry of their mothers. Furthermore, the ranking matrons of the various clans conducted assemblies that nominated, censured, and even recalled the *sachems*. Successful warriors, great orators, and men who earned recognition for other achievements could also acquire the status of chief, but they could not be voting members of the village council and they could not pass their titles on to their descendants.

The confederacies, such as those of the Huron and the Five Nations Iroquois, knitted various nations and villages together. Confederacies, whose members included the *sachems* of the member clans, promoted harmonious inter-village relations and co-ordinated external affairs, particularly warfare. Decision making at all levels was by consensus of the decision makers—a practice common to all Native groups, irrespective of their particular political organization. Significantly, the councils lacked any coercive powers; normally, kin and peer pressure ensured compliance. Once a council reached a decision, its members customarily selected one of their best orators to announce it. After contact, Europeans often mistook these "speakers" for prominent leaders.

On the Pacific slope, lineage members representing one or more clans gathered in villages of several hundred or more to pass the winter months. Their daily lives were strongly influenced by a well-developed system of inherited social rank and a great concern for status. Coastal nations each comprised three classes: chiefs or nobles, commoners, and slaves. In addition, each chief had a place in a finely graded hierarchy. At the time of contact, the Wet'suwet'en, for instance, had twenty chiefs of different rank. Slaves were either members of other groups who had been captured during raids or the descendants of these unfortunate people.

Unlike the Iroquoians, the Pacific Coast people did not use village councils and confederacies to manage their internal and external affairs. Instead, feasts, or potlatches, provided a public forum to deal with any matters of general interest. The funeral feast is an example. After the death of the head of a house, his or her rights and obligations had to be passed on to a successor. The house accomplished this by hosting a funeral feast. During this rite, a family member—usually the heir of the deceased—distributed gifts to all the invited guests—everyone who was affected in any way by the death. By accepting the gifts, they acknowledged their approval of the new order. Chiefs also held potlatches to restore tranquillity when murders or other acts of violence threatened peace within or between villages. Besides these more serious concerns, feasts were held for pure enjoyment. Given its wide-ranging functions, the potlatch was the central institution in these societies.

In the Subarctic and Arctic regions, social organization tended to be egalitarian. People spent most of the year in migratory hunting groups composed of a few closely related hunters and their wives, children, parents, and grandparents. The Inuit reinforced the bonds between families: a man would establish a life-long partnership with another man, and the two partners shared resources, and sometimes wives, pledging to support and protect each other.

Political leadership was fluid in the sense that group members followed the man who was best suited to lead them in the task at hand. Usually the "situational leader" was a married elder who was a superior hunter, a generous man, a skilled orator, or a good conciliator. When a number of local boreal-forest groups came together to form a summer camp, the winter headman who commanded the greatest respect became the camp's leader. Among some Subarctic groups, such as the Swampy Cree and northern Ojibwa, there may have been a tendency towards hereditary leadership, provided that the heir-apparent was competent. Likewise, among the Inuit of the western Arctic, the summer village headman inherited his position from his father. In northern Quebec, a man had to meet several requirements before he could be a headman: he had to own an umiak, be a noted hunter, and have kinship status that gave him control over several male relatives. The village headman's position was very important because he had the responsibility of organizing whale-boat crews. As in all other areas, good leaders were those who were skilful at gaining a consensus.

Arctic and Subarctic hunting groups used the same territories every year. When natural calamities, such as forest fires, temporarily ruined hunting or trapping

Igloos near Port Harrison (Inoucdjouac), Quebec, about 1910. These ingenious snow-block dwellings are among the best-known features of traditional Inuit culture. Usually several igloos were clustered together and connected by passageways.

prospects, hunting parties obtained permission from neighbouring groups to use portions of their traditional land. There was little need for sharply demarcated territories. Because individuals had to marry outside their winter group, the groups were knitted together by regional kinship networks. Thus, all Arctic and Subarctic hunters had a vested interest in the responsible use of their own land's resources as well as those of their neighbouring kin. What was crucial was the establishment of social bonds, not rigid territorial boundaries.

The social and political life of the Plains buffalo hunters shared some of the characteristics of both the Iroquoian and Pacific-slope clan-based societies and Subarctic and Arctic societies where this type of organization was weak or absent. Partly this was because camp sizes on the plains varied with the seasons. The population of a winter buffalo-pound village, for instance, ranged from twenty-five to one hundred or more, which was about the same size as the summer encampments of the boreal-forest groups. During the late summer, on the other hand, the buffalo-hunting and sun-dance camps could number more than one thousand inhabitants, about the size of the winter villages of the Iroquoian and Pacific-slope nations.

In Plains societies, a chief and an informal council of elders, chosen for their leadership abilities, oversaw the affairs of the summer and winter camps. When several groups gathered in the summer, the oldest and most respected winter leader acted as spokesman for the combined group. As in other regions, decision making by consensus prevailed, and persuasion rather than coercion was the preferred way for elders to implement their individual and collective wills. Associations of adult male warriors, popularly known as "warrior societies," enforced rules as necessary. Society members could seize a defiant person's property and impose physical punishment; however, this was rarely necessary.

Although Plains nations were very concerned about social status, its attainment was largely an individual quest of men. Typically, a major goal for a man was to become a member of a warrior society. These societies were the most prestigious of all the various men's associations. To be eligible for membership, a man had to earn status and wealth through demonstrations of fighting and hunting prowess as a member of other, lower-ranked organizations. Among the Siksika people, for example, associations existed for different age groups: boys in their early teens, young adult men, and older men who no longer hunted or engaged in warfare. Each society had its own entry requirements, and a man usually bought the emblems and rights to the rituals of a society from one of its members, who in turn purchased access to a higher-ranked association. Often men who had gained a great

Running Rabbit (left) painting a lodge cover at the Blackfoot South Camp, Alberta, 1905. Traditionally, men sometimes painted key events of their lives on their tipi covers.

deal of respect and status publicly proclaimed it by lavishly decorating their dwelling with pictographs that recalled their best-known achievements.

Seeking Revenge and Peace

Inter-nation relations in Native Canada, like those among societies the world over, vacillated between war and peace. Young men sought to gain prestige through their exploits in combat. This was especially the case in Iroquoia, the Plains, and the Pacific Coast regions. In these societies, it was commonplace for the relatives of a person who was killed by foreign raiders to seek revenge. However, although skirmishes were common, they predominantly involved small raiding parties and led to limited bloodshed. Usually the attackers were satisfied after they had killed a few opponents and taken some prisoners. The exceptions to this practice seem to have occurred in areas where nations fought over disputed territory or had deep-seated animosities towards one another. For example, the Inuit and various Dene groups west of Hudson Bay seem to have fought each other along the border between their lands long before Europeans arrived on the scene. The reasons are not entirely clear. And the Swampy Cree often lashed out at their Inuit neighbours after poor hunting seasons. It seems that they blamed their misfortunes on Inuit sorcery.

Native people developed various ways to counteract divisive forces and facilitate the work of peacemakers. They often paid compensation to aggrieved relatives to prevent or break a feuding cycle within a group; the people who caused the injury, or their relatives, made the payment. Alternatively, as happened among the Plains nations, a chief would make the peace offering and thereby reestablish harmony among his followers.

In Native Canada, diplomacy and trade were intertwined. Gift giving was the cement of inter-nation diplomacy. Leaders of unrelated nations met and presented gifts of equal value to each other as symbolic gestures of good will. Often the exchange was a lengthy affair, which involved feasting, speech making, and the ritual smoking of the calumet, a long-stemmed, decorated tobacco pipe. Exchanges of this kind were an integral part of inter-nation trade because they served to create or renew peaceful relations between groups that were a prerequisite for regular commerce. This explains why peace chiefs or heads of lineages usually controlled external trade. When the leaders of different groups were keen to establish long-lasting bonds, they often arranged marriages between their respective kin.

SPIRITUAL AND CEREMONIAL LIFE

Aboriginal Canadians made no distinction between the natural world and the spiritual one, believing that the world around them was governed by a panoply of spirits. Accordingly, they sought the good will and help of these powers by

This whimsical rendering of Iroquoian warfare involving an assault on a fortified, probably temporary, defensive encampment was drawn for Baron de Lahontan's New Voyages to North America, *1703.*

showing them respect through a variety of public and private ritual practices. They were assisted in some of these rites by persons who had special powers to commune with the spirit world.

The Huron considered the sky spirit, which controlled the weather and helped humans in need, to be the most powerful. They thought lesser spirits, the *oki*, could influence human affairs. A healer was a man who had an *oki*, or familiar spirit, which revealed to him in visions and dreams the cause of illnesses. Curing societies, which were usually led by an important headman, also played a major role in healing. The Huron believed there were three major reasons for sickness— natural causes, witchcraft, and the unfulfilled desires of a person's soul—and they turned to healers and curing societies to help them deal with these problems. To the Huron, dreams were the language of the soul, and healers paid particular attention to their patients' dreams when providing treatment. By taking appropriate ritual action, Huron medicine men were able to deal effectively with common emotional problems. The healing ceremonies served, in essence, as a kind of individual and group psychotherapy.

Like the funeral potlatch of the Pacific Coast people, the Feast of the Dead was the most important public ritual that the Huron and other Iroquoians observed. This ten-day celebration took place whenever a local field-rotation cycle had run its course—usually after ten to twelve years—forcing a village to relocate elsewhere and begin again. Under the supervision of a chief, the celebrants dug a large common grave outside the old settlement, where they buried the remains of their loved ones along with a wide variety of grave offerings to honour the spirits of the deceased. This ceremony not only paid homage to dead relatives and friends but also gave villagers the opportunity to renew bonds with nearby satellite communities, with relatives who had moved away, and with friends from other Iroquoian settlements who were invited to take part. Thus, the feast established harmony between the worlds of both the living and the dead.

The summer sun dance was the grand ceremony of the Plains people. It took place in July or August, following a buffalo hunt undertaken especially to obtain food for the elaborate feast. Every aspect of Plains culture was symbolically represented in the event, which, like the Huron Feast of the Dead, served to renew bonds between the several related winter groups that took part. Participants formed a circular camp with an opening facing the rising sun and erected a ceremonial pole and lodge at the centre. During the exciting three-day feast, the celebrants danced and consumed great quantities of meat, particularly buffalo bosses and tongues. Usually a man, aided by his relatives, acted as host and distributed gifts to the guests.

"Making a brave" was the highlight of the sun dance. A number of young men fulfilled vows to undergo self-imposed, painful trials as offerings to the spirits and proof of their own bravery. The men tethered themselves to the centre pole of the camp with lines attached to wooden skewers impaled under the skin of their pectoral muscles. They then danced around the pole until the skewers tore loose. Often the dancers also fastened buffalo skulls or horses to their backs with skewers and ropes and dragged or led them around until they ripped free. Because the men were forbidden to drink water while they danced, Europeans sometimes called this ceremony the "thirsting dance."

The dog feast of the Plains Cree was another important ritual. It served a variety of purposes, one of which was to publicly transfer certain powers from

A European depiction of the Huron Feast of the Dead. This celebration took place about every ten years and brought kin from surrounding villages together for spiritual and social renewal.

one person to another. The ritual took place around a sod altar inside a specially built tipi. Guests ate ceremonial dog meat.

Pacific Coast people raised ceremonial life to a high art. Their ceremonial season took place during the gloomy and stormy winter months. The Kwakwaka' wakw of the central coast thought of winter as the sacred or "secret" season. Numerous secret societies—the Kwakwaka'wakw alone had eighteen—sponsored the winter feasts and potlatches. Like Plains organizations, these associations were hierarchical; members tended to be of the same sex and social position. Each association had a mythical ancestor, and its members carefully guarded the society's secrets. New members were initiated at sacred winter dances organized under the careful supervision of a master of ceremonies. Entire villages watched the dancers, who performed with a great sense of drama, wearing elaborate costumes and carved

"Making a brave" during a sun dance at Fort Edmonton, 1884. The sun dance was the most important ceremony on the annual ritual calendar of Plains buffalo hunters.

wooden masks. By taking part in these collective rites, the novices sought the protection of guardian spirits.

Tamananawas dances, staged by secret societies, were also part of the winter rituals. Coast Tsimshian groups performed so-called dog-eating dances. *Tamananawas* dances also were common along the central coast among the Kwakwaka'wakw, the Nuxalk, and the Bella Bella. Male dancers, who had female assistants, were said to be possessed by a human-eating spirit. At the end of the ritual, the dancer performed a "tame dance" to announce he had come back from the spirit world, and his female relatives joined in to celebrate his return. According to anthropologists, it is not entirely clear that cannibalism ever took place during these ceremonies, because the dancers employed a variety of illusionary tricks; mostly they engaged in ritual arm-biting. Most groups, in fact, thought cannibalism was abhorrent. Through this ceremony the people acknowledged that if their need to kill ever got out of control and became a compulsion, they would suffer terrible consequences.

Spiritual life extended well beyond these elaborate ceremonies, however. Like groups elsewhere, Pacific Coast people engaged in a variety of daily practices and rituals to show their deep appreciation of and respect for the spirit world for pro-

These Tsuu T'ina men were photographed in a sweat lodge on a reserve in Alberta in the early 1900s. Sweat lodges were used for important purification rites by Aboriginal people throughout Canada.

viding for their basic welfare. Understandably, salmon-spawning streams were particularly revered. Some groups, such as the Nuxalk, avoided throwing animal bones into the rivers and prevented their dogs from eating fish bones for fear of offending the salmon spirits.

Here, as elsewhere in Native Canada, there were important rites of passage for boys and girls—puberty ceremonies to mark their coming of age, and ritualized training to prepare them for the responsibilities of adulthood. It was commonplace to mark the beginning of menstruation by the ritual seclusion of young women. In her book, *Life Lived Like a Story*, the anthropologist Julie Cruikshank describes this custom as it used to be practised in southwestern Yukon at the turn of the twentieth century. She based her account on the narrative of Kitty Smith, a high-status woman of Tlingit and Tagish parentage, born about 1890, who was secluded for four months. Speaking about her own experience in the third person, Smith said, "When she's a women ... they put her away—put her under that hat [a specially decorated woman's bonnet]. It's covered with little sticks—porcupine quills. They make a little place for her away from camp. No men are there, just women. They teach her to sew, sew for everyone. She sews skins—gopher-skin robe.... They put string between your fingers. Yeah! So you're going to be handy—a good sewing lady. Whoever sews with porcupine quills is going to teach you to fix them. And you're going to learn [to make] Indians' own fishnet; they're going to show you, just like a doll's [model]." Smith also described various other practical life skills and rituals the older women taught her while she remained in seclusion. At the conclusion of Smith's rite of passage, her grandmother held a potlatch in her honour to announce her new adult status. Like female exclusion rites elsewhere, the one Smith experienced crucially bound the different generations of women together.

Most Subarctic people and the Inuit did not hold elaborate religious ceremonies; nonetheless, they too sought the benevolence and assistance of the spirit world through special feasts and ritual observances. The Cree, for example, believed that the Great Spirit, or *Manitou*, had placed all living creatures under the care of lesser spirits, or keepers of the game, who were responsible to him. For continued success, a hunter or fisher had to show respect and appreciation to the appropriate spirit for being permitted to make a kill. Often this involved adhering to rules that prescribed how the hunter should dispose of the remains of his prey.

Although religion was a highly personal affair in the north, religious specialists played an important role. One religious and healing rite that Algonquian-speaking visionaries performed was the Shaking Tent; the healers conversed with the spirit world in a lodge specially constructed for that purpose. Ojibwa spiritual leaders formed a fraternity, the *midewiwin* or Grand Medicine Society, which became the most important religious institution in their traditional culture. According to Chief George Barker of the Bloodvein Reserve of Manitoba, novitiates had to pass through four levels of initiation before they became full members. They learned ritual healing practices from a head medicine man, who was an expert at using herbal remedies. "A special spot was selected, one which had at least four or five different herbs growing on it," said Barker. "When this place had been chosen, an enclosure was built around it. The head medicine man would pray to reveal which illnesses could be cured from the roots of these herbs.... The healing properties of such roots were fantastic. Medicine men would travel far each year in search of specific herbs for curing certain illnesses. They were always careful to place tobacco where they pulled the roots out. This was important to appease the spirits." Medicine men preserved the sacred symbols of the Grand Medicine Society on birchbark scrolls and used them to teach new members.

Today we are only beginning to appreciate just how effective traditional Native medicine was. It would take European immigrants centuries to appreciate the knowledge that the various nations had accumulated through careful observa-

An Ojibwa man poses outside a structure used in a Shaking Tent ceremony at Long Lake, Ontario, about 1910–20. This anti-sorcery and curing rite was common among eastern Algonquian-speaking people.

tion over thousands of years. At first most newcomers dismissed it as superstition in the belief that their "Western science" was superior. Certainly Aboriginal healers had never before experienced the epidemic diseases that Europeans inadvertently brought with them. They could not combat them—nor could the newcomers, for that matter—until the late nineteenth century, long after Native populations had been repeatedly devastated. The havoc the new diseases wrought would ultimately undermine the position of traditional healers and spiritual leaders in Native society and make it easier for Christian missionaries to make inroads.

CHAPTER 3

LEGENDS OF THE FIRST ENCOUNTERS

What great creatures are these? Do they come from the sun or the moon? Do they give us light by night or by day?

—Polar Inuit meeting John Ross, Arctic explorer, 1818

It is difficult to imagine what the people of Native Canada thought about the first Europeans who arrived on their shores. Fleeting impressions of these encounters, which took place beginning in the late fifteenth century, are found in Native legends. They reveal that the Native people were just as curious about and wary of the world beyond their own as the Europeans were. The legends provide clues about how news of the strangers spread from one group to another and also suggest some of the reasons why Native nations helped the newcomers explore their land. But perhaps most important, traditional stories about first contact provide reasons to reconsider the myths the intruders created about the contact experience.

"MEN OF STRANGE APPEARANCE"

In Atlantic Canada, sustained contact with Europeans began about five hundred years ago. In the case of the Mi'kmaq, it probably took place sometime between 1500 and 1534. Their legends say the event was foretold to a young woman in a dream: "When there were no people in this country but the Indians ... a young woman had a strange dream. She dreamed that a small island came floating in toward the land. On the island were tall trees and living beings. Among them was a man dressed in garments made of rabbit skins." According to the story, the woman followed the

A Mi'kmaq pictograph of a European sailing vessel. The single mast, raised stern, and apparent gun ports in the drawing suggest a type of ship called a yacht, which was designed for inshore work and for fighting. Such ships were uncommon before the 1630s, which means the pictograph likely dates from the mid-seventeenth century or later.

custom of consulting the wise men and prophets in the hope of finding out what the dream meant. The elders had no answers, but the next day an extraordinary event explained it. "When they got up in the morning, they saw what seemed to be a small island that had drifted near to the land and became fixed there. There were trees on the island, and what seemed to be a number of bears were crawling about on the branches. All the Mi'kmaq men seized their bows and arrows and spears, and rushed down to the shore to shoot the bears. But they stopped in surprise when they saw that the creatures were not bears but men. And what seemed to be a small island with trees was really a large boat with long poles rising above it." The visitors "lowered a strangely built canoe into the water" and paddled to shore. A man dressed in white "made signs of friendship, by raising his hand toward heaven and he spoke in an unknown language." After the exotic visitors departed, the Mi'kmaq prophets questioned the woman again about her dream. They were upset that the event had been revealed to a young woman instead of to themselves.

Nearly half a continent away, the Ojibwa first met the newcomers a century or more later than the Mi'kmaq did. Again legend has it that the encounter was foretold in a vision, this time a prophet's. His dream disturbed him so much that he fasted and took sweat baths for several days. His people worried, fearing impending warfare or famine had been revealed to him. Finally the prophet broke his silence with astounding news: "Men of strange appearance have come across the water.... Their skins are white like snow, and on their faces long hair grows. These people have come across the great water in wonderfully large canoes which have great white wings like those of a giant bird." The visionary added, "The men have long and sharp knives, and they have long black tubes which they point at birds and animals. The tubes make a smoke that rises into the air just like the smoke from our pipes. From them came fire and such a terrific noise."

The Ojibwa legend goes on to say that it took the prophet a day to tell his story and that his audience was spellbound by it. In fact, they were too impatient to wait for the strangers to find them. When the storyteller finished, the other prophets and chiefs "all agreed at once that they should prepare a fleet of several canoes and send it eastward along the Great Lakes and the great river. There at the big water, their messengers should find out about these strange people and, on their return home, should make a report to the tribe." These envoys travelled far to the east of Lake Superior to a clearing where "even the largest trees had been cut down quite smoothly." They were impressed because their own stone-headed axes could not be used to chop down such large trees or to cut anything so evenly. The party collected some of the wood shavings as evidence of this new technology and headed onwards until they finally met the strangers. After visiting with them, the messengers returned home eager to tell their relatives about what they had seen.

Their story caused considerable excitement, and souvenirs of the journey were in great demand. "Everyone crowded round, to see the things the men had brought back: the shavings, the pieces of wood cut with sharp tools, the gaily-coloured cloth. This cloth was torn into small pieces, so that each person might have one." In addition, "to impress other chiefs and other tribes, the Chippewas

[Ojibwa] followed an old custom. In former days, they had bound scalps of their enemies on long poles and sent them from one tribe to another; now they fastened splinters of wood and strips of calico to poles and sent them with special messengers." Some Ojibwa believe that the other nations of Lake Superior first learned about the Europeans from the hand-to-hand circulation of these exotic articles and the repetition of the stories the messengers passed along with them.

The "moon's people" is what the Cowichan of eastern Vancouver Island called the newcomers. Like the other nations of the Pacific Coast, they had no contact with Europeans until the late eighteenth century—nearly three centuries later than the Mi'kmaq and two centuries after the Ojibwa. According to their legend, a despondent chief climbed a mountain behind his village to die. When the chief reached the summit, "he turned round to take one last look at the ocean. He saw the moon rising in the distant sky. On the moon-path, a few minutes later, he saw a beautiful big canoe, bigger than any he had ever seen. It had large white wings, like a giant sea-gull flying." The chief concluded that this had to be "the moon's canoe" and that "the children of the moon must be coming down to the earth. Something unusual is going to happen. Will all of us die, or are our enemies coming to attack us?" He rushed back to his village with the news that the moon's people were on their way but was greeted with howls of laughter and scorn. However, the next day the villagers were startled to see a "big canoe" just offshore.

The Cowichan say that their ancestors then called an urgent council meeting to determine what to do. They decided "to select twelve men, clean in body and in heart" and send them out to greet the moon's people. The chief who had first sighted the strangers was so curious about them that he could not wait for a report from the ambassadors, and he jumped into their canoe as they pushed off. The party received a warm welcome aboard the ship. The strangers offered them what seemed to be "bones and blood" on shiny plates. The story continues: "When they had finished eating, the moon's people passed their fingers over the Indians' clothes, which were made of sea-otter furs. They seemed to like the feel of the fur so much that one of the young men suggested to the others, 'Let us make them a present of our clothes.'" While on board the ship, the visitors reportedly showed the Cowichan men the wonders of the "fire-stick" by shooting a duck in flight.

As the ambassadors were preparing to leave, the captain of the ship gave them shining dishes. "The Indian chief hung them up in his lodge, where they shone brightly, just like the moon. Over and over again, the twelve young men told the story of their visit to the wonderful canoe, where they saw the wonderful children of the moon. That was the first time any of them had seen white men or tin dishes, the first time they had handled a gun or tasted molasses and biscuits."

SPREADING THE NEWS

Although the Mi'kmaq, Ojibwa, and Cowichan had very different cultural traditions, lived in very different environments, and made first contact at progressively later times, there are some significant common elements and themes to the stories. In each instance, the oral tradition suggests the people were forewarned of the arrival of Europeans. The Mi'kmaq and Ojibwa legends say the warning came in dreams, which were commonly used by storytellers to enhance their authority and power. It is likely that they learned about the presence of the newcomers elsewhere on the continent from overlapping storytelling and trading networks.

Storytelling was a lively art and an important part of life in communities across Native Canada, as it was among other non-literate Aboriginal groups around the world. The best storytellers were held in high regard for their eloquence, imagination, and sense of drama and humour. This means, of course, that the written words we have today do not do justice to their stories. Nonetheless, there is little doubt that a raconteur's tales about a personal encounter with Europeans, or the rumoured experiences of the encounters of others, would have captivated listeners and increased the status of the storyteller. If exotic goods accompanied the fantastic account, so much the better. Contact stories provided a few members of every group with a powerful incentive to search out the newcomers. As the Ojibwa legend suggests, and later European accounts confirm, Native people sometimes travelled remarkable distances to obtain comparatively few European articles.

All this indicates that after the very first contacts were made on the Atlantic and Pacific coasts, most Native people were not surprised by the arrival of Europeans in their territory. In fact, European explorers often record that when they first arrived in a new area, it was not uncommon for the local people to tell them about the presence of other Europeans in distant lands. Nicolas Jeremie, a Frenchman who was stationed at Fort Bourbon on the western shore of Hudson Bay between 1694 and 1714, reported: "The natives say that after several months travel to the west south west they have found the sea on which they have seen large canoes (they mean ships), with men who have beards and who wear caps, and who gather gold on the shore of the sea." Undoubtedly they were referring to

Spaniards operating either on the California coast or, more likely, in the Gulf of Mexico. It is unlikely, but not impossible, that any of Jeremie's informants had actually visited either place.

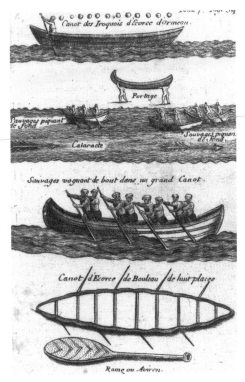

When the French explorer Pierre Gaultier de Varennes, Sieur de La Vérendrye, pushed the French trading-post frontier to the Lake of the Woods region of present-day Ontario in the late 1720s, he asked two Cree he met there about the territory beyond. They told him "… positively that there are whites [somewhere to the southwest], and that they have seen wood sawn into boards; these people, too, use boats, according to the description they give of their canoes. This appeared to astonish them a good deal, because in all that great extent of country such a thing as an axe or gun is never seen. There are a great many different kinds of wood there, and the animals are strange to them." He concluded, probably correctly, that the two men were referring to the Spanish colonial

A drawing of Native people using a canoe, published in Baron de Lahontan's New Voyages to North America, *1703. The European-looking men, the depiction of their paddling methods, and the appearance of the canoe all indicate that the illustrator had no firsthand knowledge of the subject.*

frontier to the southwest and not to the English presence on Hudson Bay and James Bay. Certainly the trees and animals found in north-central Canada would not have been unfamiliar to the Woodland Cree. So, remarkably, the Native people in the heart of the continent were receiving news and circulating stories about events that were occurring thousands of miles away on unknown shores.

The Scottish explorer-trader Alexander Mackenzie had a similar experience about seventy years later, during his voyage to the Pacific Coast. At the headwaters of the Peace River, he encountered the Athapaskan-speaking Tsek'ehne people, from whom he wanted "to gain such information respecting the country as I concluded it was in their power to afford me." Although the Tsek'ehene did not tell him how to reach the coast, since they had never travelled there themselves, they were

In this drawing, Inuit greet Sir John Franklin's second overland expedition to Great Bear Lake and the Arctic, 1824–25. These people hoped the expedition would herald the beginning of direct trading contact with Europeans. They had little to offer that interested European traders, however, and regular trade had to await the expansion of commercial whaling from Alaska later in the century and the development of a strong market for arctic fox in the early twentieth century.

plugged in to a trading network that extended more than three hundred miles to the west over rugged terrain. The network probably involved at least four different groups—the Tsek'ehne; the western Athapaskan-speaking Carrier of the upper Fraser River area, who spoke a dialect different from that of the Tsek'ene; the Tsimshian-speaking Gitxsan; and the coastal Tsimshian of the Skeena River watershed. Mackenzie noted that the Tsek'ehne had iron tools "they obtained from the people who inhabit the bank of that river [Fraser River] ... in exchange for beaver skins, and dressed moose skins. They represented the latter as traveling, during a moon, to get to the country of other tribes, who live in houses, with whom they traffic for the same commodities; and that these also extend their journeys in the same manner to the sea coast, or, to use their expression, the Stinking Lake, where they trade with people like us, that come there in vessels as big as islands." Mackenzie's report demonstrates that distance, difficult terrain, and language diversity did not stop the movement of goods and exchange of ideas in Native Canada.

This sampling of oral traditions also shows that Aboriginal people were very interested in the world that lay beyond their own homelands. Even though the Europeans were frightening at first because of the power of some of their goods—particularly firearms—most Native people quickly overcame their fear and sought regular contact. The idea that Europeans explored Native Canada is part of the mythology that the newcomers created to justify seizing territory and to glorify their own deeds in the bargain. In reality, Aboriginal men and women guided European "explorers" across the continent. They also established the trading and provisioning networks that Europeans subsequently took over and welded to their own expanding empires during the age of mercantilism.

Clearly, at the beginning of contact, Native people held the upper hand—or at the very least an equal one—for long periods and over vast areas. The ways they greeted Europeans tell us a great deal about their confidence and excitement at the prospect of exploring new opportunities, long before things went terribly wrong and they found themselves pushed into ever-shrinking niches of their former homelands.

CHAPTER 4

WELCOMING THE
NEWCOMERS

The Beaver does everything perfectly well, it makes kettles, hatchets, swords, knives, bread,
and in short, it makes everything.

—Innu trading captain, early seventeenth century

Why did Native people react to the arrival of Europeans by welcoming them to the far corners of their land and guiding them nearly every step of the way? In addition to their desire to learn more about the newcomers and their world, they saw in the early fur trade a mutually rewarding opportunity. Over the years, this enterprise served as the crucible in which the two parties forged customs for interacting with each other. These traditions outlasted the fur trade itself, and some are still with us today.

A FLEETING ENCOUNTER

The very first visits of Europeans to Native Canada are shrouded in mystery. For many years, Norse sagas suggested that Vikings had made landfalls somewhere along the northeastern coast of North America. Archaeologists confirmed this in 1960, when they discovered the remains of a small Norse settlement at L'Anse aux Meadows on the northern tip of Newfoundland. Excavations indicated that Vikings had arrived here at the end of the tenth century and had displaced an unknown Aboriginal group at the site.

We do not know how the local people reacted to the Viking pioneers. The absence of fortifications at L'Anse aux Meadows suggests that they did not threaten the newcomers. In fact, the archaeological remains hint of little contact of any kind between the two groups. The discovery of the ruins of several Viking houses, a smithy, and a carpentry shop has led archaeologists to conclude that the visitors built boats there. Norse accounts indicate that the likely purpose of the visit was to

European artists often portrayed the beaver anthropomorphically. Here Native hunters are shown pursuing the animal with metal trade axes, which were used with ice chisels to open frozen beaver lodges. These two European wares were essential components of a trapper's equipment until the steel-spring leg-hold trap came into widespread use in the late eighteenth century.

obtain timber and furs, which were shipped back to Greenland. At that time, the Vikings were the great fur traders of the Baltic region. They apparently came to Native Canada with the expectation of trading. The Norse legends suggest that the local people were interested in acquiring metal tools and weapons, but that the northern seafarers refused to exchange weaponry for furs. In any event, the Vikings quickly abandoned the site. They had pushed westward across the north Atlantic during a warm climatic phase. As weather conditions deteriorated, they withdrew eastward. By A.D. 1100, the would-be settlers had vacated L'Anse aux Meadows and shortly thereafter Aboriginal people reoccupied the location.

Another five hundred years passed before adventurers from the Old World returned to the same general area. They came back during the so-called Age of Enlightenment, when overseas exploration and expansion would see Europeans sail around the world. A Genoese named John Cabot led the way, sailing under the flag of Henry VII of England. After an eight-week voyage, Cabot arrived on June 24, 1497, somewhere in Native Atlantic Canada—most likely northern Newfoundland or Labrador in the vicinity of Belle Isle. Like his Italian contemporary Christopher Columbus, Cabot hoped to find a route to the rich markets of Asia by sailing west. His erroneous belief that he had found an unknown northeastern corner of the Asian continent sent him back to England, claiming the land for Henry VII. Cabot's apparent success won him backing for a second expedition, from which he never returned.

Cabot's initial voyage to the rich cod fisheries of the Atlantic region whetted the appetites of other Europeans, particularly the Portuguese. Between 1500 and 1528, they probed most of the outer coast between Hudson Strait and what is now northern New England. This renewed contact with Europeans had a sinister aspect for nations living along the Atlantic. The Portuguese expeditions established that the region was not part of Asia and that the inhabitants, unlike those of Central and South America, had little to plunder or trade. On the other hand, these unknown people excited the curiosity of the Portuguese at home and might make good slaves. With this possibility in mind, one of the early navigators, Gaspar Corte-Real, sent two caravels back to Portugal with Native captives on board.

Although Europeans regularly took people from Native Canada to Europe against their will until well into the seventeenth century, they quickly gave up on the idea of developing a slave trade. Instead, they continued their search for a passage to Asia through northern North America. Following in the tradition established by their Spanish contemporaries in Mexico and South America, they also looked for new civilizations to plunder. Jacques Cartier, the French explorer, is the best known of these early visitors. In 1534 he ventured into the Gulf of St Lawrence, and the next year he travelled up the well-populated St Lawrence valley as far as the Iroquoian village of Hochelaga (Montreal). The accounts of his two expeditions are the first extensive European commentary on the Mi'kmaq and the only detailed descriptions of the St Lawrence valley Iroquois in their homeland. They give us a clear idea how these people reacted to the European and his compatriots.

According to Cartier's journals, the first contact was a clumsy, rather comical affair. On the last day of June 1534, while Cartier and his crew were sailing along the northeastern shore of Prince Edward Island, they saw boatloads of people crossing a river, but sea and wind conditions prevented them from making contact. The next day the explorer reported seeing a Mi'kmaq man "running behind our boats, which were coasting the shore, and making many signs to us to turn back." When the French wheeled about, though, the anonymous man "took to his heels." Intent on demonstrating his good intentions, Cartier "landed, and laid ... a knife and a woolen belt on a stick, and thereupon returned to our vessels." With these tentative steps, contact began.

The two nervous groups finally connected at Chaleur Bay on July 6. This time

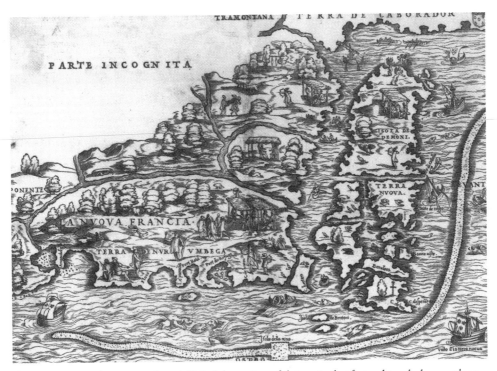

European cartographers commonly embellished the portions of their maps that featured poorly known places with imaginative sketches of people and their environment. This mid-sixteenth-century map shows Aboriginal people of New France living a life of ease in a hunter's Garden of Eden.

a large party of Mi'kmaq travelling in forty to fifty canoes met Cartier while he was exploring the shoreline in one of his small boats. Once again the Mi'kmaq made peaceful overtures: "A great number of these people leaped ashore with a great shout, and made signs to us to land, holding up skins on the ends of sticks." On this occasion, it was Cartier who proved to be timid. Being greatly outnumbered, he did not "trust their signs" and tried to retreat to his ship. The Mi'kmaq persisted, however, and surrounded the boat. Frightened by their action, Cartier shot "two fire-lances" over their heads in an attempt to drive them off. Only after a second volley did the Mi'kmaq hurry away, enabling Cartier to reach his ship.

The next day, a party of Mi'kmaq returned to a point near Cartier's anchorage, where they signalled their wish to barter. A much-relieved Cartier "likewise made signs to them that we wished them no harm, and in sign of this two of our men landed to approach them, and bring them knives and other ironware, with a red hat to give to their chief." The Mi'kmaq readily understood this diplomatic gesture and a brisk trade ensued. Cartier said the Mi'kmaq showed "great and marvellous joy to possess this ironware and other said articles, dancing continually and going through various ceremonies.... [T]hey gave us all they had, keeping nothing back; and were compelled to go away stark naked, making signs to us that they would return on the next day with more skins." When Cartier met another group of nearly three hundred Mi'kmaq several days later, everyone knew what to do. The Mi'kmaq sent the Europeans a present of cooked seal meat; the French replied with gifts of mittens, knives, necklaces, and other miscellaneous items. With this traditional peace offering out of the way, the two groups got down to business, bartering until the Mi'kmaq once again had parted with all their furs, including the clothing off their backs.

Cartier's meetings with the Mi'kmaq demonstrate just how difficult it was for these two groups of wary strangers to trade, even when one party was enthusiastic about doing so. The Mi'kmaq's eagerness to obtain French goods also strongly suggests that they were already accustomed to bartering with Europeans, albeit irregularly. They had probably dealt with cod fishermen who had been visiting the area since Cabot's time. In fact, linguists have suggested that a few of the Mi'kmaq words that were recorded in Cartier's journal may be of a Portuguese trade-pidgin derivation.

In any event, Cartier followed traditional Native diplomatic and trading practices when he bartered with the Mi'kmaq. Perhaps he had gathered information about these practices from fishermen or other European explorers who had preceded him. Particularly noteworthy is Cartier's gift of a red hat to one of the Mi'kmaq leaders. Throughout Native Canada, the presentation of "a captain's outfit," key components of which were a hat and coat, became a customary way for Europeans to acknowledge Native leaders. The practice endured into the twentieth century.

Shortly after Cartier left the Mi'kmaq, he encountered people from the St Lawrence valley Iroquoian village of Stadacona at one of their summer mackerel-fishing camps located north of Chaleur Bay near the tip of the Gaspé Peninsula. The Stadaconans were keenly interested in trading with him, but they had very few furs to offer. Nonetheless, the two parties exchanged presents and bartered until the Stadaconans had nothing left to exchange for Cartier's wares. After this auspicious beginning, relations turned sour, however, when Cartier committed two *faux pas* in terms of Native diplomacy. First, he claimed the land for the French Crown by erecting a cross on which he inscribed Long Live the King of France. Donnacona, the principal headman of the Stadaconans, immediately denounced this act. Cartier wrote, "When we had returned to our ships, the chief, dressed in an old black bear-skin, arrived in a canoe with three of his sons and his brother.... And pointing to the cross he made us a long harangue, making the sign of the cross with two of his fingers; and then he pointed to the land all around about, as if he wished to say that all this region belonged to him, and that we ought not to have set up this cross without his permission." To appease the chief, Cartier deceived him by indicating that he had merely erected a navigation marker so that he could find the location again when he returned from France.

Cartier's second, and even more offensive, deed was to kidnap two of Donnacona's sons. He lured the young men to his ship by promising to give them presents. Cartier wanted to use them as guides for an expedition to their homeland he planned to make the following summer. If the explorer had followed Native diplomatic traditions by offering two of his own men as replacements, Donnacona would not have been alarmed and angered. By not doing so, Cartier had committed a hostile act and placed his relationship with the Stadaconans on a very bad footing.

In 1535 Cartier returned with his two captives, who were reunited with their father, but he promptly made another series of blunders, which would prove even more costly to his ambitions in the long term. First, he set up a winter camp in the vicinity of present-day Quebec City without securing prior permission from the nearby Stadaconan villagers. Next, he rebuffed Donnacona's attempt to cement an alliance with him. He then travelled through the Stadaconans' territory to visit the Hochelagans without asking for permission to do so, and without taking along a guide or interpreter. Although the Hochelagans enthusiastically received him in their large fortified village, he rejected their hospitality—staying with them less than a day. The suspicious-minded Cartier did not trust his hosts in spite of their lavish displays of good will; he preferred the "safety" of his own camp. He also may have been rude because he was disappointed to learn that the St Lawrence River did not lead to Asia.

During the winter, many of Cartier's party were weakened by or died of scurvy. The explorer tried to hide their misfortune from the Stadaconans, fearing the latter would attack his sick men. He was badly mistaken. Once the Stadaconans learned of the plight of the Frenchmen, they taught them how to make a drink from white-cedar fronds that was rich in what we now call vitamin C. Meanwhile, Donnacona boosted Cartier's spirits by telling him stories about a metal-rich kingdom to the west called Saguenay. Bruce Trigger, the pre-eminent scholar of the Canadian Iroquoians, suspects that Donnacona was referring to the area of high-grade native copper located in Lake Superior country. Cartier, of course, thought the chief was speaking about gold and silver, and he began to devise a scheme to search for booty there, rather than continue the search for a passage to Asia. For his new plan to be feasible, he would have to establish a colony near the vicinity of his winter camp to serve as a base of operations.

Getting backing for this risky venture now became Cartier's main concern. He decided that Donnacona could help in this regard in France, so he abducted the hapless chief, his sons, and seven other Stadaconans, including at least one woman, and set sail in the summer of 1536. During the course of the winter, Donnacona entertained François I and his court with fictional accounts of the riches of Saguenay. These stories had the effect Cartier desired—the king decided to back the establishment of a colony. In the hope of regaining his freedom and that of his sons, Donnacona repeatedly assured his captors that he would guide them to the fabled kingdom. The French, however, had no intention of allowing any of their captives to go home. One reason was Cartier's belief that the chief represented a potential threat to his scheme. By the time the colonial expedition set sail in 1541, all but one of the unfortunate hostages had died of various ailments.

On his return to the St Lawrence valley, Cartier selected a site for the proposed colony near Stadacona, again without permission. Understandably, the Stadaconans were now openly hostile to the French intruders. The villagers and their neighbours assailed the tiny French settlement over the winter, killing thirty-five or more of the colonists. Continued Stadaconan aggression, food shortages, and scurvy forced the disheartened survivors to withdraw in 1543. Cartier's greed, antagonistic acts, and failure to adhere to indigenous diplomatic customs had sealed their fate. The Stadaconans made it very clear that settlement would be difficult here, or elsewhere, without the local people's support, which would not be forthcoming if the French or other Europeans ignored their customs.

For the time being, the newcomers were not interested in any further attempts to settle in the St Lawrence region. There was simply no prospect of reaping the sorts of quick and lucrative rewards that the Spanish had found to the south. But the cod fishery continued to expand, and commercial whaling became a major enterprise in the Gulf of St Lawrence by the middle of the sixteenth century. Basques, who were particularly active in this industry, established several whaling stations along the north shore of the gulf to process their catches.

The growing cod fishery and whaling industry brought increasing numbers of fishermen and whalers to the region, and they eagerly bought furs and skins from Native people with European goods. The sale of Native products in Europe provided a welcome supplement to their modest fishing and whaling incomes.

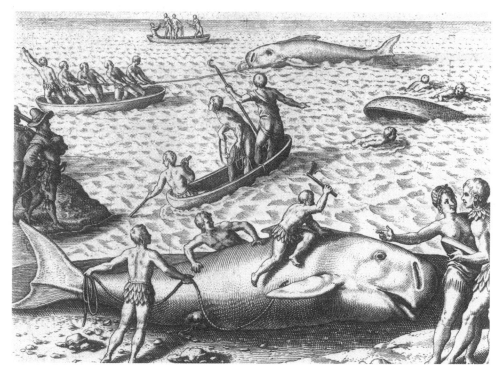

An etching of Aboriginal people, most likely Innu, participating in European whaling activities in the Gulf of St Lawrence at the beginning of the seventeenth century.

Unfortunately, few records exist of the informal trade, so it is difficult to estimate the quantities of goods that changed hands. Nonetheless, historians conclude that some Native groups, notably the Mi'kmaq, obtained enough European metal weapons during the sixteenth century to gain a military advantage over their neighbours. They used their superior weaponry to expand hunting and trapping territories so that they could better supply their European trading partners. Before the end of the century, the Mi'kmaq had driven the Stadaconans from their traditional summer fishing places in the Gaspé area, and by the early seventeenth century they occupied the entire peninsula. Later, they forced the neighbouring Maliseet out of portions of the eastern sections of the St John's River watershed.

The disappearance of the St Lawrence valley Iroquoians was the most dramatic and puzzling change to take place during the fishery- and whaling-based fur-trade era. All the people visited by Cartier between 1534 and 1536 had vanished by 1600. Trigger makes a strong case that they were the victims of warfare among nations. As early as 1534, the Mi'kmaq killed up to two hundred Stadaconans in a confrontation in the Gaspé area. The Stadaconans also could have suffered at the hands of other Iroquoians from the southwest, particularly the Mohawk, who may have been trying to gain direct access to Europeans in the gulf after Cartier's time.

Today we have no idea how many St Lawrence valley Iroquoians may have survived the warfare, and we do not know for certain where they sought refuge. Most likely some would have fled to the Algonquins of the Ottawa River region and to the Innu of the Saguenay River region. Perhaps Hochelagan refugees trekked to the Abenaki country of present-day northern New England. What we do know is that the arrival of the newcomers led initially to increased bloodshed among nations and to major population dislocations.

SELLING OLD WINTER COATS TO FOREIGN FOOLS

As the sixteenth century drew to a close, the gathering momentum of a fashion whim gave Europeans a powerful incentive to trade with Native people in North America on a much grander scale than in the past. Europeans developed an insatiable appetite for felt hats, which became the rage after the middle of the century—remaining so for nearly three centuries. Hatters created their finest products using felt made from the underfur, or "wool," of beaver pelts. Consequently, the demand for this raw material skyrocketed and the hat industry became the driving force behind the fur trade. By the time the craze began, however, the beaver had been nearly exterminated in Europe; it was plentiful only in Siberia and northern North America. The stage was now set for merchants to specialize in the fur trade, in the process freeing it from its old links to the fishing and whaling industries.

Of great importance to Aboriginal people was the fact that western European felt makers had not yet developed an industrial process to extract the unwanted guard hairs from the beaver pelts to obtain the prized underfur. The Russians had perfected a process for doing this, but they refused to share their technological secret. Understandably, they wanted to profit from their invention by processing pelts for foreigners. This of course greatly increased the cost of producing felt in western Europe. Native people offered a solution to this problem by selling the Europeans their used winter beaver coats. Because they wore these garments with the hair side turned inward, the guard hairs eventually fell out. Felt makers could use coat-beaver skins, called *castor gras* by the French, without having to send them to Russia first. As a result, coat beaver became the staple of the fur trade by the closing decades of the sixteenth century. Europeans no longer looked on Native clothing with the disdain evident in Cabot's or Cartier's memoirs. Winter coats had become soft gold.

The development of a strong market for coat beaver radically changed the fur trade. By the time this market shift occurred, the Mi'kmaq and Innu were already seasoned fur traders with nearly eighty years of experience dealing with Europeans; however, geographic circumstances made it harder for the Mi'kmaq to take advantage of the new economic development. Their homeland and population were too small to sustain large-scale beaver harvests. Although they tried to deal with this problem by using force to displace their Stadaconan and Maliseet neighbours, this was an ineffective way to increase coat-beaver supplies. The most valuable beaver coats had to have been worn for one or more years (ideally two or three). Seizing portions of neighbouring nations' territories and driving them away certainly would yield some booty and a slightly expanded resource base, but it would not secure a larger supply of coat beaver on a continuing basis. In short, the larger the number of people living within a trading network, the greater the success of the Native fur traders. The key to increased coat-beaver supplies lay in expanded trading networks.

The Innu were in a much better location to expand than the Mi'kmaq. The Saguenay River gave them access to the interior of the eastern and central Subarctic, which was prime beaver country. They wasted no time in taking advantage of their strategic position by extending their trading connections west and northwest to the upper Ottawa River and to James Bay. Lac St Jean on the upper Saguenay River became a major rendezvous for these entrepreneurs. As the first major Native trade brokers, or middlemen of the fur trade, the Innu carried European goods inland to other nations and brought back the furs they purchased with the imported items. This activity drew them into a tighter alliance with the Algonquian-speaking groups of the Ottawa valley and the four-nation Huron confederacy of Georgian Bay.

In their new economic role, the Innu were able to skilfully out-manoeuvre their European trading partners. Well before the turn of the century, Tadoussac, at the outlet of the Saguenay, had become the main centre for trade. The Innu soon realized that they could reap greater benefits in a competitive market if they waited until the ships of rival traders appeared in the harbour before agreeing to do any bartering. The Europeans complained that this tactic had turned the trade into an auction, thereby making it impossible for the Old World merchants to realize their customary profits. For their part, the Innu apparently thought the Europeans were

An Innu man builds a canoe using traditional methods in the early 1900s. These light craft enabled the Innu to create one of the earliest post-contact trading networks.

foolish for letting themselves be manipulated. In 1634 Father Le Jeune, a Jesuit priest, wrote that the Innu "say it [beaver] is the animal well-beloved by the French, English and Basques,—in a word, by the Europeans." Le Jeune noted that his Native host "was making sport of us Europeans, who have such a fondness for the skin of this animal and who fight to see who will get it; they carry this to such an extent that my host said to me one day, showing me a beautiful knife, 'The English have no sense; they give us twenty knives like this for one Beaver skin.'" What Le Jeune seemingly did not know was that the Innu obtained their furs from their partners in the interior at much lower prices than they charged the Europeans for them.

   Soon, however, the Europeans learned they could obtain cheaper furs, and more of them, if they dealt directly with the Innu's suppliers. Obviously, the inland trading partners welcomed this turn of events because it offered them not only the prospect of receiving cheaper goods directly from the Europeans but also the chance to develop their own trading empire beyond the newcomers' reach. This set of conflicting economic aspirations would characterize the commercial fur trade throughout its history and would drive it forward across the continent between the early seventeenth century and the late eighteenth century. Each time a new group of Native middlemen emerged, European traders moved to outflank them. Native entrepreneurs were always in the forefront, drawing new groups into the fur trade, while European explorer/traders followed in their wake. The golden age of the Innu in the fur trade was brief, as it would be for a succession of groups who replaced them as middlemen on the westward-moving trading frontier.

Pierre Chauvin de Tonnetuit and his associates launched the first French effort to bypass the Innu. After receiving a monopoly on the fur trade from the French Crown in 1599, they sought to establish themselves by winning over the Innu. Chauvin did so by promising to help them subdue their Mohawk foes, who were trying to gain control over the region and the fur trade. Initially he restricted military assistance to the provision of hatchets, knives, and other weapons—excepting firearms. This arrangement appealed to the Innu because it enabled them to offer French hatchets and knives as inducements to persuade neighbouring Algonquian-speaking groups to help them in their struggle against the Mohawk. They also offered some of the groups the additional incentive of direct trading access to the French at Tadoussac. The strategy worked, and by 1603 the Innu had formed large mixed war parties and pierced deep into Mohawk territory.

Success for the Innu came at a price. They became dependent on the French for support and lost most of their bargaining power with them as a consequence. When the French moved forward from Tadoussac to the north shore of the St Lawrence River, they gained direct access to some of the Innu's trading partners. The Innu had to accept this economic setback and console themselves with the prospect that the new settlement would shield them from Mohawk raiders and draw the French directly into the ongoing conflict. These were worthwhile considerations, inasmuch as the valley had become a hotly contested "no-man's land" well before Samuel de Champlain established his Habitation of Quebec in 1608.

It was not long before the French had to take an active part in the rapidly escalating armed struggle. In the summer of 1609, Champlain and two of his men joined roughly sixty Algonquians and Huron in an attack on about two hundred Mohawk who were camped at Lake Champlain. This was apparently the first time the Mohawk had ever encountered European firearms. The harquebuses fired by Champlain and his men were crude weapons, but they terrified the Mohawk, who fled. The triumphant Algonquians and Huron, following in hot pursuit, killed several of their enemies and took a small number of captives.

The French would later have cause to wonder about the wisdom of the alliance they had made against what turned out to be the powerful "League of Houdenosaunee," or Five Nations, comprising the Mohawk, Oneida, Onondaga, Cayuga, and Seneca. When the French arrived in Native Canada, this Iroquois confederacy was still in its initial stages of development. Member groups, particularly the Mohawk and Seneca, were actively seeking to increase their numbers and territory through raiding activity beyond their traditional homelands in what is today New York State. The French presence in the St Lawrence valley, and the French alliance with the Algonquian-speaking groups and the Huron confederacy, momentarily threatened to upset the balance of power in the region, to the detriment of the Five Nations.

As these events were unfolding, the inland allies of the French wasted no time capitalizing on the new economic and strategic situation. The Algonquian-speaking Allumette of the Ottawa valley, for example, encouraged the French to establish a forward post near present-day Montreal so they would have better access to trade goods. By this time the Allumette had established themselves as middlemen between their northern and northwestern neighbours and the French. Because they wanted to prevent the French from disrupting this existing trading arrangement, they refused to let Champlain pass through their territory in 1613 to visit the Huron. They did, however, appreciate his offer of gifts and his promise to help them repel the marauding Iroquois. Champlain made these diplomatic gestures in the hope they would gain him right of passage up the Ottawa River at a later date.

His overtures paid off two years later. By then, pressing strategic concerns forced the Allumette to change their minds. They and their Algonquian-speaking allies needed the help of the Huron to combat the Oneida and Onondaga, who were raiding the lower Ottawa River country with increasing impunity. As a reward for their support, the Allumette granted the Huron the privilege of passing through their country to visit the French, subject, of course, to the payment of tolls. Given this new arrangement, the Allumette had little reason to deny Champlain the right to venture up the Ottawa River en route to Huronia—provided that he, too, paid a toll.

While he was a guest of the Huron, Champlain took part in another military campaign that had the effect of cancelling many of the gains he had made on his 1609 adventure. This time he accompanied the Huron on a raid south of Lake Ontario, which ended in the siege of a well-fortified village. Unlike before, however, French firearms had little impact on the course of the fighting. The Huron

An illustration from Champlain's account of his voyages in New France showing an unsuccessful Huron attack on an Iroquoian village south of Lake Ontario in 1615. Elements of the drawing, such as the construction of the inner palisade, are reasonably accurate, whereas the outer wall and village layout are fabrications by the artist.

had to withdraw after several of their men were killed; Champlain himself was wounded. This defeat destroyed the psychological edge that the French and their allies had gained earlier over the Iroquois. It marked the end of the opening phase of contact.

CHAPTER 5

NEW FRIENDS AND FOES

It has happened very often, that where we were most welcome, where we baptized most people, there it was in fact where they died the most; and, on the contrary, in the cabins to which we were denied entrance, although they were sometimes sick to extremity, at the end of a few days one saw every person prosperously cured. We shall see in heaven the secret, but ever adorable, judgments of God therein.

—Father Gabriel Lalemant, 1640

A new era of Native diplomacy, trade, and warfare began when the Dutch arrived on the Hudson River and built Fort Orange near the confluence of the Hudson and Mohawk rivers in 1624. Rival European powers were now located on two of the major gateways to the heart of the continent, and both were eager to make commercial and military alliances with the two Aboriginal power blocs in the lower Great Lakes and St Lawrence River valley hinterland—the Huron confederacy and its Algonquian-speaking allies, and the League of the Five Nations. Although the Native people gained powerful new confederates and exacted more favourable rates of exchange from the Europeans in the bargain, in the end they paid a heavy price in bloodshed and the destruction of several Native nations. Furthermore, while the various nations battled one another, their European allies became firmly entrenched in the region and missionaries began to undermine traditional beliefs.

MISSIONARIES ON THE TRADING FRONTIER

Winning the trading loyalties of Native people was essential to the success of French imperial policy: the Crown had tied the fur trade to its colonial expansion plans through the practice of granting merchants trading monopolies on the condition that they used some of their profits to establish colonies. Cartier's experience

A reconstruction of a traditional Huron longhouse at the Sainte-Marie-among-the-Hurons mission near present-day Midland, Ontario. Archaeological data, such as the distribution of old supporting poles and hearths, combined with the accounts of French explorers and missionaries, provide the information needed for such a reconstruction.

had also made it clear that Native people could either help a colony succeed or destroy it. Once the French had to face rival European claimants for territory in the Atlantic and eastern Great Lakes regions, the retention of Native groups as military allies became increasingly important.

The Crown turned to Catholic missionaries to Christianize Native people, while simultaneously introducing them to French ways, in an attempt to make them loyal allies. A variety of tactics was used to win converts, including the promise of preferential trading privileges. Given that acculturation became a goal of the state, it is not surprising that all the major religious institutions in France supported the strategy, even if some of the missionaries in the field did not. A few Jesuits, for instance, believed that groups like the Huron could adopt the Catholic faith even as they retained most of the other aspects of their traditional culture.

In the beginning, the acculturation program focused on promoting inter-racial marriages, providing education, and persuading Aboriginal groups to abandon their hunting lifestyle. By encouraging common-law marriages between French men and Native women, the authorities hoped to create one people, replacing the indigenous population in the process. These unions came to be known as *mariages à la façon du pays*. Although canon law prohibited the marriage of Catholics to "pagans," priests often blessed such couples anyway and sometimes baptized their children. The French Crown reversed its position at the beginning of the eighteenth century and began to discourage such unions in the belief that interracial marriages were producing a "bad race" in North America. However, the Native people and Frenchmen in the interior paid little attention to colonial or Church policies. They continued to form unions as they pleased, for many reasons, including, in keeping with Native traditions, the cementing of trading and military alliances.

The education program began at an early date. Priests taught children at the missions, and they also sent a few "novices" to France in the hope of creating a male Native "elite" who would be able to lead the evangelical and acculturation efforts among their people. An Innu boy called Pastedechouan was among the earliest to make the trip. In 1620 the Récollets sent him to France, where he studied for five years. Tragically he could no longer speak his mother tongue when he returned, and he felt out of place back home with his kinfolk. The Jesuits eventually had to take him in and employ him as a language teacher in Quebec City. But by this time, Pastedechouan could not find comfort in either culture. He became an alcoholic and starved to death in the forests north of the city. Pastedechouan's misfortune was a harbinger of things to come for many other Native people who became trapped between two cultural worlds, unable to find a place for themselves in either. Despite early problems of this sort, training Native children with the view of using them to win over their kinfolk remained an important aspect of missionary work for years, especially among Protestant sects.

In the early years of the seventeenth century, the French sent a few Native girls overseas for training, to prepare them either for marriage to French settlers or for a religious vocation. When the Ursulines came to Canada in 1639, they brought one young Native woman named Louise with them. The arrival of the order largely ended the practice of sending Aboriginal girls to France. Thereafter, the children studied at convents in the colonies, where the instruction they received was intended to make them suitable marriage partners for Christian men.

Soon after contact, the idea took hold among the newcomers that they would have to settle Native people in fixed locations before they could "civilize" and Christianize them. In subsequent years, missionaries of all denominations shared this opinion. It was the Jesuits, though, who took the first steps in a process that would lead to the establishment of the reserve system in Canada. In 1637 they created the Sillery reserve near Quebec City with the financial backing of Noel Brulart de Sillery, a wealthy nobleman. It was modelled on settlements the Jesuits had established in Brazil in 1549. The priests hoped to relocate Innu hunters and Algonquin on this reserve beside French farmers. They thought the settlers could teach the displaced Native people how to farm while the priests kept a close eye on their spiritual development.

The experiment at Sillery was not encouraging. The Algonquin hated their new sedentary life and were unable to feed themselves from their fields. Colonial and missionary authorities concluded that locating reserves adjacent to French settlements was a bad idea. They believed that each group picked up only the worst aspects of the other's culture. Consequently, the authorities decided that reserves should isolate and protect Native people from the evils of settler society so that the priests and Native catechists could teach them the arts of civilization before integrating them into French society. Using this line of thinking, the Jesuits concentrated their missionary effort in Huronia. The Récollet fathers, who began their missionary work in New France in 1615, had already learned that efforts to convert the nomadic groups of the boreal forests were exhausting and unrewarding. The Huron and other Iroquoian-speakers, however, already practised agriculture, spent substantial portions of the year in their villages, and were remote from French settlements along the St Lawrence River. In short, they seemed to be ideal candidates for conversion.

CONFLICTING INTERESTS

At the same time that the French missionaries were gaining a solid toehold in Huronia, the Five Nations were being well armed by their Dutch allies at Fort Orange and were ready to take advantage of their military strength. They intensified their raiding activity to the north of Lake Ontario and changed their fighting methods. No longer satisfied merely to secure booty and a few captives, they decided to destroy their opponents. The explanation for this change of tactics has been that the Iroquois lived in a marginal beaver-producing country and had been unable to gain peaceful access to the northern fur trade through a trading alliance with the northern nations. Recently some scholars have suggested that the Iroquois took captives and pressured other groups to merge with them in order to replace the population losses they had sustained in post-contact epidemics.

This portion of a map by J. B. L. Franquelin shows an imaginary Native camp adjacent to Quebec City in 1699. Innu Catholic converts and refugees from the Beaver Wars in the eastern Great Lakes region began settling in the Quebec City area in the early seventeenth century.

Whatever their reason, in 1647 and 1648 the eastern Iroquois fell on the Algonquin bands of the lower Ottawa River and sent them fleeing in terror. During the next three years, the Iroquois focused their assaults on the upper Ottawa valley area, the Nipissing region, and Huronia—the key to the French trading network at that time.

The Huron confederacy failed to mount a co-ordinated response to the crisis, owing, in large part, to the social disintegration taking place in their villages as a result of disease and Christianization. Epidemics had killed many of their elders, who normally would have provided leadership, and had weakened their Algonquian-speaking allies as well. (Initially, Native people believed that sorcery practised by the "black robes" was responsible for the epidemics.) Meanwhile, missionaries had created social rifts that set "Christians" against "traditionalists." French imperial policy dictated that firearms be traded only to converts, although their Iroquoian enemies had unrestricted access to the new weapons.

Beleaguered by these and other problems, the Huron suffered a series of crushing defeats, especially in the spring of 1649. Such setbacks led them to abandon and burn their remaining villages and look for refuge elsewhere. Some Huron joined their trading partners; others sought refuge at the fortified Jesuit mission of Sainte-Marie-among-the-Hurons. Fearing that they could not hold out against an Iroquois onslaught, the French relocated the mission to nearby Christian Island in Georgian Bay. Although it was a more defensible site, the island lacked the resources needed to feed the large number of Christian Huron refugees who gathered there. During the winter of 1649–50, hunger and disease took a terrible toll, and the Jesuits decided to abandon the island the following June. At least three hundred of the remaining Huron took refuge at French mission stations, notably

Lorette near Quebec City. Other refugees moved west to the upper Great Lakes or joined their Iroquois enemies. Huronia ceased to exist.

With the Huron essentially out of the picture, the Iroquois turned their muskets on their defeated enemy's neighbours and trading partners. The Petun, who lived near the present-day town of Collingwood, Ontario, were the first to feel their blistering fire; many of them escaped to the Green Bay area of what is now Wisconsin, where they joined forces with exiled Huron and became known as the Wyandot. Next, it was the Nipissing's turn. The Iroquois attacked in the winter of 1649–50, scattering most of them to the west. In 1650 and 1651, the Neutral experienced a similar fate. The Ottawa and other groups, the Ojibwa among them, who had been major trading partners of the Huron moved away to the safety of the southern Lake Superior country to avoid the risk of attack. However, even before they cleared the southern Ontario peninsula of rival nations, the Iroquois had launched massive incursions into the lower Michigan peninsula and much of present-day Ohio and eastern Illinois. As a result of their wide-ranging warfare, they reigned supreme—if only momentarily—in the eastern Great Lakes territory.

Although the French trading system lay in tatters, various Native groups wasted little time stitching it back together. In 1654 the Wyandot and some Ottawa from the upper Great Lakes area arrived in Montreal (founded in 1642) to barter furs they had collected from their neighbours. Other up-country nations soon followed their lead. Some of these middlemen linked up with Cree living southwest and west of James Bay. Meanwhile, a few Innu groups, particularly the Chicoutimi from the vicinity of Lac St Jean and the Attikamek of the St Maurice River country, took advantage of the disruptions in the St Lawrence valley to strengthen their old trading connections with the Eastmain Cree.

The Iroquois had little choice but to watch these developments from the sidelines between 1654 and 1658, partly because the Five Nations, with the exception of the Mohawk, had signed a peace treaty with the French. The accord was short-lived, however, and the Iroquois resumed their offensive in the early 1660s. Between 1661 and 1665 they raided the upper Michigan peninsula and Cree territory as far northeast as Lake Mistassini in northern Quebec. These attacks threatened the security of New France, and the French government reacted by dispatching a regiment to the colony. In January 1666, a force of twelve hundred men carried out an abortive raid into Iroquois territory. The following autumn, as another French force was about to invade their land, four of the Five Nations renewed peace with the French. Only the Mohawk again held out. Some of them favoured coming to terms, but an anti-French faction held sway. The French force fell on the hold-outs and burned four villages, thereby discrediting the hostile Mohawk. This paved the way for a temporary peace and the establishment of Jesuit missions among these people, some of whom readily converted, partly to cement the new alliance. Others resisted, and enmity grew between the two groups. Beginning in 1667, Mohawk and Oneida converts to Christianity began to migrate to the Montreal area. Eventually they settled at present-day Caughnawaga (Kahnawake). Over the years, other Iroquois immigrants formed two additional reserve communities—Oka (Kanesatake) and St Regis (Akwesasne)—in the same general vicinity.

After the English takeover of New Netherland in 1664, the English and the French fought for control of the Hudson River–Mohawk valley corridor and the St Lawrence valley. Both led to the heart of the continent and converged on the homeland of the Five Nations. Whoever won the allegiance of these people, or seized their land, had the best chance of establishing an inland colonial empire. Certainly the English grasped this strategic fact immediately. New York colonial officials continually encouraged the Five Nations to take an aggressive stance towards New France and its Aboriginal allies. Merchants at Albany (formerly Fort Orange) gave the Iroquois the means to do so by supplying them with firearms and other weapons, as well as an array of cheap trade goods to sweeten the deal.

The conflicting interests of the Five Nations and the French, particularly those of the governor of New France, Louis de Buade, Comte de Frontenac, also helped to provoke armed conflict. Frontenac, who received his first appointment in 1672, promoted colonial expansion and the further development of the fur trade, partly to bolster his sagging personal fortune. In 1673 he ordered the construction of Fort Frontenac on the eastern shores of Lake Ontario, and by 1682, the year he was recalled to France, he had established an impressive string of outposts extending southwest as far as the Mississippi River, just below its junction with the Ohio. Needless to say, the Iroquois watched this invasion with growing resentment. They had claimed hunting and trading rights to the land where Frontenac's outposts were situated after their victory in the Beaver Wars of the 1640s and '50s. In 1680, they retaliated. Seven hundred Iroquois warriors punished the Illinois for trading directly with the French by destroying one of their villages and taking several hundred captives. In the heat of the conflict, they wounded at least one Frenchman who was in the area. This action, and the impending threat of an attack on the St Lawrence valley colony, led colonial officials in 1683 to begin placing military garrisons at posts in the Great Lakes area in the hope of deterring the Iroquois.

The Iroquois were not intimidated, however, and continued their raids, forcing the French to take more drastic measures. In 1685 the home government dispatched sixteen hundred soldiers to the colony for defensive purposes. Two years later, the next governor of New France, Jacques-René de Brisay, Marquis de Denonville, drew together a force that included some of these men, colonial militia, and Native reinforcements (mostly old enemies of the Iroquois). He launched an attack on the Seneca. After a brief skirmish with this large invading force, the Seneca wisely decided to withdraw and fight another day. The French force had to content itself with setting fire to some abandoned villages and destroying food supplies. In the end, Denonville's raid had not cowed the Seneca or their allies in the league. Instead, he merely provoked another round of retaliatory raiding that lasted until the end of the seventeenth century.

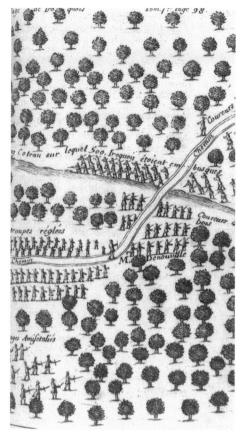

A sketch depicting a battle during the campaign of Governor Jacques-René de Brisay, Marquis de Denonville, against the Seneca in 1687.

Towards the end of this period, the Iroquois faced growing pressure from another quarter. Some of the Ojibwa groups decided to avenge the murders of their kinfolk and other intolerable acts. In the 1690s they fell on the Iroquois who had moved into the southern Ontario region following the collapse of Huronia. In the opening battle of their campaign, Ojibwa warriors in some seven hundred canoes landed near the outlet of the Saugeen River on the east side of Lake Huron and overcame a sizable party of the enemy. They cut off the heads of their vanquished foes and stacked them in a pyramid—an event that led to the clash being aptly named the Battle of Skull Mound.

Other equally ferocious encounters followed in the same general area. When the Iroquois began to retreat, the Mississauga Ojibwa chased after them up the Severn River, across Lake Simcoe, and on to the Rice Lake area, where

This quill design embroidered on a birchbark box was inspired by a rock painting near Lake Couchiching, Ontario. It portrays the victory of the Ojibwa over their Iroquoian enemies as represented by the clubbing of a Mohawk warrior. During the closing decade of the seventeenth century, the Ojibwa drove the Iroquois south of Lake Ontario.

another pitched battle took place. The Ojibwa triumphed yet again, and after several other skirmishes the Iroquois abandoned the area to the now-powerful southern Ojibwa.

The seemingly endless conflicts in the eastern Great Lakes and St Lawrence valley area eventually exhausted everyone, and by the beginning of the eighteenth century the various nations and their rival European backers entered into serious peace negotiations. After protracted talks, the various warring parties concluded a peace in Montreal in 1701. The large number of Aboriginal nations who concurred in this agreement showed how widely the Beaver Wars had affected northeastern North America in the previous century. Representatives of the Ottawa, Huron, Mississauga, Nipissing, Algonquin, Timiscimi, Ojibwa, Potawatomi, Menominee, Winebago, Mesquakie, Mascoutin, Miami, Illinois, Kickapoo, Abenaki, and all the Five Nations except the Mohawk, were present. Shortly thereafter, the reluctant Mohawk gave their approval. Significantly, the Iroquois pledged to remain neutral

*A West Coast leader wearing a traditional crested headdress
and a woollen trade blanket. Chiefs inherited the rights to display the
symbols that belonged to their clan.*

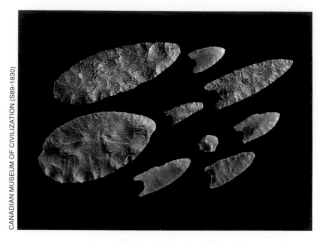

These chipped-stone tools and weapons establish the presence of large-game hunters in present-day Nova Scotia about 8500 B.C. These early people were highly skilled in working stone. Quarried from sources as far as 30 miles from the site, the stone was carefully selected and designed for a wide spectrum of tasks, from hunting to fine craftsmanship.

Plains parflèche *and case. Women used buffalo hide to make a variety of food-storage and cooking containers.*

Snow goggles from the eastern and western Arctic, which the Inuit used to prevent snow blindness.

Athapaskan Slavey dolls, displaying traditional and European dress.

Traditional maple-syrup- and sugar-making equipment from the Great Lakes region:
sugar cone (mould), sap spile, sap bucket, sap trough, and sap skimmer.

Inuit earrings.

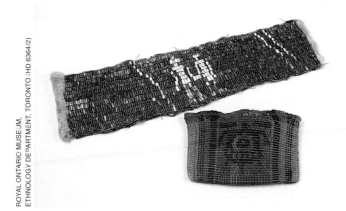

Eastern woodlands wampum belt and pouch.

Kayaks enabled Inuit hunters to pursue their quarry along the edges of ice sheets.

A romantic watercolour painting of a mid-nineteenth-century Native camp north of Quebec City.

*Naskapi or Montagnais moccasins, c. 1930. They are made of
sealskin that has been dyed with spruce root.*

An amulet from the plains, c. 1885. It was used during girls' puberty ceremonies. The beaded turtle, which symbolizes procreation, contained an umbilical cord.

This Assiniboine dancer's shirt was made about 1905 at Carry the Kettle Reserve, Saskatchewan.

Hare people of the lower Mackenzie River valley dancing.

*A collection of many of the trade goods Native consumers prized
during the eighteenth and nineteenth centuries. In addition to the items
displayed here, a wide array of yard goods and clothing also figured
prominently on their shopping lists.*

in any future conflicts between England and France. They did so because they could no longer sustain the heavy losses the Ojibwa and other allies of the French were inflicting on them. In the future, they would have to rely on their diplomatic rather than their military skills to protect their interests.

New Opportunities for Northern Nations

The focus of the fur trade began to shift to the beaver-rich lands of the upper Great Lakes and beyond after the Wyandot and Ottawa reopened commerce with the French in 1654 by venturing to Montreal. When they returned to their homeland, Frenchmen followed them. One, Médard Chouart Des Groseilliers, was dispatched there by colonial officials with instructions to encourage other Native people to follow the Wyandot's example. Des Groseilliers succeeded. Trade with the upper Great Lakes people expanded rapidly in the late 1650s, leading to the rise of Montreal as the new focus of the French fur trade. Hundreds of Native people visited the city every year to take part in trading fairs. They brought furs obtained through exchange with groups who lived as far to the northwest as Lake Nipigon. Inevitably some of the colonists wanted to engage in this lucrative carrying trade. Increasing numbers of these *coureurs de bois*—French settlers who were unlicensed traders—headed out to the upper Great Lakes region. In 1656, for instance, Native guides helped thirty or more Frenchmen make the trek, including Des Groseilliers and his brother-in-law Pierre Esprit Radisson.

The two adventurers learned from the Cree that the best fur country lay beyond Lake Superior. It was prohibitively expensive to reach overland from the St Lawrence, however, and Iroquois raiding parties remained an ever-present danger. The Cree told Des Groseilliers and Radisson about a "Bay of the North," which the pair thought might offer an alternative route to the region. They were determined to try it. In the late 1660s they sought the backing of the French government for the venture, but were rebuffed by officials who opposed westward expansion. The two Frenchmen then turned to England. Prince Rupert, a cousin of King Charles II, liked their idea, and he persuaded Charles II and his court to back a trading expedition into Hudson Bay. In the summer of 1668, Des Groseilliers and Radisson set out for the bay in two small sailing vessels. Although only one ship managed to complete the voyage, it returned laden with prime winter beaver. The sales of these coat beaver yielded a handsome profit for the investors and encouraged them to establish regular trading connections with the Native people of Hudson Bay. To do this they founded the Hudson's Bay Company (HBC) and obtained a royal charter from Charles II on May 2, 1670.

Acting in a manner that was typical of European governments at the time, Charles II granted the HBC title to Rupert's Land, a vast area that included all the land draining into Hudson Bay—roughly one-third of Native Canada. Although the Crown gave no thought to the interests and rights of the region's residents, the company's directors came to realize that it would be wise to obtain their consent to the HBC's presence. On May 29, 1680, they gave the following instructions to the company's Canadian governor, John Nixon: "Wee judge [it] would be much for the interest & safety of the Company, That ... In the severall places where you are or shall settle, you contrive to make compact wth. the [Native] captns. or chiefs of the respective Rivers & places, whereby it might be understood by them that you had purchased both the lands & rivers of them, and that they had transferred the absolute propriety to you, or at least the only freedome of trade." The directors added: "You should cause them to do some act wch. by the Religion or custome of their country should be thought most sacred & obliging to them for the confirmation of such Agreements."

Today, we have no way of knowing what the Cree thought about these or similar ceremonies. There is little doubt, however, that they and their Assiniboine confederates were at least willing to allow a few trading posts on their lands in order to take advantage of the new economic possibilities the English traders offered. Both would gain direct access to European goods and would no longer have to rely on Ottawa, Ojibwa, Nipissing, and Innu brokers. Instead, they could establish trading empires of their own and they moved quickly to do so. Just ten years after the founding of the HBC, Governor Nixon wrote to the London headquarters: "I am informed, there is a nation of Indians called the Poyets [Dakota Sioux] who have had no trade with any Cristian nation.... It would be greatly to the advance of our trade if we could gaine correspondence with them.... For they would faine have a trade with us but are affrayed to break through our neighbouring Indians for want of armes ... our Indians [Assiniboine and Cree] are affrayed that they [the Dakota] will breake doune to trade with us, for by their good-will, they would be the only brokers between all strange Indians and us."

As long as the middlemen supplied the HBC with enough furs, the London directors were content to "sleep by the frozen sea," according to one company critic. Their French rivals had no intention of letting them do this, however. For one thing, the first shipments of fur from Hudson Bay had demonstrated that the

English would have access to superior-quality beaver in this region. For another, it was very risky to let the English build up a northern Native alliance through trade. In 1672 colonial officials dispatched Father Charles Albanel, an experienced Jesuit missionary working at Tadoussac, overland to James Bay with orders to spy on the English operations and stake a French counterclaim to the region.

Between 1673 and 1685, the French built four small "opposition" posts in the southern watershed of James Bay to reinforce the French claim. When these did not seriously disrupt HBC operations, the French resorted to force. In 1686 Governor Denonville sent an expedition to James Bay, which seized three HBC posts, Moose Factory, Fort Charles, and Fort Albany. The Cree at Moose Factory were instrumental in the French victory there. They failed to sound the alarm when the attackers crept close to the small fort, apparently because they were angry about the way the local HBC trader had been treating them. In any event, the French assault heralded the beginning of a series of attacks and counterattacks in which naval forces from each country struggled, unsuccessfully, to eject their rivals from the shores of James Bay and Hudson Bay. The local Cree for the most part watched the intermittent contest from the sidelines. It mattered little to them who held the posts, provided that trade goods were plentiful.

MAINTAINING A DELICATE BALANCE

Far away from this small drama beside Hudson Bay, the War of the Spanish Succession erupted in Europe in 1702. Because England and France were on opposite sides yet again, the conflict affected their Aboriginal allies in both positive and negative ways.

The war came at a time when the French fur trade was in crisis because of a glut of beaver on the Paris market. Fur prices and profits had plummeted, reducing colonial revenues in the process. To stop the drain on the treasury, Louis XIV ordered the closure of all the western posts in 1697, with the exception of Fort St Louis des Illinois on the upper Illinois River. He prohibited colonial officials from issuing any new trading permits or allowing any colonists to travel beyond the settled area of the St Lawrence.

These restrictions drew an icy response from New France's northwestern Native allies. Few of them wanted to travel to Montreal after having grown accustomed to alternative outlets closer to home. Because these groups had the option of trading with the Cree and the HBC, the French could not afford to ignore their

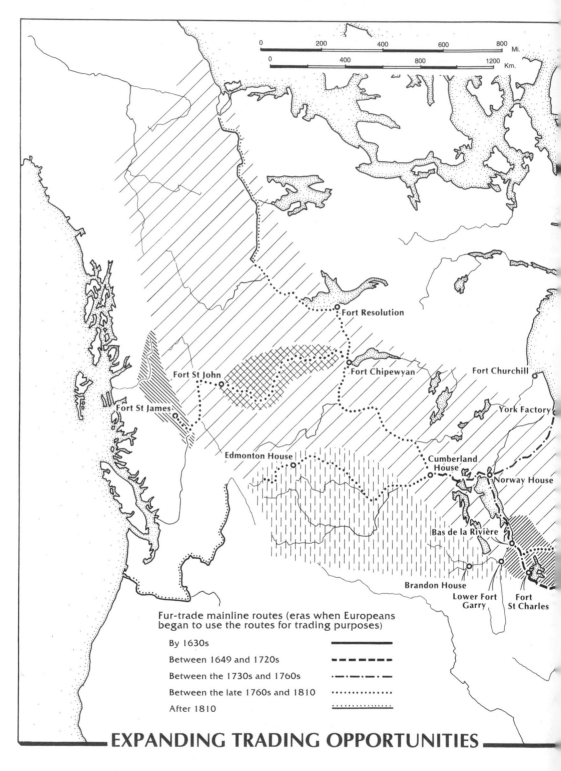

0   200   400   600   800 Mi.

0   400   800   1200 Km.

Fort Resolution

Fort St John

Fort Chipewyan

Fort Churchill

Fort St James

York Factory

Edmonton House

Cumberland House

Norway House

Bas de la Rivière

Brandon House

Lower Fort Garry

Fort St Charles

Fur-trade mainline routes (eras when Europeans began to use the routes for trading purposes)

By 1630s

Between 1649 and 1720s

Between the 1730s and 1760s

Between the late 1760s and 1810

After 1810

EXPANDING TRADING OPPORTUNITIES

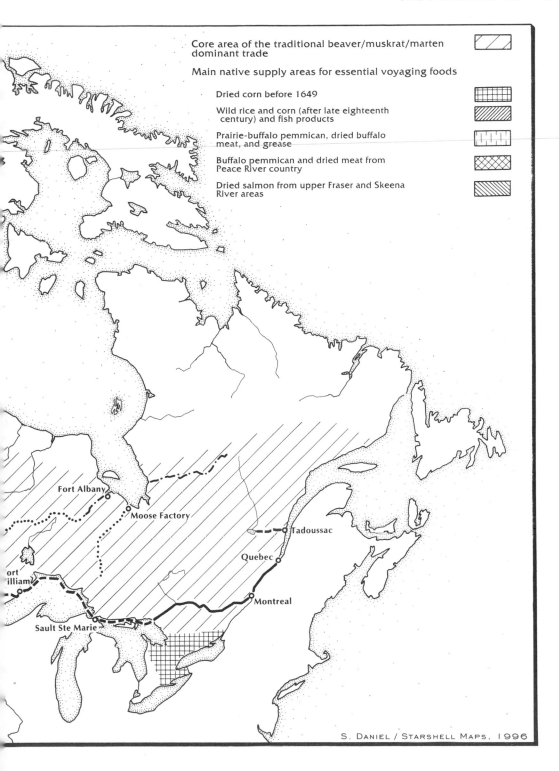

Core area of the traditional beaver/muskrat/marten dominant trade

Main native supply areas for essential voyaging foods

Dried corn before 1649

Wild rice and corn (after late eighteenth century) and fish products

Prairie-buffalo pemmican, dried buffalo meat, and grease

Buffalo pemmican and dried meat from Peace River country

Dried salmon from upper Fraser and Skeena River areas

Fort Albany

Moose Factory

Tadoussac

Quebec

Montreal

ort illiam

Sault Ste Marie

S. Daniel / Starshell Maps, 1996

interests. The harsh reality was that New France had to continue the fur trade to hold its Native allies or risk creating a power vacuum in the northwest. Recognizing this fact, the imperial government decided to retain Michilimackinac on the strait between Lakes Michigan and Huron (although it subsequently abandoned this post in 1701), Fort St Joseph des Miamis on the Maumee River, Fort St Louis des Illinois, and Fort Frontenac on Lake Ontario, but it reduced the official price for beaver and continued to prohibit the issuing of new trading licences. Colonial authorities made a show of closing all other posts; in fact, most of them continued to operate surreptitiously. The *coureurs de bois* also continued to comb the countryside collecting furs and selling them wherever they could—often at Albany—in contravention of official regulations.

This clandestine trade ultimately helped the French hold their northwestern Native allies during the War of the Spanish Succession. The various nations engaged in the fur trade paid close attention to rates of exchange and the quality of merchandise European traders offered them. Albany traders were able to pay Native people the highest prices for their beaver following the collapse of the French fur market. Furthermore, the Albany merchants offered cheaper, and generally better-quality, English goods. This put the English, and their Iroquois allies, in the best economic position to sustain and extend their influence in the upper Great Lakes region through trade. The *coureurs de bois* helped reduce but not eliminate this threat to New France by offering English goods from Albany at competitive prices.

By the beginning of the eighteenth century, the Wyandot, Miami, and Ottawa from the Great Lakes region wanted to bypass their Iroquois intermediaries and the *coureurs de bois* and deal directly with Albany's merchants. Although

Each truce in the seventeenth-century Iroquoian wars allowed for new voyages of exploration and trade, and the French soon built sailing vessels to cover the Great Lakes. This engraving, from Louis Hennepin's Nouvelle découverte d'un très grand pays dans l'Amérique *(Utrecht, 1697), shows the building of Robert Cavelier de LaSalle's ship* Griffon.

the Iroquois balked initially at such an arrangement, they soon agreed to grant the three northern groups access rather than risk renewed conflict with them, but this created a crisis for the colonial government of New France. If their northwestern allies established strong commercial links with the Iroquois and the Albany traders, the French would lose their influence with them. Short of using force, how could they prevent this traffic from getting out of control? In 1701 colonial officials made their first effort to address the problem by building a well-manned garrison (initially called Fort Pontchartrain and later Fort Detroit) at Detroit to serve as the nucleus for a small colony of settlers and a gathering place for various allied Native nations. They hoped that their Native allies would eventually relocate their villages there, forming a French-Aboriginal settlement that would intimidate the Iroquois and preempt any English expansion into the region. The plan backfired. The settlement proved to be a convenient place for the Iroquois and the Algonquian-speaking allies of the French to trade with one another. By 1710 the trading alliances developed at Detroit and at Albany were strong enough for the Iroquois to view the French with increasingly menacing eyes; they even offered to join English colonists on any raids they might organize against New France.

The next French move to curry Native favour met with greater success. The governor of New France, Philippe de Rigaud, Marquis de Vaudreuil, reopened the post at Michilimackinac and sold trade goods there at artificially low prices to cajole the Ottawa and other upper Great Lakes groups into not travelling farther south. As a further inducement, he ordered a lavish annual distribution of presents, including special medals for prominent chiefs. These measures had the desired effect. The continuing smuggling activity of the *coureurs de bois* also helped the French, because it not only enabled them to pay their allies their good prices for furs, but also discouraged the English merchants in Albany from pushing westward themselves in search of beaver. In this way, the French checkmated the Anglo-Iroquois alliance sufficiently to retain their allies and hold the peace in the northwest. However, their allies came to expect gifts, competitive rates of exchange, and quality merchandise.

Farther east, a very different set of circumstances led to conflict in the Atlantic region during the War of the Spanish Succession. Neither the French nor their allies wanted peace in this area. The Abenaki, for instance, saw the war as an excellent opportunity to strike a severe blow at the Massachusetts Bay colony, which was steadily encroaching on their lands. French authorities encouraged the Abenaki to attack the English settlement and sent French colonists to take part in their raids.

In 1702 and 1703 combined parties of Abenaki, French colonists, and some Kahnawake Mohawk carried out deadly assaults against several frontier communities in New England. By participating in these campaigns, the French hoped to stop English naval attacks on Acadia and reinforce their own ties with the Abenaki. They did so knowing that the Iroquois had pledged to remain neutral and would stay out of the fight. The French also knew that it was unlikely that the New Englanders would have much success in mounting counterstrikes overland. They were correct. The only major success the English colonists achieved in Acadia was at Port Royal in 1710.

THE IMPACT OF EARLY CONTACT

In many respects the end of the War of the Spanish Succession in 1713 concluded the opening phase of the land-based fur trade and Native-white relations in northeastern North America. During this period, the fur trade had an enormous impact on Native economic life. This probably would not have been the case had the Native groups disliked European goods. However, they readily adopted them into their cultures and many, such as the Huron, buried relatives with their prized European possessions.

Native people quickly learned to appreciate the military and utilitarian advantages of the new trade articles. The acquisition of metal hatchets, knife blades, and projectile points, as well as firearms and ammunition, altered the balance of military power among Native groups. But the new weapons and tools also made subsistence and commercial hunting easier. For example, metal axes and ice chisels were excellent tools for breaking open frozen beaver lodges in winter.

Other goods, particularly brass and copper kettles, had a dramatic impact on domestic life. Cooking food in containers made from bark, hide, or paunches was tedious work because the vessels could not be placed over an open flame. Heated stones were used, but when they cooled, they had to be replaced. Metal pots, on the other hand, could be used to simmer food untended for hours over the fire. They were also much less fragile, and therefore more portable, than traditional ceramic ware. Not surprisingly, boiled fish and meat, stews, and soups became a mainstay of the post-contact diet both at home and while travelling.

The fur trade also brought about other fundamental changes in Aboriginal diets. The Algonquin and the Nipissing, for instance, developed an appetite for corn as a result of their expanded economic dealings with the Huron. As groups began to travel more extensively for trading and warfare purposes, their demand for portable food increased. When Huronia collapsed in 1649, the Ojibwa took up corn cultivation and carried it with them as they moved west and northwest. Farther east, the Innu who lived close to the French began to use flour, which the colonists provided.

Native people also liked European clothing materials. The women made excellent apparel from hides and furs, but such garments provided little warmth when wet and dried very slowly, which was a liability to people who were highly mobile and spent much of their time on or near water in cool weather. In comparison, cotton and woollens dried comparatively quickly and woollens were warm even when wet. At first women used European yard goods to line and decorate traditional garments. They also were fond of using trade beads, buttons, and other items to adorn their clothing.

By 1700 most of the Atlantic and eastern Great Lakes people—the ones heavily engaged in trade—had thoroughly integrated European goods into their economies. The growing demand for a wide range of these imports greatly stimulated inter-regional trade. The need to pay for the new goods, largely in coat beaver, became one of the driving factors. Most winter groups probably produced only a limited number of coat-beaver pelts, given the wearing time that was required before they were salable. To increase the number of coats they had to sell, Native entrepreneurs sought out new trading partners. Inter-nation rivalries and the efforts by Europeans to bypass middlemen also encouraged the expansion of the fur trade into new territories.

Native people obviously benefited in many ways from their involvement with Europeans in this early period, but there was another—darker—side. The fur trade allowed the Europeans to gain a toehold in Native Canada. Increased inter-nation trade and involvement with the newcomers meant that foreign epidemics spread rapidly and with devastating impact. Warfare claimed more lives after the introduction of European weapons and changes in the reasons for fighting. Finally, Native participants in the fur trade took the first steps on the long road leading to economic interdependence with their guests.

CHAPTER 6

TRADE AND WAR IN THE WESTERN INTERIOR

You told me last year to bring many Indians, you see I have not lied, here are a great many young men come with me; use them kindly.... Let them trade good goods.... Let the young men have more than measure: roll tobacco cheap, kettles thick.... [G]ive us good measure in cloth, let us see the old measure: do you mind me, the young men love you by coming to see you.

—Trading captain's speech, *James Isham's Observations on Hudson Bay*, 1743

B y the middle of the eighteenth century, Native people had carried the fur trade northwest as far as the Athabasca River and Peace River country. As French explorers and traders followed them, a multiracial and multicultural society emerged around the trading posts that began to dot the landscape. In the Subarctic, the expansion of the fur trade unsettled old balances of power between nations, leading to new alliances, conflict, and significant population movements. Meanwhile, on the prairies, a revolutionary change in the lives of the Plains nations was in its early stages.

THE ERA OF THE NORTHERN TRADERS

While the Native people of the eastern Great Lakes and St Lawrence River valley struggled to cope with shifting inter-nation and European alliances, the Assiniboine, Cree, and Ojibwa strengthened their hold on the northern fur trade. The Assiniboine, who lived in the region extending from Lake of the Woods to the forks of the Saskatchewan River, were at war with their Dakota Sioux enemies to the south. The origin of the enmity between the Assiniboine, who were Siouanspeakers, and their former Sioux relatives is unrecorded, having occurred some-time during the pre-contact era. With the arrival of Hudson's Bay Company traders, the Assiniboine were able to obtain a steady supply of firearms and metal weapons to use in their ongoing skirmishes. Understandably, they, and their Cree allies, denied the Sioux access to the suppliers of this weaponry. French expansion into their territory, however, provided the Sioux with an alternative source of supply. The growing intensity of the warfare between these two enemies made it unsafe for either group to live in the area between the northwestern shores of Lake Superior and the lower Red River. Consequently, the Assiniboine moved off in a northwest-erly direction, and by about 1725, they had deserted the southeastern sections of their homeland. Although some remained in the woodlands, most groups took up buffalo hunting in the parklands and grasslands.

During this period, Cree migrated west and northwest from present-day northern Ontario to take advantage of new trading opportunities in the Nelson River drainage area. In the territory between the Saskatchewan River and the upper Churchill River, they moved into areas already occupied by other Cree. But along the Churchill River and in the lands immediately to the northwest, the Cree began pushing into the lands of the Dene, and considerable bloodshed took place. In the middle and lower Churchill River region, it was the Dene who took the brunt of their blows. Far to the northwest, the Dunne-za, who lived along the Athabasca and lower Peace rivers, also suffered from the Cree advance. They took flight westward up the Peace River, pushing the Tsek'ehne before them into Native land in what is now British Columbia. Apparently the Cree raided even beyond the Rocky Mountains; remains of their war camps were still visible at the close of the eighteenth century along the upper reaches of the Peace River and its tributaries.

The Treaty of Utrecht, which ended the War of the Spanish Succession in 1713, proved to be a catalyst for more changes to the population map of the western interior. The agreement awarded control of Hudson Bay to the English, yet it left the interior beyond the boundaries of New France open to the traders of both countries. Although this forced the French to abandon their posts on the bay, they retaliated by building a series of new inland posts, which encircled James Bay and Hudson Bay and cut off the HBC posts from the surrounding hinter-land. An interconnected network of major waterways—the Native trading net-work—linked the French posts to Montreal. Native groups along the way welcomed the French and the new economic and military opportunities they brought with them.

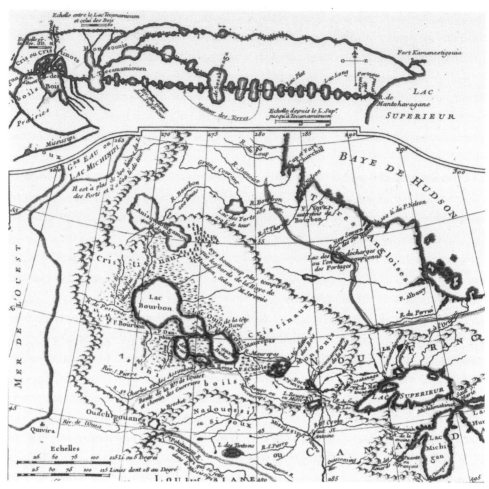

Ochagach's map of the canoe route leading west from Lake Superior to central Manitoba (inset above Philip Bauch's 1754 map) helped guide Pierre Gaultier de Varennes, Sieur de La Vérendrye on his exploration of the Canadian West. All European exploring expeditions depended on Aboriginal guides, ambassadors, interpreters, provisioners, and labourers.

Pierre Gaultier de Varennes, Sieur de La Vérendrye, headed the French advance, beginning in 1727. As commander of the northwestern posts, he was responsible for developing the fur trade beyond Lake Superior and continuing the search for the elusive western sea. From the Cree, La Vérendrye heard embellished accounts of Lake of the Woods and the large lakes of central Manitoba. One of his informants was a Cree chief named Tacchigis, who met La Vérendrye at Kaministikwia post on Lake Superior during the winter of 1728–29. Tacchigis knew the Lake Winnipeg country first-hand. His description of a great "River of the

West" (probably Rainy River) and of the Missouri River valley and its Native inhabitants provided by an unnamed slave from the grasslands persuaded the French explorer to head west.

In preparation for the journey, La Vérendrye arranged for a Cree by the name of Ochagach to guide his party. Little is known about this man except that La Vérendrye was confident he was loyal to the French and would not desert the expedition en route. The Frenchman wrote in his diary, "I gave him a collar by which, after their manner of speaking, I took possession of his will, telling him that he was to hold himself in readiness for such a time as I might need of him." Ochagach drew a now-famous map that showed, in a style reminiscent of modern bus- or subway-route maps, the canoe route leading from Lake Superior to Lake Winnipeg. Another band of Cree from the Lake of the Woods visited La Vérendrye that same winter, and their leader, a very elderly man named Mateblanche, produced a nearly identical map.

Aided by Cree maps and guides, La Vérendrye built a line of posts from Lake Superior to the lower Saskatchewan River between the late 1720s and early 1750s. He also visited the Mandan villagers to the southwest. These seemingly harmless activities actually unleashed forces that radically changed the Aboriginal world of the upper Great Lakes region and the western interior. First, La Vérendrye's posts displaced the northern Ottawa and Ojibwa nations of the Lake Superior country from their positions as middlemen in the French fur trade. These groups had been struggling to maintain their role as intermediaries since the 1690s when *coureurs de bois* started to push past them. La Vérendrye's incursion into the boundary-waters area of what is now northern Ontario and Minnesota was even more disruptive, because he allied himself with the Cree. Their Dakota enemies, who were already allies and trading partners of other Frenchmen located farther south in the upper Mississippi River area, regarded La Vérendrye's alliance with the Cree as a breach of faith. In 1736 the Dakota attacked some of the explorer's forces near Fort St Charles on Lake of the Woods, killing nineteen men, including one of La Vérendrye's sons. As the violence escalated, the northern Ojibwa broke their alliance with the Dakota and joined forces with the Cree and Assiniboine. One long-term consequence of this new pact was that the northern Ojibwa began to migrate into former Cree territory in present-day northwestern Ontario, where their descendants live today. The warfare in the Mississippi River headwaters' country continued well into the nineteenth century and eventually spilled over into the Red River valley.

La Vérendrye's actions in the interior provoked only a slight reaction from the HBC, which remained committed to doing business at its bayside posts. It

This depiction of the interior of a Cree lodge was drawn by Robert Hood of John Franklin's 1819–21 overland expedition to the Coppermine River. By the time of Hood's visit, the western Cree had been involved in the European fur trade for more than 150 years. The metal trade kettle made it much easier for women to prepare food.

dispatched the occasional small expedition inland to check on French activities and to encourage the various Native groups to trek to the bay. It also asked Assiniboine and Cree clients to act as ambassadors on the company's behalf, sending them away with small assortments of goods to distribute to potential trading partners. In doing this, the company officers badly misread the situation, because their emissaries were using every means at their disposal to protect the lucrative trading networks they had built. They were highly successful in blocking others from visiting HBC posts. The Cree and Assiniboine maintained their hegemony south of the Churchill River until 1774, when the company moved inland to establish direct contact with Native trappers.

North of the Churchill River, the Cree lost ground, beginning in 1717, when the HBC built Fort Churchill to gain direct access to the Dene. A remarkable Dene woman named Thanadelthur (Jumping Marten) was largely responsible for this turn of events. She had been captured by Cree raiders in 1713 but escaped shortly thereafter. In 1714 she made her way to York Factory and discovered to her surprise that the "stone house people," a term the Dene used to describe the HBC traders, supplied the Cree with their new weapons. She was

A painting by Franklin Arbuckle showing Thanadelthur making peace between Cree and Dene warriors. This remarkable Dene woman, a former captive of the Cree, established regular trading relations between her people and the Hudson's Bay Company in the early eighteenth century.

determined to gain access to these arms for her people so that they could fight back against their Cree foes. Thanadelthur also realized that the household goods the English had to offer could make her life, and that of other Dene women, much easier. In 1715 she enticed the chief factor at York Factory, James Knight, to send an expedition to her nation by telling him of its furs and yellow metal (native copper).

Thanadelthur guided the party, which included 150 Cree who had promised Knight they would make peace with the Dene. Starvation forced the expedition to break up into smaller parties, and one of these attacked a Dene group, putting the whole enterprise in jeopardy. Thanadelthur, however, persuaded her people—after talking for days until she was hoarse—not to seek revenge. She arranged a temporary peace with the local Cree and returned to York Factory, where she lobbied to have her brother made a trading captain and a post opened for the exclusive use of her people. Eventually Knight agreed. Tragically, before work on the new post began, an epidemic swept through the Native population at York Factory, and Thanadelthur died in February 1717. Before she died, she trained a young company servant to be an emissary to her people by instructing him in their customs and telling him how to trade with them.

Once armed with a steady supply of English weapons, the Dene lashed back at the Cree and began to build their own trading network with other Athapaskan-speaking people who lived farther inland, towards the middle and lower Mackenzie River valley. The increased involvement of the Dene in the fur trade had two dramatic effects on this group: it drew them into the full boreal forest to trap furs and it forced them to learn how to use canoes. At first, they had journeyed to Hudson Bay on foot, taking up to three years to complete a return trip, with loads probably limited to under one hundred pounds a person. Canoes greatly reduced downstream travelling times and allowed the Dene to carry substantially more.

Doing Business

In their descriptions of the evolving trading practices of Assiniboine and Cree middlemen, HBC records reveal that a small number of influential Native leaders controlled the business. At York Factory, the post that collected the largest number of furs, fewer than twenty Aboriginal trading captains brought in most of the post's returns in the 1740s. This meant that post managers, or chief factors, had to do everything in their power to curry the favour of the leaders, the "lieutenants" who accompanied them, and other followers. Gift exchange remained the most important way of doing this. As competition with the French heated up, the exchange ceremonies became more and more elaborate.

Trading parties put ashore to dress in their finest clothing just before coming within sight of York Factory. According to HBC traders' descriptions, once properly attired "they re-embark and soon after appear in sight of the Fort, to the number of between ten and twenty [canoes] in a line abreast of each other. If there is but one captain his station is in the centre, but if more they are in the wings also; and their canoes are distinguished from the rest by a small St. George or Union Jack, hoisted on a stick placed in the stern of the vessel." When the flotilla of canoes drew near York Factory, "several fowling-pieces are discharged from the canoes to salute the Fort, and the compliment is returned by a round of twelve pounders." After landing, the visitors set about making camp while the trading captains and lieutenants walked inside the fort to pay their respects to the post commander and his officers. Andrew Graham, who was in charge of York Factory in the late eighteenth century, described what happened next: "Chairs are placed in the room, and pipes with smoking materials produced on the table. The captains place themselves on each side of the Governor.... The silence is then broken by degrees by the most venerable Indian...." This leader announced "... how many canoes he ... brought, what kind of winter they have had, what natives he has seen, are coming, or stay behind, asks how the Englishmen do, and says he is glad to see them." Then it was the factor's turn to welcome them, saying "he has good goods and plenty; and that he loves the Indians and will be kind to them. The pipe is by this time renewed and the conversation becomes free, easy and general."

In the course of this speech making by both sides, the factor gave the most prominent Native leader a "captain's outfit." In Graham's time, this attire must have been striking: "A coarse cloth coat, either red or blue, lined with baize with regimental cuffs and collar. The waistcoat and breeches are of baize; the suit ornamented with broad and narrow orris lace of different colours; a white or checked shirt; a pair of yarn stockings tied below the knee with worsted garters; a pair of English shoes. The hat is laced and ornamented with feathers of different colours. A worsted sash tied round the crown, an end hanging out on each side down to the shoulders. A silk handkerchief is tucked by a corner into the loops behind; with these decorations it is put on the captain's head and completes his dress."

Following this first round of the exchange, the company officers and the Native leaders trooped out of the fort and on to the camp for another round of speeches. The meeting took place in a specially prepared tent where "a clean birchrind or beaver coats are spread on the ground for the chief to sit on." After receiving the factor's presents—mostly brandy, food, and tobacco—"the Chief then makes a speech to his followers, and then orders his lieutenant, or some respectable person, to distribute the present, never performing this himself."

One or more days of revelry followed before the band made their return gift of furs (called the *puc'ca'tin'ash'a'win* in Cree) to the chief factor. The trading captain collected a fur pelt from each of his followers and presented them on their behalf during a grand calumet, or pipe-smoking, ceremony. Chief Factor Graham noted that the ceremony was "necessary to establish confidence, [and] it is conducted with the greatest solemnity.... The Captain walks in with his calumet in his hand covered with a case, then comes the lieutenant and the wives of the captains with the present, and afterwards all the other men with the women and their little ones." According to Graham, "The captain covers the table with a new beaver coat, and on it lays the calumet or pipe; he will also sometimes present the Governor [chief factor] with a clean beaver toggy or banian to keep him warm in the winter." Then the Native leader offered his group's gift. A period of silence followed, which the factor eventually broke by lighting the pipe and passing it around.

In the next part of the ceremony, the trading captain and the factor exchanged lengthy speeches. In the course of his address, the Native leader reconfirmed his people's friendship towards the HBC, mentioned any of the troubles his followers had experienced with the previous year's supply of company goods, and detailed the hardships they had experienced over the winter. Before concluding, the captain politely demanded that his people receive fair treatment—or they would trade with the opposition. In reply, the post manager told his clients that the company laboured very hard on their behalf and that it would treat them better than anyone else would. Only after the completion of the ceremony were the two parties ready to barter.

The trading itself was highly structured. Each Native client transacted his or her own business through a so-called hole-in-the-wall, or small wicket, situated in a wall between the warehouse and the trading room. The HBC conducted its affairs this way to minimize pilfering. The trading captain, on the other hand, kept a watchful eye on the proceedings from behind the counter on the warehouse side to make sure that the clerks adhered to the agreement he had struck with the chief factor regarding the general prices for furs and goods. Prices were expressed in terms of *made beaver*, or the value of a prime winter beaver pelt. The HBC trader offered a customer a price for his or her entire bundle of furs, taking into account the quality and variety of pelts it contained. The client dickered with him over what that price should be.

Although barter was commonplace, credit transactions predominated from the beginning. Regular hunters, trappers, and trading partners received "outfits" of staple goods as advances to carry them over the winter. Hatchets, knives, firearms, ammunition, trapping tools, net lines, and twine were the main subsistence items, but a few other goods—particularly tobacco—were also included in an outfit.

York Factory was the Hudson's Bay Company's most important trading post before 1774. The post's clerks kept detailed records of trade-goods inventories and sales, expressing prices in made beaver, which equalled the market value of a prime winter beaver pelt.

Credit trading was very compatible with the Aboriginal tradition of sharing food and material goods with close friends. The cyclical nature of animal populations meant food and fur shortages were recurrent, so when a trader developed social and economic bonds with a particular Native group, they would have expected him to provide what they required in times of need. Conversely, the group recognized an obligation to return a trader's kindness as soon as they were able to do so. These considerations would explain why Native people who dealt with the HBC initially saw their debts as being personal obligations to individual traders rather than to the organization. From the European perspective, advancing outfits was a way of staking a claim to the furs their clients would harvest in the future, thereby preventing them from falling into the hands of competitors. Credit also ensured that a trader's clients always had the tools they needed to hunt and trap, even when the number of furs in their bundles did not provide enough income to buy these necessities. Credit trading proved to be one of the enduring features of the business; Native people believed they had a right to it.

Kinship ties reinforced economic bonds between traders and local Native groups. At first, the HBC directors prohibited their officers and men from becoming too "familiar" with Aboriginal women. In 1682 they wrote to Governor John Nixon, "We are very sensible that the Indian Weoman resorting to our Factories are very prejudiciall to the Companies affaires, not only by being a meanes of our Servants often debauching themselves, but likewise by embeazling our goods and very much exhausting our supplies." They continued, "It is therefore our possitive order that you lay your strict Commands on every Chiefe of each Factory upon forfiture of Wages not to Suffer any Woeman to come within any of our Factories." This policy was completely unrealistic. It did not take into account Native trading practices or the social needs of men and women. Aboriginal women and their kin sought trading privileges through marriages with the newcomers, and the lonely company men welcomed female companionship. Many long-lasting liaisons resulted, which drew HBC traders, as well as their French counterparts, into local Native social orbits. These "country marriages" often had heartbreaking consequences for Native women when their spouses retired to their homelands, or when their children were sent away for schooling.

At the end of the eighteenth century, the HBC directors recognized that they could not prevent inter-racial liaisons and country marriages, so they lifted the ban against fraternization. By that time many people of mixed ancestry lived near the posts and among the various nations. HBC men called them "mixed-bloods," "country-born," or "citizens of Hudson Bay." The French called their offspring of mixed descent *bois-brûlé* or *Métis*.

Although Native people developed strong ties with traders, it did not prevent them from using the rivalries between the English and the French for their own advantage. They sharply criticized merchandise to pressure the traders to bring in the quality and variety of goods they wanted, and they also used comparative shopping to press for better rates of exchange. In 1728 Thomas McCleish, who was chief factor at York Factory, wrote to the London directors complaining bitterly about the withering criticism he was receiving from his clients: "Never was any man so upbraided with our powder, kettles and hatchets, than we have been this summer by all the natives, especially by those that borders near the French." McCleish added a warning: "The natives are grown so politic in their way in trade, so as they are not to be dealt by as formerly … now is the time to oblige the natives, before the French draws them to their settlement … for here came at least forty canoes of Indians this summer, most of them clothed in French clothing that they traded with the French last summer. They likewise brought several strong French kettles and some French powder in their horns, with which they upbraided us with, by comparing with ours."

On the northern trading frontier, alcohol was not yet having a disruptive influence on Native societies. Nonetheless, James Isham noted that among the Cree, "These Natives are given very much to Quarrellg, when in Liquor having Known two Brothers when in Liquor to Quarrell after such a manner, that they have Bitt one anothr. nose, Ears, and finger's off, Bitting being common with them when in Liquor.—they also are Very Sulky and sullen, and if at any time one has a Resentment against another, they never show itt, till the Spiritious Liquor's work's in their Brains, then they Speak their mind freely." The Cree, like all the nations of pre-contact Canada, had no prior experience with an intoxicant as powerful as the alcohol in brandy or rum. Because they lived most of the year in small, closely knit groups, where survival depended on conformity and co-operation, they had few outlets to express the personal resentments that inevitably arose. Drinking alcohol, which impairs judgement and reduces inhibitions, facilitated the expression of these feelings.

Unfortunately, the way Native people and Europeans dealt with each other in the fur trade encouraged alcohol abuse. Rival traders attempted to court the favour of Native groups by displaying greater generosity than their opponents. Their expenses spiralled upwards as a result. To reduce costs, traders gave away larger quantities of watered-down alcohol. They also encouraged their Native clients to buy more alcohol to address another business problem. Because their mobile lifestyle made the accumulation of goods impractical and social mores discouraged it, trappers harvested only the number of pelts they required to satisfy their immediate demand for goods. When competitive fur markets sent fur prices soaring, trappers responded by harvesting fewer pelts, much to the dismay of European traders. However, once the trappers became addicted to alcohol, this changed, because they mostly drank it at or near the trading posts. It was too heavy to carry inland. In the early decades of the northern fur trade, when Native groups visited posts infrequently, their members had little opportunity to become addicted. Greater access in later years would lead to abuse.

Tobacco, on the other hand, could be easily carried and fetched good prices. Native people were particularly fond of Brazil tobacco—a molasses-treated tobacco that was twisted in long ropes and sold in bundles called "carrots." The HBC went to great lengths to obtain the finest Brazil for its clients from the tobacco markets of Lisbon and Oporto, Portugal.

By the mid-1700s, the inland nations sold a substantial portion of their highest-valued lightweight furs, such as prime beaver and marten, to French traders. In return, they usually bought lightweight high-priced goods. These were the only kinds of commodities that the French could afford to handle in any quantity, because their lengthy overland canoe transportation system linking Montreal to the far northwest had very limited capacity. Native people turned to the HBC for a greater variety of merchandise; the company had the advantage of cheap ocean transportation right to the doorsteps of its posts. For the same reason, the English traders could accept lower-valued, bulky furs. Some of the nations in what are now Manitoba and Saskatchewan responded to this situation by beginning their annual trading round with a visit to the French posts. Afterwards some of them would continue on to Hudson Bay to buy items that were not available from the French. Those who chose not to make the arduous voyage gave their kinfolk the balance of their furs along with a "shopping list" of the things they wanted purchased on their behalf at the HBC posts.

THE BEGINNINGS OF A REVOLUTION ON THE PLAINS

Although the fur trade had an impact on the lives of the Plains peoples by the mid-eighteenth century, there is little doubt that the most profound change taking place among them at the time was their acquisition of horses. At a much earlier date, the Spanish had introduced the animals to the southern plains. From there they spread

Before obtaining horses, Plains people used dogs as beasts of burden. Initially they described horses as "big dogs" and used them only as pack animals. By the late eighteenth century, Plains groups were becoming skilled equestrians.

northward through Native trading networks and horse-raiding activities. La Vérendrye did not see any horses in the southern Manitoba area in the 1730s, but he did find them at the Missouri River Mandan villages during his visit there in 1739. Shortly thereafter, Plains Assiniboine and Cree began to acquire horses, and by the middle of the eighteenth century their western neighbours, members of the Siksika confederacy, had them too.

Horses greatly increased the mobility of those nations who had enough animals for everyone, and they quickly became the primary symbol of wealth on the plains. In these very competitive and highly status-conscious societies, a man's social position was soon dependent on the number of horses he possessed and the daring he displayed in getting them. Men sometimes took their best horse into their lodge at night to protect it from marauders. Taking such animals was a great coup that earned the raider the highest esteem of his compatriots. As a result, inter-nation conflict rapidly escalated as horse raiding became a central feature of Plains culture.

At the same time that the Plains Assiniboine, Siksika, Cree, and Ojibwa were

An Assiniboine child's sketch of an Assiniboine warrior killing a Siksika enemy. Before the 1770s, the Assiniboine supplied the Siksika with Hudson's Bay Company trading goods in exchange for furs. After the company moved inland, this trading partnership broke down.

acquiring horses, they were buying firearms through the fur trade. The smooth-bore flintlock muskets were not well suited to buffalo hunting on horseback, however. For this reason firearms did not become important hunting weapons until later, when percussion-cap muskets and rifles became available in the nineteenth century. It was in the realm of warfare that firearms had their first major impact. By the mid-eighteenth century these armed equestrians were well on their way to becoming unrivalled military forces. Until the destruction of the buffalo herds in the late nineteenth century altered their way of life, they would represent a threat that the Europeans and Canadians could not ignore.

CHAPTER 7

OPPORTUNITIES
IN THE
FUR TRADE

*I have told you that we believe in years long passed away, the Great Spirit was angry
with the Beaver, and ordered Weesaukejauk (the Flatter) to drive them all from the dry land
into the water; and they became and continued very numerous; but the Great Spirit has
been, and now is, very angry with them and they are now all to be destroyed. About two
winters ago Weesaukejauk showed to our brethren, the Nepissings and Algonquins the
secret of their destruction; that all of them were infatuated with the love of the Castorum of
their own species. . . . We are now killing the Beaver without any labour, we are now rich,
but [shall] soon be poor, for when the Beaver are destroyed we have nothing to depend on to
purchase what we want for our families. . . .*

—Fur trader/explorer David Thompson's recollection of an Ojibwa elder's
story, late 1790s

Between 1763 and 1820 the Native people of the western
interior were drawn into a no-holds-barred fight between
the Montreal-based merchants, assisted by the Iroquois and
other eastern nations, and the Hudson's Bay Company. Although this contest for
control of the northwestern fur trade eliminated many Native middlemen, it created alternative opportunities for Native people as trappers, provisioners, and labourers. It also sent fur prices soaring and trade-goods prices tumbling. These benefits
proved to be costly, however. The bitter fight led to violence in the so-called
Pemmican War and to the widespread depletion of numbers of fur-bearing animals,
the destruction of game, and alcohol abuse.

GUIDING EUROPEAN EXPLORERS

After the fall of New France, a full-scale effort to reoccupy the old French trading area began in 1765, when the Montreal fur trader Alexander Henry obtained a monopoly on the Lake Superior-region trade from the commander at Michilimackinac. Three years later, the pace accelerated sharply when the British government stopped regulating the fur trade according to the terms laid down by the Royal Proclamation of 1763. This edict addressed a number of pressing Native concerns. Of relevance here, it specified that only licensed traders could take part in the fur trade in "Indian territory" beyond the settled colonies. In 1768, however, the Crown concluded that administration of the business was too costly and passed the responsibility on to colonial authorities, who promptly opened the trade to everyone.

Montreal-based merchants responded quickly by re-establishing or constructing posts at Sault Ste Marie, Grand Portage, the outlet of the Winnipeg River (Fort Bas de la Rivière), on the lower Assiniboine River, at the outlet of the Dauphin River, on the Saskatchewan River near Cedar Lake, at The Pas, and Nipawin. From these bases, they dispatched scores of men to comb the country for furs. In undertaking the expansion program, the Montreal traders openly flouted the provisions of the HBC charter that granted the London company exclusive trading rights in Rupert's Land. The company's factors merely sent a few traders to the interior for exploration purposes and invited various Native groups to visit the bay-side posts.

A cartouche from William Faden's 1777 Map of the Inhabited Part of Canada, *from the French Survey. This is a fanciful and simplistic portrayal of the fur trade, which was a complex business that accommodated disparate Aboriginal and European economic traditions.*

The surviving accounts of one of these early HBC expeditions provide some very good insights into the role Native people, particularly women, played in European exploration. The expedition was the 1770–72 overland journey of Samuel Hearne from Prince of Wales's Fort (later Fort Churchill) to the mouth of the Coppermine River. Native reports describing this region as being rich in minerals (copper and tar) had prompted Moses Norton, the mixed-blood chief factor of the fort to send Hearne on a gruelling thousand-mile trek on foot to investigate. From two previous attempts, Hearne had learned three hard lessons. First, expeditions faced certain failure without first-class Native guides; those selected for his first two journeys proved to be totally unsuitable. Second, visitors did not lead guides in their homeland; one had to follow them, at the pace they set for themselves. With these lessons in mind, Hearne chose Matonabbee, a Dene chief who was part Cree, to lead the third attempt. Born at the Prince of Wales's Fort some forty-five years earlier, he had become a prominent trading captain there.

Matonabbee taught Hearne the third, and probably most important, key to success: bring Native women. Hearne said that Matonabbee "attributed all our misfortunes to the misconduct of my guides, and the very plan we pursued, by the desire of the Governor [Norton], in not taking any women with us on this journey, was he said, the principal thing that occasioned all our wants." According to Hearne, Matonabbee explained this by pointing out that "[w]hen all the men are heavy laden, they can neither hunt nor travel to any considerable distance; and in the case they meet with success in hunting, who is to carry the produce of their labour? Women were made for labour; one of them can carry or haul, as much as two men can do. They also pitch our tents, make and mend our clothing, keep us warm at night; and, in fact, there is no such thing as traveling any considerable distance, or for any length of time … without their assistance."

Most of the territory that Matonabbee guided Hearne through was within the trading sphere of Dene groups. But part of their journey led them into the Dene-Inuit borderlands where an age-old conflict continued between the two groups. Hearne was deeply shaken as he watched Matonabbee's people attack a camp of sleeping Inuit and ruthlessly kill all the men, women, and children. Subsequently, the HBC made repeated but unsuccessful efforts to end the violence. It may be, however, that the organization's very presence intensified the strife in some areas, as the Dene and Inuit tried to limit each other's access to firearms and goods.

About the time Hearne and Matonabbee undertook their epic trip, the HBC realized that it would face ruin unless it altered the way it was dealing with the

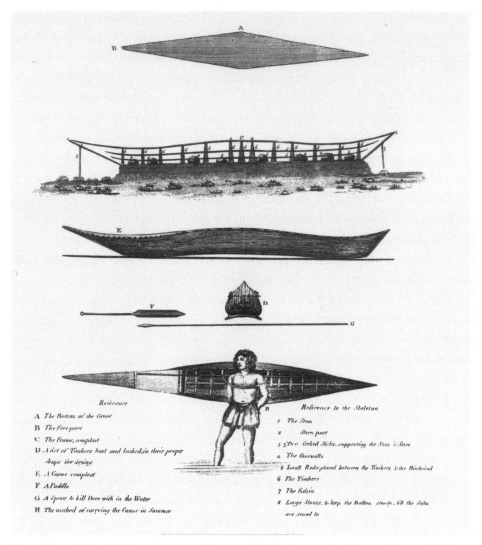

Samuel Hearne's sketch of the construction of a canoe. Skilled male canoe-builders usually carved the frames, ideally from cedar, and assembled the craft. Women raised the birchbark covering material and prepared the white-pine or spruce-root watap, *which the builders used to join the frame and stitch the bark pieces together. Women also collected spruce or pine tar for waterproofing.*

intruders from Montreal. Native groups were taking advantage of the new trading opportunities closer to home. As a result, the company's opponents were acquiring most of the prime fur and winning the allegiance of key Native groups in the bargain. To address this threat, the HBC launched a major expansion program in 1774 with the construction of Cumberland House on the Saskatchewan River.

Competition soon became cutthroat as the two rivals embarked on a trading-post building spree. Neither the American War of Independence nor the Napoleonic Wars in Europe, with their North American offshoot—the War of 1812—checked it. Before it came to an end, the rivalry brought chaos to the greater northwest and disaster to many Aboriginal groups.

By the time the HBC built Cumberland House, its rivals had been persuaded by the Dene to expand into the fur-rich Athabasca and Mackenzie river areas. The Montreal traders had to amalgamate their small partnerships to muster the financial resources, equipment, and manpower that they needed to reach this new fur bonanza. In the 1770s they began to join together in the Saskatchewan River area, and in 1779 they rallied under the banner of the North West Company (NWC). This new enterprise, like the smaller partnerships it absorbed, united merchant-suppliers located in Montreal with their various fur-trading associates—the so-called wintering partners—who managed operations in the interior and shared the profits.

The Nor' Westers faced formidable obstacles. The Athabasca-Mackenzie region could not be reached from Montreal in a single canoeing season because of the shortness of the open-water period, and the small northern Native canoes lacked the cargo capacity the new company needed. The NWC solved the first problem by organizing a system of canoe brigades and the second by building much larger birchbark canoes. The grandest of these was the massive *canot du maître*, or Great Lakes canoe, which was about twelve yards long and one and one-half yards across the beam. It could carry at least five thousand pounds of cargo plus a crew of six to twelve. The company used these canoes on the route between Montreal and the western shores of Lake Superior, but beyond Lake Superior, numerous rapids, falls, and countless portages precluded their use. In their place, the Nor' Westers employed the smaller *canot du nord*. Only eight yards long and slightly more than a yard across the beam, it carried half the cargo and crew of its larger cousin.

Although the Nor' Westers designed these two types of birchbark canoe, some Native groups, particularly Ojibwa who had moved into the Lakehead area, quickly specialized in building the *canot du nord* for the company. Along all the NWC's routes, Native people sold the cedar root, birch rind, and tar that were needed to build and repair the craft. They also constructed countless numbers of small traditional canoes, which were well suited for travelling between the burgeoning number of outposts and the various district headquarters.

Provisioning the NWC crews provided another economic opportunity for Native groups. The French-Canadian and Iroquois voyageurs who paddled the

Ojibwa women mending a birchbark canoe at their camp at Northwest Angle, Lake of the Woods, in 1872. A bark-covered lodge appears in the background. Birchbark continued to be used extensively by the Ojibwa for a variety of purposes long after the introduction of European goods through the fur trade.

company's canoes between Montreal and Fort William did not have time to hunt or fish for their needs en route. They came to be known as the *mangeurs du lard*, or pork eaters, because they subsisted on a diet of melted pork fat and hominy made from corn. While travelling, the men supplemented their diet with "country foods" purchased from local Native people. Country foods included staples, such as meat, and delicacies, such as maple sugar, which was prepared in maple bushes throughout the Great Lakes forest region. The NWC explorer Alexander Mackenzie reported that at Sault Ste Marie, Ojibwa "and the other inhabitants [about a dozen Canadians who had intermarried with them] make a quantity of sugar from the maple tree, which they exchange with the traders for necessary articles, or carry it to Michilimackinac, where they expect a better price. One of these traders was an agent for the North-West company." Aboriginal people also sold a variety of fish, particularly whitefish, to the brigades, and some Ojibwa groups bartered small quantities of potatoes.

Beyond Lake Superior, the diet of the voyageurs changed abruptly. In Rainy River and Winnipeg River country, they purchased sturgeon, whitefish, wild rice, and corn from the local Ojibwa residents. Long before the Ojibwa began to live in this region, La Vérendrye's men had bought the same food products (excepting corn) from the Cree. Subsequently, the Ojibwa introduced corn and squash cultivation to the district as well as sugar making, using the Manitoba maple. To capitalize on the growing demand of fur traders for these provisions, the Ojibwa expanded their production and towards the end of the century increased their prices markedly.

For the leg of the journey between the lower Winnipeg River and the upper Churchill River, the Nor' Westers turned to the Plains nations for provisions—especially pemmican. The voyageurs worked incredibly long days; they rose before the light of dawn and usually paddled until well past sunset. Because the daily calorie expenditure of the crews was staggering, they needed a highly concentrated source of calories and protein. Pemmican was the ideal food. In addition, the Nor' Westers bought large quantities of dried meat and fat. They also developed a taste for traditional Aboriginal delicacies such as buffalo tongues and bosses. Obtaining adequate supplies of the provisions was so important to the success of the NWC that it built a string of parkland forts. These posts shipped the foodstuffs they collected to depots at Bas de la Rivière and Cumberland Lake, where they were picked up by the passing Athabasca brigades.

Martha Goodrider drying berries on the Sarcee reserve, Alberta, in the early 1900s. In the Plains region, the most highly prized berry was that of a deciduous shrub of the rose family, which the Cree called the saskatoon.

The Prairie Assiniboine and Cree were eager to supply the fur traders but at maximum prices. To back up their demand for high prices for their buffalo tongues, bosses, dried meat, grease, and pemmican, they resorted to clever pressure tactics. Their practice of setting fire to the prairies near the posts in the autumn to keep the buffalo herds away during the winter was particularly effective. Denied the opportunity to hunt buffalo in the winter, the traders faced the prospect of food shortages—even starvation—if they did not buy their food from neighbouring Native people. Because this trade was so lucrative and compatible with their way of life, by the early nineteenth century most of the Plains nations devoted more of their energy to buffalo hunting and food processing than to trapping furs for exchange.

When the HBC moved inland beginning in 1774, it had to take a somewhat different approach to the development of its transport system than the NWC. York Factory, which eventually became the company's primary western supply base, lay beyond the limit of usable canoe birch, so it could not buy canoes, or the materials to build them, from local Swampy Cree bands. Although Fort Albany was situated in the canoe-birch zone, neither the company men nor the local Cree knew how to build craft as large as the *canot du maître*. Drawing on the maritime traditions of its Scottish servants, the HBC men developed an alternative vessel—the broad-beamed wooden York boat. By heaving hard at the oars on the major rivers, or hoisting sails on the larger lakes, a crew of five to seven York boatmen could haul a cargo of up to six thousand pounds. There was a catch, however. Because these boats were too heavy to portage, crews had to drag them overland. To make this task bearable on difficult portages, they cut "roads," trimmed and laid down small trees to serve as rollers, and pushed and pulled the boats over them.

The HBC operated several boat-building works to maintain a fleet of these crucial craft. The facilities at Moose Factory and York Factory on the bay side, and those inland at Oxford House, Norway House, and Fort Edmonton were the most important. At first Orkney servants of the company handled the construction and repair of the York-boat fleets. By the late nineteenth century, the mixed-blood descendants of these men had learned boat-building skills as apprentices and had become the backbone of this small but essential industry.

Even before they came to grips with their respective transportation challenges, the rival groups of traders had embarked on an era of destructive competition for furs and provisions that pushed their network of posts into the Mackenzie River basin and over the Rocky Mountains to the Pacific slope. The Nor' Westers took the initiative in 1778 when the Yankee ruffian and seasoned trader Peter Pond

The York boats were too heavy to carry over difficult portages, so Hudson's Bay Company men built portage "roads" and hauled the boats over them on wooden rollers.

ventured up the Churchill River and into Athabasca country with four canoeloads of goods. He had received reports of a country teeming with furs from the region's Cree and Dene, who wanted the opportunity to trade without having to undertake the arduous trip on foot or by water to Prince of Wales Fort or York Factory. When Pond arrived on the scene, the local people offered him more furs than he could stuff into his canoes. The trader wanted more than furs, however; he dreamed of finding a route to the Pacific Ocean. But his bad temper led him into violent confrontations with fellow traders, and he was forced to retire in 1789 without realizing his goal.

Pond's protégé, Alexander Mackenzie, took up the search for a river to the Pacific Coast. First he moved Pond's advance base from the lower Athabasca River to the shores of Lake Athabasca, where he established the first Fort Chipewyan. He then hired the Aboriginal men and women he would need to carry out his grand scheme in the late spring of 1789. "We were accompanied also," Mackenzie wrote, "by an Indian, who had acquired the title of English Chief and his two wives, in a small canoe, with two young Aboriginal people; his followers in another small canoe." The two women helped paddle the canoe, and made and repaired moccasins and clothing, and the men served as interpreters and hunters. The leading Native man "was one of the followers of the chief who conducted Mr. Hearne to the copper-mine river [Matonabbee had died in 1782], and has since been a principal leader of his country-men who were in the habit of carrying furs to Churchill Factory ... and till of late very much attached to the interest of that company. These circumstances procured for him the appellation of the English Chief."

Mackenzie's journal is a one-sided account of his trip, intended as self-promotion, but it does provide us with a picture of the kind of strained relations that sometimes existed between Native guide-interpreters and European explorers. Setting out from tiny Fort Chipewyan, the Nor' Wester was optimistic about reaching the Pacific Ocean. Imagine his bitter disappointment a month later when the river that now bears his name led him to the Arctic coast. On the way back to Fort Chipewyan, Mackenzie took out his frustrations on the English Chief. He accused him of frightening off a camp of unidentified Native people and pilfering some of their belongings. His guide "was very much displeased that I had reproach'd him, and told me so. I [had] waited [for] such an Opportunity to tell him [what I thought of] his Behaviour to me for some time past, that I had more reason to be angry than he, that I had come a great way at great Expence to no Purpose, and that I thot. he hid from me a principal part of what the Aboriginal people told him respecting the Country &c. for fear that he should have to follow me, and that his Reason for not killing game, &c. was his Jealousy." Apparently the English Chief reacted strongly to this tonguelashing. Mackenzie said he "got into a most violent Passion, and said, we spoke ill, that he was not jealous, that he had not concealed any thing from us, and that till now there were no Animals, and that he would not accompany us any further tho' he was without Ammunition."

This bad-tempered exchange makes it clear that Mackenzie, like all the European explorers before him, had to learn the hard way that it was not wise to "lead" Native guides through their own country. He had to make amends the next day "as I could not well [do] without them." We have no way of knowing whether the English Chief withheld information he gathered from informants. He and his followers were clearly seasoned traders, and the chief may well have tried to screen information to protect potential trading secrets. After all, a succession of native middlemen had done so since the days of Champlain. In any event, Mackenzie had embarked on the wrong river and neither his guides nor the local people they queried knew the way to the Pacific Ocean.

Although he was frustrated and angry, Mackenzie did not give up his quest. In the autumn of 1792, he again set out from Fort Chipewyan, but this time he and his party headed west up the Peace River. Warfare between the Cree and Dunne-za for control of the Peace River country had ceased, and the Cree's westward expansion had ended in the vicinity of Vermilion Falls (Fort Vermilion, Alberta). A smallpox epidemic, which ravaged nations in much of the western interior in 1780 and 1781, may have been partly responsible for this turn of events; it hit the Cree particularly hard, momentarily sapping their military strength.

Mackenzie spent the winter of 1792–93 near the confluence of the Peace and Smoky rivers in a small trading post his men built. In the spring he soon learned that crossing interior British Columbia, known then to Europeans as New Caledonia, was much more challenging than the route to the Arctic. The terrain of the cordilleran country was extraordinarily rugged and most of the major rivers had terrifying white-water stretches. Mackenzie frequently had to make major decisions about the route when faced with several tempting possibilities. Once again, he had to depend on the information provided by his Aboriginal guides and interpreters, and once again he was not comfortable with the situation and only grudgingly admitted his need.

The guides teased him about his arrogance. On June 23, 1793, for instance, he called them together to determine whether it was better to continue to follow the river they were on (the Fraser), or abandon it and head to the Pacific Coast along one of its branches (the Black Water River, which is now called the West Road River). He wrote in his journal, "At the commencement of this conversation, I was very much surprised by the following question from one of the Indians: 'What,' demanded he, 'can be the reason that you are so particular and anxious in your inquiries of us respecting a knowledge of this country: do not you white men know everything in the world?' This interrogatory was so very unexpected, that it occasioned some hesitation before I could answer it." Once Mackenzie regained his composure, he replied that "we certainly were acquainted with the principal circumstances of every part of the world; that I knew where the sea is, and where I myself then was, but that I did not exactly understand what obstacles might interrupt me in getting to it; with which he and his relations must be well acquainted, as they had so frequently surmounted them."

Mackenzie opted for the western route over that of the Fraser River, wisely believing his informants had correctly stressed the dangers of the latter. What he did not know was that his guides had also minimized the distance and difficulties of proceeding via the Black Water River. Travelling partly by canoe and partly by foot, Mackenzie reached the Bella Coola River at Friendly Village on July 17, 1793. There he obtained new canoes and continued onwards, feasting on salmon and dishes of fish roe at successive Nuxalk villages as he went. Three days later, he finally reached the Pacific Ocean at North Bentinck Arm.

The two-hundred-year-old European overland quest to reach the Pacific had ended at last. Native men and women had guided the newcomers from coast to coast. Most had welcomed the Europeans into their territories, usually in the hope of improving their trading position or gaining new allies in struggles against old foes. They allowed the strangers to move into other nations' territories only reluctantly, seeing a golden economic opportunity pass with them.

The Legacy of Expansion

From the 1780s to the early nineteenth century, the HBC and the NWC built numerous posts throughout the sprawling country between James Bay and the Moose River to the southeast, and between Lake Athabasca and the lower Peace River to the northwest, as each tried to counter the advances of the other. Between 1797 and 1804, the New NWC (better known as the XY Company because of the brand marks it used) joined in. The XY Company included a number of dissidents from the NWC, Mackenzie among them. The ruthless competition among the three rival companies had positive and negative effects on the lives of the Native people who became entangled in it.

On the positive side, the companies flooded the countryside with trade goods, and no Native group had to travel very far to buy them. In the contest to win the business of local Native people, the HBC men and the Nor' Westers showered their clients with presents. Most hunters and trappers began to receive the kind of treatment the French and HBC had previously reserved for trading captains; they gained access to liberal credit and they were given ever more favourable rates of exchange.

The proliferation of trading posts and the growing number of canoe and boat brigades plying between them created a soaring demand for manpower at the time of the Napoleonic Wars in Europe and the War of 1812 in North America. Under these circumstances, it was very difficult to recruit men in Europe, so the HBC turned to the mixed-blood population of Rupert's Land during the beginning phases of its inland expansion program. (It was partly the need to hire these men that had led the company to abandon its hundred-year-old prohibition against country

Francis Hopkins's oil painting Voyageurs at Dawn *(1871). The North West Company built the country's first transcontinental business enterprise by expanding Aboriginal canoe-building technologies to produce the* canot du maître *for use in the Great Lakes area and the smaller* canot du nord *for transport in the northwest. Traditionally, Iroquois, who helped man the brigades, camped in this fashion while en route.*

marriages.) The HBC also needed Native men for brigade duty and other work. From its inception, however, the HBC had a policy of not hiring "Indians" full-time because the directors were eager to keep trappers in the bush, generating the industry's wealth. Even in this time of labour shortages, it still hired "Indian men" only for part-time summer work. One result of this policy was that the designations "Indian" and "mixed-blood" came to have more of a lifestyle than a racial connotation. Indians did most of the trapping and for the most part lived a traditional lifestyle, whereas mixed-bloods worked as full-time and part-time company workers. The HBC also actively recruited French Canadians and Iroquois, mostly Mohawk, in Lower Canada.

The Montreal-headquartered NWC led the way in recruiting Iroquois, who played a crucial role in the fur trade of the western interior. Initially, the company retained Mohawk from the Montreal area for brigade work. It considered these men to be superior even to French Canadians. As the NWC trader Colin Robertson explained, "I have frequently heard the Canadian and Iroquois voyagers disputed as regards their merits, perhaps the former may be more hardy or undergo more fatigue, but in either a rapid or traverse, give me the latter, for their calmness and presence of mind which never forsakes them in the greatest danger." The fearless men usually signed one- to three-year contracts to work as voyageurs, and a few hired on to serve as interpreters. In the interior, the NWC needed fur and provision hunters at many of its posts. Consequently, a substantial number of these men later signed additional contracts to serve in these capacities.

The heaviest recruiting of Mohawk took place after 1790, during the height of the trading companies' battle for furs and provisions. Between the early 1790s and 1815, the North West and XY companies hired more than 350 Mohawk. Most were hired by the NWC between 1800 and 1804, when the company was expanding rapidly. After 1815, the HBC responded by hiring these talented men too, using them to muscle its way into the crucial Peace River country, which had game resources essential to westward and northern expansion from Lake Athabasca. The NWC had been using strong-arm tactics to bar the entry of its old rival into the Peace River valley. In hiring Mohawk, the HBC hoped to gain an aggressive labour force that was not as easily intimidated as Orkney men were. The strategy worked and broke the NWC's hold on the territory.

The ballooning labour forces of the trading companies meant that there were many more mouths to feed. Most of the men had families to provide for, and this added to the problem. By today's standards the food allowances were mind-boggling; HBC men were entitled to nine pounds of fresh meat a day, or the equivalent in dried provisions. The companies hired armies of Native hunters and fishers to stock the larders of the trading posts. Fisheries operated by local men and women were often the main food suppliers of posts in the boreal forests where game resources could seldom support permanent establishments. On the prairies and in the parklands, Native nations continued to cash in on the mushrooming provision market. They also benefited from the heightened demand for hides and babiche (leather pack-cords), which were used in packaging furs and trade goods for transportation and storage.

THE PEMMICAN WAR

The HBC and NWC contest for sources of food for their employees culminated in the Pemmican War at Red River. In 1810 Thomas Douglas, 5th Earl of Selkirk and a major shareholder in the HBC, persuaded the company to establish an agricultural colony in the Red River valley to provide additional foodstuffs and, in time, a new pool of labour. On June 12, 1811, the company gave Selkirk a land grant of 116,000 square miles in what is now Manitoba and North Dakota.

Selkirk wanted to avoid any trouble with local Native people over the establishment of the new community. He instructed his first governor, Miles

Macdonell, to proceed cautiously and offer to purchase the land if the Native residents objected to the plan. Selkirk also ordered Macdonell to build a well-fortified post to intimidate them. As it turned out, his strategy was unnecessary. When the first settlers arrived at Red River in 1812, Chief Peguis and his Ojibwa followers welcomed them. The Peguis group members were themselves newcomers to the area. They were in the vanguard of the westward-moving Ojibwa and had been welcomed to the area by the Cree.

Unlike Peguis's band, the Nor' Westers were very hostile to the colonists. With good reason, they regarded the Selkirk scheme as a direct provocation. The colony lay astride one of their major provision-supply lines from the prairies, and it threatened the flank of their trade route from Lake Superior to Athabasca. They were determined to deter settlement. Their first move was to persuade the prairie Métis to join them as allies, so NWC provocateurs appealed to this group's growing sense of identity to spur them into action against the new settlers. They reminded the Métis that because the Aboriginal ancestry of their mothers gave them a birthright to the land, the HBC had no right to grant any part of the territory to Selkirk or anyone else without their consent.

The Métis rallied to the Nor' Westers' cause, and the bungling Macdonell played right into their hands. Unable to feed themselves from the start by farming, the colonists had to turn to the local Ojibwa and Métis for supplies of pemmican, meat, and grease. To deal with the problem of chronic food shortages in the settlement and to assert his authority over the region, Macdonell issued a proclamation early in 1814 that banned the export of most provisions from the "Territory of Assiniboia" for one year. The following July, he banned the hunting of buffalo on horses near the settlement to prevent Métis from stampeding the herds out of reach of settlers and local Ojibwa. Writing later of the ban, Macdonell noted, "The people in general were well pleased with the restriction, as only a few of these [Métis] had hunting horses, about five or six, the chief of whom was Beaulino, the Northwest hunter." Of course the Métis ignored the edict. Not only did they prefer to hunt on horseback, but they were also intentionally keeping the buffalo herds away from the local posts and the colony in order to monopolize the provision trade, a well-established Native tactic.

Although the Nor' Westers did not really object to the ban against "running" buffalo on horseback because it served their interests too, they decided to oppose it as a ploy to undermine Macdonell's authority. The harassed governor reported: "Repeated accounts reached us from fort Daer [Pembina] that the cattle [buffalo] were driven from our hunters by Beaulino ... and others running them on horseback ... that our hunters could not kill a sufficiency of cattle; that when they would be crawling on their bellies after a herd of buffalo on the snow, a party of horsemen would come before them and drive away the herd."

As the Pemmican War heated up, the local Ojibwa and Métis chose opposite sides. The Ojibwa rallied behind Macdonell because they were also disadvantaged by the hunting practices of the Métis. Most of the Métis were firmly behind the NWC. Agents of the company helped them draft a petition to the Prince Regent in which they claimed the land and asserted that the HBC was taking it, along with their right to hunt. After a few minor skirmishes, the two opposing groups had a major confrontation on June 19, 1816, on the open plain, just northwest of the forks of the Assiniboine and Red rivers. At a place called Seven Oaks, Robert Semple, who had become governor of the colony in 1815, and a group of his men tried to stop a party of Métis from attacking the settlement. In the bloody encounter that followed, the Métis, commanded by one of their own leaders, Cuthbert Grant, killed the governor and twenty of his men. One Métis died in the fight. Immediately afterwards, the Nor' Westers and their Métis allies forced the colonists to abandon the settlement.

Selkirk was on his way to the colony with new settlers, a group of discharged Swiss soldiers, when he heard about the Battle of Seven Oaks. He retaliated by raiding Fort William at the head of Lake Superior, where he seized a number of the NWC wintering partners for treason and conspiracy and confiscated a large quantity of furs as indemnity for the losses he had suffered at Red River. Selkirk then continued on to Red River and re-established the colony. Violence prevailed in the northwest for another six years. In the long term, the greatest significance of these hostilities was that they helped reinforce the evolving sense of nationhood among the Métis, a people who already thought of themselves as different from either of their ancestors. Today, Métis elders believe that the Michif language, which was in its formative stages of development at the beginning of the nineteenth century, contributed to this sense of solidarity.

The conflict also led to the signing of the first land treaty in the northwest. To ensure the continuing support of Peguis's people, Selkirk decided to obtain their consent before new settlers occupied a portion of their lands. In the summer of 1817, a treaty was signed, under which the chief and his elders granted the colonists the right to use the land lying within two miles of the riverbanks of the Red and Assiniboine rivers (as far west as Portage la Prairie); at the forks of the Red

River, and at Pembina the corridor extended to six miles. In exchange, Selkirk agreed to a yearly payment "consisting of one hundred pounds weight of good and merchantable Tobacco" to the Ojibwa at the forks and to the Cree at Portage la Prairie. It is somewhat ironic that the first western land treaty was concluded by groups that were both newcomers to the region. Much later, just two years before his death in 1864, Peguis complained that the colonists had not abided by the terms of the agreement. By that time, the settlement extended well beyond the two-mile corridor and had begun to encroach on his people's land. The Cree, on the other hand, never accepted the treaty and maintained that Peguis had no right to negotiate it in the first place.

The fur trade had an adverse impact on the region's Native people in several other important ways. The wild

Cuthbert Grant, of Cree and Scottish descent, led the Métis to victory at the Battle of Seven Oaks, June 19, 1816. He also played a pivotal role in the establishment of a Métis settlement on the White Horse Plains, west of present-day Winnipeg, in 1824.

and relentless scramble for furs and country food depleted fur and game animals in the woodlands south and east of the Churchill River. The areas that suffered first, and to the greatest degree, lay near the major travel routes, supply depots, and trading posts. The exhaustion of beaver stocks in the territory between Lake Winnipeg and James Bay, known to fur traders as the "Petit Nord," is a good example. Once this had been prime beaver country, but by the 1790s the beaver had become scarce all along the north shore of Lake Superior, the Rainy and Winnipeg rivers, the east side of Lake Winnipeg, and the Hudson Bay and James Bay lowlands. By 1800 beaver were in short supply in the lands bordering the Hayes and Albany rivers, and by 1820 they were scarce throughout the region. Large-animal populations were wiped out too. As early as 1800, caribou herds had vanished from the Hudson Bay and James Bay lowlands, radically altering the economic lives of the Swampy Cree. Twenty years later, caribou and moose were so scarce in Rainy

River country that the HBC had to import buffalo hides so that some of the local Ojibwa could make moccasins for themselves.

Buoyant fur and provision markets alone do not account for this spreading crisis. The proliferation of trading posts meant that Native groups had ready access to trade goods. The cargo capacity of their small traditional canoes no longer set limits on their consumption, as it did when they had had to travel great distances to trade. Indeed, during this era, trading-post Native groups became commonplace; they lived very close to company establishments and visited them at will. The ready availability of trade goods promoted greater consumer demand, which could only be satisfied by obtaining more furs as payment.

Mohawk and other newly arrived groups (mostly Nipissing, Ojibwa, and other Algonquian-speakers) had an even more devastating impact on northwestern wildlife. The NWC hired Mohawk trappers wherever local nations did not produce the quantities of furs desired or where they refused to switch their allegiance from the HBC to the NWC. In some districts, the NWC used these people to strip the country of furs in the hope of bankrupting the XY Company. In the end, neither company could sustain the ruinous practice, and they merged in 1804.

The Mohawk were the best trappers in the northwest; they devoted themselves single-mindedly to the endeavour, whereas local people incorporated commercial trapping into their normal seasonal round of activities. The Mohawk routinely used European steel-spring leg-hold traps in conjunction with castorum bait, which they made from the sex glands of male beavers. This combination led to the indiscriminate slaughter of male and female animals. One Nor' Wester said the skilled and ruthless immigrant trappers were largely responsible for seriously depleting the beaver population of the Saskatchewan district by 1802. They then moved on to the Athabasca and Peace River country, where they had a similar impact on fur stocks just before the HBC moved into the region. In fact, by that time Mohawk trappers were already working beyond the Rocky Mountains in New Caledonia, where the NWC had constructed Fort McLeod (1806) and Fort St James (1807). Needless to say, local people often resented the depredations of the intruders. Nonetheless, many Mohawk remained in the West as "freemen," or men without contracts, when they retired from the NWC. They intermarried with local women and eventually lost much of their cultural distinctiveness.

In addition to eroding the economic base of woodland Native people, the fur trade struck at the heart of their social organization. Rampant abuse of alcohol was the major culprit. In the prairie and parkland areas, Native trading parties routinely sent one or two emissaries to a post to announce their arrival in the area. Stiff competition forced traders to send these messengers back to their kinfolk with small supplies of alcohol and tobacco to encourage them to stop at their post rather than a rival's. The visitors would receive more presents as soon as they arrived at the post. Aboriginal people bought greater quantities of liquor each year and the traders sold, or gave away, wooden casks to help them to carry it away. Once spirits became readily available locally, alcohol abuse became endemic.

The fight for the business of local nations undermined the ability of elders to lead their people. Traders appointed local persons to represent them if the chief refused to do so. The competing traders then showered their respective "captains" with goods to promote them in the eyes of their fellow group members. In the end these efforts proved to be counterproductive: establishing rival leaders simply created new social problems, which repeatedly surfaced during drinking bouts at the posts and promoted domestic and inter-nation violence. Sometimes fur traders found themselves caught in the crossfire. By 1820 it was clear to Native people and traders alike that the fur trade could not survive much longer unless some kind of order was restored.

CHAPTER 8

THE SEA-OTTER BONANZA

Captain Cook, he was out there lost in the fog when Maquinna's great-grandfather took a bunch of warriors out and guided his ship in. The people then helped nurse the crew back to health. They were in poor shape. They stayed across in Resolution Cove for over a month, repairing their ship. During that time, Captain Cook and his crew used to go to Yuquot [Friendly Cove], treat the ladies in a real mean way, and raid whatever they could get their hands on: smokehouses and sun-dried fish. Then they left for Hawaii or somewhere.

—Ray Williams, Yuquot, British Columbia fisherman

The conflicting imperial ambitions of Russia and Spain brought Europeans to Aboriginal Canada's Pacific Coast for the first time in the 1700s. The Russians crossed the Bering Strait in 1741 in their search for fur, and by the 1770s they had moved from the Aleutian Islands into mainland Alaska. The Spanish, fearing that this advance posed a threat to their northern California frontier, sent Capt. Juan Pérez to the northwest coast in 1774 to claim the area for Spain. Only four years later, the British mariner Capt. James Cook sailed into the area in search of the elusive Northwest Passage. The coastal Native nations recognized that all these intruders had much to offer and, by all accounts, greeted them enthusiastically at first. Very soon the Asian, European, and West Coast Native worlds became intertwined in a lively, sometimes violent, trading system unlike any that had developed east of the Rocky Mountains.

A MUSICAL WELCOME

The Pérez expedition's first contact with coastal people occurred near Langara Island in July 1774, when a Haida canoe approached the Spanish ship. The chief in the canoe spread feathers on the water around the ship as a sign of friendship.

Another dugout canoe then approached and its crew welcomed the visitors by singing. Next the Haida offered the Spanish some dried fish, probably halibut, which was their most important food, and they accepted some "trifles" in return. After this encounter, Pérez continued north until he met another group of Haida in the Cape Muzon area on the northwestern tip of the Queen Charlotte Islands. This party was much larger; it numbered about two hundred people travelling in twenty-one enormous canoes. Like the Haida at Langara, this group played drums and timbrels and sang and danced, to signal that they meant their visitors no harm. The Spaniards were impressed by the array of clothing their hosts wore, which included well-tailored sea-otter coats, blankets, woven shirts, and woollen blankets. They also marvelled

This is a highly romanticized depiction of a Nuu chah nulth family standing in front of a fish-drying rack. All West Coast societies were organized around extended families, rather than the small nuclear family portrayed here.

at the variety of household items the Haida carried in their canoes. These included beautifully carved wooden platters and bowls, horn spoons, and bentwood cedar boxes.

After turning south, towards the end of July, Pérez encountered Nootka Sound villagers on the west coast of Vancouver Island. Initially these people seemed to be wary of the Spaniards. A day after the expedition's arrival, however, about a hundred villagers paddled out to trade. They offered sea-otter skins, pear-shaped basket hats, and woven blankets in exchange for the exotic wares the Spanish had to offer.

When Captain Cook visited the same area in 1778, two Nuu chah nulth canoes came out to the ships, and an officer reported that one ambassador "worked himself into the highest frenzy, uttering something between a howl and a song, holding a rattle in each hand, which at intervals he laid down, taking handfuls of red Ocre and birds' feathers & strewing them in the Sea." Once Cook's ships had anchored, another

An etching of Nuu chah nulth masks and rattle based on a sketch by John Webber, 1778. Intricately carved of cedar and painted, these items were part of the ceremonial dress dancers wore at potlatches, or feasts. Chiefs greeted the first European visitors with chants and rattle accompaniments.

villager came alongside in a canoe to dance. "The only performer appeared in a mask which was made of wood, not badly painted in the manner they generally do their faces, of these he had two expressing different countenances which he changed every now and then. Over his body was thrown a fine, large wolfe Skin with Hair out-wards and a neat border worked around its edges." The dancer "jumped up and down in his canoe with his arms extended, he moved his head different ways and shaked his fingers briskly, while he was acting in this manner [on a plank platform] all the other Indians sat down in their canoes and sung in concert and struck the sides of their canoes with the but [butt] end of their Paddles keeping exact time."

After the singing and dancing ended, the local chief delivered a lengthy wel-coming speech. One of Cook's midshipmen reported that at the conclusion of this address the chief took off his "hat made of cane and in the shape resembling a buck's head" and presented it to the visitors. Cook's men gave him a large axe in return, which apparently pleased the chief a great deal. During the month Cook remained to repair his ship, the Nuu chah nulth engaged in a lively trade with his crewmen.

TRADE WITH THE "IRON MEN"

Cook's crew was astonished to find out that the sea-otter pelts they had bought with various metal goods for about a shilling a skin could be resold in Canton for ninety pounds sterling each—an astronomical profit of 1,800 per cent! In the early 1780s, this news appeared in the official and unofficial accounts of the voyage and fired the imaginations of seafaring merchants from Britain, Boston, and Russia. The run on sea otters began immediately.

West Coast Native nations were delighted by the wonderful articles the new-comers had to offer. Their desire to obtain as many as they could was a golden business opportunity for the European and American traders. In 1794 an American captain, Josiah Roberts, arrived in the Queen Charlotte Islands with a variety of trade goods and about 250 elk hides. He had soon sold his wares, but the Haida still had another 800 sea-otter skins to sell. Not wanting to pass up the chance to buy more skins, Roberts stripped his ship. His effort yielded an eclectic array of items for sale. The Haida snapped up swivel guns, tablecloths, bed sheets, cabin curtains, deep-sea lines, seines, a longboat, an anchor, a powder horn, ship's crockery, sails, a mirror, officers' trunks, seamen's clothing, rockets, seal oil, women's garments hastily fashioned on board from old sails, iron bangles, and, last but not least, a Japanese flag.

Although the groups had wide-ranging and adventurous tastes at the outset, they quickly narrowed their focus. They became particularly fond of metal tools for woodworking and metal weapons and firearms for warfare. The Haida valued imported metal so highly that they called their suppliers "iron men." Sheets of copper and woollen blankets were also prized. Traditionally Native copper and Chilkat blankets had been symbols of wealth everywhere on the coast; European and American substitutes therefore found a ready market. By the beginning of the nineteenth century, cotton cloth and clothing had also become very popular.

Once the sea-otter trade was firmly established, the newcomers began to complain about Aboriginal trading practices. Many traders sailed more than halfway around the globe to do business, and not surprisingly, they were impatient about the lengthy pre-trade ceremonies. Many also complained that the Native groups seemed to enjoy haggling over prices. No doubt West Coast people, who were seasoned traders from affluent societies, did regard bargaining as a kind of "sporting" contest. Women often played essential business roles and the foreign traders were distressed to discover that they were extremely tough minded. In 1791 one observer said of the Haida, "In direct opposition to most other parts of the

Sardine [herring] fishing at Nootka 1792, *an enhancement of a drawing by Atanasio Echeverria. West Coast Native groups fished for herring close to shore in the spring using hand-held dip nets, beach seines, and fish rakes (long comblike instruments with barbs that impaled the fish).*

world, the women maintain a precedency to the men in every point insomuch as a man dares not trade without the concurrence of his wife. Nay, I have often been witness to men being abused by their wives for parting with skin before their approbation was obtained." Another witness said of the Nuu chah nulth, "The Women, who managed the traffic ... were more exorbitant in their demands than the Men."

The Native people realized they could demand high rates for sea-otter pelts as long as the newcomers vigorously competed with one another to obtain them. Along the western coast of Vancouver Island, villagers pushed their prices upwards so sharply that 1792 rates were twice those of 1778. In a 1792 comment that recalls Innu dealings with rival Europeans at Tadoussac two hundred years earlier, the English captain George Vancouver said barter rates "manifestly proved, that either a surplus quantity of European commodities had been since imported into this country, or more probably, that the avidity shewn by the rival adventurers in this commerce, and the eagerness of an unrestrained throng of purchasers from different nations, had brought European commodities in low estimation [by Native people]." Three years later, the villagers doubled their sea-otter prices again. The peak year of competition proved to be 1801, when at least twenty-five vessels visited the coast, prompting an officer of one of the ships to remark that "[t]he Indians seem astonished at the number of ships they see, & they have sense enough to advantage by it, in demanding a large price for their furs."

The inflationary trends of this period are best illustrated by the decreasing number of pelts required to purchase foreign goods. On the west coast of Vancouver Island, the price the Nuu chah nulth paid for a sheet of copper declined from four skins to one during the first five years of contact. On the Queen Charlotte Islands, the Haida paid one skin for one musket in 1801; in 1802, they demanded three muskets for each pelt.

The nations on the outer coast (the Queen Charlotte Islands and Vancouver Island) soon faced a problem, however. Overhunting had reduced sea-otter stocks to very low levels and the people lacked a large hinterland to tap for land furs such as beaver, river otter, and marten. In this respect their situation was similar to the one the Mi'kmaq had faced much earlier on the Atlantic Coast. In part, the island villagers dealt with the problem by acting as middlemen to more remote mainland groups. They also kept a sharp lookout for new trading opportunities. It did not take

A potato field behind a Native village at Fort George, British Columbia. After contact, coastal groups, especially the Haida, produced large quantities of potatoes for sale to European traders and other Native nations. An elevated food cache appears in the background on the right.

them long to notice, for example, that the larders of the European and American ships often ran low by the time they dropped anchor on the Pacific Coast. The islanders quickly set up a provisioning trade, selling the crews salmon and venison.

In 1791 a ship's captain showed the people of the Clayoquot Sound how to grow potatoes and onions. To his astonishment, they uprooted the sets the next day, brought them back to his ship, and offered them for sale. However, in 1795 another ship reported that the Friendly Cove Nuu chah nulth were cultivating abandoned Spanish vegetable gardens. The Spanish had established plots there during their building and occupation of Fort Santa Cruz de Nutka from 1789 to 1795. Their crops included potatoes, beans, and cabbages. In the years that followed, cultivation spread rapidly along the coast. Of a growing array of crops, the potato became the most important and was traded between coastal villagers themselves and with European and American visitors. The Haida, in particular, became very adept at cultivating and trading this vegetable. By the mid-1820s, they were sending fleets of forty to fifty canoes filled with potatoes to the mainland to trade with the Nisga'a living on the Nass River and the Tsimshian of the lower Skeena River. By then the Haida were also carving argillite souvenirs for sale to the visiting sailors.

DETERIORATING RELATIONS

At first, the coastal people fitted trading with the newcomers into their seasonal round of activities. The trading season commenced in the spring when the mainland villagers went to the outer coast to fish and collect shellfish, and ended in late summer, when they headed upriver to fish the fall runs of salmon. In this respect, the sea-otter trade did not have a disruptive impact on the traditional economic cycles of the various nations. However, relations with the newcomers deteriorated as competition escalated. A key reason for this was the foreigners' attempt to offset the falling value of their merchandise by selling defective or poor-quality goods, by diluting trade alcohol, and by using short measures when possible. Their clients responded in kind. One ruse involved stretching "the tails of land-otters unto those of sea-otters." Another consisted of colouring and stretching pelts that were of poor quality and substandard size. Native people learned to inspect the goods they were buying very carefully before leaving the ships for home, and they avoided captains who had acquired reputations for being disreputable.

Historians hold divided opinions about the extent of the violence that took place between Native people and the newcomers on the coast, but the historical geographer James Gibson believes that it was commonplace for several reasons. First, the newcomers and the Native people did not regard each other as equals. Most of the British and American crews were uneducated men who often received harsh treatment from their commanding officers. According to Gibson, this led the crews to view their Native hosts as "saucy," "daring," and "insolent" whenever the latter demanded to be treated with respect during social and business encounters. They grew especially resentful of these demands when the villagers began to drive sea-otter prices up. The Native groups, on the other hand, regarded the cutting of wood and the drawing of water on their respective homelands, or fishing in their coastal waters, as thefts of property and acts of trespass.

Some of the nastier skippers aggravated the situation by kidnapping chiefs to ransom them for furs. A Haida chief named Altasee was twice lured aboard ship and shackled in irons. Sometimes the trading ships attacked whole villages. In 1792 an American ship under the command of Capt. Robert Gray levelled the two-hundred-house Nuu chah nulth settlement of Opitsat in Clayoquot Sound. Gray said he had done it in reprisal for a previous attempt by the same Nuu chah nulth to seize his ship by surprise. Two months later, he attacked another village, killing seven residents merely because they "would not agree about the rate of exchange for furs. "Although Gray was probably one of the most ruthless captains to sail the coast, others committed similar acts of violence. Needless to say, such incidents provoked hostile responses from the Nuu chah nulth and others who were similarly abused. The attempts by foreign traders to bypass the villagers living on the outer coast, who had established themselves as middlemen for mainland people, was an added source of friction.

One of the most famous incidents of Native retribution took place in 1803, when the Nuu chah nulth Chief Maquinna and his followers captured the American trading ship *Boston* and killed all the crew except the armourer and sailmaker, who remained in captivity for two years. The purpose of the assault was to avenge a long series of insults and murders suffered by Maquinna's people since the commencement of trade in 1785. That year, a ship's captain slaughtered more than twenty Nuu chah nulth by firing a cannon on their canoe in retaliation for the theft of a chisel. Maquinna himself had been assaulted aboard a ship. His hosts exploded a charge of powder under the seat they had given him, leaving him permanently scarred. In 1811 the Nuu chah nulth struck again by laying siege to a three-hundred-ton American ship, the *Tonquin*. All thirty of its crewmen and as many as two hundred Nuu chah nulth died in the melee. The attackers were possibly avenging the abduction of about a dozen of their kinfolk the year before by the crew of the *Mercury*.

This collage of Vancouver Island Native leaders was apparently copied from sketches made by the Spanish during their exploration of the island in 1792. Chief Tetacu, on the lower right, was the ranking chief of the Juan de Fuca area and guided the Spanish explorers through the strait. Maria de Tetacu, his wife, is beside him. Chief Maquinna is pictured to her right. He was the paramount chief of Nootka Sound when Capt. James Cook arrived there in 1778.

Native groups thought all the intruders belonged to one country and therefore shared the guilt equally for any transgressions. As a result, innocent ships often suffered for the crimes of others. Similarly, British and American traders held villages responsible for the actions of one person, leading ship captains to destroy entire coastal settlements.

Although some of these confrontations ended in bloodshed, epidemics of disease caused far greater population losses. Because so many ships plied the coastal waters, West Coast people had very high exposure to extremely contagious foreign pathogens. Their custom of living together in large settlements and in communal dwellings increased the risk of contracting diseases. The first recorded coast-wide epidemic took place in 1775, when a Spanish expedition inadvertently introduced smallpox. The next reported outbreak of the disease took place in 1801, but it seems to have affected only the southern Vancouver Island and lower Fraser valley nations. Localized outbreaks of other infections, such as influenza, likely occurred; however, because ships did not visit the entire coast each trading season, outbreaks could easily occur without Europeans' awareness. Historical demographers estimate that the region's population began a sharp decline immediately after contact as a consequence of epidemics and continued to fall until the end of the nineteenth century. As early as 1804, the Nuu chah nulth had lost half of their people. Over the years smallpox, which visited the coast again in the 1830s, 1850s, and 1860s, remained the biggest single killer.

The sea-otter trade affected the lives of West Coast people in various ways. There is no question that the volume of goods reaching the coastal area between 1790 and 1820 far exceeded the quantities that traders managed to carry into the western interior during the same period. The combined imports of the Hudson's

Bay Company and North West Company probably never exceeded four shiploads a year, while ten to fifteen ships usually visited the Pacific Coast every year. Of all the goods in their holds, metal tools were perhaps the most important. They were a great boon to these woodworking people and no doubt contributed to a florescence of wood carving; for instance, at contact Europeans observed carved poles in the settlements of various nations. Large freestanding monumental poles, or totem poles, were largely absent. Soon after the maritime fur trade began, totem poles became commonplace throughout the region.

Within a decade of the establishment of the sea-otter trade, firearms and ammunition became staple trade items. At first some of the ship captains tried to moderate this traffic to maintain their own military superiority, but in the end the Native demand for firearms was too irresistible for the profit-minded foreign traders. By the early nineteenth century, the coast was inundated with muskets and pistols, and many Native warriors became expert at using them. Besides making inter-nation conflicts more deadly, uncontrolled weapons sales enabled the coastal people to defend themselves against the newcomers in a more conclusive manner. One visiting ship officer observed as early as 1793 that "[t]he shameful practice of putting Fire Arms and Ammunition into their Hands have made some of the Tribes so formidable, that several of the Traders who are weakly manned cannot enter their Harbours with Safety." In other words, as happened elsewhere on the continent, ready access to firearms likely led to escalating levels of violence.

The sea-otter trade probably had its greatest impact on the social sphere. One reason the coastal people were so eager to participate was that it provided them with new symbols of wealth that could be used at potlatches to validate status. This became increasingly important as the number of deaths due to epidemics grew: many hereditary leaders as well as their own heirs died, and their kinfolk and other persons often competed for vacant positions at funeral and other feasts. Sometimes this triggered "potlatch wars," in which contending parties tried to outdo one another with displays of generosity or the destruction of wealth until they established a new order. Flooding the coast with trade goods encouraged this practice.

The reckless pursuit of the sea otter could not, of course, continue indefinitely. The peak harvest seems to have taken place about 1795–96—only ten years after the enterprise began. About eighteen thousand sea-otter pelts were taken by American ships to Canton in 1800, but by the early 1840s, barely two hundred were collected each year by all the countries involved. The sea-otter trade was fast becoming only a memory of the early contact experience.

CHAPTER 9

CHOOSING SIDES

When a white army battles Indians and wins it is called a great victory, but if they lose it is called a massacre and bigger armies are raised. If the Indian flees before the advance of such armies, when he tries to return he finds that white men are living where he lived. If he tries to fight off such armies, he is killed and the land is taken away.

—Chiksika, elder brother of Tecumseh, 1779

By the mid-eighteenth century, it was becoming clear to Native people that unless they refocused their diplomatic and military strategies, the rising tide of European settlers would overrun them. When the American War of Independence began, most nations joined whichever side they thought was more likely to protect their interests. For some, the choice had painful consequences. The once-powerful Five Nations, for example, fractured when some of the confederates decided to remain loyal to the British while others chose to support the Americans. After the fighting ended, many groups fled to British North America as Loyalist refugees. In the end, however, peace among Europeans proved to be as menacing as war.

ALLIES AND ENEMIES OF THE FRENCH

The Abenaki had attempted to halt the northward flow of colonists into their homelands east of the Hudson River and Lake Champlain by joining the French cause during the War of the Spanish Succession. They tried the same tactic again between 1739 and 1748, when Europe became embroiled in yet another series of conflicts known as the War of the Austrian Succession. England and France were again on opposite sides, and hostilities spilled over into North America, when the British Royal Navy and a force of New Englanders successfully laid siege to Louisbourg in June of 1745. The Abenaki promptly joined the fray on the French side to strike back at their old colonial foes. Over the next two years their warriors fought beside French colonists, and together they attacked many frontier settlements between Albany and the Atlantic Coast northeast of Boston.

A painting of an Iroquois council fire. Male councillors represented their matrilineal clans and extended families. The ranking matrons of the clans nominated, and also could censure or recall, their representatives.

Meanwhile, the nations of the eastern Great Lakes region watched the unfolding war closely, waiting for economic opportunities. They did not have to wait long. The loss of Louisbourg disrupted commerce between France and the colony. As a result, the prices of French goods rose sharply, and some post commanders ran out of merchandise for trading and gift giving. At the same time, traders from the colony of Pennsylvania began carrying greater quantities of cheap goods into the Ohio valley. To gain access to these goods, Native groups from the eastern Great Lakes area gave the Iroquois agents of traders in the Thirteen Colonies a cordial welcome. They also listened intently to their schemes, which included launching a general uprising against the French. Many of the traditional Aboriginal allies of New France were receptive to this idea by 1747, yet very few acted. Some Huron burned the mission at Detroit and harassed the French traders who were located there. But other Native nations did not take part in an uprising, deterred by the French reinforcements sent to the region after the attack on Detroit.

The peace treaty of 1748 and the restoration of Louisbourg to France enabled the French to resupply New France, cut their prices for trade goods by 50 per cent, and renew the liberal distribution of presents to loyal allies. However, the Thirteen

Fort Niagara figures prominently in Native history. Here a combined British and Iroquois force, which included William Johnson and Joseph Brant, dealt a crushing blow to French and Native defenders during the Seven Years' War. During the American War of Independence, five thousand Loyalist Iroquois took shelter in the fort.

Colonies' traders still threatened to undermine New France's network of Aboriginal alliances in the Great Lakes region. In 1752 officials in New France (the colony was popularly referred to as Canada, to distinguish it from Acadia) took the bold step of dispatching a combined force of Canadian militia and two hundred Ottawa and Ojibwa from Michilimackinac to attack and destroy the key colonial American distribution centre of Fort Pickawillany on the Great Miami River, a tributary of the Ohio. The Ottawa and Ojibwa participated partly because they had been promised a share in the expected booty. Immediately afterwards, the French secured the area south and southwest of Lake Erie by building several posts in the western Pennsylvania area.

This work had barely been completed when an even greater European conflict decisively erupted in 1756—the Seven Years' War. In this global contest, which was also France's final struggle against England to establish an empire in North America, the French adopted a military strategy that depended heavily on their Native allies. It involved employing Aboriginal warriors and Canadian militia in lightning raids all along the British colonial frontier while regular army troops defended the French central colony. During the first four years of the war, Native and Canadian forces penetrated deep into the heartland of the New England and midatlantic-seaboard colonies, terrorizing colonists wherever they went. To this day, Americans still refer to this conflict as the French and Indian War.

Although New France's Native allies quickly joined the hostilities, the Iroquois, traditional supporters of the British but having pledged in 1701 to remain neutral in any British-French conflict, held back, not wanting to commit themselves until the tide of battle was clear. At first the French appeared to be winning; nonetheless, the Iroquois waited. When a British and colonial force set out for Fort Niagara in 1759, a party of one thousand Iroquois went along and watched from the sidelines. Once the attackers gained the upper hand, the Iroquois jumped in and helped overcome the French and their allies. Fort Niagara was a major victory for the English, because it meant that their foes no longer commanded the southeastern Great Lakes and Ohio country. Shortly after the fall of Fort Niagara, the French forces suffered a crushing defeat on the Plains of Abraham, overlooking Quebec City. With the arrival of additional British reinforcements in the spring of 1760, further French resistance was futile and hostilities ceased.

A depiction of the death of Gen. James Wolfe on the Plains of Abraham, 1759. The Iroquoian warrior in the left foreground symbolizes the importance of these British allies during the Seven Years' War.

PONTIAC'S UPRISING

The French surrender shocked their Native allies, who faced an uncertain economic and political future. But they were not the only ones. Of immediate concern to all Native groups was the English threat to end the long-standing tradition of giving lavish presents and offering highly favourable trading terms to buy their loyalty or neutrality. The groups living near Lake Erie and the Ohio River were even more alarmed by the actions of the Thirteen Colonies' traders whom they had welcomed into their midst. Soon it became clear that a number of these men were acting as advance agents for development companies intent on seizing control of Native land.

Unrest mounted steadily between the time the British forces began occupying former French strongholds in 1760 and 1761 and the signing of the Treaty of Paris in 1763. The Seneca, for example, were calling for an uprising against the British as early as 1761. The Delaware prophet, Neolin, from Ohio country, preached that Native people did not need foreign trade goods to survive and warned that the intruders prevented Native people from achieving eternal happiness. Pontiac, who lived near Detroit, embraced these ideas. Although he is the most famous Native leader from this area, little is known about him. Born of mixed Ottawa-Ojibwa ancestry about 1720, he had become a noted Ottawa war chief by the end of the Seven Years' War. As the war drew to a close, Pontiac decided to act on Neolin's teaching by rallying various eastern Great Lakes groups together in order to push the British and colonists out of the region. Eventually substantial numbers of Ottawa, Ojibwa, Potawatomi, Sauk, and Wyandot agreed. After a year of discussions and planning, they launched their massive campaign. Between May 9 and June 22, 1763, they seized nine forts in the region and laid siege to Detroit and Pittsburgh.

The successful surprise attack on the well-armed British garrison at Michilimackinac is probably the best-known incident. An influential local Ojibwa chief named Minweweh planned it. He staged a game of lacrosse, a traditional Native sport, with the visiting Sauk outside the fort gates on June 2, 1763. During the match, he cunningly had one of his men hook a ball over the garrison walls. The players rushed inside, apparently in hot pursuit of the ball, and once there they took control of the fort.

At its peak strength, Pontiac's combined force numbered just under nine hundred men, but this small corps dealt a heavy blow to their enemies. Keeping the alliance together proved to be an impossible task, however. The approach of winter, the need to resume the fur trade, disagreements about the treatment of prisoners, and news of the peace agreement between England and France worked against Pontiac.

Wabbicommicot, the most powerful Ojibwa chief in the area of present-day Toronto, played a key role in ending the hostilities. He was a close friend and ally of local British officers, particularly the commander at Fort Detroit, and he was worried about the disruptive impact a war would have on the local fur trade. For these reasons, Wabbicommicot opposed Pontiac's call to arms and warned the British that an uprising was coming. In the autumn of 1763, he came to the aid of his friend at Fort Detroit, which had been under siege since May 9. When word spread of Wabbicommicot's overture, other members of Pontiac's alliance followed the Ojibwa chief's lead and quit the fight, ending the siege. Negotiations aimed at ending the general uprising took place at Fort Niagara in 1764 and at Sir William Johnson's home, Johnson Hall in the Mohawk valley, in 1765. Johnson had been appointed superintendent of Indian Affairs for the Northern Department ten years earlier. At the Johnson Hall meeting, Wabbicommicot agreed to be Johnson's peace emissary to Pontiac. The Ojibwa chief presented Pontiac with a wampum peace belt and persuaded him to accept Johnson's offer of peace. When Pontiac finally met Johnson, he pointedly told him that the French had been tenants of the lands on which they had built their forts and, therefore, they did not have the right to transfer any territories to the British. The Native nations were willing to allow the British to occupy the old French forts, but they did not give their consent for the establishment of new settlements. Furthermore, Pontiac insisted that Native hunting territories not be disturbed.

Even before Pontiac's uprising, the British were aware of a number of the problems that concerned the Ottawa chief. Officials in London were taking steps to address them in order to maintain peaceful relations on the settlement frontier and to win Native people's allegiance in the event of any future conflict with the increasingly troublesome Thirteen Colonies. The British government drafted a policy statement, which formed the basis of the Royal Proclamation of 1763. Issued on October 7, this edict stated it was just, reasonable, and in the interests and for the security of the British colonies that "the several Nations or Tribes of Indians with whom We are connected, and who live under our Protection, should not be molested or disturbed in the Possession of such Parts of Our Dominions and Territories as, not having been ceded to or purchased by Us, are reserved to them, or any of them, as their Hunting Grounds." A second crucial clause stipulated that "no Governor or Commander in Chief in any of our Colonies or Plantations in America do presume for the present, and until our further Pleasure be known, to grant Warrants of

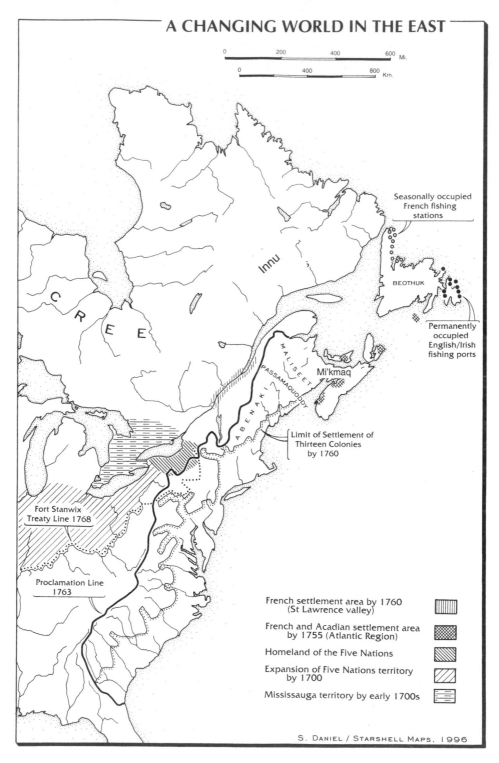

A CHANGING WORLD IN THE EAST

0   200   400   600 Mi.

0   400   800 Km.

Innu

C R E E

Seasonally occupied
French fishing
stations

BEOTHUK

Permanently
occupied
English/Irish
fishing ports

MALISEET

PASSAMAQUODDY

Mi'kmaq

ABENAKI

Limit of Settlement of
Thirteen Colonies
by 1760

Fort Stanwix
Treaty Line 1768

Proclamation Line
1763

French settlement area by 1760
(St Lawrence valley)

French and Acadian settlement area
by 1755 (Atlantic Region)

Homeland of the Five Nations

Expansion of Five Nations territory
by 1700

Mississauga territory by early 1700s

S. Daniel / Starshell Maps, 1996

Survey, or pass Patents for any Lands beyond the Heads or Sources of any Rivers which fall into the Atlantic Ocean from the West and North West, or upon any Lands whatever, which, not having been ceded to or purchased by Us as aforesaid, are reserved to the said Indians." To reinforce this provision, the declaration asserted that it was the Crown's intention "to reserve under our Sovereignty, Protection, and Dominion for the use of the said Indians, all the Lands and Territories not included within the Limits of Our said Three new Governments [Quebec, East Florida, and West Florida], or within the Limits of the Territory granted to the Hudson's Bay Company, as also all the Lands and Territories lying to the Westward of the Sources of the Rivers which fall into the Sea [Atlantic] from the West and North West as aforesaid."

Within the "Indian Territory," as defined above, the imperial government barred settlers from buying or occupying land without first obtaining special permission to do so from the government. Additionally, any colonists who were homesteading on unceded lands in this territory were supposed to "forthwith remove themselves from such settlements." To prevent the fraud and corruption that had characterized most previous "sales" of Native land, the edict banned purchases by private persons. In the future, Native groups could dispose of their lands only by selling them to the Crown "at some public Meeting or Assembly of the said Indians, to be held for that Purpose by the Governor or Commander in Chief of our Colony respectively within they shall lie."

Despite the Royal Proclamation's assurances, Pontiac remained very suspicious of the British. In 1765, when he initially but reluctantly agreed to come to terms with them, Pontiac allegedly said, "The English are the most cruel of enemies, with whom there is no guarantee for any conventions they might enter into as to what regards their country and who conceal their resentment until they would have an opportunity to satisfy it." In many respects this was a prophetic statement. The Crown in years to come often lacked the will to uphold the spirit or the provisions of the proclamation; it was a document born of expediency rather than from a deeply held sense of moral obligation towards Native people.

REVOLUTIONARIES AND LOYALISTS

The Thirteen Colonies had participated in the struggle against the French partly with the goal of securing the heartland of the continent for their development schemes. For this reason, they considered the establishment of a western "Indian

Territory" to be a betrayal of their interests. In the 1768 Treaty of Fort Stanwix, Native groups endorsed the essential provisions of the Royal Proclamation and agreed to establish a boundary line that set aside western New York, northwestern Pennsylvania, and all the region north of the Ohio River for Native nations. Subsequently, as a clash between the home government and the colonies appeared ever more likely, British officials decided it would be wise to take steps to cement the allegiance of French Canadians, too. The proclamation of the Quebec Act of 1774 was the first step in this process. However, a key provision of the decree redrew the 1763 boundaries of the colony to include the "Indian Territory" that lay between the Ohio River, the upper Mississippi River, and southern Rupert's Land. This was a significant unilateral alteration of the Fort Stanwix agreement.

When the American War of Independence finally began in 1775, the Iroquois found themselves in an extremely awkward position. Their long-standing covenant with the British remained in effect, but now the house of their ally was divided into two warring factions. Both camps recognized the strategic importance of Iroquois country and lobbied hard for the league's support. The Iroquois leaders had to answer two crucial questions, Which side was more likely to win, and Which one would protect their interests? Unable to agree on the answers, in 1777 they "covered the council fire of the league" so that each nation could make its own decision. The Cayuga and most of the Onondaga and Seneca joined the British. But the Oneida and Tuscarora (the latter refugees from North Carolina who had been adopted into the league, making it the League of Six Nations, in the early 1720s) threw their lot in with the Americans.

The Mohawk chose the British because American colonists were already overrunning their country. In addition, one of the Mohawk war chiefs, Joseph Brant (Thayendanegea), and his older sister, Molly (Konwatsi'tsiaiénni), were closely connected with Sir William Johnson. Joseph Brant was born about 1742 into an influential family at Cayahoga (near present-day Akron, Ohio) and grew up in the Mohawk settlement of Canajoharie, located on the lower Mohawk River. At the age of nineteen, he enrolled for two years in Moore's Charity School for Native children in Connecticut, where he learned to read and write in English. While there he also converted to Christianity. When Joseph was a young teenager, his sister became Johnson's third wife. This made her even more influential among her people than she already was as head of a society of Mohawk matrons. Understandably, Joseph and Molly were staunch supporters of the British. Joseph fought alongside Johnson in the Seven Years' War at Fort Niagara in 1759, and he refused to join those who rallied to Pontiac in 1763.

Fighting raged throughout Pennsylvania and New York between 1777 and 1779. Joseph Brant and his followers played a key part in the Loyalist offensive. Their attacks provoked counterstrikes by combined American-Native forces, the most catastrophic of which took place in 1779. Troops from Fort Stanwix destroyed the Onondaga villages in April, and a raiding party sent into Cayuga and Seneca country in August burned forty villages and destroyed their winter food supply of corn, as well as a substantial quantity of vegetables. This forced some five thousand Iroquois to flee to Fort Niagara and British protection.

The next year, sixty-four Native forces totalling just under three thousand warriors struck all along the frontiers of New York, Pennsylvania, and Ohio. By that time, however, it was apparent that the British were losing the war, which made their Native allies increasingly apprehensive about their own future. In 1779 the governor of Quebec, Sir Frederick Haldimand, quickly reiterated that the government would uphold its guarantee that all Native Loyalists would have their property rights restored as soon as hostilities ceased. But the elders of the Iroquois Loyalists remained sceptical; they feared that their interests would be overlooked when peacemaking began. As the war began to go badly for the British forces, the elders had good reason to doubt that their ally could compensate them for the property losses they had suffered in what is now New York State.

Brant was one of the key spokesmen who confronted colonial officials about Native concerns over property. They admired the influential Brant and tried to mollify him by appointing him captain of the Northern Confederate Indians. But the Mohawk leader refused to be so easily bought off. Just before receiving his commission, he reminded Haldimand of the promises the Crown had made to the allied nations at Fort Stanwix in 1768. Brant and his followers were not satisfied with the governor's noncommittal reply, and they harboured growing suspicions about British intentions.

Although Brant and his people had good reason to worry, Haldimand likely was sympathetic to their concerns. He also feared the possibility of another rebellion similar to the one led by Pontiac. In response to the growing crisis, he devised a solution that took into account some of Brant's views. Significantly, he accepted the Mohawk leader's idea that it would be wise to establish a colony of Native Loyalists on the settlement frontier of British North America to block any further American encroachments. In the spring of 1783, Haldimand took steps to implement this plan. He dispatched a surveyor to the location he had chosen for the proposed settlement—the fertile shores of the Bay of Quinte near present-day

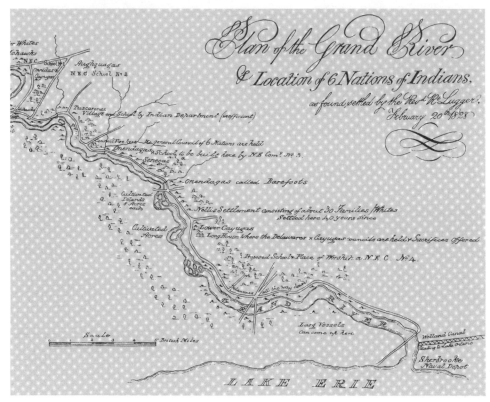

A map of the Six Nations reserve on the Grand River, 1828. Joseph Brant persuaded British colonial officials to establish a refuge for the Iroquois Loyalists who had followed him during the American War of Independence. The British purchased land on the Grand River from the Mississauga in 1784 and granted it to Brant and his people.

Kingston, Ontario. Brant preferred the Grand River valley where he would be able to maintain contact with the Seneca in New York. While Brant and Haldimand were dickering about this issue, the Americans and the British concluded a peace treaty. In it the Americans agreed to "protect" their former Aboriginal enemies, provided that they gave up most of their traditional territories in New York State. These terms stiffened Brant's resolve to maintain close contact with his relatives on the American side of the border and he insisted on the establishment of a settlement on the Grand River.

Other Mohawk leaders disagreed with Brant. Chief John Deserontyon was the most important of them. He had aided the British during the Seven Years' War, Pontiac's Uprising, and the American War of Independence. Although he, too, was very angry about being forced to leave New York, Deserontyon was against a Grand

River location because he feared this area would eventually be exposed to American settlement pressures. He preferred the comparatively isolated Bay of Quinte. In the end, Haldimand had to abandon his plan of creating a unified Iroquois community and yield to the wishes of these two leaders by establishing separate settlements.

Land for the settlements was Native land. In March 1784 a tract was purchased from the Mississauga for Brant and his followers. Initially, the Mississauga resisted the idea of providing land for their old foes. However, at least one of their leaders, Pokquan, decided that the Iroquois were preferable to European settlers and that Brant's knowledge of the British could be useful to his people in the future. On May 22, 1784, the Mississauga assembled at Fort Niagara, along with British officials and representatives of the Six Nations, and they graciously agreed to make the lands next to the Grand River available to Brant and his followers. We do not know how much pressure the British exerted on the Mississauga to make this concession, but it is certain that some of them were not enthusiastic about the arrangement. At the assembly Pokquan may have tried to put a positive gloss on the agreement by declaring to the British officials, "Your request or proposal does not give us that trouble or concern, that you might imagine from the answer you received from some of our people the other day, that difficulty is entirely removed, we are Indians, and consider ourselves and the Six Nations to be one and the same people, and agreeable to a former, and mutual agreement, we are bound to help each other...." Turning to Brant, the chief continued, "Brother Captain Brant, we are happy to hear that you intend to settle at the River Oswego [Grand River] with your people, we hope you will keep your young men in good Order, as we shall be in one Neighbourhood."

The British concluded their first major purchase of Native land in Upper Canada by giving the Mississauga presents and a cash payment of £1,180/7/4

This illustration appeared in A Primer for the Use of the Mohawk Children, *which was published in 1786. Joseph Brant and his followers believed that it was important for Six Nations children to receive a European education, but not at the expense of their Iroquoian heritage.*

for their "fraternal agreement." The displaced Six Nations people began to settle in their new homeland during the winter and spring of 1784–85. The first refugees to arrive numbered approximately 1,600 people and included 450 Mohawk, 380 Cayuga, 200 Onondaga, 125 Tuscarora, 75 Seneca, and a few Oneida. Seven years later, a group of Moravian Delaware refugees obtained Ojibwa consent to settle nearby in the upper Thames River valley at Moraviantown. Upper Canada thus became a refuge for Britain's Native allies, who had little choice but to leave their traditional territories and take up lands purchased from their ancient enemies.

In the Atlantic region, the Mi'kmaq and the Maliseet wavered during the American War of Independence. Most of them wanted to remain neutral, but some of the younger men were sympathetic to the American rebels. They wanted to use the conflict to gain trading concessions and to eject settlers who had taken up lands on the Saint John River in the 1760s. During the early phases of the war, the British paid little attention to these small groups, who did not seem to be a major threat. The Americans, in contrast, courted their favour from the outset. The initial success of the rebel forces in the north, particularly Benedict Arnold's foray into Quebec in 1775, made the Maliseet and some Mi'kmaq receptive to Yankee overtures. In the winter of 1776, a group of Maliseet joined Kahnawake and Penobscot leaders at Gen. George Washington's camp near Boston. At this conference the Kahnawake Mohawk, who had also been impressed by the rebel attack on Quebec, concluded a treaty. For the time being, however, Washington merely wanted a pledge of neutrality from the others in return for the promise that his forces would protect them against any British attacks.

The following summer, a deteriorating military situation forced Washington to change his mind. His need for more soldiers led him to ask the Continental Congress for the authority to enlist Penobscot, Maliseet, and Mi'kmaq warriors. While Washington was obtaining this approval, a delegation from the latter two groups visited Massachusetts government officials and pressed them for better terms of trade at Machias, a post at the outlet of the Machias River on the western shore of the Bay of Fundy. In a treaty concluded on July 19, 1776, the authorities agreed to this request and the Mi'kmaq and Maliseet delegation recognized the independence of the United States, agreed to supply men for the rebel army, and promised to encourage other Native nations to do the same. Mi'kmaq leaders, however, promptly denounced the treaty, telling British officials that the young men who had signed it lacked the authority to do so. In 1777 the Royal Navy sent a thirty-four-gun man-of-war to the Saint John River to intimidate those who had sided with the rebels. This had the desired effect, and in 1778 the two groups concluded the Treaty of Fort Howe with the British, under which they pledged their loyalty to the Crown and renounced their earlier agreements with the Americans.

In the northern New England–southern Quebec areas, most of the eastern Abenaki, led by the Penobscot, cast their lot with the American rebels when the war began. They took part in the attack on Quebec in 1775–76 and fought in local skirmishes. In the opening phase of the rebellion, some of the western Abenaki, who lived beyond the Merrimack River, sided with the Americans and others with the British. The Missisquoi, who lived near the present Vermont–Quebec boundary, sought shelter in the St Lawrence valley as they had done previously during the Seven Years' War. Groups living on the lower St François River at Odanak, in present-day Quebec, remained neutral. When the war ended, few of the Missisquoi returned to their traditional territory; most joined the Abenaki at Odanak. Years later, in 1805, the Crown granted additional lands for these people farther up the St François River at Durham, Quebec, to relieve the overcrowding at Odanak that had been caused by continuing immigration from New England and natural population growth.

THE LAST WAR

Although the 1783 Treaty of Paris ended hostilities between Great Britain and the United States, the Native nations living in the region between Lake Erie and the Ohio River continued fighting against the new republic until 1794. They had compelling reasons for doing so. The peace accord made no provisions for the various Native groups that had participated in the war. As far as the Americans were concerned, they thought they had gained rightful title to Native lands by virtue of the treaty. Even before the war officially ended, would-be pioneers had moved across the Fort Stanwix Treaty line in anticipation that the territories lying beyond would be thrown open to settlers. Between 1784 and 1789, Americans pressured the Iroquois, Shawnee, and Delaware into a series of treaties, under which they surrendered large tracts of the upper Ohio valley. Other western Native nations refused to recognize these agreements, maintaining that various groups had not been properly represented at the negotiations.

A collective Native response was in order. Many of the nations had already taken steps in that direction during the American War of Independence when they organized the Western Confederacy. Its purpose was to hold settlers behind the Fort Stanwix line by creating a mutual defence alliance. All member nations agreed to aid any fellow members if they were attacked by the Americans. When the nations of the Western Confederacy rejected the bogus treaties, several skirmishes took place. These initial encounters led to a major clash in 1791, when an army of about a thousand members of the confederacy attacked and routed fourteen hundred American troops near the later site of Fort Recovery, close to the present western boundary of Ohio.

Up to this point, the Ojibwa confederates from Upper Canada had not taken part in any of the clashes. However, they played a major role in the next crucial confrontation that took place three years later at Fallen Timbers, on the southwestern shore of Lake Erie. This time, a disciplined American army of three thousand regular and militia troops triumphed over a badly outnumbered and disorganized Native force. They destroyed nine towns and torched cornfields along the Maumee River belonging to Delaware, Shawnee, Miami, Wyandot, and Ottawa.

This crushing defeat forced the confederacy to abandon their fight to hold the Fort Stanwix Treaty line of 1768. In the Treaty of Greenville, concluded in 1795, eleven confederate nations (the Ojibwa among them) yielded most of present-day Ohio except for the northwestern corner. In the Jay Treaty, concluded in 1794, Britain agreed to withdraw all the military posts it continued to operate in American territory. In return, it obtained important concessions giving Native people unrestricted movement across the border (a right that continues to the present) and granting British traders and settlers the right to remain. These provisions enabled officials in British North America to continue their tacit support of Native resistance to American expansion through the traditional avenues of trade and gift giving with various nations living south of the border. In turn, this would guarantee British control of the Upper Canadian peninsula by making sure that Native groups in the region would aid the British in any future conflicts with the Americans.

The grievous defeat at Fallen Timbers and subsequent loss of territory led the great Shawnee war chief, Tecumseh, to work tirelessly, and with considerable success, to rally his dispirited confederates. By all accounts, the twenty-six-year-old visionary leader was an impressive man. A British army officer described him as being "five feet nine or ten inches; his complexion light copper; countenance oval, with bright hazel eyes, beaming cheerfulness, energy and decision." In Shawnee councils Tecumseh argued strongly against reaching any accords with the victorious Americans, and he took steps to rebuild an alliance of western nations to fight against further encroachment on Native lands. Meanwhile his half brother, Tenskwatawa—better known as the Prophet—preached a return to traditional religious beliefs and values. Like Neolin before him, the Prophet urged his followers to abandon their dependence on the material goods the invaders provided.

In 1807 the various nations held councils throughout the territory extending from New York to Illinois country. The assembly that Tecumseh convened at Greenville, located near the western boundary of present-day Ohio, was one of the most important. Although he had invited the Iroquois of New York and the Six Nations of the Grand River to attend, they declined, partly because British colonial officials had lobbied against the participation of Brant's people. Nonetheless, Tecumseh pressed forward and encouraged the other members of the Western Confederacy to adopt a decidedly more militant stance. Additional Native land

After the American War of Independence, Tecumseh, a famous Shawnee leader, welded the various nations of the eastern Great Lakes region into an alliance to halt the expansion of the American settlement frontier beyond the Ohio River. Tecumseh and his confederates joined the British in the War of 1812.

surrenders in the lower Ohio River valley encouraged more groups to rally to his cause. Tecumseh's success led the governor of Indiana Territory, Gen. William Harrison, to conclude that Tecumseh and his followers posed a threat to settlers. He attacked the Shawnee leader's home base at Prophetstown (Indiana) beside the Tippecanoe River on November 7, 1811, while Tecumseh was away recruiting support. In the well-known Battle of Tippecanoe, the governor delivered a devastating blow to Tecumseh's people.

Eight months after the Battle of Tippecanoe, the United States declared war on Great Britain. Most Canadian schoolchildren are taught that the War of 1812 was a heroic struggle in which Laura Secord and Maj.-Gen. Isaac Brock played crucial roles in thwarting the last American attempt to seize territory in present-day Canada. In reality, it was two intertwined contests. One was an American-Native war that really began at Tippecanoe and took place mainly in the Mississippi valley and the lower Great Lakes area. The other for the most part involved American and British naval and land forces operating in the St Lawrence River valley and along the Atlantic and gulf coastal areas.

That Upper Canada did not fall into American hands was largely due to the successes of allied resident Native warriors in key battles during the first year of the war. Three clashes stand out. In the summer of 1812, British allies played central roles in the taking of strategic forts of Michilimackinac, Dearborn (Chicago), and Detroit. Those involved in the successful assault on Fort Detroit included Tecumseh and his men, approximately 280 Mohawk from Kahnawake and Akwesasne, another 100 Iroquois from the Grand River settlement, and about 100 Ojibwa from the Thames River area.

On June 24, 1813, the Iroquois played a pivotal role in another major American defeat at Beaver Dams (Thorold, Ontario) on the Niagara Peninsula. This time they ambushed an invading force of about 500 men. Acting under their own command, the Native force inflicted heavy losses on the invaders. The Americans surrendered to the British lieutenant, James Fitzgibbon. Afterwards, a wag said of the battle that the Kahnawake Mohawk fought it, the Six Nations Iroquois got the plunder, and Fitzgibbon got the credit. This defeat and one at Stoney Creek convinced the Americans that it was highly risky to venture very far afield from their fortified positions on the Niagara frontier.

When this opening phase of the war ended, the allied nations and a handful of British troops and colonial militia clearly held the upper hand. Soon, however, the Americans mounted several important counterattacks and shifted the tide in their favour. The destruction of the British Great Lakes fleet at Put-in-Bay on Lake Erie, in early September 1813, was a turning point because it cut the main British supply line to Fort Detroit. The British decided their only option was to evacuate the fort and its satellite, Fort Malden.

The order to withdraw from Detroit enraged Tecumseh, who had assembled a large force of two thousand to three thousand men, and led to a division in the ranks of the allied nations. One-third of them chose to cross over to the American side and seek peace with their old adversaries. Their defection set the stage for an American invasion of Upper Canada and a calamitous battle on the Thames River. General Harrison, who had taken over command of the Ohio Territory, led the strike force. He sent nearly five thousand men by ship across Lake Erie and they chased the retreating British-Native force up the Thames River, finally pinning them down near Moraviantown. The Americans were triumphant. Early in the melee they killed Tecumseh, and legend has it that a call immediately circulated among his warriors: "Tecumseh is dead! Retreat! Retreat!" The battle's British and Native survivors took flight to the head of Lake Ontario, while Harrison's army returned to Fort Detroit where they fortified their position.

To this day, conflicting stories are told about what happened to the remains of Tecumseh. Some accounts say that the Americans mutilated the great chief's body where he had fallen. Shawnee tradition holds that Tecumseh's compatriots temporarily buried him near the battlefield, intending to return later for his remains. A group of warriors supposedly did make an unsuccessful attempt to locate the burial site. According to a Shawnee story, "No white man knows, or ever will know, where we took the body of our beloved Tecumseh and buried him. Tecumseh will come again!"

Although the Americans held the balance of power in the area west of Lake Ontario after the battle of Moraviantown, their defeats at the hands of Britain's Native allies at the beginning of the war dissuaded them from venturing into Upper Canada at that time. Instead, they set about making peace with their Native adversaries in the area south of the Great Lakes. In October 1813, Harrison reached an armistice with those groups who had switched sides when the British evacuated Fort Detroit. In July 1814 the Americans concluded the second Treaty of Greenville with 1,450 Native people, who included Wyandot, Delaware, Shawnee, Seneca, and Miami. In the accord, these groups pledged to fight for the United States.

Although Native warriors played an important role in battles west of the Niagara Frontier during the War of 1812, to the east they mostly stayed on the sidelines. One of the reasons they refused to be drawn into the conflict was that the Mississauga and the Six Nations of Upper Canada, and the Seneca, Tuscarora, and Onondaga of New York, did not want to fight against one another. It took lavish gift giving and arm twisting by British officials, in conjunction with the early military successes in the west, to persuade the two Upper Canadian groups to play auxiliary roles. Likewise, the New York groups responded to American calls to arms only after intensive lobbying.

Of the sixty-three battles that took place to the east of Moraviantown during the course of the war, only seven skirmishes involved significant numbers of Native warriors on either side and only at the Battle of Beaver Dams did they predominate. In general, the Native nations took part only when military expeditions threatened them by operating near their settlements. If they found themselves opposing their cousins from south of the border, it caused great consternation among their ranks. For instance, in July 1814 five hundred American Iroquois faced three hundred Six Nations people, Ojibwa, and other British allies at the Battle of Chipewya near the confluence of the Welland and Niagara rivers, and the American forces won. This clash and other similar incidents led the Six Nations to call a council at Burlington Bay (Ancaster, Ontario) to consider adopting a neutral position. Over the vigorous objections of the local British commander, a delegation of Iroquois from the United States accepted an invitation to attend. At this conference the Native nations agreed to restrict their military participation in the war.

The only clash in which Native warriors played a major role after the conference took place at Brants Ford (Brantford, Ontario) in November 1814, when the Six Nations took up arms to defend their community on the Grand River against an impending American assault. The United States dispatched an invading force to seize the valley because it provided easy access to the heart of Upper Canada from Lake Erie, which was now an American lake, thanks to the earlier victory at Put-in-Bay. The Americans had little trouble defeating the British regulars and militia on their way to the ford. However, extended lines of communication, the exhausted state of the troops, and the impassable river forced the Americans to abandon their plan to carry on to the head of Lake Ontario. Instead, they scorched the surrounding countryside before beating a retreat.

Great Britain and the United States fought to a standstill, ending the war with the signing of the Treaty of Ghent in December 1814. The Native people were the big losers. The death of Tecumseh at Moraviantown crippled the Western Confederacy, even though his second-in-command, Oshawanah, an Ojibwa from Upper Canada, tried to carry on. Despite the success Native warriors had had in holding Upper Canada for the British, the Americans were in the ascendancy in the heart of the continent. The Native allies of the British had good reason to feel bitter and to be fearful. In 1818 the Ojibwa chief Ocaita from Drummond Island in Lake Huron stated their case succinctly and with great emotion:

> Though many of our young men were mixed with the earth [killed] we were
> happy, and took to your chiefs [army and militia officers] the hair of a great
> many of the heads of your enemies; and tho' we were enjoying ourselves and
> everything going on well, we were astonished one morning to hear by a little
> bird, that you had buried the Hatchet and taken our enemies by the hand....
> My heart now fails me. I can hardly speak. We are now slaves and treated
> worse than dogs. Those bad spirits [Americans] take possession of our Lands
> without consulting us, they deprive us of our English traders.... Our chiefs

did not consent to have our lands given to the Americans, but you did it without consulting us; and in doing that you delivered us up to their mercy. They
are enraged at us for having joined you in the play [war] and they treat us
worse than dogs.

With the close of the War of 1812, the efforts of eastern nations to preserve their
ancient homelands through the formation of European and American alliances and
participation in their wars came to a sorry end. After almost one hundred years of
intermittent warfare, they had managed to secure only widely scattered tracts of
land in British North America. And even these enclaves were not safe.

CHAPTER 10

FIGHTING THE LOYALISTS FOR LAND

When your white children first came into this country, they did not come shouting the war cry and seeking to wrest this land from us. They told us they came as friends to smoke the pipe of peace; they sought our friendship, we became brothers. Their enemies were ours. At the time we were strong and powerful, while they were few and weak. But did we oppress them or wrong them? No! ... Time wore on and you have become a great people, whilst we have melted away like snow beneath an April sun; our strength is wasted, our countless warriors dead.

—Shinguacouse, Ojibwa chief, 1849

At the signing of the Royal Proclamation in 1763, Native groups still occupied most of their original lands in the east. However, they rapidly lost nearly all their Atlantic homelands, the territory south of the St Lawrence River, and most of present-day southern Ontario. Undoubtedly the single most important reason for this rapid transformation was the American War of Independence and the Loyalist migration to British North America that it triggered. Loyalists were not natural allies of the various Native nations, even though they had fought on the same side. They coveted "unsettled" Native land the same way Americans did. Because they believed land was owed to them in appreciation of their loyalty, they did not feel bound by the provisions of the Royal Proclamation.

In eastern British North America, the Loyalist migration forced the Aboriginal inhabitants to change the nature of their struggle for a land base. Instead of waging an armed fight, they increasingly had to engage in a war of "paper talk." Needless to say, verbal warfare put the Native nations at a great disadvantage. On the battlefield their skills in guerrilla-style combat had given them an advantage. In the ensuing confrontation, they battled faceless bureaucrats and politicians according to rules and interpretations the outsiders imposed.

The Mi'kmaq and Beothuk

Before the American War of Independence, a small number of Europeans had settled in three areas—along the southern and eastern shores of the Bay of Fundy (Acadia), in the St Lawrence valley between Quebec City and Montreal, and beside the sheltered bays of Newfoundland's Avalon Peninsula, where the cod fishery was concentrated. The tidal-flat farming system of the Acadians barely interfered with the lives of the Mi'kmaq because it did not impinge on the large tracts of tribal hunting grounds. By contrast, in the St Lawrence valley, more than seventy thousand colonists had cleared extensive stretches of land to establish their river-based farms. However, this territory had been a hotly contested no-man's land after the St Lawrence valley Iroquois abandoned it in the sixteenth century, so the colonists of New France were not as disruptive as might be suggested by their large-scale clearing of the forest.

Circumstances were very different in Newfoundland during the pre-Loyalist era. European cod fishermen established seasonal fish-drying stations on many traditional Beothuk camping places. Worse, the intruders cleared land and recklessly burned the forests surrounding their operations on the Avalon Peninsula. Understandably, the local people did not welcome the fishermen. For their part, the newcomers resented the Beothuk, who sometimes plundered the drying stations during the winter to obtain nails and metal scraps. The opposing interests of the two groups were a recipe for disaster.

This painting of Demasduwit, or Mary March, is the only known portrait of a Beothuk. After earlier efforts to establish peaceful relations with her people failed, colonial officials offered a £100 reward to anyone who could make contact. In 1818 local fishermen surprised a camp of Demasduwit's people, who fled. She was captured and taken back to the colony, where she died of consumption on January 8, 1820. For many years this haunting portrait was mistakenly thought to be that of her niece, Shanawdithit, who was captured in 1823.

An imaginary and misleading portrayal of a British effort to reach out to the Beothuk. When colonial authorities finally realized that these people were facing extinction, they sent expeditions in 1768 and 1811 in abortive efforts to establish peaceful contact. It was too late. Years of bloody encounters with cod fishers had left the Beothuk distrustful and fearful. They hid from the first expedition, and because of a misunderstanding they killed two members of the second party.

The expansion of the local cod fishery in the seventeenth and eighteenth centuries saw the Beothuk pushed out of the northern coastal portion of their homeland by the French and the eastern section by the English. Faced with these pressures, the Beothuk withdrew inland to the Red Indian Lake–Exploits River area. By the late eighteenth century, they found themselves cut off from the marine resources that had always sustained them. Continuing skirmishes, starvation, and European diseases (especially tuberculosis) took a heavy toll and eventually led to their extinction. The last known survivor was a young woman named Shanawdithit. Colonial officials captured her in 1823 in the hope of saving her, but she died of tuberculosis six years later in St John's.

While the world closed in on the Beothuk, the Mi'kmaq and Maliseet of the mainland came under relentless pressure from the Loyalists, who settled in the Atlantic area in large numbers. Between 1776 and 1784, an estimated 13,500 arrived in the New Brunswick area—particularly the fertile Saint John River valley—and another 19,000 colonized Nova Scotia. The two Native groups suddenly found themselves swamped by an alien population with a voracious appetite for their land and fisheries and very little sympathy for their well-being.

The Royal Proclamation of 1763 should have protected the Mi'kmaq's land. The edict recognized two types of Aboriginal territory. One category, referred to as "Indian Country," or the "hundred per cent reserve," encompassed all territories lying beyond the colonial boundaries at the time of the conquest. In the other category were all those districts that had been reserved for Native people "within those parts of our colonies where, We [the Crown] have thought proper to allow settlement." The decree also specified that only the Crown could purchase these lands and only at a public meeting. Nonetheless, the new Loyalist government of Nova Scotia took the position that the Royal Proclamation did not apply to the colony. The Mi'kmaq experience in Nova Scotia (which included Prince Edward Island

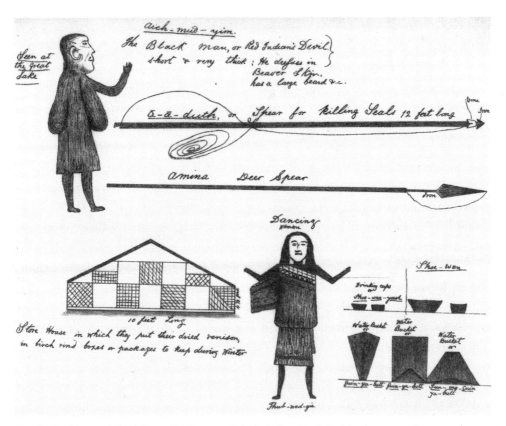

Sketches by Shanawdithit (also spelled Shawnandithit), the last Beothuk. After her capture in 1823, she provided most of the information we have about her ill-fated people in a series of interviews with settlers and through pencil drawings.

from 1763 to 1769 and New Brunswick until 1784) serves to highlight the general problem they faced in the Maritimes—and foreshadowed what other groups would confront from coast to coast.

In Nova Scotia, colonial politicians held the view that Britain had gained title to the area by defeating France and its Native allies. In other words, the Mi'kmaq had lost their lands to the British by right of conquest. Significantly, the Lords of Trade in London, who had drafted the Royal Proclamation of 1763, did not challenge this interpretation. In the Atlantic region, they simply left the matter in the hands of local colonial officials. As a result, the Mi'kmaq found themselves in the terrible position of having to petition the colonial government for grants to occupy the territories they traditionally used. The Mi'kmaq were particularly anxious to protect shoreline areas along the rivers and coasts for their use, because fishing and shellfish collecting remained crucial to their economy. However, the newcomers coveted the same areas. These strips of land included the fishing harbours, most of the best agricultural land, and the bulk of the water-power sites that were needed to develop mills for grain, lumber, and so on.

Between 1782 and 1784, the Nova Scotia government responded to the Mi'kmaq petitions by granting them ten "licences of occupation," but these were almost useless because the areas awarded were never surveyed and could be claimed by newcomers with ease. Nevertheless, the politicians thought they had taken care of the "Indian problem." The assembly even abolished the office of superintendent of Indian Affairs, which was a carryover from earlier times when the Mi'kmaq had been a credible military power in the region. Unfortunately, there was little the Mi'kmaq could do. An observer of the local scene in 1787 explained why: "[T]heir weakness, added to their prudence, will certainly prevent them from making any disturbances."

Over the years, colonial officials showed only sporadic interest in helping the Mi'kmaq, who experienced increasing economic deprivation. Between 1793 and 1838, politicians held six inquiries. Their studies recognized identical causes for the Mi'kmaq's situation: the destruction of game, fur, and fish resources; the lack of any refuge for the traditional Mi'kmaq way of life; and the group's failure to develop a new agriculture-based livelihood. The colonial assembly offered economic assistance to the Mi'kmaq, but it was very stingy, allocating only enough funds to pay for blankets, coats, and some seed. The assemblymen were unwilling to make long-term financial commitments. This might not have been a serious problem for the Mi'kmaq had the government dealt with the land issue in a meaningful way in the first place. Instead, between 1784 and the early 1840s, Nova Scotia approved various schemes to grant land to Mi'kmaq bands and individuals, but once more officials rarely surveyed the tracts properly and they did not eject intruders who invariably squatted on the most desirable sections.

The Mi'kmaq tried to fight back. In the 1840s they took their first tentative political steps aimed at halting this pernicious process. Chief Paussamigh Pemmeenauweet, an important leader for over twenty-five years, addressed Queen Victoria directly and powerfully in 1841:

> I cannot cross the great Lake to talk to you for my Canoe is too small, and I am old and weak. I cannot look upon you for my eyes [do] not see so far. You cannot hear my voice across the Great Waters. I therefore send this Wampum and Paper talk to tell the Queen I am in trouble. My people are in trouble.... My people are poor. No Hunting Grounds—No Beaver—no Otter—no nothing. Indians [are] poor—poor for ever. No Store—no chest—no Clothes. All these Woods once ours. Our Fathers possessed them all. Now we cannot cut a Tree to warm our wigwams in Winter unless the white Man please. The Micmacs now receive no presents, but one small blanket for a whole family.... Pity your poor Indians in Nova Scotia.
>
> White Man has taken all that was ours. He has plenty here.... Let us not perish. Your Indian Children love you, and will fight for you against all your enemies.

Pemmeenauweet's petition, which was witnessed by other Mi'kmaq leaders, moved the Queen, who instructed the colonial secretary to look into the matter. The outcome was the Nova Scotia Indian Act of 1842, which was based on the recommendations of the reform-minded politician Joseph Howe. It provided for an Indian commissioner who was supposed to supervise reserves, take action against squatters, work with the chiefs to promote agricultural settlement, and arrange for the admission of Mi'kmaq children into local schools. It was the first of many such acts passed in various parts of British North America that would "protect ... this helpless race, and elevate them in the scale of humanity" by taking an assimilation approach.

Howe became Indian commissioner. As one of his first official actions, he undertook yet another survey and concluded that the Mi'kmaq population was declining so rapidly—it numbered just over 1,425 in 1838—that they would disappear by the 1880s. Like others before him, Howe lacked the resolve to protect the Mi'kmaq reserves. Making matters worse, the education provision of the Indian

An Encampment of Micmac Indians at Point Levi, *1839. This painting gives the misleading impression that the living conditions of the Mi'kmaq were idyllic at the time. In reality, colonists had impoverished these people by pushing them off most of their land. Ironically, artists liked to paint the Mi'kmaq in shoreline settings, which were among the fertile places most highly prized by the land-hungry Loyalist settlers.*

Act proved to be ineffective. There were three primary reasons: the school boards did not want to admit hungry, shabbily dressed Mi'kmaq children into their classrooms; the assembly refused to pay the bills to educate them; and key officials asserted that the effort was a waste of time because the Mi'kmaq had to become farmers before formal schooling would have any positive influence on them.

Given these attitudes, it is easy to see why so little ever came of the initiative generated by Pemmeenauweet's letter. It was easier—and much less costly—to blame the Mi'kmaq for their increasingly grim situation. Nonetheless, Mi'kmaq leaders did not lose heart. In 1848, ten of them sent a petition to the assembly: "Some of your people say we are lazy, still we work. If you say we must go and hunt, we tell you again that to hunt is one thing and to find meat is another. They say to catch fish, and we try. They say make baskets, but we cannot sell them. They say make farms, this is very good; but will you help us till we cut away the trees and raise the crop. We cannot work without food. The potatoes and wheat we raised last year were killed by the poison wind [potato blight]. Help us and we will try again."

Although a few colonial officials thought that the Mi'kmaq could be saved by turning them into farmers, a new Indian commissioner—William Chearnly—took office in 1853 and convinced the assembly that these people were doomed. Any expenditures of substantial public funds for education and health services, he argued, would be useless; instead, the government should give the unfortunate Mi'kmaq a few blankets and greatcoats to help them in their final days. This became policy, and it remained in place until 1862, when a new commissioner again tried to encourage agricultural development by subdividing reserve lands into hundred-acre lots. The government thought that leasing these plots to Mi'kmaq individuals would give them a strong incentive to work the land, but the Mi'kmaq wanted to hold the land in common in keeping with their traditions. Another major problem was that the program was supposed to be funded by money received from cash-poor squatters. Not surprisingly, this arrangement did not end the continuing erosion of the Mi'kmaq land base—the root cause of their difficulties.

TAKING NATIVE LAND IN THE CANADAS

In Quebec the takeover of Native land proceeded along two divergent paths, both of them quite unlike the one followed in the Maritimes. Article 60 of the Montreal Articles of Capitulation of 1760 guaranteed "The Savages or Indian allies of his most Christian Majesty [of France], shall be maintained in the Lands they inhabit; if they chuse to remain there; they shall not be molested on any pretence whatsoever, for having carried arms, and served his most Christian Majesty." At the time of the conquest, the Native people of New France occupied two types of land: scattered reserves located within the settled part of the colony, and large hunting territories that lay beyond the settled areas.

The Catholic Church, acting through its various religious orders, served as trustee for the reserves' Native converts. In some instances, such as at Sillery and Lorette, this meant that the French Crown granted the lands to the Native people and the Church acted as their legal trustee. In other instances, such as at Kahnawake, the religious order received a royal bequest to develop the tract on behalf of the residents. Regardless of the precise arrangement, the understanding was that these land grants would revert to the Crown if the Native inhabitants abandoned them.

Although the Royal Proclamation of 1763 specifically excluded the new colony of Quebec from its provisions, the imperial government decided that it should ensure that the nations living there remained loyal to the Crown by giving them the same protection as those living elsewhere in British North America. Accordingly, a month after issuing the edict, the home government informed the Quebec governor, James Murray, that "[o]ur Province of Quebec is in part inhabited and possessed by several Nations and Tribes of Indians, with whom it is both necessary and expedient to cultivate and maintain a strict Friendship and good Correspondence...." Murray was "... upon no Account to molest or disturb them in the Possession of such Parts of the said Province as they at present occupy or possess." With regard to the Royal Proclamation, the home government told the governor, "It is Our express Will and Pleasure, that you take the most effectual Care that Our Royal Directions herein be punctually complied with." Immediately after the British government expanded the colony in 1774 under the terms of the Quebec Act, the new governor, Guy Carleton (later Lord Dorchester), received orders stating that Native lands should continue to be protected as specified in the 1763 decree.

The end of the American War of Independence and the arrival of approximately two thousand Loyalists in Quebec led to an abrupt change in British policy towards Native land there. The key priority became making land available for the newcomers. In 1791 the colonial government of Quebec passed an ordinance that allowed *bona fide* settlers to take up the "Waste Lands of the Crown." In effect, this meant that any settler who took an oath of allegiance to the Crown could settle on Native land. Those who did not could be fined and ejected for having settled on it!

In the year when this ordinance came into effect, the British Parliament passed the Constitutional Act, which divided Quebec into the colonies of Upper Canada and Lower Canada. The division would be important for Native people because the two Canadas followed divergent policies towards Aboriginal land. In Lower Canada the guidelines laid down in the Royal Proclamation of 1763 were largely ignored and settlers advanced steadily on Native land. Even the reserve lands held in trust by religious orders for Catholic converts were not safe. Settler encroachment on one of them, at Oka (Kanesatake) on the shores of Lake of Two Mountains, ultimately led to an armed confrontation there in the summer of 1990.

At Oka, the French government made a seigniorial grant to the Seminary of St Sulpice of Paris in 1717, and augmented it with additional lands in 1733. In 1784, the Sulpicians of Paris transferred their rights to the land to the Sulpicians of Montreal, who subsequently treated it as their exclusive property. When the order began to sell parcels of the reserve to settlers, the Mohawk charged it with violating its sacred trust and launched legal challenges on several occasions. Oka's Mohawk residents, who had moved there from Montreal in 1721, and the Nipissing and Algonquin,

In 1717 the Seminary of St Sulpice of Paris established a Native village near Oka, Quebec, on the shore of Lake of Two Mountains. Subsequently this settlement became the Kanesatake reserve. In 1739 the missionaries built a calvary on the hill as a pilgrimage for the local Aboriginal people, who visited it before setting off on their autumn hunts.

who had joined them shortly thereafter, hunted and fished in territories adjacent to the reserve, as did Native people living on other reserves in the St Lawrence valley. But immigrants moved onto these lands too, disrupting the reserve economies. This set the stage for a number of Native land claims and disputes. As early as 1822, the people of the Kanesatake reserve claimed (unsuccessfully) all the Ottawa River valley between their reserve and Lake Nipissing in an effort to halt the settler advance.

Until the end of the War of 1812, Upper Canada was highly vulnerable to attack by American forces. Consequently, courting Native support remained a corner-stone of British policy there until 1816. The earlier practice of adhering to the principles of the Royal Proclamation of 1763—or at least giving the appearance of doing so—continued. Accordingly, the Crown obtained Native land by negotiating treaties with various Ojibwa groups. All these accords were simple purchases in which the government made a single payment in cash and goods to the groups surrendering their land. Supposedly these were all voluntary sales. However, there is good reason to suspect that in many cases the Crown applied considerable pressure to obtain Ojibwa consent. A common ploy was to tell the Native people that if they did not sell their land, squatters would take it anyway. With the possible exception

St Regis Reserve (*Akwesasne*), *in the early nineteenth century. It was one of the earliest Iroquoian reserves to be established. Near present-day Cornwall, Ontario, it straddles the borders of Ontario, Quebec, and New York State.*

of the Grand River treaty creating Brant's reserve, probably none of the early treaties is better known than the 1787 Toronto Purchase, confirmed in 1805. In it the Mississauga surrendered title to all the land within what is now the greater metropolitan area of Toronto and the adjacent counties to the north, for a modest payment of "one thousand pounds Province currency, in goods at Montreal prices, to be delivered to us." Significantly, none of these early treaties made provisions for the setting aside of reserves because large tracts of territory were still available outside the areas settled by colonists. Ojibwa groups who sold some or all their territory simply migrated to adjacent areas, essentially retreating peacefully as the Loyalists advanced. Ojibwa oral tradition says that the reason that their ancestors were willing to do this was because the Crown promised to protect Native fisheries, which were so central to their economic life. Historian Mike Thoms' research shows that initially the Crown fulfilled this promise by amending colonial fish conservation legislation.

After the War of 1812, the character of the land surrenders changed in a fundamental way. In 1818 the Lords of the Treasury in England decided that in future the colonies, instead of the home country, would have to pay for acquisitions of Native land, but these governments had little money. Upper Canada's lieutenant-governor, Sir Peregrine Maitland, devised an ingenious solution. In essence, he turned to the Native people for credit. Maitland proposed to pay them annuities in perpetuity rather than the traditional lump sum at the time a treaty was signed. To obtain the income it would need to pay the annuities, the government would resell land to development companies and settlers on credit. The annual interest payments of these buyers would supposedly fund the scheme. The arrangement never did operate as smoothly as Maitland had envisaged, but it became very popular with Native people because it guaranteed them and their descendants a small annual income. Annuity payments became an integral part of all later treaties with the Crown, and records show that this provision helped accelerate the rate of land surrenders after 1818. It is important to remember that the annuity payments are essentially deferred payments for land purchases—not a kind of welfare payment.

By the 1820s, the steady westward advance of settlers was making it painfully clear to the Ojibwa that they were rapidly running out of lands to retreat to. They needed reserves. As a result, by the end of the decade, provisions for reserves became a common feature of the land surrenders. Missionaries and social reformers strongly supported this development; they wanted the Native people to retain enough land to enable them to become self-supporting farmers. This of course raised the issue of where to locate the reserves. Some thought that Native groups should live near settlements where they could learn new ways by observing the immigrant farmers. Others favoured the alternative strategy of placing reserves in remote areas, arguing that this would shield the Native people from the worst aspects of colonial society. Government officials and settlers liked this idea, thinking it would draw Native people away from developing areas; needless to say, the bands' preferences were usually ignored.

Perhaps the most notorious scheme to remove Native people to isolated areas was the one Lieutenant-Governor Sir Francis Bond Head put forward in the 1830s. Bond Head was convinced that nations living in the south would be better off if they moved north away from colonial settlements. The first he wanted to relocate were the Saugeen River Ojibwa. On August 9, 1836, 1.5 million acres of their land on the Bruce Peninsula had been purchased by his government for the benefit of land speculators and some of his political supporters. The site he had in mind for their relocation was Manitoulin Island in Lake Huron. On the same day the Bond Head–Saugeen Treaty was concluded, Bond Head met fifteen hundred Ottawa and Ojibwa at the Native settlement of Manitowaning on Manitoulin Island. He distributed presents to them to obtain their agreement to "make them [Manitoulin and the adjacent islands] the property (under your Great Father's control) of all Indians whom he shall allow to reside on them."

Gift-giving at Wikwemikong, Manitoulin Island, in the 1840s.

The Saugeen group strongly objected to Bond Head's plan. They rallied the support of church groups to their cause—particularly the Anglicans, the various Methodists, and the recently organized and influential London-based Aborigines' Protection Society. These supporters petitioned the British Colonial Office to block any forced removal. They informed it that contrary to Sir Francis's claims that most Native people could not be "civilized," many groups were making good progress, they were adopting the Christian faith, and their farming operations were increasingly productive. The Saugeen campaign paid off and the Colonial Office did not approve the forced relocation scheme.

The legality of the Bond Head–Saugeen Treaty was also in question at this time. Sir Francis claimed that the Saugeen River Ojibwa had willingly given up their land, even though only four of their people had signed the agreement and they lacked the authority to do so. The general superintendent of Wesleyan Missions, Joseph Stinson, reported that the lieutenant-governor "endeavoured to persuade them, and even threatened them, by telling them that he could not keep the white people from taking possession of their land, that they (the Indians) had no right to it only as hunting-grounds...." Stinson continued, "They told him they could not live on the Mundedoolin Island, that they would not go there, that they wanted land that they could call their own." In spite of the band's and Stinson's strong objections, and the fact that a grand council had not been called for the surrender according to the provisions of the Royal Proclamation, Bond Head had his way and the land surrender was upheld. In the end, the Saugeen group had to accept small reserves on the Bruce Peninsula.

This example and other similar incidents illustrate the fact that the land-cession treaties of Upper Canada often merely created the illusion that colonial officials were abiding by the rules of the Royal Proclamation. Too often the southern Ojibwa groups who signed the early treaties did not fully understand what they meant or feared offending government officials if they refused to co-operate. Chiefs who made the agreements frequently lacked the authority to sign them; in some instances these men handed over land that did not belong to them or their followers. In addition, government agents usually made verbal concessions to persuade the bands to sell. Routine promises included guarantees of the right to hunt and fish at traditional places, assurances that settlers would not be allowed to encroach on the remaining Native lands, and the provision of education for those who wanted it. For the most part, the Crown ignored the oral versions of treaties.

The Ojibwa of Upper Canada probably would have given up their lands even if officials had not resorted to their various ploys. Other pressures gave them little choice. By the beginning of the nineteenth century, they were already greatly outnumbered by immigrants. After the War of 1812, the rapid expansion of the American settlement frontier into the Midwest swept away their traditional allies. This meant that they were now isolated and of little value as a potential military force. The changing political landscape had undermined their bargaining position with the government.

New economic circumstances also weakened them. The spread of non-Native settlement into the area to the east of Lake Simcoe and into the Niagara Peninsula eroded the land base they needed for hunting, trapping, and fishing to the point that these activities yielded small returns. Meanwhile, groups living near the shores of Lake Ontario and other settled tracts had become highly dependent on trade goods and on alcohol. For these reasons the more southerly Ojibwa welcomed the prospect of receiving an annuity income. By the 1840s, the Ojibwa had signed away most of the arable sections of present-day southern Ontario, except for substantial tracts in the remote and beautiful Bruce Peninsula. But even here, settlers were pressing in, and by the late 1850s the peninsula's Ojibwa retained little more than some barren offshore islands.

The 1841 amalgamation of Upper and Lower Canada as the colony of Canada (creating Canada West and Canada East) had no immediate impact on land-acquisition policies. By this time, however, the firmly entrenched settler society of Canada West had little interest in continuing the long-established surrender formalities. When non-Native miners began uncovering copper deposits along the north shore of Lakes Huron and Superior in the late 1840s, the Crown Lands Department issued a number of mining licenses for the area, even though the Aboriginal people had not surrendered any of the territory. Leaders of the local Ojibwa and Métis settlements reminded the colonial government of their sovereignty in the area; in 1848 a party of Métis and Ojibwa from Canada and the United States burned a Lake Superior mining operation to stress the point (an event known as the Mica Bay War). The local Métis threatened to invite their relatives living at Red River to join the struggle if the government did not respond. At this important juncture, the governor general of Canada, James Bruce, 8th Earl of Elgin, intervened and wrote the colonial secretary in London to say, "I am much annoyed by a difficulty which has occurred with some Indians on the shore of Lake Superior." He explained that the previous governor general had given licenses to certain mining companies "with out making arrangements with the Indians." As a result of these interventions, the colonial government negotiated the Robinson-Huron and Robinson-Superior treaties in 1850.

The two treaties encompassed more territory than all the previous Upper Canadian cessions combined. The agreements included the major elements of previous treaties—annuities, a distribution of gifts at the conclusion of negotiations, and the establishment of reserves—and some very important new provisions. The most significant addition was the written guarantee that the Métis and Ojibwa could always hunt, trap, and fish on undeveloped Crown lands. Government treaty negotiator William Robinson reported that this clause, and his promise that they would be able to sell the produce of their hunts to incoming settlers, persuaded the Aboriginal people to agree to the treaties. Undoubtedly he would not have added this provision if the lands included in the Robinson treaties had been valued for agriculture rather than for mining. Mining development did not require large tracts of land, and indeed, in this remote area it seemed likely to be confined to scattered small properties along the shores of Lakes Huron and Superior. Government officials doubted that most of the area inland from these two lakes would ever be developed; therefore, it made good sense to grant the Métis and Ojibwa the right to continue using it. The Métis living beyond the Ojibwa reserves, especially those who operated small family farms at Sault Ste Marie, remained concerned about their land rights, however. To win them over, Robinson agreed to present their petition about this issue to the government. Although he did so subsequently, their property rights never were secured and most of them were displaced eventually.

The conclusion of the Robinson agreements extended the surrendered area to the limits of the colony's political boundaries. Long before this happened, how-ever, settlers had begun to encroach on the reserve lands of Canada West. In at least one notable instance—that of the Six Nations reserve—the Native people eagerly facilitated the process. As soon as he had taken up residence in his new homeland, Joseph Brant began awarding grants of land to settlers. By 1797 the Six Nations had given away, sold, or leased some 350,000 acres of the nearly 675,000 they had originally received. The chief and those who backed him did so for several reasons. First, they wanted to award grants to Brant's friends and those of other Iroquois leaders. Second, Brant concluded that the tract his followers had received was much larger than they could farm or develop in other ways, and that settlers eventually would surround the reserve, cutting off the Six Nations from their hunting lands. However, if they sold and leased lands to settlers, they could generate an annuity. And finally, Brant argued that settlers could teach the Six Nations new farming methods and build some of the facilities, such as grist and sawmills, that his people would need.

Not surprisingly, Brant's land deals were controversial. Some of the young Iroquois men questioned his motives and wisdom, but the fact that they were silenced by their "mothers and aunts," the traditional wielders of power, suggests that Brant had widespread support. In 1796 he obtained the formal backing of thirty-five of the chiefs, who "[c]onsented for themselves, and their posterity: and to and for their future benefit and support ... to Surrender a part thereof as aforesaid to His Majesty in order and upon the express Condition of the same being regranted to such person or persons as the person hereinafter appointed by them shall Nominate." They designated Brant as "our true and lawful attorney for us and In our names and in behalf of our said several Nations." Nonetheless, colonial officials, especially Lieutenant-Governor John Graves Simcoe, argued that Brant had violated the provisions of the Royal Proclamation of 1763, which dictated that Native land be sold only to the Crown. Simcoe also thought Brant set a bad precedent—one that would encourage unscrupulous land speculators to grab more Six Nations territory. Certainly this was a reasonable concern. Simcoe refused to allow any further surrenders, which left the legal status of the earlier sales in doubt. After lengthy wrangling and bullying by Brant, who threatened to attack the capital in 1797, the executive council of Upper Canada approved the Six Nations grants and leases.

Although the colonial government, particularly Simcoe, showed genuine concern about the disposal of Six Nations lands in the late eighteenth century, land-hungry settlers and the politicians who served them put heavy pressure on most of the other reserve lands of Upper Canada. As in the Atlantic colonies and Lower Canada, newcomers freely squatted on the most desirable parts of these tracts. In 1856 the legislative assembly of Canada appointed a commission to investigate "Indian affairs." The commissioners, whose sympathies lay squarely on the side of colonial settlers, concluded that "[t]he hardy pioneer who in advance of his fellows, plunges with a half sullen resolution into the forest, determined to make a home for himself, is not likely to be over scrupulous in respecting reserved lands." They added, "In a country like Canada the tendency to take possession of waste lands is irresistible, and the feelings of the country at large will always sympathize with the Squatter who is earning his living by his labour."

The commissioners' observations explain why the Ojibwa of Canada West fared little better than their counterparts elsewhere in British North America. Settler societies simply had no vested interest in protecting Aboriginal economic interests, no matter how legitimate. On the contrary, immigrants came primarily to

In the nineteenth century, many Ojibwa living in southern Ontario became successful farmers.

acquire land, so they believed that reserving tracts for Native hunting, trapping, fishing, and collecting purposes could not be justified when they could put it to more intensive uses such as agriculture, forestry, and mining. Rationalizing their appetite for land in this way, colonists had no qualms about whittling away Native reserves. Even those groups who managed to develop highly productive farms could not escape the pressure to give up their lands.

The Credit River Ojibwa were one of the groups Lieutenant-Governor Bond Head wanted to move to a common reserve on Manitoulin Island, even though they had made great strides towards becoming successful farmers. The chief of this band, Joseph Sawyer (Kawahjegezhegwabe), predicted that Bond Head's proposal would be a disaster for his people: "Now we raise our own corn, potatoes, wheat; we have cattle, and many comforts, and conveniences. But if we go to Maneetoolin, we could not live; soon we should be extinct as a people; we could raise no potatoes, corn, pork, or beef; nothing would grow by putting the seed on the smooth rock." Eventually, in 1847, Sawyer's people had to yield to the mounting pressure of settler encroachment on their lands. The government refused to grant the band secure title to its reserve, so instead of letting settlers take their land for nothing, the Credit River band accepted the government's offer for it and relocated to the Grand River valley.

Chief Sawyer's complaint points out some basic conflicts in government policy that have persisted to the present. The government had a fiduciary obligation to protect Native economic interests, but it also had to finance and promote development and settlement. On the one hand, it had a vested interest in encouraging the economic advancement of Native people so that they would not become chronic burdens on the public treasury; on the other hand, it did not want to help Native people compete against settlers in the marketplace. By resettling most of the southern Ojibwa bands into areas where they had little chance of participating in the emerging agricultural economy, the settler society pushed the Ojibwa to the economic and geographic margins of Canada West before Confederation. Other groups would suffer the same fate when Canada colonized the prairie West after 1867.

CHAPTER 11

THE CHANGING ORDER IN THE NORTHWEST

No one who ever saw one of these plain hunters come in to Fort Garry after the season's work on the Saskatchewan, could fail to see that he was a person in exceedingly comfortable material circumstances. In his train he had any number of carts (with ponies for each and to spare), and these were laden with the choicest viands in the shape of buffalo meat, marrow fat, beaver-tail, etc., while he also had a goodly supply of furs that would bring handsome prices.

—R.G. MacBeth, *The Making of the Canadian West*, 1898

In Rupert's Land and the northwest, most Native people did not have to confront land-hungry settlers until the latter half of the nineteenth century. They did, however, have to face a renewed Hudson's Bay Company, which gained a strong monopoly hold on the fur trade in most areas. This enabled it to dominate many aspects of the economic lives of the northwestern nations. The principal exceptions were the Plains people. The advance of American trading companies down the Red River and up the Mississippi and Missouri rivers offered them an alternative market for their furs and buffalo robes and hides. Such highly favourable economic circumstances helped the Plains buffalo hunters reach their zenith and enabled the Métis to develop a highly diversified and prosperous economy, which supported a vibrant new culture.

THE FUR-TRADE MONOPOLY

Mounting economic and political pressures had forced the HBC and the NWC to merge in 1821. The cutthroat competition of the previous thirty years had brought both enterprises to the brink of ruin. In the boreal forests, it had led to the serious depletion of fur and game resources, particularly beaver, woodland caribou, and moose. This bleak situation left the two competitors with little choice but to join forces, particularly after the British Parliament began pushing them in this direction to end the violence between the two, and the alcohol trading. The politicians made the elimination of liquor from the business one of the terms of the monopoly trading licence it granted to the amalgamated organization.

A Hudson's Bay Company trading room on the prairies, 1849. Contrary to popular myth, Aboriginal people were sophisticated customers who had well-defined tastes and a sharp eye for quality merchandise.

The job of restructuring the HBC's fur trade under the new licence fell to George Simpson, an experienced HBC trader. In 1821 the London directors appointed him governor of the sprawling Northern Department, which included all of present-day Canada west of Ontario. Five years later he also took control of the Southern Department, comprising all of present-day northern Ontario. Finally, in 1839 he rose to become governor of all HBC overseas operations in British North America. These responsibilities gave Simpson an unprecedented influence over the lives of a large majority of the Native people of British North America.

Under Simpson's leadership, the company devised a complex strategy to rehabilitate the fur trade of Rupert's Land. The new governor began by introducing a program that sought to place beaver harvesting on a sustained-yield basis in the central Subarctic. It banned the sale of steel-spring leg-hold traps in 1822 (except in frontier regions where American opponents were working) and introduced harvest quotas for various districts in 1826. The company closed posts in areas where beavers were particularly scarce, and it opened new ones in places where they were plentiful. It established open and closed trading seasons for beaver pelts, discouraged beaver trapping in the summer when the skins were of little value, and encouraged Native people to hunt other fur-bearing animals, particularly muskrat, where and when ecological and economic conditions were favourable.

Most Native groups strongly opposed this radical program to reduce the trapping and trading of beaver. They depended on their beaver-trapping income to buy essential supplies, and the meat of this animal was a mainstay in the diet of those who lived in areas where hunters had depleted moose and woodland caribou. Native people also may have objected to the plan because they looked at the depletion problem from a very different perspective than did the HBC. Some believed that every time an animal offered itself to the hunter in death, its spirit was released to create a new creature. Most believed that the welfare of animals rested with the gamekeepers of the spirit world, and that successful hunting depended on maintaining the good will of these supernatural forces by performing certain rituals. However, the gamekeepers could order the destruction of game even if such rituals were carried out. For example, the explorer and trader David Thompson wrote that the Ojibwa believed the Great Spirit had shown the Nipissing and Algonquin how to destroy beavers with castorum bait because it was angry with the animal. Although Native people often ignored the company's regulations for these reasons, the program worked sufficiently well that beaver populations did rebound. By the early 1840s, the HBC was able to revoke most of its restrictions. Ironically, by this time the silk hat had become so fashionable in Europe that the felt-hat market collapsed, sending beaver-pelt prices tumbling.

While the HBC tried to increase beaver stocks in southern Rupert's Land, it worked to create a "fur desert" in the borderlands of western British North America. The border ran along the 49th parallel between Lake of the Woods and the Rocky Mountains, according to the terms of an 1818 agreement between Great Britain and the United States. The company hoped that if fur-bearing animals along this boundary were killed, American traders would find it unprofitable to cross into its domain. Accordingly, Governor Simpson encouraged Native groups living in the prairies to strip the borderlands of furs. He also employed brigades of white "mountain men" to do the same in Oregon country to discourage Americans from entering New Caledonia.

To offset reduced beaver harvests in the areas set aside for conservation, Governor Simpson tried to develop new areas, such as the fur-rich lower Mackenzie River and the upper Yukon River drainage basins. But distance proved to be a major obstacle. These regions were far removed from York Factory, which remained HBC's central supply base until the establishment of steamboat companies and railway lines later in the century. Until then, York-boat brigades carried goods inland from Hudson Bay to the main forwarding base at Norway House, north of Lake

Winnipeg. The Athabasca, Peace River, and Mackenzie River district brigades brought their returns out to this post, and picked up their inbound outfits there. This labour-intensive transportation system severely limited the amount of freight that the company could haul inland. By all accounts it did not have the capacity to deliver enough goods to the Mackenzie River basin to satisfy the demand of the various Athapaskan-speaking groups who lived there. Consequently, the company's fur returns from the area remained well below their potential, and the local people were less dependent on trading posts than most other groups, with the exception of the central and western Inuit who had not yet been drawn into the fur trade.

Big Foot, a Copper Indian chief, and his son at Fort Providence, Great Slave Lake, 1820. Although this man's musket, powder horn, and European clothing materials indicate the influence of the fur trade, the logistical problems the Hudson's Bay Company faced supplying this area meant that local Native demand for goods greatly exceeded the available quantities.

After the merger, the renewed HBC also moved quickly to eliminate redundant trading posts and to trim its bloated labour force. Between 1821 and 1826, 1,233 men, or just over 60 per cent of the company's labour force, were laid off. Many were Métis from the parkland and grassland posts and mixed-bloods of Aboriginal-Scottish descent. Substantial numbers of these men moved to the Red River settlement with their families. During the 1820s, this migration radically transformed the character of the fledgling community. By 1831 the Métis residents numbered 1,300, and by 1870 they numbered almost 6,000 of the total population of almost 11,500. English-speaking mixed-bloods totalled about 4,000 in 1870. Europeans and French Canadians made up the balance. "Indians" were not included in the census.

In addition to cutting staff, Governor Simpson hoped to take advantage of the company's monopoly by slashing operating costs associated with long-established trading practices. He tried, for example, to eliminate gift giving, but he badly underestimated how much Native people still valued the institution. They refused to let him abolish it. Simpson had to be content with giving less lavish presents. Thus, "steady and reliable" hunters and trappers continued to receive presents—usually tea, tobacco, sugar, and a few other "trifles"—when they came to trade, or to commemorate the sovereign's birthday, or to celebrate Christmas and the New Year. A chief or "Indian of considerable influence" received a suit of clothes, and the aged and infirm were given an ammunition allowance, which they remitted to good hunters in exchange for food.

Simpson also wanted to overhaul the credit trading system. He wrote: "Heavy Debts are ascertained to be injurious to the Trade and of little benefit to the Indians, it is therefore understood that no more shall be given than there is a reasonable prospect of being repaid." Once again the company's clients balked. They prevented Simpson, and all the senior managers who followed him, from eliminating this aspect of the business, because they still believed that the amount of credit the HBC provided was a measure of its good faith and trust in them.

Finally, Simpson thought, again mistakenly, that the elimination of competition would make it possible for the company to improve its profit margins by importing lower-quality merchandise. Aboriginal consumers again rebelled. In this instance the London directors backed them. They believed that the HBC had an obligation to supply their loyal customers with high-quality merchandise, particularly where basic staples such as firearms and blankets were concerned.

In the end, the most important retailing change that took place after 1821 was the elimination of alcohol sales by company traders. Tea became the major substitute. Later flour became an essential item where country foods were limited or the HBC wanted to turn the attention of hunters away from large-game hunting and towards fur trapping. For the most part, Native people used flour to make an unleavened pan bread called bannock. In time, tea and bannock became the key ingredients of every trapper's bill of fare in the bush, and today they remain northern traditions.

As a monopoly, the HBC seemed to hold the whip hand in the Subarctic fur trade between 1821 and 1870, but it still relied on Native people in a wide variety of ways. In particular, its survival depended on maintaining a large pool of cheap, experienced Native labour in the bush. It was this realization that forced the company's directors and managers to move cautiously with reforms. Radical changes that adversely affected the quality of bush life risked accelerating the migration of Native people from areas where resource depletion was already a problem.

The York Factory district was one of the areas from which substantial numbers of Native people emigrated. They were drawn to the growing Red River settlement to the southwest. Its best-known resident historian in the mid-nineteenth century, Alexander

Assiniboine Hunting Buffalo *by Paul Kane. Buffalo ponies that were not easily spooked by the thundering herds became prized possessions of Plains hunters in the eighteenth and nineteenth centuries.*

Buffalo Rift *by A. J. Miller. Before they had horses to drive the herds over cliffs to their death in the summer, the Plains buffalo hunters used fire.*

A Family from the Tribe of the Wild Saulteaux Indians. *Peter Rindisbacher of the Red River colony specialized in drawing scenes of Native life on commission for Hudson's Bay Company traders and a succession of the colony's governors.*

After contact, West Coast artists combined European cloth and buttons to produce prized button blankets that depicted traditional symbols in new styles.

Clal-lum Women Weaving a Blanket *by Paul Kane. West Coast women were master weavers who used a wide variety of techniques and materials. The Clallum are Central Coast Salish people from the Juan de Fuca Strait area.*

Shooting the Rapids *by Frances Hopkins shows a crew of voyageurs skilfully manoeuvring a* canot du maître *in dangerous water. The North West Company relied heavily on these craft and hired a large number of Iroquois from the Montreal area to man them.*

Squall on Lake Superior *by Henry Warre. This painting gives the viewer a sense of the risks voyageurs faced when they crossed the Great Lakes and the large lakes of Manitoba.*

Moose Factory in the mid-nineteenth century. The boat-building works is portrayed behind the boats floating on the river. The unmarried officers' quarters and the chief factor's house are situated to the left, beyond the flagpole.

Thayendanegea (Joseph Brant) *by William Berczy. As one of Britain's most important Loyalist allies, this Mohawk leader and statesman was the driving force behind the creation of the Six Nations reserve on the Grand River, Ontario.*

*This Peter Rindisbacher painting, which shows a Métis man
and his two wives, indicates that the Métis developed a
distinctive culture of their own that set them apart from their
Aboriginal and European ancestors.*

*Arriving Red River colonists are welcomed by Peguis's band of Ojibwa, November 1, 1821.
Peguis and his followers played an important role in helping the colonists establish themselves.*

Winter Fishing on the Ice of the Assiniboine and Red Rivers, 1821, *by Peter Rindisbacher.*
Fisheries were an essential part of Native economies in most areas of Canada. Aboriginal fishers played
important roles in sustaining many trading posts.

Ross, complained that the Aboriginal people "began to edge themselves in; not indeed to labour themselves, but to partake, if possible, in the fruits of our toil." Governor Simpson moved to check this influx by maintaining a small outpost at Netley Creek and another one at the mouth of the Winnipeg River. He thought that if the migrants were able to obtain food, trade goods, and credit at these posts, they would not go on to Red River. The migration slowed, but it did not stop because many of these people had kinship ties to Métis and mixed-blood residents of the settlement.

Besides offering food and shelter, Red River settlers provided summer farm work. Ross recognized that this work might encourage the nomadic hunters to take up farming, which he thought was desirable. He claimed that a Swampy Cree from Oxford House, who originally came to the settlement to visit a daughter and stepson, was the first "Indian" to settle permanently at Red River and take up agriculture. Most of the Ojibwa and Cree migrants established themselves just north of Lower Fort Garry, where the Reverend William Cockran of the Church Missionary Society had established a Native settlement. Teaching Native people how to farm was one of the society's primary goals; however, the missionaries' "pupils" refused to abandon their old ways entirely. Instead, like the Métis and many of the mixed-bloods, they combined the old livelihoods and the new ones—a very sound economic survival strategy.

THE MÉTIS

While the Ojibwa and Cree were trying to find new niches in the evolving fur-trade economy, the Métis took centre stage and became the most potent economic force in the region. One of their achievements was combining buffalo hunting with farming and other activities. Their farms, like others in the settlement and those of the St Lawrence and the Great Lakes, were laid out in long narrow lots that reached back from the wooded riverbanks to the open grasslands. River frontage provided water, shelter in the woods, and ease of travel. At that time, no one believed that the open prairies behind the farms could be cultivated. Instead, they were used as a common hayfield.

Like their Plains relatives, the Métis undertook two major buffalo hunts annually. In late summer and early autumn, they headed out into the open grasslands to hunt buffalo for hides and to make grease, dried meat, and pemmican. In winter they went out again, but during this season their primary objective was to obtain buffalo robes and fresh meat.

Although their Plains roots are evident in the organization and execution of these expeditions, the Métis made several important innovations. The most obvious

The Métis built their Red River carts of local wood and used rawhide to hold them together. Unlike this family, most Métis used horses to pull their carts because oxen were too costly.

one was the extensive use of the two-wheeled Red River cart to haul their belongings and transport the returns of the chase. We do not know who introduced these vehicles to the area, but their appearance suggests a French-Canadian or possibly a Scottish heritage. During the first two decades of the nineteenth century, they became commonplace in the Red River valley. The Métis fashioned their carts entirely from local wood held together with strips of buffalo hide. No metal was used. The earliest carts had straight-spoked wheels, but later ones used dish-shaped wheels, which provided more stability. When one side of each wheel was covered with buffalo hides, the cart could be used to ferry cargo across rivers.

In his memoirs of this period, Louis Goulet, a Métis, wrote that when the community decided to mount an expedition, "the news was announced from the pulpit and by criers in as many parishes and missions as possible, telling people that if anybody wanted to join a buffalo-hunting caravan, all they had to do was be at a certain place on a certain day at a certain time." According to Goulet, the reason for calling the assembly "was just about always the same: to elect a first and second leader along with a council of at least twelve. We also decided on the rules of order for the march. Each member of the executive who took part in the expedition had a voice in the assembly." The two leaders and the council served the same roles on the hunt that the chiefs and elders did among the Plains nations. They made laws that were intended to ensure everyone's safety. Goulet said these laws usually included a ban on drinking alcohol, a prohibition against leaving camp without council authorization, and a stipulation that participants had to wait for a signal from the appointed guides before doing anything. "The council's decisions were law," he noted, "entirely and everywhere, for the duration of the journey." Councils imposed fines for minor infractions and distributed the payments they received to those in need. Violators could receive severe punishment— even a death sentence—for very serious transgressions. Goulet recounted one instance when a council ordered the execution of an entire family because it had broken all the rules including those pertaining to "robbery and immorality."

Goulet left us a vivid description of a typical expedition heading out into the prairies:

> The hunters brought their wives and children with them, in carts covered with leather or canvas hoods, to protect them from sun, rain, wind and even snow. We used to call those covered carts carrachetehounes. It was an awe-inspiring and unforgettable sight to see hundreds of oxcarts loaded with human clusters, making their way towards the buffalo country in three or more parallel lines. What made this scene of an entire population on the march even more picturesque was a noisy assembly of dogs, hundreds of them, who always tagged along with the travelers. Their barking made a chorus for the incessant din of wooden hubs thirsty for grease, squealing all day long and announcing our presence for miles around.

By the late eighteenth century, the use of horses had revolutionized summer buffalo-hunting techniques. "Running" a herd on swift buffalo ponies became the common practice. Bows and lances were better suited to this type of hunting than the cumbersome and slow-loading smooth-bore flintlock or percussion-cap musket.

The Métis hunting expeditions grew steadily in size over the years and brought prodigious quantities of food, hides, and robes back to Red River. Each cart carried about nine hundred pounds. In 1820 the hunters set out in approximately 540 carts; by 1840 they used just over 1,200. This represented an increase in capacity from slightly less than half a million pounds to more than one million pounds over a twenty-year period. The fresh and processed meat products of the Métis were the mainstays of their diet and prominent articles in their commerce. There is no question that the Red River colony would have failed without this food. The colonial farmers faced a seemingly never-ending succession of setbacks due to early and late frosts, recurrent droughts, plagues of locusts, and frequent floods. When they did manage to bring in a harvest, they lost most of it to vermin or poor processing and storage facilities.

Another market for their meat products—the fur traders—was not as lucrative as it once had been, and the Métis had to compete with the Plains Assiniboine, Cree, and Ojibwa for a share of it. In 1840 the HBC needed 55,886 pounds (sixty-two cart loads) of dried meat and pemmican to feed its Northern Department employees. Clearly this demand, coupled with that of the colonists, was not sufficient to support commercial buffalo hunting on the scale that the Métis practised. The market for buffalo robes and hides that developed in the eastern United States became their primary market. The Métis shipped 26,000 to 200,000 robes, which were used for carriage robes and heavy winter coats, from the northern plains annually between 1815 and 1830. The HBC was not able to be a major player in this business because of its high transportation costs. Buffalo robes were simply too bulky to export by boat to York Factory or by canoe to eastern North America.

The Métis traded at two major outlets. Fort Union, situated at the junction of the Yellowstone and Missouri rivers, just south of the border, was the most important one because it was in the heart of buffalo-hunting country. In 1844 the Métis also established regular contact with St Paul, on the upper Mississippi River, by building the Red River Trail. By the mid 1850s the cartmen hauled as many as seventy-five hundred robes to this alternative market. The development of the robe market had important implications for Métis women and the women of the Plains nations. Because they processed the robes, the production capacity of a hunter's wives and daughters determined how many robes he could trade annually. This crucial role women played in generating wealth was one of the reasons Plains men took more than one wife.

In the 1860s the high demand for leather in the post–Civil War United States created a market for buffalo hides that was many times larger than the one for robes

Tanning a hide on the Sarcee reserve, Alberta, in the early 1900s. Strong export markets developed for buffalo robes and hides in the nineteenth century. Native hunters depended on their wives and daughters to prepare them.

A train of Red River carts meets a York-boat brigade. The Hudson's Bay Company relied heavily on Native labourers to supply its Northern Department posts by York boat and Red River cart.

had ever been. Buffalo hides made ideal belts for use in the power-transmission systems that drove mills and factory machinery during the early stage of industrialization. The rapid expansion of the hide market sounded the death knell for the once-bountiful prairie buffalo. Well before this new threat developed, however, the herds were already in retreat. The Red River hunts had begun to take their toll on the buffalo of the southern Manitoba district as early as the 1820s. Comparatively few animals existed there after 1850. By 1860 the herds were declining sharply in the Saskatchewan River valley downstream from Fort Edmonton.

The Métis and some of their mixed-blood neighbours directed their entrepreneurial energies in other directions as well. Operating freighting businesses was one of them. The tortuous courses of prairie rivers made moving goods across the plains by boat and canoes a time-consuming and tedious chore, so the Métis contracted to haul HBC supplies overland by cart from the Red River colony to Fort Carlton in Saskatchewan country and to Fort Edmonton. On this journey, the noisy and dust-choked caravans carved deeply furrowed trails that are still visible today.

While these developments were taking place, other mixed-blood people and Métis established themselves as "free traders" and competed against the HBC. A number of elements encouraged them. When American traders expanded their operations into the northern plains of the United States in the 1820s and 1830s, they threatened to take a large portion of the HBC's business in the Rainy Lake, Red River, Swan River, and Saskatchewan districts. To deal with the threat as cheaply as possible, Governor Simpson opted to license a number of mixed-blood and Métis men as semi-independent traders. Under this arrangement, the licensed traders were supposed to buy their supplies from and sell their hides and furs to the HBC at preferential rates. The scheme failed—the Americans simply offered much better terms. Because the company refused to grant enough licences to satisfy the demand for them, a lively clandestine traffic developed between the Americans and unlicensed traders. When the HBC tried to restrict this commerce, the Métis and mixed-blood "free traders" led a free-trade movement. One of their tactics was to petition London for self-government in 1848 in the hope of undermining the company's authority.

A test of the Métis' growing strength came with the Sayer trial, when local HBC officials tried to crack down on the offenders in 1849 by bringing a fellow countryman, Pierre Guillaume Sayer, to trial at Red River on the charges that he had violated the company's charter by trading furs illegally. Sayer refused to appear when the court was ready to begin on the morning of May 17, 1849. Instead, he remained outside the courthouse in the protection of a large group of armed Métis and mixed-blood supporters. He sent two "delegates of the people" in his place to protest the proceedings. Adam Thom, who presided as recorder of Rupert's Land (essentially the chief civil justice), persuaded one of the delegates, James Sinclair, known locally as the "chief of the half-breeds," to act as Sayer's defence counsel and the trial proceeded in the afternoon. Sayer entered the courtroom and testified in his own defence, asserting that he had not violated the company's trust in him because he had traded only with his Métis relatives. At the conclusion of the trial, the jurors convicted him, but they recommended clemency.

HBC officials now found themselves in a difficult position. With a menacing mob surrounding the courthouse, they had little choice but to accept the jury's recommendation; otherwise, a violent outbreak was a certainty. Clearly, the Métis wielded the real power in the settlement, although the company controlled the local administration and the civil court. As the courtroom emptied, one of the jurors came to the door and shouted, *"Le commerce est libre! Le commerce est libre! Vive la liberté!"* Apparently the crowd outside took up the chant, which history proved to be correct. Never again did the HBC try to enforce its monopoly in the prairies. Instead, it took steps after the trial to accommodate Métis' interests by giving them representation on the council that governed the settlement.

RACISM IN THE HUDSON'S BAY COMPANY

Although the HBC trimmed its labour force in the early 1820s, its demand for workers increased again at the end of the decade. One reason was that the developing economies and higher wage rates of the St Lawrence valley and northern Scotland made it harder for the company to recruit workers from these traditional areas. The HBC therefore turned increasingly to the "Indian," Métis, and mixed-blood communities to meet its requirements. However, the company's policy prohibiting the hiring of Native people for anything other than seasonal (mostly summer) work or specific tasks remained in place. The majority of Native men were hired as crews on the boat and canoe brigades, as unskilled labourers at posts in the summer, and as provision hunters for posts in the winter. As fur and game depletion became widespread again later in the century, this short-term employment became vital to hunters and trappers. Without such earnings, increasing numbers of them could not afford to buy basic necessities. Post managers took advantage of the situation by awarding coveted summer work only to their most reliable hunters. In this way they developed hiring practices that reinforced the company's goal of keeping a labour force in the bush.

Native women also played crucial economic roles at the posts. They produced and repaired essential footwear (moccasins and snowshoes), chopped wood, collected canoe-birch supplies, made canoe sails, provided tanned hides and pack cords, re-dressed furs for shipment to London, grew vegetables, snared hare, and caught and preserved fish. Indeed, women made significant contributions to the larders of many posts until well into the twentieth century. In northern Ontario, for instance, the "old fisherwoman" provided Fort Severn with most of its fish in the late 1870s. Nearby, at Martin Falls Post, "Old Betsy and her daughter" fished, built smoking lodges, smoked the whitefish others brought in, and visited the various fishing stations carrying messages from the post manager to the fishers. Additionally, women continued to trap and trade furs, and they produced and sold large quantities of isinglass, a dried gelatin prepared from the air bladders of sturgeon. The HBC had promoted the isinglass trade from the earliest days of its operation, but Native women had always thought the payment they received was too low, considering how time-consuming its production was. After 1821 rising prices on the European market made this activity worthwhile.

Mixed-blood employees of the HBC fared somewhat better during this period than their Native counterparts, although not as well as they had before the merger. Prior to 1821, it was possible for the men to work their way up the company ladder and become senior officers. Afterwards, the HBC developed a two-tiered structure. Mixed-blood and Métis men holding seasonal and permanent jobs occupied the rank in the labour hierarchy just above that of the Native seasonal workers.

The highest position a man of mixed descent could hope to attain in the company was that of a semi-skilled or skilled tradesman—for example, a boat builder, bricklayer, carpenter, cooper, gunsmith, or blacksmith. A man learned these trades by apprenticing, often with men recruited in Scotland. Bowmen and sternmen played essential roles in the brigades and these positions continued to be held mainly by mixed-bloods and Métis.

The HBC looked for its officers outside Rupert's Land and the northwest. Most continued to come from Scotland, but a few came from Lower Canada. The officer recruits, who usually joined the firm as clerks, trained on the job under the watchful eyes of post managers. The upper echelons of the officer class were occupied by the profit-sharing chief factors and chief traders. Collectively these men shared 40 per cent of the fur-trading profits of the company.

Understandably, the men of mixed ancestry resented the new, racist arrangement, which blocked them from attaining the most prestigious and lucrative positions in the company. They were not alone. Many senior men in the officer class had married Native women and raised children with them. Predictably, they wanted their sons to have the opportunity to follow in their footsteps. Pressure from these ranking officers eventually forced the HBC to create the position of apprentice postmaster explicitly for the mixed-blood sons of officers. The trouble was that this move merely emphasized the company's discriminatory hiring practices. It was willing to hire raw European recruits as junior officers, but it expected young mixed-blood men to serve a seven-year apprenticeship, even though they had grown up around posts and were much more familiar with the enterprise than European immigrants were. Few ever completed the apprenticeship to become full-fledged officers. In the stratified labour force that emerged after 1821, a man's opportunity depended heavily on his ethnic background. Those of mixed descent were barred from the top; "Indians" were kept at the bottom.

The HBC hierarchy had a strong impact on the development of the multi-cultural society that evolved at Red River and around the larger company establishments throughout Rupert's Land and the northwest. Active and retired senior officers living in Red River, some with white wives, dominated the English-speaking elite. Other members of this class included the Protestant clergy, British female schoolteachers, and a handful of mixed-blood merchants and free traders. Scottish and mixed-blood farmers ranked below them. (Many of the latter also worked for the company part-time and engaged in buffalo hunting.) By cutting off advancement possibilities to mixed-blood men, the HBC also limited their chances, and those of their spouses, to improve their social status. The social status of Métis men and women was not as seriously affected because they rarely socialized with the English-speaking community. Their own elite included the priests, the more influential members of a small group of French-Canadian immigrants (who first arrived at Red River in 1818) and their descendants, and the most successful Métis free traders.

The attitudes, racial prejudices, and social practices of Governor Simpson and the settlement's Protestant missionaries had a great impact on its residents—especially the women of mixed extraction. Although country marriages between traders and Aboriginal women had once been commonplace, by the turn of the nineteenth century it was more fashionable for wintering partners of the North West Company and officers and clerks of the HBC to marry Métis and mixed-blood women, who usually were more European in appearance and behaviour. Senior officers with mixed-blood daughters often tried to arrange a match between them and promising young clerks of the company. When they retired to Canada or Scotland, these officers often "gave their wives" to their comrades at the post, a practice they called "turning off." Alternatively, the women returned with their children to their Native kinfolk. These customs provided for the welfare of the offspring of interracial unions and offered the female members of the fur-trade society a chance to enhance their status through marriage. However, in the 1820s Governor Simpson advocated new marriage customs that would make these women extremely vulnerable to poverty and social uncertainty.

Simpson's own relationships reveal the realities of what life was like for the women. In 1821, shortly after his arrival in the northwest, he formed a liaison with Betsey Sinclair, the mixed-blood daughter of a deceased high-ranking HBC officer and an Aboriginal woman. Although he had a child with her, Simpson did not regard the relationship as binding in any way. When he grew tired of her companionship in 1823, he instructed another company officer to marry her off to a clerk. Three years later he began a relationship with Margaret Taylor, who was the mixed-blood daughter of the sloop master at York Factory and the sister of his personal servant of many years. The governor had two daughters with Margaret before he left for England in 1830, where he married his cousin, Frances Simpson. As soon as the governor returned to Red River with his English bride, he promptly arranged a marriage between Margaret and a French Canadian who was living in the settlement.

Simpson then let it be known that he frowned on the practice of allowing HBC men to marry Aboriginal women or those of mixed ancestry. He took this position partly because he held Native people in extremely low regard and partly

A Hudson's Bay Company marriage contract, 1837. From the beginning of contact, European men and Aboriginal women married à la façon du pays. Initially, the HBC barred its servants from entering into such unions, but eventually it was forced to accept the practice, which it formally legitimized by issuing marriage contracts.

because he believed "country wives" exerted too much influence over their husbands. On an inspection tour in 1825, he complained about three senior officers in the Columbia District, saying the men were "so much under the influence of their Women … that what they say is Law and they can not muster sufficient resolution in themselves or confidence in their Ladies to be 5 Minutes on end out their presence." Finally, Simpson disliked the fact that his officers and servants were raising large families with their Native wives. Although these unions tied the HBC into Aboriginal kinship circles, and gave it access to their furs, they also created obligations that could be costly for the company. "Almost every man in the District [Columbia] has a Family," Simpson grumbled, "which is productive of serious injury and inconvenience on account of the great consumption of Provisions; but by changing men from this evil, will be remedied and the women and Children sent to their Indian relatives."

As with the other reforms he attempted, the governor learned that he could not overturn well-established practices at will without placing the business at risk. Country marriages continued because there was no alternative for most men at that time. White women would be few and far between in the northwest for many years to come. Nonetheless, the example set by Simpson and other senior men who subsequently brought European wives to their posts, or married English schoolteachers at Red River, undermined the status of the mixed-blood spouses of their fellow officers. And officers who married women of mixed ancestry had to face the reality that their career prospects would be compromised as a result. By mid-century, the fur-trade accounts became filled with racist slurs against "Indian" and, to a lesser extent, mixed-blood women. Writing in 1830, the fur trader James Hargrave also blamed European women for this development, saying, "This influx of white faces has cast a still deeper shade of the faces of our Brunettes in the eyes of many."

The Protestant clergy generally frowned on interracial marriages, too. Nor did they approve of marriages outside of the church *à la façon du pays*. As a result of the clergy's pressure, many couples eventually "solemnized" their unions in churches at Red River and other settlements. However, away from major settlements, it was impossible for the missionaries or the company to impose a more rigid social order based on class and race. Even at Red River, the task proved to be difficult, given the polyglot character of the population and its diverse economic activities.

It is not clear to what extent Red River's two different groups of mixed-descent people interacted with each other or shared common goals. Some historians believe that the Protestant community of Scots and mixed-bloods had little to do with the Catholic French Canadians and Métis. Certainly these communities lived in different parts of the settlement. Most of the mixed-bloods and Scottish farmers were located on the west bank of the Red River to the north of its confluence with the Assiniboine. The French Canadians lived in the parish of St Boniface, opposite the outlet of the Assiniboine River, and the Métis lived south of the forks along the west bank of the Red River. There also was an outlying Métis community at Portage la Prairie. Other scholars stress that in spite of their cultural differences and the physical distance between their communities, strong ties bound the two groups together. For example, some mixed-bloods participated in the buffalo hunts, and buffalo hunters and farmers continued to buy each others' products. Intermarriage also took place. Nonetheless, sectarian tensions seem to have increased over time, and the clergy were mainly responsible. Beginning in the early 1860s, immigrants from Canada West aggravated the situation. The newcomers disdained the mobile lifestyle of the Métis and did not believe that the long-time residents, or their Aboriginal kinfolk, had any valid rights to the land. They also loathed the HBC, regarding it as an impediment to their own economic interests.

The Canadian immigrants were harbingers of the future. This new breed of settler dreamed of turning the prairies and parklands into wheat fields, but they did not envisage the Plains nations, the Métis, or the mixed-bloods having any role to play in the process. Their dream was incompatible with the traditional land-use practices of the Native groups, which required large open areas for buffalo hunting and extensive common grazing and hay fields behind their Red River lots.

CHAPTER 12

PLACED ON A LITTLE SPOT

[O]ur families are well, our people have plenty of food, but how long this will last we know not. We see your ships, and hear things that make our hearts grow faint. They say that more King-George-men [settlers] will soon be here, and will take our land, our firewood, our fishing grounds; that we shall be placed on a little spot, and shall have to do everything according to the fancies of the King-George-men.... We do not wish to sell our land nor our water; let your friends stay in their own country.

—An anonymous Sechelt chief speaking to Gilbert Sproat, Port Alberni, August 1860

Beyond the Rocky Mountains, the years between 1821 and the early 1870s were ones of accelerating change and dangerous disputes. First the sea otters all but disappeared, forcing the fur trade to move inland. The race between Americans and the Hudson's Bay Company to settle the Pacific Northwest began in 1821 and lasted until 1846. The Americans won easily. As a result, Great Britain and the United States concluded the Oregon Boundary Treaty in 1846, which gave the Americans control of the Native territory south of the 49th parallel. To establish a stronger British presence in the remainder of the area and to ward off any further Yankee expansion, the Colonial Office gave the HBC the go-ahead to establish an agricultural colony on southern Vancouver Island and to develop resources elsewhere on the island. The colony had barely established itself when a sequence of gold rushes began in the coastal region. These various developments signalled the beginning of a new economic order in the West that would present new opportunities to Native people; it would also threaten their future and security as the newcomers began to expropriate Native lands and resources.

An engraving of Saveeah, chief of the Kootcha-Kootchin, one of the northwesternmost Dene groups, 1847–48.

HEREDITARY LEADERS AND THE HBC

When Governor Simpson curtailed beaver exploitation in Rupert's Land during the 1820s and 1830s for conservation purposes, he tried to compensate by expanding operations in other districts, including New Caledonia, the former North West Company fur-trading area to the west of the Rocky Mountains. This proved to be a very difficult and costly effort. The declining stocks of sea otter had encouraged coastal nations, particularly the Tsimshian of the lower Skeena River, to make a major effort to expand their inland trading networks. The HBC officers found themselves battling head to head with these experienced traders.

HBC trader William Brown's account of his time in New Caledonia gives us a clear picture of this conflict in the territories of the Babine, Gitxsan, and Wet'suwet'en during the 1820s. The company dispatched Brown to Babine Lake, where he established Fort Kilmaurs (also known as Old Fort Babine) in 1822. He intended to use this post as a base to extend the company's sphere of operations northwestward. Brown found himself in a very unfamiliar world. Because he had spent his earlier career in various districts to the east of the Rocky Mountains, he was unaccustomed to dealing with hereditary leaders who exerted considerable control over the use of resources on their lands and who dominated inter-nation trading relations.

A succession of coast Tsimshian chiefs bearing the hereditary name Legiac led the Native opposition to the HBC. When Brown arrived on the scene, these people were in the process of strengthening their ties with the Gitxsan and Wet'suwet'en. The Tsimshian already held regular trading fairs at the forks of the Skeena and Bulkley rivers, and some Gitxsan and Wet'suwet'en undertook frequent expeditions to the coast. Brown learned that he would have great difficulty breaking into this exchange network because the Tsimshian, who had access to trading ships plying the coast, were able to provide goods at much cheaper rates than he could. To address this problem, Brown resorted to an old Nor' Wester strategy. He instructed the company to import moose hides from districts lying to the east of the Rocky Mountains. The Babine, Gitxsan, and Wet'suwet'en were willing to pay premium prices for the scarce commodity, which they presented as gifts to guests at funeral feasts. The trade in moose skins remained a feature of the company's business in Skeena country until the turn of this century, when provincial conservation legislation unfortunately banned the traffic in game-animal hides.

The Babine tossed other obstacles in Brown's way. Like most of the nations living on the Pacific slope, the Babine were experienced fish sellers. They knew Brown would have to depend on them for fresh and dried salmon because game was not abundant in their country—or in most areas of New Caledonia, for that matter. Soon after his arrival, the Babine informed him that they would determine the price he would have to pay for salmon and for any fishing nets that he required. Brown had no choice but to pay their high prices.

In light of the company's conservation policies elsewhere at this time, it is ironic that the resource-management methods of the Babine, Gitxsan, and Wet'suwet'en proved to be the biggest barrier to increasing the trade in beavers from the upper Skeena country. Brown quickly discovered that each chief permitted an annual harvest of only about twenty-five beavers from his house territory. These leaders, whom Brown referred to as "men of property," or "nobles," limited the harvest partly by denying most of their followers the right to hunt beavers. As well, they jealously guarded their domain against the incursions of outsiders. When Governor Simpson visited the district, he reported that the chiefs regarded any trespass on their houses' lands as being tantamount to a declaration of war. In 1826 Brown tried to get the Babine to agree to abandon their limits on the hunt at a meeting of the men of property he called at Fort Kilmaurs. After having learned that the various Carrier nations, which included the Babine and Wet'suwet'en, husbanded the beaver because they prized the animal's flesh as a ceremonial food, Brown proposed that the chiefs permit all their male followers to trap beavers, provided that these men gave the meat to the first leader who sponsored a funeral feast in any given year. The house leaders who had accepted Brown's invitation listened politely to his proposal but rejected it.

The elders also refused to give commercial trapping activities any priority, in spite of Brown's repeated call for them to do so. Instead, the Babine and Wet'suwet'en spent most of the long winter months doing what they liked best—feasting, gambling, and socializing. Furthermore, the chiefs, who handled most of the trade of their followers, refused to break their well-established trading connections with other nations. The best that Brown could do was persuade them to divide their loyalties. In this way he obtained a small share of the regional fur trade while the coastal Tsimshian held on to the largest part.

Unable to outwit its coast Tsimshian opponents, the HBC decided to try a new tactic. In 1831 it established the first Fort Simpson on the coast between the Nass and Skeena rivers (later relocating it to the Skeena River) so the company could become the Tsimshian's primary supplier. This was part of an overall strategy to establish a strong presence on the coast, which began in 1827 with the construction of Fort Langley on the lower Fraser River. In 1833 it built Fort McLaughlin on Milbanke Sound, near Bella Bella. Operating posts at these strategic locations enabled the HBC to outfit most of the key mainland coastal groups. To enhance its position even further, the company eliminated Russian competition from the north by negotiating an arrangement with the Russian American Fur Company in 1839. In it the HBC obtained exclusive trading rights in the Alaska Panhandle for an annual payment of river-otter skins; in the 1840s the payment for this concession amounted to an impressive fifty thousand pelts. As it had hoped, the company profited indirectly from the traffic into and out of the Gitxsan and Wet'suwet'en territories through Tsimshian middlemen at Fort Simpson.

NEW ZEALAND-STYLE LAND SURRENDERS ON VANCOUVER ISLAND

At the same time that the British Colonial Office was searching for someone to develop a settlement on the West Coast to act as a buffer against American encroachment, the HBC was interested in Vancouver Island for its agricultural and mineral potential—particularly coal. The Native people had shown company officers deposits at various locations on the island. In 1849 the Colonial Office accepted the HBC's proposal to establish a colony on Vancouver Island.

The settlement at Fort Victoria got off to a very shaky start because the Colonial Office chose Richard Blanshard as its first governor. He was an English lawyer who knew nothing about the region or its people. The manner in which Blanshard dealt with one group in 1850 was reminiscent of the practices of the early maritime fur traders. That year three HBC men had deserted ship in the territory of the Newitty (a Kwakwaka'wakw group) and had been murdered by some unknown assailants. The Newitty claimed that the killers belonged to a northern group, perhaps the Kitkatla or Haida, but a neighbouring and hostile Kwakwaka'wakw group living next to Fort Rupert blamed the Newitty. The magistrate at the fort was baffled. The new governor, however, resolved to take decisive action, fearing that Fort Rupert would be attacked by the surrounding well-armed Kwakwaka'wakw.

The purported wrongdoers would pay for their crimes to safeguard against any "sudden outburst of fury to which all savages are liable." At Fort Rupert, Blanshard authorized the local magistrate to offer the Newitty a reward for the arrest of the murderers. According to the governor, the Newitty responded by taking up arms, by acknowledging their kinsmen had committed the crime, and by refusing to turn them over to the magistrate. Instead, as was their tradition, they offered to pay compensation. Blanshard flatly rejected their proposal and dispatched three Royal Navy boats to the culprits' village to seize them. By the time this party arrived, the Newitty had fled north. The marines and sailors set fire to the deserted settlement, but neither Blanshard nor the naval commander thought that this was sufficient punishment. They sent the H. M. S. *Daphne* northward with Blanshard on board to force the Newitty to turn over the murderers. After a brief armed clash, the villagers retreated into the forest and Blanshard's force burned this settlement too, as well as all their canoes. In the end, the Newitty yielded up three mutilated bodies, which they claimed were those of the murderers.

This seminal episode resulted in some important interim policy changes. The Colonial Office disapproved of Blanshard's heavy-handed measures. The colonial secretary, the 3rd Earl Grey, in typical understated fashion, told the governor, "I should state for your guidance on future occasions that Her Majesty's Government cannot undertake to pro-

"Coal Tyee," or the Coal Chief, was one of the Coast Salish people who brought the coal deposits near present-day Nanaimo, British Columbia, to the attention of the Hudson's Bay Company in the 1840s. The local Salish were eager to trade the mineral to the company, but the HBC decided to develop its own mining operation after the "discovery."

tect, or attempt to punish injuries committed upon British subjects, who voluntarily expose themselves to the violence or treachery of the Native Tribes at a distance from the settlements." Legal advisers of the Crown warned the Royal Navy to move cautiously and with a great deal more tolerance in the future if British subjects were murdered by Native people and commanders did not witness the act.

Blanshard's year in office also made it clear to the Colonial Office that the HBC's Vancouver Island colony needed a governor who understood Native people, had good leadership skills, and would use force judiciously. These considerations led to the appointment of HBC Chief Factor James Douglas in 1851. Douglas was an intriguing character of mixed Scottish and "free coloured" West Indian ancestry. He was married, à la façon du pays, to Amelia Connolly, the mixed-blood daughter of Chief Factor William Connolly, Douglas's former superior officer, and Susanne Pas-du-nom, a Cree.

Early in his career, Douglas's brashness nearly cost him his life. His wife and a Carrier chief named Kwah saved him. This important story began in 1823 when two Carrier men at Fort George killed two HBC employees in a dispute over two Carrier women. The company retaliated by closing the post, which was located at the confluence of the Nechako and Fraser rivers. Local officers wanted to take more drastic measures to avenge the murder of their comrades. For several years they encouraged the Carrier to kill the murderers, but the influential Kwah repeatedly blocked his people from doing so. The chief was an elderly man who had gained fame for his prowess as a warrior. Kwah held a noble title, which he had inherited from his mother's brother, and lived in a village near Fort St James, on Stuart Lake. One of the suspects came to the village in 1828 and took refuge in Kwah's house while he was away; Carrier tradition held that those who had committed crimes could use a chief's house as a sanctuary. When he learned that the alleged offender was nearby, the young and reckless Douglas gathered up a few of his men, marched to Kwah's house, and killed the man.

Several days later, Kwah and his followers arrived at Fort St James and an ugly confrontation ensued. Douglas grabbed for a gun when he saw the angry mob, but Kwah restrained him. Amelia Douglas then seized a dagger from the father of the murdered man, but was disarmed. In the commotion, Kwah's nephew reached Douglas and, holding a sword to the trader's chest, told the chief to give the word and he would kill him. In desperation, Amelia and the wife of the HBC interpreter promised restitution and hurled gifts at Kwah's followers. The chief had already made his point, and the women's actions gave him an out. He asked his followers to take pity on Douglas and accept the presents as adequate compensation for his misdeeds. Today the event is commemorated locally by the inscription on Kwah's tombstone: "HERE LIE THE REMAINS OF GREAT CHIEF KWAH BORN ABOUT 1755 DIED SPRING OF 1840. He once had in his hand the life of James Douglas but was great enough to refrain from taking it."

The "Indian policy" that Douglas implemented as governor reflected his

Amelia Douglas, the mixed-blood wife of Governor James Douglas, was subject to discrimination in the Vancouver Island colony. One way she responded to it was by consciously presenting herself as a model of Victorian womanhood.

thirty-two years of experience in the fur trade, the long-standing practices of the HBC, and the thinking of the Colonial Office. He thought it was foolish to hold entire villages responsible for the actions of individuals, and announced that any Native people who committed crimes against settlers would be punished according to British law. He would apply "gunboat diplomacy" as necessary to that end. On the other hand, when the newcomers offended Native people, the relatives of the victims would receive compensation in keeping with ancient local traditions. Disputes among Native people were their own affair.

Today Douglas is probably best remembered in British Columbia for the way he dealt with Aboriginal title to the land. Even before assuming the governorship, he wrote to the HBC directors in London and argued that they needed to adopt a policy to facilitate the purchase of Native land. In reply the directors noted that a recent parliamentary inquiry into the land claims of the New Zealand Land Company had ruled that the Maori had a "right of occupancy," but not title to the land. Only those who had a "settled form of government" and cultivated the land could hold title. In light of this ruling, the company secretary, Archibald Barclay, instructed Douglas: "With respect to the rights of the natives, you will have to confer with the chiefs of the tribes on that subject, and in your negotiations with them you are to consider the natives as the rightful possessors of such lands only as are occupied by cultivation, or had houses built on, at the time when the Island came under the undivided sovereignty of Great Britain in 1846. All other land is to be regarded as waste, and applicable to the purposes of colonization…. The right of fishing and hunting will be continued to [the Native people], and when their lands are registered as waste, and they conform to the same conditions with which other settlers are required to comply, they will enjoy the same rights and privileges." Typically the newcomers defined Aboriginal rights in terms that were compatible with the primary development interests of the day—agricultural colonization. The land policy made no sense in terms of Native economic realities.

Douglas received Barclay's instructions in December 1849. Early the following summer, he called together the Songhee and Esquimalt, who lived at the southern tip of Vancouver Island, and negotiated the first land surrender with them. For a payment of 371 blankets valued at seventeen shillings each, he persuaded the chiefs to show their approval by making their signs on the bottom of a blank piece of paper. Douglas then wrote to Barclay and asked him to provide a text. The one the secretary supplied was a copy of the legal document that the New Zealand Land Company used to buy tracts from the Maori. Douglas copied Barclay's wording and added the details he needed to address local circumstances. It seems odd that a New Zealand document served as the pragmatic model for the first colonial land surrenders on the Pacific Coast of Canada, but apparently no one paid any attention to the well-established treaty-making traditions of Upper Canada.

One peculiarity of this first treaty is the clause stating that "our [Songhees] understanding of this Sale, is this, that our Village Sites and Enclosed Fields are to be kept for our own use, for the use of our Children, and for those who may follow after us; and the land, shall be properly surveyed hereafter; it is understood however, that the land itself, with these small exceptions becomes the Entire property of the White people for ever." In other words, Douglas bought only the "waste lands," even though the HBC did not believe the coastal people had a valid claim to them. In spite of this apparent anomaly, the remaining thirteen surrender agreements of the so-called Douglas treaties all contain the same clauses. From 1850 to 1854, the company obtained a total of 358 square miles (3 per cent) of prime land on Vancouver Island. The eleven treaties in the Fort Victoria and Saanich Peninsula and the one at Nanaimo (where local people led the HBC to coal deposits in 1851) involved various Coast Salish groups. The two signed at Fort Rupert were with the local Kwakwaka'wakw groups.

Like the early treaties of Atlantic Canada and Upper Canada, the Douglas treaties provided Native groups with a one-time payment for the lands they surrendered, but no annuities. Douglas offered annuity payments, but the local groups preferred a lump-sum payment. The cost to the company was nominal because, following the precedent of Douglas's first treaty, it paid them in goods, mostly woollen blankets. By this time the venerable HBC striped "point blanket" rivalled the traditional Chilkat blanket as a symbol of wealth. Because the company was interested in land strictly for agricultural settlement and coal mining, it readily agreed that the nations who signed the surrenders "are at liberty to hunt over the unoccupied lands, and to carry on our fisheries as formerly." This concession would have seemed innocuous to Douglas and his superiors in London, but in time it would become very significant to aboriginal fishers.

Colonization advanced at a snail's pace, so the agreement that Douglas and the various Coast Salish and Kwakwaka'wakw groups had reached worked reasonably well—for a while. Nonetheless, the handful of settlers near Fort Victoria generally thought that the governor was not forceful enough with the Songhees, and they provided him with frequent reports about Native attacks. He knew that the surrounding Native people held the balance of power. Accommodation was preferable to confrontation.

Some of the friction that arose between the newcomers and the local people took place in the Fort Victoria area and involved conflicting views of property. Native people regarded roaming cattle as wildlife available for the taking. Even more upsetting to the colonists, however, were the large numbers of Haida and coast Tsimshian who began to visit Victoria annually, beginning in 1854. These northern visitors did not have hostile intentions; they simply came to take advantage of markets in the new settlement and to find work. Nevertheless, the colonists mistrusted all Native people. Their feelings were so strong that once Douglas became the governor of Vancouver Island, Amelia Douglas was subjected to insults from prominent white women. Eventually the governor sent his daughter Martha to England to help her disguise her Native heritage. These were minor squabbles, however, compared with the serious clashes that loomed just over the horizon.

THE GOLD RUSHES

"Gold fever" hit the West in 1849, following the discovery of gold in California. Prospectors fanned out across the region, hoping to make other strikes in the western mountains. Like everyone else, Native people were caught up in the excitement. The Haida of the Queen Charlotte Islands, for instance, were hopeful that they could find enough gold in their territory to develop new trading opportunities. In 1850 Chief Albert Edward Edenshaw led HBC officers to gold deposits at Gold

Native placer-gold miners on the Thompson River. Aboriginal people are credited with making most of the major gold discoveries in the West during the latter half of the nineteenth century. Many copied white mining practices, which enabled them to go beyond the gold-panning stage to more capital-intensive sluicing.

Harbour (Mitchell Inlet). However, the Haida refused to let the company mine these deposits; they wanted to mine them themselves. They were also resentful that Americans, having heard about the gold, came in search of it without asking their permission. Before 1853 the Haida had already driven off one group of these intruders from the Gold Harbour area.

A legendary early skirmish involved the American ship *Susan Sturgis*. In 1853 this vessel was sailing in the Queen Charlotte Islands area for trading purposes and had let a small party of miners off to search for gold near Gold Harbour. The Royal Navy had warned the skipper and crew that all speculators operating in the area did so at great risk, but the Americans ignored the warning and headed north in search of Chief Edenshaw. Descriptions of the chief portray him as young, extremely wealthy, and very powerful, always on the lookout for new opportunities. He lived in the heavily fortified village of Kung, located northwest of Masset. Like many others before them, the Americans wanted Edenshaw, who was a well-known sailor, to pilot their ship. They located him at Skidegate, and he came aboard on the condition that he would be given passage to his village.

The Skidegate villagers apparently passed word overland to the Masset people that the *Susan Sturgis* could be taken easily. When the ship rounded Rose Spit (the easternmost point of Graham Island), a Masset canoe approached and Edenshaw apparently confirmed the Skidegate villagers' report. The following day Chief Weah, leader of the Masset villagers, brought twenty-five canoes alongside, under the pretence of being a trading party. They seized the crew, pillaged the ship, and burned it. Edenshaw, who received a share of the spoils, persuaded his accomplices to spare the lives of the Americans and take them to Fort Simpson, where they would likely receive a ransom in blankets from the HBC. His accomplices agreed and ransomed their captives at the fort.

The possibility of further conflict died away when the gold deposits on the Queen Charlotte Islands proved to be very small. Attention quickly shifted to the mainland. Again local Native people made the initial strikes. Rumours of impressive gold deposits in the Fraser River watershed had been circulating throughout the 1850s. By 1857 some groups living near the confluence of the Thompson and Fraser rivers had begun trading placer gold to the HBC. Douglas encouraged them, anticipating that the trade in placer gold would become another aspect of the company's commercial relationship with the residents. With that goal in mind, he ordered the construction of a post at the confluence of the Fraser and Thompson in the spring of 1858. Unfortunately, word of the gold trade leaked out, and rumours circulated in San Francisco that Douglas had sent eight hundred ounces there for minting. Thirty thousand California miners, prospectors, and "Indian" fighters quickly descended on the region. Douglas estimated that by August 1858, more than ten thousand of them were already combing the Fraser River corridor. Two years later, the rush spread into the Cariboo Mountains, and by the 1870s prospectors were combing the Skeena, Omineca, and Peace River areas.

Miners complained that Native people rustled their livestock and ruined their crops. They objected to the attempts some groups made to tax them for working diggings located on traditional Native territory. Aggravating the situation, many Native people took up residence near boom towns like Yale, where they could find work, and they often panned gold side by side with the intruders. During the summer of 1858, for instance, sixty to seventy white miners and four to five hundred Native miners worked Hills Bar on the Fraser River. This close proximity increased the likelihood of friction between the two groups.

Armed miners organized into "armies of conquest" had already effectively triggered the Indian wars of Washington and Oregon. In British territory, besides trying, often successfully, to push the local people off the gold bars, the invading rabble plundered their food supplies and destroyed their fishing, fish-drying, and camping sites. Some miners from California bragged that they would "clean out all the Indians in the land." Indiscriminate killings of Native people did take place, but the violence was not entirely one-sided. In the lower Fraser River canyon, the local people engaged the invaders in a bloody conflict known as the Fraser Canyon War during the summer of 1858. Although Douglas is usually credited with being the one who prevented the violence from spiralling out of control, Native people's recollections of the event indicate that their leaders played an important role. Mary Brent, granddaughter of the Okanagan chief N'kwala, recalled that "during the Fraseer River trouble between the Thompsons and the whites in 1858 and 1859, [N'kwala] advocated peace, although preparing for war had the affair not been settled. The Thompsons were against the miners and settlers. Although he was begged by the Spokanes and Thompsons to join them in war against the whites, he refused to allow his people to join them."

The possibility of further conflict, and the threat that Americans would take over the territory, forced Douglas and the British government to move quickly to establish order and defend the sovereignty of the Crown in the region. Even before this crisis, a British parliamentary committee had begun considering the future of the territory in anticipation of the expiry of the HBC's trading licence on the main-

land in 1858. The committee recommended against renewal wherever settlement was advanced. Parliament
agreed, ended the HBC's rule of the
Vancouver Island colony, and established
the new colony of British Columbia on
the mainland. Douglas was appointed
governor of both colonies. He gave up
his position with the HBC.

For the people of the Pacific slope,
the influx of miners and settlers that
started in the summer of 1858 represented an important turning point in
their history. The newcomers and the
growing number of deaths due to foreign diseases, especially smallpox, set in
motion a major demographic shift in
favour of the immigrant society. The
smallpox epidemic of 1862, which
began in Victoria and swept rapidly up

Songish chief's sister with fish for sale *is the
title of this photograph. Before contact, West Coast
people engaged in extensive inter-nation trading of
fish and fish products. After contact, they sold fish
to European fur traders and colonists.*

the coast and into the interior, was the worst calamity to strike the coastal people
since the epidemics of early contact. When it ended three years later, as many as
twenty thousand Native people had died, reducing their total population to about
forty thousand. The populations of some groups, such as the Haida, declined more
than 80 per cent.

The staggering death rate meant that the Native population represented much
less of a threat to the newcomers than it had a decade earlier. Worse, Douglas and
others concluded that these people were dying out. This assumption, and an
increase in racial tensions and expressions of prejudice, led the governor to change
some of his basic attitudes and policies towards Native people and their economic
rights. Believing that their only chance of survival lay in learning European ways—
particularly farming—he granted reserves only for those tracts that included village
sites, cultivated fields, and burial grounds. He no longer regarded "waste lands" as
belonging to Aboriginal nations. Furthermore, the governor took the position that
the Crown, not the Native people, held the title to the reserves, which was in
marked contrast to his stand when he had negotiated the earlier treaties. Douglas

This is a typical central Coast Salish winter settlement, which consisted of shed-roof plank houses that were built close to the water, with ready access to canoes.

changed his mind partly because he believed that reserve lands could not be protected from white encroachment unless the government kept them in trust. Regrettably, this would not be the case here any more than it was anywhere else in British North America.

Even Douglas, who wanted to protect the lands set aside for Native people, never envisaged that the reserves would become permanent features of the landscape. He thought of them as cultural waystations where missionaries and others could teach the residents Christianity and the practical skills they would need to survive in the new economic order. Believing that most Native people would eventually choose to make it on their own away from these refuges, Douglas gave them the same rights to settle off-reserve lands as white settlers.

One result of this assimilationist agenda was that Douglas did not conclude any treaties after 1854, even though the Colonial Assembly of Vancouver Island and the British government continued to recognize Aboriginal title and encouraged him to buy the lands needed for settlement. In the early 1860s, the assembly even approved expenditures for that purpose. The legislators were particularly eager that he buy Cowichan land, which was in demand. Instead, Douglas set about establishing reserves without treaties, allocating approximately ten acres, "a little spot," to each family, which was a meagre amount. Simultaneously, he opened extensive areas to white settlement. Through these actions, Douglas set the colonial governments of Vancouver Island and the British Columbia mainland on a path that was at variance with the expressed wishes of many of the First Nations, politicians, and settlers. He also set the stage for a struggle for land and resources between Native groups and successive British Columbia governments that continues to this day.

CHAPTER 13

THE MÉTIS AND "INDIAN" QUESTION

That the Dominion Parliament ... proceeded to organize a government for our country, giving to the Governor who was to administer the same, unlimited power ... assisted by a council to be chosen by himself, consisting of Hudson's Bay Company officers and Canadians; and thus your memorialists (the people) found their ancient surveys, land marks, boundaries and muniments of title, set at naught and disregarded, and a Government established over their heads, in the selection of the rulers and administration of which, they had no voice; and by this process they found that their homes, their country and their liberties, were held at the mercy of a foreign power and subject to a foreign jurisdiction.

—"Memorial of the people of Rupert's Land and North-West" to President Ulysses S. Grant, Red River, October 3, 1870

The strong desire of speculators and settlers in Canada, especially Canada West, to develop Rupert's Land and the lands beyond it—the area that comprised the Hudson's Bay Company's Northern and Southern departments and where it had suzerain rights—was one of the driving forces behind Confederation. They saw the region as a source of raw materials and a market for eastern goods. Most Canadian annexationists wanted to simply brush aside Native people and the HBC and take control of the region. The Métis refused to let them. Taking up arms in 1869 and 1870, they forced the new Canadian government to address their aspirations and some of their most pressing concerns in the Manitoba Act. The government moved more slowly to establish the legal and administrative frameworks that it believed it needed to deal with other Native people. It took a major step in that direction in 1876 when Parliament passed the Indian Act. This crucial piece of legislation consoli-

A camp of Métis, 1858.

dated earlier colonial acts dealing with the First Nations. The primary goal of the act was to encourage assimilation. It was also supposed to protect the interests of Native people, most of whom resided west of Ontario.

THE CANADIAN INVASION

Having already gained title to all the Aboriginal lands of Canada West that were suitable for agriculture, developers cast their eyes northwestward to Rupert's Land for a new area to colonize. Canadian annexationists did not want to recognize the validity of Aboriginal or HBC titles to the area they coveted. They lobbied the British Parliament to review the company's licence and colonizing activities, and they drummed up excitement about the development potential of the prairie West. Their lobbying led the Canada West and British governments to back separate well-publicized scientific expeditions to the region in the late 1850s. The Canadian excursion, led by Henry Youle Hind, and the British-sponsored party, commanded by Capt. John Palliser, provided solid information about the Plains people and those of the Rocky Mountains north of the 49th parallel, made detailed descriptions of the agricultural potential of the prairies, gave accounts of coal and other mineral deposits, and discussed possible transcontinental transportation routes.

Politicians and would-be developers and speculators paid little attention to Hind's and Palliser's ethnographic work, but they were thrilled by their discussion of the economic potential of the sprawling region. The information circulated widely and had an impact well beyond Canada. It led the International Financial Society, a syndicate of English and French bankers and stock promoters, to buy control of the HBC in 1863. The society recapitalized the company and made a highly successful public offering of its shares by promoting the development possibilities of the chartered territory. Subscribers hoped to make a windfall profit from the sale of Rupert's Land to the British or Canadian government; however, the British government had no intention of buying the territory, and the Canadian government could not afford the high price the company's directors led the shareholders to anticipate.

After protracted negotiations, Canada agreed to buy Rupert's Land for a mere £300,000 on March 8, 1869. The HBC kept one-twentieth of the lands of the "fertile belt," which Palliser had defined as the tall-grass prairies and parklands, and it retained the developed lands around its numerous trading posts (approximately fifty thousand acres). These land grants were compensation for the disappointingly small cash payment the company received. The agreement confirmed all the titles the HBC had issued to settlers (mostly in the Red River colony) before March 8. The failure of HBC directors to secure a large cash settlement left a majority of the shareholders very angry; they had expected a settlement of as much as £5 million.

The reaction of the shareholders was mild compared with that of the Aboriginal residents of the northwest, who were outraged. The company and the two governments had treated the entire affair as if it were a straightforward real-estate deal involving vacant territory, although the company had sought and obtained legal protection from land claims through the Rupert's Land Act of 1868. This act was passed by the British Parliament to facilitate the transfer of the HBC's title to Canada. It provided that the company would not be liable for "any claims of Indians to compensation for lands required for purposes of settlement." According to the deed of surrender, the Canadian government accepted this responsibility. What deeply offended Native people was that no one consulted them about their land during the prolonged negotiations.

The Métis strongly feared that the sale of Rupert's Land would hurt their economic and political interests. They distrusted Canadians, and with good reason. Following the Sayer trial, the HBC had made a greater effort to accommodate Métis interests. The Red River colony remained reasonably tranquil until Upper Canadians began to settle there and elsewhere in the northwest. These newcomers championed annexation to Canada, disdained the HBC, looked down on the hunting and trapping lifestyles of the prairie nations and Métis, and gave little credence to the company's, or the Native people's, claims to land. Dr John Christian Schultz, leader of the small but vociferous Canadian Party, was their main spokesman. From 1865 to 1868 he published the *Nor' Wester* newspaper, which championed the annexationists' cause. The immigrants from Canada West also encouraged divisions within the colony between the mixed-bloods and Métis.

By the summer of 1869, the Métis of Red River had decided to block the unconditional transfer of Rupert's Land to

"Young" McKay, a Métis Red River guide, is shown wearing traditional dress in 1859.

Canada, a decision that marked a major turning point for Native people in the West. They sprang into action when a Canadian land-survey crew arrived in August. Led by the twenty-five-year-old Louis Riel, whose father had been among the armed group of Métis at the Sayer trial, they stopped the government surveyors, informing them that Canada had no authority in the territory. In keeping with their tradition of organizing themselves with suitable leadership—the buffalo hunt provides an example of this—the Métis selected a National Committee and chose Louis Riel as its secretary.

They made a wise choice. Riel was one of the best-educated young Métis living in the settlement. As a young boy he had attended school at St Boniface in Red River. The Catholic bishop, Monseigneur Alexandre Taché, and his teachers were greatly impressed with Riel's ability and piety. In 1858, with Riel's parents' blessing, the bishop sent the fourteen-year-old Riel off to study for the priesthood at the Collège de Montréal. He proved to be a good scholar, but after seven years of intense study, Riel decided against a life of serving the Church and left the college. He found employment in the firm of a leading Montreal lawyer, where he remained for a little more than a year before returning home in 1868 on the eve of the Red River uprising.

Louis Riel (centre of second row) and his council in 1869. By use of force and skilful political manoeuvring, Riel and his supporters prevented the government of Canada from imposing an appointed government on the Red River settlement and forced it to recognize the Aboriginal rights of the Métis.

In October 1869, the Métis prevented William McDougall, lieutenant-governor-designate for Rupert's Land and the North-West Territory, from entering Red River, and shortly thereafter they seized the HBC's Fort Garry. After forming a provisional government, the Métis set about trying to pull the colony together to present a united front for negotiating terms of union with Canada.

The story of what happened next is well known. Sir John A. Macdonald and his government wanted to avoid further conflict, so they invited the people of Red River to draw up a list of demands and send a delegation to Ottawa to discuss them. At a large public meeting held in the courtyard of Fort Garry on January 19, 1870, Riel proposed that the English-speaking and French-speaking communities each elect twenty representatives to a committee that would determine how best to reply. The assembly accepted his suggestion and the Convention of Forty had their first meeting a week later. After lengthy deliberations, they drew up a List of Rights to present to Ottawa. At Riel's insistence, members of the convention also created a provisional government before they finished their work. The new government was proclaimed on February 10, 1870, with Riel as president.

In this capacity, the Métis leader dispatched three envoys to Ottawa to submit a revised list of terms. His government demanded that the new province (Manitoba) be admitted to Confederation on equal terms with the other governments; all the properties, rights, and privileges that the inhabitants of the territory enjoyed at the time of union be continued; the legislature of the province have full control over all public lands; and everyone involved in the uprising be granted amnesty. The provisional government also wanted the new province to include all of what was now, for the first time, called the North-West Territories—formerly the HBC's Rupert's Land and the North-West Territory. (Out of this was carved the province of Manitoba, and in 1905 Alberta and Saskatchewan.) Privately, Riel instructed one of the negotiators, Abbé N. J. Richot, to "[d]emand that the country be divided into two so that the customs of two populations [French Catholic and English Protestant] living separately may be maintained for the protection of our most endangered rights." In other words, Riel and his followers sought a way to join Confederation under terms that would allow these two cultures to flourish in the newly emerging country. Métis leaders knew that this would not be possible without a substantial land base.

Macdonald and his close advisers rejected the idea of handing over control of land and natural resources to the new provincial government and opposed creating large reserves for the Métis or any other group. After all, the financially strapped Canadian government had just paid the HBC £300,000 ($1,500,000) for its stake in the territory, and it had still to buy Aboriginal title. In addition, the new province the Métis wanted to create would be in a strong position to impede, perhaps even block, Ottawa's nation-building schemes, and the establishment of large areas of reserve land would likely deflect settlers southward into the United States. Nevertheless, concessions were made for pragmatic reasons.

The Manitoba Act was pushed through Parliament in 1870, allowing for the entry of the province into Confederation as a nearly equal member. Ottawa retained control of public lands and natural resources, as it would when Alberta and Saskatchewan became provinces thirty-five years later. As a further limitation on its economic and political power in the northwest, Ottawa insisted that Manitoba be of "postage stamp-size." Nevertheless, the Manitoba Act did provide the official bilingualism the Métis wanted and the educational rights the various denominations exercised "by law or practice at the union."

During the negotiations leading up to the act, one of the most perplexing issues was the Métis' concern about the land rights of those families who held HBC titles in the colony, or who squatted elsewhere on Aboriginal land, and the future rights of their descendants. The Canadian government found itself in an awkward position. An Ottawa politician expressed it tersely: "The Government had to do two things, either they had to send an army to conquer those people and force them to submit, or to consider their claims as put forward by their delegates.... [I]t would be folly to refuse such a small concession when compared with the amount of land which the Hudson's Bay Company had been allowed to retain." Faced with this reality, Parliament agreed that "half-breeds" had a valid claim because of their part-Aboriginal ancestry. It gave its approval to the section of the Manitoba Act that stipulated: "It is expedient, towards the extinguishment of the Aboriginal Title to the lands in the Province, to appropriate ... one million four hundred thousand acres thereof, for the benefit of the families of the half-breed residents...." The governor general and lieutenant-governor were given the responsibility for selecting the lots and distributing them to the children of the "half-breed heads of families" living in the province in 1870. The statute also recognized the right of "half-breeds" to occupy the long-lot farms they had already developed along the Red River. Finally, it gave pre-emption rights to settlers located "in those parts of the Province in which

The interior of a Métis house in 1874. Many Métis families prospered before the influx of settlers in the 1870s by combining commercial buffalo hunting, trading, carting, farming, and working as seasonal employees of the Hudson's Bay Company.

Indian Title has not been extinguished." The purpose of this provision was to allay the concerns of the Métis, mixed-bloods, and others who had settled beyond the boundaries of the HBC grants included within the Peguis Treaty area.

The Manitoba Act represented a major victory for the Métis, with a crucial exception—the act did not specify how the 1.4 million acres should be allocated to them. Problems arose immediately. One of the most troublesome difficulties was that officials had no idea how many inhabitants of mixed ancestry would be eligible for the grants. The government conducted two censuses (in 1870 and 1875), but they were both undercounts because many families were away hunting or engaged in other activities when the enumerators arrived. Making matters worse, the first lieutenant-governor, Adam Archibald, arbitrarily decided to include family heads in the count, even though this was in clear violation of the act. The Métis strongly objected to his unilateral action. Previously they had tried, but failed, to obtain government support for the idea of blocking sales of any allocated lands for at least a generation. Archibald flatly rejected this notion because he thought it ran counter to the trend of bringing "Real Estate more and more to the condition of personal property and abolishing restraints and impediments on its free use and transmission." Having failed to gain this concession, influential Métis did not want heads of families included among those who were entitled to receive land because these adults, most of whom were illiterate, had the right to sell their holdings immediately. Minors, on the other hand, presumably could not do so until they reached the age of majority. By making sure that only the children received warrants for parcels of land, Métis leaders thought that the land base their people had obtained would be safe during this crucial transitional period. In the end they had their way, and family heads were stricken from the list of those eligible for land grants.

Métis leaders also pressed to have the land distributed in contiguous blocks so that their people could control sizable territories collectively. Initially the government resisted this request, but in 1872 it yielded.

While government officials and the Métis wrangled over land-distribution procedures, settlers from Ontario flocked to Manitoba. At first, Ottawa gave the newcomers the right to preempt land ahead of survey crews and before the Métis had selected their reserve plots. This angered the Métis, and the spectre of violence caused the government to rescind the practice in 1871. Nonetheless, these early preemptions further complicated the land-allocation plan.

After several false starts, the government finally distributed the reserved land in 240-acre parcels in the mistaken belief that approximately 5,100 children were eligible to receive grants. In fact, 7,027 *bona fide* claimants came forward, of whom 6,034 received parcels of land and 993 obtained certificates (scrip) valued at $240 apiece instead of land. The government arrived at this figure based on the assumption that the land was worth about $1 an acre on average. Although officials had largely finished making the allotments by 1881, the process dragged on for years. Remarkably, Louis Riel's son received the last grant in 1900; he had been absent from Manitoba in 1875. The government continued to process late scrip applications as late as 1919.

Unfortunately, the Métis leaders' fear that little of the land would remain in the hands of their people for very long proved to be well founded. Speculators did a brisk business in land and scrip. A large number of Métis sold their land, or their claim to it, so that they could move west in pursuit of the retreating buffalo herds or to reestablish themselves well beyond the frontier settlements. Many of them chose the North and South Saskatchewan River valleys, but some settled as far away as the Peace River valley. In the end, the idea of giving the warrants to minors provided almost no protection for the Métis land reserves. A large number of the children conveyed their entitlements through a power of attorney.

The politically contentious issue of pardoning Louis Riel was another acute problem for the Canadian government. During the Red River uprising, a number of Canadian malcontents attempted to overthrow the provisional government and were arrested. Thomas Scott, a violent and boisterous Orangeman from Ulster, was the most obstreperous of them. Riel's government court-martialled and executed him— thereby making its only major political blunder. From that day forward, Riel was a marked man in the eyes of the Red River Canadian annexationists led by Dr Schultz, who held "indignation meetings" in Ontario to inflame public opinion against Riel. A pardon for Riel was out of the question, even though the Canadian government had promised a general amnesty on December 6, 1869, in a pragmatic gesture aimed at persuading the rebels to put down their arms. In February 1872, the Métis leader fled to the United States for safety, helped by a grateful Prime Minister Macdonald, who covered his expenses. Riel was so popular among the Métis, however, that they even elected him to the federal Parliament while he was in exile.

In 1875, the House of Commons granted an unconditional amnesty to all who had taken part in the uprising—except for Riel and two others. It gave Riel a conditional absolution; he was banished from Canada for five years. Riel spent nearly all of the next ten years in the United States, where he became a schoolteacher in

Montana. Outside Manitoba, the country remained deeply divided about how Riel and the Métis should have been treated. French-Catholic Quebec strongly identified with Riel, the Métis, and their cause. Most people in English Protestant Ontario wanted revenge against the Métis and their leader. They had to wait until 1885.

THE INDIAN ACT

After Confederation, the Canadian government faced the difficult job of developing the legal framework it needed to discharge the responsibility for Aboriginal affairs it had inherited, with reluctance, from the imperial government. It took nine years before Parliament passed the first Indian Act in 1876, which combined all laws affecting Indian people. The consolidated act provided for the uniform treatment of "Indians" everywhere in Canada.

The act defined "Indians" as being men who belonged to a band that held lands or reserves in common, or for whom the federal government held funds in trust. The wives and children of these men also had Indian status. Women who married outside the status-Indian community—and their children born of the marriage—lost their Indian status and all rights associated with status and band membership forever. This provision violated long-standing post-contact marriage practices. Ostensibly, it was intended to protect Indian lands from white opportunists. Indian men were free to choose a non-Indian partner, who then acquired Indian status. According to the act, all "legal" Indians were wards of the federal government and were to be treated as minors without the full privileges of citizenship. (In this and subsequent chapters, the term "Indian" is applied to those who were defined as such under the 1876 act and its various revisions.)

The new legislation placed Indian reserve land in the trust of the Crown and stated that this land could not be mortgaged or seized for defaulted debts, nor could it be taxed. In the spirit of the Royal Proclamation of 1763, it specified that reserve lands could be sold only with the approval of a majority of the adult band members and the superintendent-general of Indian Affairs. Furthermore, only the Crown could purchase it. The government was supposed to hold the proceeds from any such sales in trust, although 10 per cent of the revenue could be paid directly to band members. Likewise, timber and mineral resources on reserve land could not be harvested or removed unless the same procedures for obtaining consent had been followed.

Parliament made no provision in the act to accommodate the different kinds of Aboriginal governments that existed at the time of Confederation. It simply

A census taker visiting a Cree village in 1881. The Canadian government did not know how many Aboriginal people lived in the prairie West when it negotiated treaties with them in the 1870s, even though these agreements committed it to a variety of per capita payments. Subsequently, politicians in Ottawa became alarmed when the Native population proved to be larger than they had expected.

stated that elected chiefs and councils would govern all bands for three-year terms. Only the adult males could vote. Band councils were given various responsibilities, including overseeing public works and the suppression of "intemperance." Concerning the latter, the Indian Act outlawed the manufacture, sale, or consumption of liquor on reserves. Because the government aimed to "civilize" all Indians eventually, the original legislation included a provision for enfranchisement. As a first step towards becoming a full-fledged Canadian citizen, an Indian had to prove that he was literate in English or French, of good moral character, and free of debt—terms most Canadians would have found it difficult to meet. Next, the applicant had to obtain an allotment of reserve land and manage it for three years in the same way a non-Indian would. At the end of this probationary term, the superintendent-general of Indian Affairs could make the candidate a full-fledged citizen and give him title to his allotment. Subsequent amendments to the Indian Act made enfranchisement easier in the hope of encouraging assimilation. A 1920 amendment (repealed two years later) and one reintroduced in 1933 gave the superintendent-general the power to enfranchise Native people without their approval. Most resisted because, until 1960, they lost their Indian status when they gained full citizenship rights.

Superficially, the Indian Act of 1876 created a structure that was designed to teach Native people democratic principles, while it protected their interests until they could stand on their own feet as Canadian citizens. The reality was that the act allowed the federal government to interfere in all aspects of Indians' lives, because Parliament had the right to amend it without first obtaining their permission. The government frequently amended the act over the years to push forward its own agenda for these people. In short, the act created a special class of people designated solely on the basis of their race, and it established a means for governing them autocratically.

Because Canada had assumed the responsibility for governing Indians very reluctantly, the government did not give any priority to their needs. In this respect the new country was no different from its colonial predecessors. The Indian Affairs Department began its existence as an unwanted stepchild in the public service. In the 1860s a separate branch had been created within the colony of Canada's Crown Lands Department, and the commissioner of that department also served as chief superintendent of Indian Affairs. For the first eight years after Confederation, the Department of the Secretary of State for the Provinces looked after Indian affairs. In 1873, federal politicians created the Indian Lands Branch, shifting the portfolio to the Department of the Interior, which mainly promoted western development. Simultaneously, a short-lived Board of Commissioners was appointed to administer Indian affairs in Manitoba, British Columbia, and the North-West Territories. Two years later, the board was replaced with a system of superintendents and agents, but a commissioner for the North-West Territories was retained. In 1880 Parliament created a separate Department of Indian Affairs, but its minister also held the portfolio of minister of the Interior.

This constant restructuring shows that politicians believed it was a good idea to tie Indian Affairs to the federal ministry responsible for natural resources and western development. Once established, this tradition remained in place, except for a short period between 1950 and 1966, when Indian Affairs was housed in the Department of Citizenship and Immigration. Linking the department to the ministries responsible for natural resources, immigration, and economic development was a bad arrangement for Native people everywhere in Canada. Conflicts of interest were inevitable, because the minister responsible for reserve lands and aboriginal title in unsurrendered territories also looked after the acquisition and disposition of public lands. It is hardly surprising, therefore, that the department often did not defend the interests of Native people.

CHAPTER 14

TREATY MAKING

Our hands are poor but our heads are rich, and it is riches that we ask so that we may be able to support our families as long as the sun rises and the water flows.

—Ma-we-do-pe-nais, Fort Francis chief, addressing Alexander Morris, Lieutenant-Governor of Manitoba and the North-West Territories during Treaty 3 negotiations, October 4, 1873

By the time of Confederation, Native people living in the area of old Rupert's Land sensed that dramatic changes were taking place; they were very concerned about their future. They took advantage of treaty negotiations with Canada to air their grievances about the sale of Rupert's Land and to wring concessions from the government that would help them adjust to the new economic order in ways that were compatible with their traditions. They secured treaty rights to schooling and training, as well as some protection against the economic hardships they would face if forced to abandon hunting as a livelihood. In the grassland area, Native leaders sought ways to guarantee that their people would remain a political force in the region.

NEGOTIATING THE NUMBERED TREATIES

The Métis victory at Red River was of little benefit to the western Native groups. Many of them were angry about the recent sale of Rupert's Land, because they had never relinquished their lands to the Hudson's Bay Company. The Plains Cree made their feelings known about this crucial matter during treaty negotiations at Fort Qu'Appelle, Saskatchewan, in 1874. A leader named Otahaoman ("The Gambler") told government representatives: "The Company have no right to this earth, but when they are spoken to they do not desist.... I hear now, it was the Queen gave the land [to the company]. The Indians thought it was they who gave it to the Company." Pis-Qua (also spelled Paskwaw or Pasquah), who led a band of Plains Saulteaux, pointed to the manager of the Fort Qu'Appelle post, who was acting as host to the government party, and said, "You told me you had sold our land for so much money, £300,000. We

206

want that money." By interfering with the geological survey and by blocking the construction of telegraph lines on their lands, the Plains Cree made it abundantly clear to the Canadian government that development could not proceed without their being compensated first.

Besides seeking fundamental justice, the various nations of old Rupert's Land believed that negotiating treaties with Canada offered them the opportunity to address their economic problems and to share the benefits everyone expected agricultural settlement would bring. In general, their demands indicated that most of them wanted to maintain valued traditions while participating in the new economy. They also wanted to retain some control over their own destinies within the context of the expanding Canadian state. Each group made a number of specific requests as well, according to its particular circumstances.

The Siksika leader Yellow Horse wearing a treaty coat and medals. The presentation of coats and medals to Native leaders at the conclusion of treaties was a continuation of an old fur-trade custom. English and French traders gave coats and medals to their Native trading "captains" to retain their loyalty.

The woodland nations who concluded treaties during this era faced common problems. Fur prices had begun to plummet in 1871, signalling the beginning of the long depression of the late nineteenth century, and they did not rebound until after 1885. The price collapse ravaged trapping incomes and drove Native trappers deep into debt. Treaty money offered them the prospect of relief—if trappers could obtain enough annuity money to buy their annual outfits, they would not have to turn to the traders for credit. By entering into agreements with the government, trappers also hoped to address the new threat posed by incoming prospectors, miners, and settlers. Many of these newcomers lived in or near the forests and trapped part-time or full-time to weather bad economic periods and to raise money for other activities. They often used techniques that were extremely destructive: for example, they frequently used strychnine-laced bait, which killed many of the Native hunting dogs. Prospectors set forest habitats on fire to make it easier to

Manitoba Indian Treaty-Conference with the Chiefs *appeared in the September 9, 1871, edition of the* Canadian Illustrated News. *Aboriginal people of the prairie West tried to secure their economic futures through treaty negotiations, beginning with Treaties 1 and 2, signed in 1871.*

search for gold and other mineral deposits. The woodland nations pleaded with the government to stop such abuses. The widespread depletion of fur and game in many areas, but particularly between Lake Superior and the Winnipeg River, forced many Native people to seek federal assistance in developing small-scale farming operations to help them cope with periodic food shortages.

Native economic interests ranged well beyond hunting and trapping. The Ojibwa of Rainy River country, for instance, looked for ways to profit from the new business possibilities in their district. They lived near the Dawson Road, which the Canadian government had started to build in 1858. By the early 1870s, as many as sixteen hundred people used the road annually to travel from Lake Superior to the Red River. The Ojibwa wanted to be paid for the right of passage through their territory, they expected compensation for the wood used in building construction along the Dawson Road and to fuel the steamboats, and they claimed that they owned the settlers' houses because the intruders had not paid for the timber they had used to build them. In addition, they wanted to lease access and resource rights, rather than sell their lands to the Crown.

The Ojibwa reacted in a similar way to immigrants' stories about plans for a railway and a telegraph line through their territory. In the case of the railway, they wanted the government to grant them free rides forever as partial payment for the use of their land. In 1873 an Ojibwa negotiator said, "I ask you a question—I see your roads here [Fort Francis] passing through the country, and some of your boats—useful articles that you use for yourself. Bye and bye we shall see things that run swiftly, that go by fire—carriages—and we ask you that us Indians may not have to pay their passage on these things, but can go free."

Like Native groups in British Columbia, the Ojibwa wanted to benefit from mining development. When government negotiators for Treaty 3 told the Ojibwa that their rocky and forested lands were not as valuable as those of their grassland neighbours, a wise chief is recorded to have replied, "*The sound of the rustling of the gold is under my feet where I stand; we have a rich country.* . . . [I]t is the Great Spirit who gave us this; where we stand upon is the Indians' property, and belongs to them."

The Plains groups had much more pressing concerns than the Rainy River Ojibwa. The buffalo herds were in headlong retreat towards their last refuge—the lush slopes of the Cypress Hills and the Montana territory south of the border. This meant that Métis, Plains nations, and non-Native hunters were all competing for the remaining animals within a contracting supply area. Some Plains groups had already experienced a year or more of deprivation and starvation because of reduced numbers of buffalo. Several leaders believed that their only option was to take up farming. Abraham Wikaskokiseyin (Sweet Grass), an important Cree chief and leader of the Fort Pitt band, was one of them. He and his followers wanted the government to promise to help them learn how to farm.

Other Native leaders believed that it was not too late to save the buffalo.

Abraham Wikaskokiseyin (Sweet Grass) was an influential leader of the Fort Pitt Cree.

Mistahimaskwa (Big Bear), a neighbour and close friend of Wikaskokiseyin, was among them. He blamed Métis and white hunters for ruthlessly pursuing the dwindling buffalo. Non-Native hunters were particularly objectionable: they used repeating rifles to kill countless buffalo for their hides, and they poisoned the carcasses with strychnine to destroy wolves so that they could obtain the skins of these animals too. Mistahimaskwa wanted the Canadian government to move quickly to protect the remaining herds and demanded that it set aside a large territory in the plains exclusively for Aboriginal use. He opposed the idea of having the people settle down in small scattered reserves, knowing that this would weaken their voice. Pitikwahanapiwiyin (Poundmaker), another highly influential Cree leader, held the same opinion. At the commencement of treaty talks in 1874, he replied to the government negotiators' offer to provide reserves: "The governor mentions how much land is to be given to us. He says 640 acres, one mile square for each family, he will give us. This is our land! It isn't a piece of pemmican to be cut off and given in little pieces back to us. It is ours and we will take what we want."

During the lengthy treaty negotiations, the buffalo population continued its rapid decline. Many proud and fiercely independent buffalo hunters found themselves reduced to eating gophers and prairie dogs to survive. This experience drove them to ask for assurances of government aid during times of pestilence and starvation.

Although these desperate economic circumstances made the Plains Nations apprehensive of their future, until the late 1870s they remained a powerful military threat that Canada could not afford to ignore. Alexander Morris, who was the lieutenant-governor of the North-West Territories from 1872 to 1876 and of Manitoba from 1873 to 1878, was well aware of this reality. In 1873 he reported that the Cree and Siksika, who had reached a peace accord in 1871, and their Assiniboine allies could put 5,000 mounted warriors in the field. He warned Ottawa that these nations did not think that Canada could mount a credible force against them. Additionally worrying to Morris were the overtures that Tatanka-Iyotanka (Sitting Bull), legendary chief of the Hunkpapa Lakota of the United States, was making to the Canadian tribes to ally with his people to fight against further American and Canadian expansion into their respective homelands. Morris understood that if these former enemies did forge such an alliance it would be disastrous for Canada. For these reasons, he urged the federal government to proceed expeditiously with treaty-making in the Prairie West.

At the time, Canada was primarily interested in obtaining lands in the southwestern portion of former Rupert's Land (the present-day area of northwestern Ontario and the Prairie Provinces) for railway construction and agricultural colonization. This was the area covered by Treaties 1 to 4, 6, and 7. Establishing a steamboat system on Lake Winnipeg and the Saskatchewan River and the prospects of a commercial fishery on Lake Winnipeg led the government to negotiate Treaty 5. The Klondike gold rush at the end of the century and the interest it generated in the prime fur country northwest of Edmonton, one of the jumping-off points for the gold fields in the late nineteenth century, provided a catalyst for Treaty 8. The threats of Aboriginal people living in the Peace River area to wage war against the intruding miners, prospectors, and settlers unless the government signed a treaty with them provided an added incentive for the government to come to the treaty table. Treaty 9 (and the additions to it) and a major amendment to Treaty 5 resulted from several different development pressures in the early twentieth century. The most important of these were expanded mineral exploration and mining, the growth of the pulp-and-paper industry, the development of hydroelectric-power-generating systems, and the building of a second transcontinental railway with branch lines to James Bay and western Hudson Bay. A major discovery in 1920 of petroleum at Norman Wells on the Mackenzie River in the Northwest Territories (the area east of what became the Yukon Territory in 1898) was instrumental in the negotiation of Treaty 11.

In all these cases, it is important to note that Native people asked for treaties well before the government was willing to sign them. Considerable numbers of Native people who lived beyond treaty boundaries moved into surrendered territories during poor economic times to share treaty benefits with their neighbours and relatives. This happened in northern Manitoba, for instance, during the late nineteenth century, when many Cree living outside the original Treaty 5 area moved into that district. This migration did not end until the first decade of the twentieth century, when additions to Treaty 5 brought the rest of northern Manitoba within the framework of the agreement.

Morris was commissioner, the key government negotiator, for Treaties 3, 4, 5, and 6 while he served as lieutenant-governor of the North-West Territories. Looking back on his negotiating experience in 1880, he wrote, "The Indians are fully aware that their old mode of life is passing away. They are not unconscious of their destiny; on the contrary, they are harassed with fears as to the future of their children and the hard present of their own lives." In other words, he understood what later generations of Canadians would forget—that the Native people were not wedded to their past, nor were they blind to the future.

The Canadian government, however, was not willing to negotiate with Native people on a wide range of issues; the politicians simply wanted to obtain land as cheaply as possible. They gave Morris and other treaty negotiators little room to manoeuvre. For example, they flatly rejected the Ojibwa idea of paying royalties to Indians for rights of access or for resources, preferring agreements modelled closely after the Robinson treaties of 1850—albeit with richer compensation packages. The so-called numbered treaties provided the following: annual allowances for hunting and fishing supplies; triennial clothing allowances ranging from $500 to $2,000 a year, depending on the treaty; annuities ranging from $4 to $5 for adults and children and from $15 to $25 for headmen and chiefs; and lump-sum payments of varying amounts to the chiefs and their followers when they signed a treaty. The government promised to provide schools on the reserves when the Indians requested them. The Indians had the right to pick the locations of their reserves, but the amount of allotted land varied from 160 acres to one square mile for each family of five, depending on the treaty. In response to Native concerns about the impact that alcohol trading was having on their societies, government negotiators included provisions in the treaties that banned the introduction, sale, or drinking of alcohol on the reserves.

Compared with what the HBC eventually received for its residual stake in Rupert's Land—approximately $96 million between 1891 and 1930—the Native people received niggardly compensation for the territory they surrendered. So, given their aspirations, why did they agree to these treaties? There are two likely explanations. The agreements did address many of their most pressing concerns, and officials often gave Native people the impression that they were "getting something for nothing." During Treaty 3 negotiations, government spokesmen repeatedly promised that "when you have made your treaty you will still be free to hunt

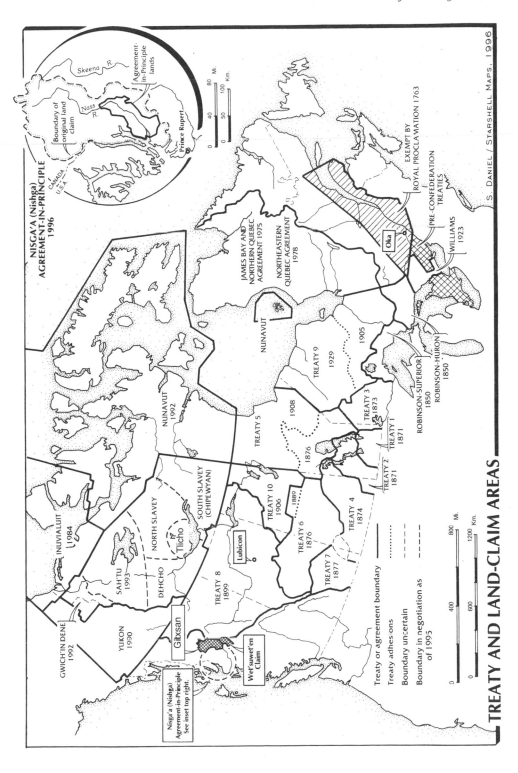

TREATY AND LAND-CLAIM AREAS

S. Daniel / Starshell Maps, 1996

NISGA'A (Nishga) AGREEMENT-IN-PRINCIPLE 1996

Skeena R.

Agreement-in-Principle lands

Boundary of original land claim

Nass R.

Prince Rupert

CANADA U.S.A.

Mi.
Km.

EXEMPT BY ROYAL PROCLAMATION 1763

PRE-CONFEDERATION TREATIES

WILLIAMS 1923

Oka

ROBINSON-SUPERIOR 1850

ROBINSON-HURON 1850

JAMES BAY AND NORTHERN QUEBEC AGREEMENT 1975

NORTHEASTERN QUEBEC AGREEMENT 1978

NUNAVUT

1905

TREATY 9 1929

TREATY 3 1873

TREATY 1 1871

TREATY 2 1871

TREATY 5 1908

1876

NUNAVUT 1992

TREATY 10 1906

1889

TREATY 4 1874

TREATY 6 1876

SOUTH SLAVEY (CHIPEWYAN)

NORTH SLAVEY

Tlicho

DEHCHO

SAH'TU 1993

INUVIALUIT 1984

Lubicon

TREATY 7 1877

TREATY 8 1899

Gitxsan

Wet'suwet'en Claim

GWICH'IN DENE 1992

YUKON 1990

Nisga'a (Nishga) Agreement-in-Principle See inset top right.

Treaty or agreement boundary

Treaty adhesions

Boundary uncertain

Boundary in negotiation as of 1995

Mi.
Km.

Cree chiefs meeting Edgar Dewdney, Indian commissioner and lieutenant-governor of the North-West Territories, at Regina, immediately after the North-West Rebellion of 1885. The controversial Dewdney is shown in the left foreground. Piapot, who was one of the Cree leaders, is second from the right.

over much of the land included in the treaty. Much of it is rocky and unfit for cultivation. Till these lands are needed for use you will be free to hunt over them, and make all the use of them you have made in the past." All the numbered treaties contain a similar clause. Later, Morris also promised during Treaty 6 negotiations, "I see them [the Indians of Treaties 1 to 5] receiving money from the Queen's Commissioners to purchase clothing for their children; at the same time I see them retaining their old mode of living with the Queen's gift in addition."

This duplicitous and very successful negotiating strategy came under attack by none other than Dr Schultz, who served as a member of Parliament from 1871 to 1882. Although he was not sympathetic to Native causes, he probably feared trouble from Plains Indians when he pointed out to the House of Commons in 1877 that the government was persuading the Indians to "part with their birth right for a mere trifle. The reserve question not being fixed, the Indian is under the impression that the country is still practically his for hunting purposes. This answers very well till the necessities of colonization force him on to the reserve." The Plains Cree and other nations would soon learn the bitter truth of Schultz's observation as their affairs were taken over by a succession of narrow-minded and mean-spirited government officials.

From the point of view of Canada's politicians, the country's relationship with the Plains nations got off to a terrible start. After 1876, the rapid rise of annuity and relief costs alarmed them. Echoing the earlier confusion about the number of Métis, officials admitted to Parliament that when they embarked on the treaty-making path, they had not known that there were so many Native people living in the treaty areas of the North-West Territories, and even as late as 1882 the government was still unsure of the numbers. It often took government agents several years after concluding a treaty to count all the Indians who lived within its boundaries. Enumerators usually missed a substantial number of people in their first censuses and many nations did not immediately sign the treaty encompassing their territory. Once a band did join, its members had the right to claim arrears annuities. Making substantial financial commitments to Native people based on incomplete information and during the depths of a depression understandably created great anxiety among Ottawa politicians.

The simultaneous collapse of the buffalo-hunting economies on the prairies contributed to their sense of alarm. By the time Palliser and Hind led their expeditions to the West, the region's people already knew that the herds were declining, and some Plains Cree had already begun to experiment with farming. However, neither the Native people nor anyone in Ottawa had expected the buffalo population to fall as rapidly as it did.

The foresight that the Plains Nations had shown in wringing the concession from the government to help them in times of famine soon came to haunt politicians. When relief expenses shot upwards in the late 1870s and passed the $550,000-a-year mark in 1882, recriminations flew back and forth across the House about the wisdom of having made this commitment. Dr Schultz stood up in the Commons and charged that "[t]he necessity for this expenditure commenced with the sanction, by the late Administration, of one of the vicious conditions of Treaty # 6 ... the result of the clause agreeing that the government should furnish food in times of scarcity—was followed by a vote for that purpose at the very next session of Parliament, and we have found the constant occurrence of a similar necessity at every session since." Shortly thereafter, Sir John A. Macdonald replied with the brutal frankness of the pragmatist that he was: "Of course the system is tentative and it is expensive, especially in feeding destitute Indians, but it is cheaper to feed them than to fight them, and humanity will not allow us to let them starve   the country will not allow us to let them starve for the sake of economy."

Regrettably, Edgar Dewdney, who served as Indian commissioner for Manitoba and the North-West Territories from 1879 to 1888, had no qualms about being ruthless. He used the threat of starvation to bend Native people to his will. When he took office, the commissioner faced two immediate problems. Many

Plains Cree resented the government's slow pace in implementing treaties 1, 2, 4, and 6. Those who had signed the treaties were unhappy because federal officials had delivered so few of the promised livestock and little of the farming equipment; they had not surveyed most of the reserves; and they had taken no steps to preserve the few remaining buffalo. Some of the most influential Plains Indian leaders refused to join Treaty 4 or 5 unless they could obtain improvements in the terms.

Mistahimaskwa, who led the largest group, was probably the most important, and certainly is the best known, of the Cree hold-outs. He refused to bind his people to the will of the Canadian government for a few gifts. "We want none of the Queen's presents: when we set a fox trap we knock him on the head; we want no bait." Morris considered Mistahimaskwa and his followers troublemakers for expressing their concerns.

Mistahimaskwa and other Plains Cree leaders proved to be extremely tough opponents. He and two close allies, Minahikosis (Little Pine) and Piapot, relentlessly pursued the idea of creating an Indian territory for all the Plains Nations. Collectively, these three commanded the loyalty of about 50 per cent of the Indians living in the Treaty 4 and Treaty 6 areas. They set their sights on establishing the proposed reserve in the Cypress Hills, located in the southwestern portion of Treaty 4. This area still teemed with wildlife and it was close to the few remaining buffalo herds, which now mostly roamed on their last refuge in Montana. However, skirmishes between the Plains Cree and American Native groups in 1879 made it clear to the Cree that they would no longer be able to hunt in the United States. Consequently, Minahikosis and Piapot decided to join Treaty 4, and in 1879 they applied for adjacent reserves in the Cypress Hills near Fort Walsh.

If Mistahimaskwa had joined his two allies and the federal government had granted their requests for contiguous reserves, they would have created the unified Indian territory they sought. In the spring of 1880, the goal seemed attainable when Canadian officials indicated that they were willing to grant Minahikosis and Piapot the reserves they wanted, but shortly thereafter Dewdney overruled his officials. Fearing that a large Native settlement could be a threat to government authority in the region, he decided to prevent the Plains leaders from establishing one. This was in clear violation of treaty provisions that gave them the right to select their reserve sites. In the autumn of 1879, the commissioner tried to force treaty hold-outs to sign up by telling them that only those who had signed treaties could expect food relief. He hired Indian agents and farm instructors to serve as spies and rewarded Indians who were compliant. To drive the Cree from the Cypress Hills, he ordered the closing of Fort Walsh and the withdrawal of all government services in the area so that the local groups would have no one to turn to if they needed help. The Cree decided to head north in 1882, mostly because any further access to the Montana herds had been blocked by the Americans, and they faced the prospect of severe food shortages in the Cypress Hills without access to government assistance. In the end, Mistahimaskwa yielded to the wishes of his people and signed Treaty 4.

Although they had faced numerous setbacks, the Cree remained resolute in their pursuit of a unified territory. They now attempted to obtain adjoining reserves farther north in the vicinity of Indian Head and Battleford, Saskatchewan. Dewdney responded by threatening to cut off the rations of any Indian who attended councils to plan such actions. He also said he would arrest chiefs (on trumped-up charges, if necessary) who took part and have them incarcerated. Mistahimaskwa, Piapot, and others persisted in spite of this terror tactic, and they might have succeeded had the North-West Rebellion of 1885 not overtaken them.

THE NORTH-WEST REBELLION OF 1885

Trouble had been brewing in the North and South Saskatchewan River valleys ever since the Red River crisis of 1870. Métis and mixed-bloods had established some large settlements—the most notable being Batoche, St Laurent, and Prince Albert. French and English Canadians had also moved into the territory, and land-development companies had begun staking out substantial blocks of land. There were two reasons for the high interest in this region: it lay in the heart of the fertile belt, and until 1881, the transcontinental railway was supposed to traverse it. (In 1881, the Canadian Pacific Railway chose a shorter, more southerly, route.)

Well before the 1880s, the Métis and other settlers in the Saskatchewan River valley had been trying to obtain title to the lands they had developed to protect them from encroachment by newcomers or speculators. Local Métis petitioned Ottawa for recognition of their claims as early as 1873. Over the next few years, they sent numerous other written appeals, but all they received in reply were terse acknowledgements and a promise of future consideration. The English-speaking mixed-bloods were treated in a similar fashion. It was not until 1879 that the federal government added a clause to the 1872 Dominion Lands Act that gave the governor general the authority "to satisfy any claims existing in connection with the extinguishment of the Indian title, preferred by mixed-bloods resident in the North-West Territories outside the limits of Manitoba ... by granting land to such persons,

Isapo-nuxika (Crowfoot), a very influential Siksika leader, and his family. Isapo-nuxika refused to let his people join the North-West Rebellion of 1885 in the belief that a violent confrontation would be futile.

to such extent and on such terms and conditions, as may be deemed expedient." Yet the government did nothing further about the issue. Recognition of the validity of their claims was of little value to the Métis without an accompanying offer of land grants. The slow pace of the land survey, disgruntlement over other provisions of the Dominion Lands Act, and the lack of a representative territorial government all added to the feelings of unease among longtime residents.

The Canadian government did not address these problems in time to ward off the North-West Rebellion of 1885. The estimated $5 to $20 million that it cost to subdue the Métis, and the handful of Indians and mixed-bloods who joined them, far exceeded the few hundred thousand dollars it would have cost the government to settle Métis land claims. The great question is this: Why didn't the government act decisively and prevent this terrible incident from taking place?

Regardless of how this misadventure is explained, the fact remains that the Métis and the Plains Cree were the ones who paid dearly for it. A number of factors worked against them. In May 1884 the English- and French-speaking communities sent a delegation to Montana territory to beg Louis Riel to come and assist them. Although Riel was well established in his new home, he had not forgotten his Métis roots. He had always been a deeply religious man, but now he thought of himself as a prophet destined to establish a new religion in the northwest. This belief set him on a collision course with the Catholic clergy, many of whom had supported him earlier at Red River. Their opposition hurt the cause. On the eve of the outbreak, the mixed-bloods and other settlers also broke ranks with the Métis when the government yielded to some of their demands. Finally, the West was not as isolated as it had been in 1870. Ottawa had built the roads, steamship facilities, and railways needed to promote immigration, establish a viable agricultural economy, and protect their investments. In particular, although gaps remained in the CPR line, it was sufficiently complete to enable the federal government to dispatch heavily armed troops shortly after the fighting began.

On March 18 and 19, 1885, the Métis formed a provisional government and an armed force at Batoche, to the northeast of what is now Saskatoon. Riel was elected president and Gabriel Dumont was chosen as military commander. The new government issued a Revolutionary Bill of Rights, in which the Métis claimed ownership of their farms. Fighting began on March 26 at Duck Lake, when a party of North-West Mounted Police (NWMP) and volunteers, who were on their way to Batoche, clashed with Métis defenders. The rebels were triumphant.

Dumont, a legendary buffalo hunter, proved to be an excellent guerrilla fighter and leader. Guerrilla fighting offered the Métis their best chance, given the economic climate and other problems the Canadian government faced. As it turned out, the Canadians did not have to fight this type of war. In May Riel insisted that Dumont switch tactics and have his forces dig in at Batoche. However, Dumont did not have the men, the heavy weapons, or the stockpiles of ammunition he needed to fight a protracted defence there. On May 12, 1885, his mixed force of three hundred Métis, Cree, and Lakota suffered a crushing defeat at the hands of the much larger Canadian force, which was armed with artillery and a new, frightful weapon—the Gatling gun.

Gabriel Dumont was the leader of the Saskatchewan Métis before the North-West Rebellion of 1885. He led the Métis forces during the conflict. Afterwards, he fled to the United States, where he appeared in Buffalo Bill's Wild West Show as a marksman. He returned to Saskatchewan in 1888 and died there in 1906.

Riel surrendered shortly after the Battle of Batoche. The government promptly tried, convicted, and hanged him for treason. The Métis were deeply offended.
Their descendants have waged a campaign for a posthumous pardon for him, which
has thus far been unsuccessful.

The Rebellion played into Dewdney's hands by giving him the long-awaited
opportunity to use force to end the struggle of Plains Cree for more autonomy. Until
the outbreak of hostilities at Duck Lake, the Cree had steadfastly refused all Métis
entreaties to join them. The experience of their American cousins south of the border, particularly those of Sitting Bull's people who had defeated General Custer at the
Little Big Horn River in 1876, made it clear that armed conflict, even if temporarily
successful, ultimately led to disaster for Native people. The Cree troubles began
when the people living on several reserves in the vicinity of Battleford learned of
the engagement at Duck Lake and concluded that it would make the local
Department of Indian Affairs agent more receptive to their pleas for extra rations.
They decided to travel to the town and demand clothing, sugar, tobacco, powder,
and shot. Pitikwahanapiwiyin accompanied them, apparently with the intention of
being one of their spokesmen. However, as the large party approached Battleford,

Battle of Batoche, *1885*, Illustrated War News. *After initial successes in a series of small skirmishes,
the Métis, Cree, and Lakota forces were defeated at Batoche on May 12, 1885.*

The Cree leaders Mistahimaskwa (front row, second from left) and Pitikwahanapiwiyin (front right) after their surrender in 1885. Both men were sentenced to three-year prison terms on trumped-up charges.

the agent and all the townsfolk fled in terror, fearing an attack was imminent. They took refuge in the NWMP barracks. Following this unexpected turn of events, the destitute Cree helped themselves to the abandoned larders of the town and plundered some of the stores before retreating to Pitikwahanapiwiyin's reserve.

Elsewhere, dissident groups on various reserves, including Mistahimaskwa's, took advantage of the hostilities to seek retribution against settlers and government agents for past offences. These were the very kinds of incidents that Dewdney could use to justify destroying the Cree political leadership. Although he quietly informed officials in Ottawa that he believed the Cree acts of violence at Battleford and Duck Lake were simply actions of desperate people driven more by hunger than anything else, Dewdney publicly claimed that the Cree had joined forces with the Métis. He issued an official proclamation warning the Cree that those who left their reserves would be considered rebels. Those who had taken up arms were forced to surrender, and Dewdney used the courts to have Mistahimaskwa and Pitikwahanapiwiyin tried and convicted on trumped-up treason-felony charges. When the two chiefs emerged from Stony Mountain Prison, after serving only part of their three-year terms, they were broken men. Using these tactics, Dewdney succeeded in placing the Cree under the yoke of the federal government just in time for the great "wheat boom" of the 1890s, when three million European immigrants responded to the Canadian government's promises of free land.

CHAPTER 15

IT IS A STRICT
LAW THAT BIDS
US DANCE

It is a strict law that bids us dance. It is a strict law that bids us distribute our property among our friends and neighbours. It is a good law. Let the white man observe his law, we shall observe ours.

—An anonymous Kwakwaka'wakw chief addressing the anthropologist Franz Boas in British Columbia, 1896

After the North-West Rebellion, the federal government redoubled its efforts to assimilate Native people into the dominant white culture. Their plan had two components, both aimed at destroying the viability of Native societies. The first outlawed key cultural institutions, and the second sought to "re-educate" aboriginal children. The policies implemented by politicians and Department of Indian Affairs bureaucrats at this time amounted to a plan for cultural genocide. They were put into effect in a particularly heavy-handed fashion in the West, where officials still regarded the Plains and coastal nations as potential threats to orderly settlement. Initially, most missionaries not only lobbied Parliament to pass the legislation needed to implement the assimilation policies but also helped to administer and monitor the programs. In the economic sphere, officials sought, with varying degrees of success, to undermine the communal orientation of Native economies.

BANNING THE POTLATCH

On the West Coast, the move to ban certain cultural practices began well before 1885. Missionaries were convinced that the potlatch seriously impeded their efforts

222

to convert the Native population, because one of the purposes of the ceremonies was to reinforce traditional beliefs and practices. According to a Methodist missionary from Nanaimo, "the Church and school cannot flourish where the 'Potlatching' holds sway.... Thus all the objects or advantages to be secured by good government are frustrated by this very demoralizing custom." Most Indian agents, who represented the Department of Indian Affairs at the local level, agreed.

To whip up support for their position, missionaries and Indian agents drew the attention of politicians and the public to those aspects of feasts that seemed the most contradictory to the customs and values of their own society. They stressed repeatedly that coastal

Totem poles at Kitwanga, Gitxsan territory, 1915.

nations "wasted" valuable time attending potlatches when they should have been employed elsewhere in more profitable pursuits. This, of course, was not a new charge. In the early nineteenth century, HBC traders often complained to London that the Babine and Wet'suwet'en caught few furs in the winter because they spent most of their time "feasting and gambling." Like the fur traders before them, the new critics could not understand why Native people amassed a prodigious quantity of material goods only to "squander" it at feasts—"bankrupting" themselves in the process.

The public destruction of wealth certainly was an aspect of the feasts that disturbed many outsiders whose European traditions placed a high value on the private accumulation of material goods. However, this usually took place during a so-called potlatch war. It is likely that such competitive ceremonies were uncommon before contact, given that the social order would have been more stable. The high degree of instability that characterized later societies was the result of massive depopulation caused by repeated epidemics; the movement of many Native people to trading-post sites, villages, and towns; increased per capita wealth; and the disruptive work of missionaries and Indian agents. In the late nineteenth and early twentieth centuries, "competitive potlatching" was one of the ways coastal groups tried to establish a new social equilibrium. It became increasingly common among the Kwakwaka'wakw, who had suffered very heavy population losses but had prospered materially from their extensive participation in the evolving industrial economy, especially the commercial fishery. Feasting provided ambitious chiefs with an opportunity to extend their power and influence beyond traditional bounds. By engaging in "competitive potlatching," however, coastal nations played into the hands of their critics. Indian agents, for instance, claimed that coastal Native people often had to turn to them for help after giving away all their possessions at the ceremonies.

Even this dimension of potlatching probably was not as abhorrent to the missionaries and Indian agents as the fact that elders used the ceremonies to maintain their influence over the younger generation and to promote traditional values. In 1881 the agent at Cowichan wrote that "these dances have been sadly on the increase during the present winter, and many young men have impoverished themselves and their families because they had not the moral courage to oppose the custom. Indeed, this want of courage or inability to withstand the sneers of the old people always forms one of the greatest drawbacks to the advancement of the Native races on the coast." Coastal Native people who had been converted to Christianity often parroted this argument, as did those who resented chiefs who exceeded traditional bounds of chiefly power.

Missionaries raised other objections about Native customs. Traditionally West Coast families arranged the marriages of their children because inheritance determined a person's titles and privileges and those of his or her relatives. Among matrilineal groups, such as the Kwakwaka'wakw, traditional marriage customs gave the impression that young girls were being "sold" for the goods exchanged when the marriage pledges were made and the unions celebrated. Missionaries charged that this was scandalous. Even more shocking to them was that some Native women engaged in prostitution to raise money to pay for family-sponsored potlatches.

In 1873 Dr I. W. Powell was appointed Indian superintendent for British Columbia. Siding with the missionaries, Powell advocated appointing more agents in the remote north and banning the potlatch altogether. Gilbert M. Sproat, British Columbia's first Indian reserve commissioner, also took up the cause. After touring the province, he wrote to Prime Minister Macdonald in 1879 to voice his worries about the "evils" of the potlatch. When Macdonald took up the issue in the House of Commons in the spring of 1883, he did so not out of concern for the coastal

Dancing in elaborate ceremonial costumes was an integral part of a potlatch. Colonial settlers, who in this photograph are watching from a railway bridge, enjoyed the ceremonies, and many of them did not support government and missionary efforts to ban the events.

nations but for fear of the physical threat that they represented to settlers. "There are a large number … of the said Indians," Macdonald told the House, who "are now, I believe, very profitably employed in the [salmon] canneries and establishments of that kind. Indians are now employed as miners and they work very well. But it must be remembered that they are not white men, and civilized, and must be strictly watched…. They are very suspicious and easily aroused; the white population is sparse and the Indians feel yet that they are lords of the country in British Columbia." It is hardly surprising, therefore, that Macdonald and other politicians were sympathetic to the idea of eliminating a ceremony that brought West Coast Native people together.

Because he was eager to avoid a costly subjugation program requiring the use of police, Macdonald issued an Order in Council on July 7, 1883, directing Indians to abandon the custom. Macdonald thought "such a Proclamation from the well-known loyalty of the Native people generally and their reverence for Her Majesty the Queen will go far to induce them to abandon the heathenish custom of 'Potlack.'" However, the continuing clamour for tougher measures led the Macdonald government to amend the Indian Act on April 19, 1884, making it a misdemeanour for anyone to encourage or participate in the potlatch "or in the Indian dance known as the 'Tamanawas.'" Violators would be subject to imprisonment for a minimum of two months and a maximum of six months. Subsequently, Section 3 of the Indian Act came to be widely known as the Potlatch Law.

The coastal nations had no intention of abandoning this important institution, and geography helped them preserve it. Most areas of coastal British Columbia remained beyond the easy reach of Indian agents until well after the turn of the century. Nations living in these remote areas flouted the Canadian law. For instance, four years after the imposition of the ban, the magistrate living at Hazelton on the Skeena River visited the Gitxsan village of Kitwangak to tell the people there that they had to refrain from any further potlatching. Later a local missionary told the magistrate, "They replied, that the law was a weak baby, and in several speeches defied you, and the Government." In more accessible areas, the people took a more tactful approach and simply pointed out the hardships the new law created for them. They said that those who owed debts to their kinfolk and others before the passage of the law wanted to be allowed to repay their obligations. Some of them wrote letters to Powell. The letter of Tummeen, the son of Chief Lohah of Comeakin, is typical: "I am not a chief, only a boy, but I owe nearly $200 worth of property. My father has always tried to keep the law and teach us to do so. But if he is not allowed to return his debts, in public, the disgrace will be more than he can bear.... My father, Lohah, has always helped white men even against the old or bad Indians, and if Mr. Powell does not help him now he will always be laughed at."

Many settlers did not support the war against potlatches. They enjoyed watching them; many local merchants profited when the participants stockpiled goods for redistribution; and they feared that violence might erupt if the government used force to suppress the feasts. Citing this last concern, the provincial MLA Henry Dallas Helmcken, the grandson of Sir James Douglas and a lawyer representing Nisga'a potlatchers, introduced a resolution in the provincial Parliament in April 1897 that urged the immediate repeal of Section 3. Subsequently, the legislators asked the federal government to investigate Indian complaints about the Potlatch Law.

Indian agents were supposed to help enforce the law by collecting evidence and planning court actions against suspected violators, but there were not enough agents in British Columbia to do this and Parliament lacked the will to appropriate money for enforcement costs. The British Columbia government did not co-operate either, taking the position that the Indian Act was a federal responsibility. Provincial officials refused to allow the police to help Indian agents, and they denied them the use of provincial jails.

The federal government was forced to backtrack. Powell told the Native people that they could hold ceremonies to "witness a return of gifts made on some former occasion." He granted this permission on the understanding that once people had discharged their debts they would stop potlatching. Of course, this was folly.

In 1889 British Columbia and Ottawa worked out an arrangement whereby the province agreed, with great reluctance, to provide the police and jails needed to enforce Section 3. It did so on the understanding that local constables would consult Indian agents before taking any actions against violators. Just as the enforcement program was set to begin, however, it suffered a setback when a local justice of the peace arrested, convicted, and sentenced a Kwakwaka'wakw man for violating the Potlatch Law. The case was appealed to Matthew Begbie, the first chief justice of the Supreme Court of British Columbia. He overturned the summary conviction, noting that "[d]ifferent people appear to have very different notions as to what the word [potlatch] means." The judge made it clear that the statute would have to be changed so that it fully described the acts that were prohibited. Begbie's ruling came at a time when Indian Affairs also wanted to move against Plains Indians' sundance ceremonies, so federal officials drafted an amendment to the Indian Act that covered all ceremonial redistribution of wealth. In 1895 Parliament passed the amendment as Section 114, banning "any Indian festival, dance, or other ceremony of which the giving away or paying or giving back money, goods or articles of any sort forms a part, or is a feature, whether such a gift of money, goods or articles takes place before, at, or after the celebration."

The growing effort to stamp out the potlatch intensified new divisions in the Native community. Many Christian converts opposed the ancient custom and urged the government to enforce the law. They deeply resented the attempts by traditionalists to claim their hereditary titles and rights because they did not confirm them in the customary way. At the turn of the century, the conflict between the "anti-potlatchers" and the traditionalists came to a head in Nisga'a country. The Christian chiefs charged their potlatching kinfolk with stealing "our names, fishing streams & hunting grounds." In 1899 the local Indian agent reported that these chiefs had warned that the government would have to eliminate the practice because "wherever it is allowed to exist, no other government is respected or obeyed by the Indians." The Nisga'a chiefs wrote to the superintendent-general of Indian Affairs in Ottawa: "We want to follow the Queen's law and the Indian Act, but the Potlatch Law will not agree to the Queen's law." Because they claimed to represent the majority of the Nisga'a, the new Indian superintendent for British Columbia, Arthur Vowell, believed them. Nonetheless, he opted to follow the same lenient approach of his predecessor. He warned agents not to interfere with exchange ceremonies provided that no one destroyed any property. He was particularly anxious that the law not be enforced at public gatherings, fearing that violence would be the result if it was.

Officials continued to have difficulty stamping out the potlatch. Native people frequently held the ceremonies in isolated locations and posted lookouts. They also devised ways of continuing the old custom in modified forms that were either less offensive to anti-potlatchers or harder to detect. The so-called disjointed potlatch was one of these clever schemes. It involved distributing gifts and establishing debts several months after a public gathering for dancing and singing took place. Because no public gift giving occurred at the ceremony, the participants could avoid prosecution. Holding a "private potlatch" was another strategy. In this instance a person sent two messengers out to visit various people in their homes to give them presents—usually money, which was not readily identifiable as a potlatch gift. One of the envoys took care of distributing the gifts, while the other wrote down the names of the recipients and the amounts they were paid. Some Native people did not attempt to dodge the law at all; instead, they chose to defy it openly. A few Indian agents sympathized with their Aboriginal clients and refused to make a concerted effort to carry out official policy. Unless local missionaries complained, the Department of Indian Affairs usually did little to prod these reluctant agents into action.

Circumstances changed, however, when Duncan Campbell Scott took charge of Indian Affairs in 1913. Scott, who is best remembered as an accomplished poet, was a dedicated career civil servant and a loyal Conservative. His biographer, Brian Titley, writes that despite being well educated, Scott harboured most of the negative stereotypes about Native people that were common in his day. Scott thought Native people had been unreliable allies in the past and "a real menace to the colonization of Canada." Like many government officials before and after him, he presumed that Native people were a dying people and this belief guided his policies as the director of the department. Scott looked forward to a day when they would no longer exist as distinct nations and would adopt all the ways of the dominant society. In his opinion, "the happiest future for the Indian race is absorption into the general population.... [T]his is the object of the policy of our government." Scott dedicated his career to achieving that end.

In his effort to stamp out West Coast Native culture, Scott found a willing ally in William Halliday, the infamous Indian agent for the southern Kwakwaka'wakw who was stationed at the Namgis (Nimpkish) village of Alert Bay, just off the northern coast of Vancouver Island. In his annual reports to Ottawa for the years 1911 to 1913, he complained that the people under his jurisdiction continued to hold potlatches. Shortly after Scott became superintendent-general, he ordered Halliday and his other agents to enforce the Potlatch Law, thereby ending the conciliatory approach initiated by Powell. Scott had little to fear in making this change. By the turn of the century, the influx of settlers and the steeply declining Native population meant that Aboriginal people no longer posed a credible threat, except perhaps in central and north-coastal territories, where white settlers remained in the minority.

Halliday wasted no time. When the Namgis of Alert Bay, the Nimpkish people, assembled to head off to their summer employment at the coastal salmon canneries, he read them the law and decried the evils of the potlatch. Halliday related that after listening quietly and respectfully, the Nimpkish "said they would think about what I said and let me know what they thought after they came back from fishing." In the autumn, Chief Bagwany decided to challenge Halliday by calling the neighbouring nations to a potlatch. Halliday charged him, and one of his co-conspirators, Ned Harris, with violating Section 114 of the Indian Act. The two chiefs were tried twice in Vancouver. At the first trial, the jury could not decide whether the potlatch was a religious ceremony with fixed rules. The following day, Harris and Bagwany were retried and convicted on the charge that dances had been held at the "festival." The jury recommended mercy, and the judge gave the two suspended sentences. A number of other arrests and convictions of Kwakwaka'wakw people followed over the next decade; at subsequent trials, judges were not so lenient and many defendants went to jail.

Probably the most notorious aspect of the potlatch-suppression program involved the government's use of extortion to pry ceremonial regalia from West Coast people. In the 1920s the government stepped up enforcement. Those who were convicted in the flurry of prosecutions in 1922 were told they would not be given prison terms if their fellow villagers surrendered to authorities all their masks, rattles, whistles, coppers, and other "potlatch gear." The Alert Bay and Cape Mudge people agreed, and the government paid the owners the modest sum of $1,450.50 for several hundred of their treasured possessions. Officials shipped this precious heritage to the Victoria Museum (later the Canadian Museum of Civilization) in Ottawa and to the Royal Ontario Museum in Toronto. The government also sold thirty-three articles to the Heye Foundation Museum of the American Indian in New York.

In the end the potlatch not only survived, albeit in modified form, but even flourished among some groups such as the Gitxsan and Kwakwaka'wakw. The ban lasted until 1951, when it was simply left out of the revised Indian Act.

Today the consensus among historians seems to be that the extent to which the potlatch ceremony diminished in significance or was altered in a Native group depended more on the influence of the local missionaries than on the application of the law. Missionaries appear to have been particularly successful among the Haida, coast Tsimshian, some Nisga'a, and many Coast Salish groups. Initially Native nations often turned to the new religion for economic reasons. Many missionaries operated stores, for example, which provided goods more cheaply than traditional sources, such as the HBC. In addition, the missionaries taught them new skills, helped them run a variety of non-traditional enterprises, and were frequently in the vanguard of the defence of Aboriginal economic rights—especially land claims. Finally, missionaries operated hospitals and taught at the schools Native children attended.

ATTACKING THE SUN (THIRST) DANCES

Sam Steele, superintendent of the North-West Mounted Police (renamed Royal Canadian Mounted Police in 1920), was one of the first government officials to regard the continuation of the sun or thirst dance as a potential threat to Canada's colonization of the West. After attending the ceremony at a Kainaiwa (Blood) encampment in 1889, he warned headquarters: "Old warriors take this occasion of relating their experience of former days counting their scalps and giving the number of horses they were successful in stealing. This has a pernicious effect on the young men; it makes them unsettled and anxious to emulate the deeds of their forefathers." Officials in Indian Affairs shared this worry. They also thought that ceremonial activities diverted the Plains nations from "more important" activities. In particular, the department expected them to devote the summer months to farming. Indian agents and their superiors thought that it was outrageous for their clients to spend up to six weeks every summer dancing and feasting in the old way.

A Siksika sun-dance circle, 1943. The 1884 amendment to the Indian Act, known popularly as the Potlatch Law, was also intended to curtail the sun dance. Until the law was repealed in 1951, Plains groups continued the ceremony by eliminating the banned elements or by disguising them.

Indian Affairs' first attempt to put an end to the sun dance involved using the "pass system." Officials originally introduced the system as a temporary measure aimed at halting the spread of the North-West Rebellion of 1885. Maj.-Gen. Frederick Middleton first proposed the scheme to the Indian commissioner for Manitoba and the North-West Territories, Edgar Dewdney. He said that it would be wise to issue a proclamation to "[half]breeds and Indians" telling them to return to their reserves and remain there. Middleton also suggested that those who refused should be treated as rebels. Dewdney replied that he lacked the authority to issue such an edict; nonetheless, he did circulate a warning to the Native people in the North-West, informing them that anyone who was absent from his or her reserve without a pass would be arrested as a possible "hostile."

When the conflict ended, Dewdney was prepared to lift the restriction; he had no authority under the Indian Act, or any other legislation, to make it permanent. In fact, it violated the provisions of some of the treaties that gave Native people the right to hunt and trap freely on undeveloped Crown lands. However, the idea did not die at this time, mainly because an important official in the Department of Indian Affairs—Hayter Reed—supported it.

A meeting of the hereditary council of the Six Nations, 1898. The Six Nations resented the provisions of the Indian Act that provided for elected councils and facilitated Indian Affairs' autocratic control over their lives. In 1890 the chiefs petitioned Ottawa for self-government by asking that their people be exempt from the provisions of the act. The petition set off a long-running battle with officials from Indian Affairs and a minority group of dissidents on the Six Nations reserve, who favoured democratic reforms. In the end, the department succeeded when Parliament passed a bill in 1920 abolishing the hereditary system.

Reed was a vengeful and rigid man who rose rapidly through the ranks of Indian Affairs. He became assistant Indian commissioner for Manitoba and the North-West Territories in 1884, took over the role of commissioner in 1888, and was appointed deputy superintendent-general of the department in 1893. Reed thought Native people had no right to be consulted about government policies that might affect them. Holding them responsible for all their misfortunes, he regarded Indians as the "scum of the prairies." He favoured hanging rebel leaders to teach Native people a lesson and openly applauded the natural deaths of traditional chiefs in subsequent years because he regarded them as bad influences.

Given his outlook, it is not surprising that Reed strongly supported the idea of curtailing freedom of movement for Native people in the West. He acknowledged that the treaties guaranteed them this right, but he noted that these agreements also forbade them to trespass on settlers' land. On this basis Reed proposed that towns, villages, and farms be declared off limits to Indians. Moreover, he thought that a pass system could be introduced even without a proper legal foundation. In 1886 the government introduced this shameful scheme, which required Plains Indians to carry passes for all off-reserve activities. To obtain a pass, a person had to get the approval of the local farming instructor and the Indian agent who issued the passes, which gave these officials dictatorial control over the lives of Indians. Agents denied passes to anyone they thought was troublesome, and the police backed them up by patrolling the borders of the reserves day and night looking for absentees. In this way Indian Affairs essentially imprisoned Native people on reserves.

Although rigorously enforced in the beginning, the pass system fell into disuse after the early 1890s because no one feared the Native people once the memory of the North-West Rebellion had faded. In addition, it was clear that the absence of legislative authority for the system meant that it would never withstand a legal challenge by Indians. As a result, officials began to look for new ways to control Native people.

The 1895 amendment to the Indian Act, which spelled out more clearly what practices were forbidden by the Potlatch Law, strengthened the department's hand. While this amendment was being drafted, Indian agents from the prairies had asked their superiors if the new provisions could also be applied to the prairie bands. Department officials in Ottawa successfully pressed the government for changes that would make it an indictable offence under Section 114 to take part in any "celebration of which the wounding or mutilation of the dead or living body of any human being or animal forms a part or is a feature."

Although Indian Affairs now had the authority to stop the ceremonies, Reed wanted to move slowly and carefully to avoid provoking a hostile reaction from the Plains nations. The presence of North-West Mounted Police at celebrations discouraged the participants from performing the illegal rituals. Like some West Coast groups, several bands were prepared to alter their ancient sun-dance customs rather than risk the imposition of a total ban on the dances. They discontinued the distribution of gifts and eliminated the bloody "making a brave" parts of the celebration. Some groups also shortened the length of the dance and discouraged their children from leaving school to join in. In this way they hoped to ward off criticism about those features of the rituals that had not been banned but nevertheless were frowned on by missionaries and Indian agents.

As on the West Coast, Indian agents on the plains held widely differing views about whether to zealously pursue the department's objective of stamping out ancient traditions. Some readily granted their wards the right to hold dances if they promised not to engage in the forbidden aspects. Others opposed Native dances in any form, believing that such events undermined the department's basic goal of turning the people into subsistence farmers. Sometimes agents acted ruthlessly. In 1903, for instance, the agent responsible for Piapot's reserve in Saskatchewan arrested a man named Etchease for holding a dance at which, apparently, nothing was given away except a supper for the guests. Etchease received a three-month jail sentence! In a particularly notorious case, a nearly blind ninety-year-old man from Fishing Lakes, Saskatchewan, was convicted of "dancing" and given a two-month sentence of "hard labour." This merciless action created such a public outcry that the department had to give the "offender" a suspended sentence.

Although episodes of this kind tended to evoke public sympathy for Native people, most local missionaries largely supported the hard-line approach to enforcement. They generally shared the belief of their West Coast comrades that the fastest way to convert Native people to Christianity was to eliminate those cultural institutions that passed on old ideologies and value systems to new generations. Only a handful of them favoured a more tolerant approach.

At the same time, local public support for the Indian Affairs department's effort to undermine Native cultures began to weaken. White settlers no longer believed the Indians were a threat. In fact, they became interested in Native ceremonies and wanted to include them in their county fairs and stampedes. For their part, most nations were eager to participate. However, such public celebrations of Native culture, even if highly transformed, undermined the work of the department. Predictably, the senior civil servants, with their Victorian mindset, were scandalized at the prospect of "half-clad" Aboriginal men dancing before white women and children. They were even more worried that press coverage of the events would give the outside world the perception that the Plains people still lived the way they always had. Consequently, when organizers of the 1908 Dominion Exhibition, the forerunner of the Calgary Stampede, invited various nations to participate, the deputy superintendent-general of Indian Affairs, Frank Pedley, asked the minister of Agriculture to make any financial support for the exhibition conditional on the cancellation of the authentic "Indian performance." Pedley was too late; the donation had already been made. In later years, politicians successfully pressured the department to allow Native groups to participate in the Calgary event.

Federal bureaucrats did not abandon their struggle in the face of this kind of opposition. After he became head of the department in 1913, Scott used the same heavy-handed tactics in the western interior as he did on the coast. He drafted a revision to the Indian Act, which Parliament approved in 1927 with little dissent, that banned the Native people in the four western provinces or in the territories from engaging in Native dances off their own reserves and from appearing in public exhibitions in "aboriginal costumes." An offender was subject to a fine of $25 and a one-month prison term. Agents still had discretionary power, however, so enforcement continued to be uneven.

Tom Three Persons and his wife, Ambush Woman, in 1912. He is wearing the championship medal he won at the first Calgary Stampede. Native people had taken part in the predecessor of this event, the Dominion Exhibition, since its inception in 1886.

Despite all the efforts of Indian Affairs, the Plains people continued to hold sun dances. Numerous accounts indicate that in the late 1920s their gatherings were as lavish as ever. Furthermore, many participants openly flouted the law prohibiting them from attending ceremonies off their own reserves. The North-West Mounted Police usually attended, but took no action, provided that the celebrants did not drink alcohol or distribute gifts openly. Dancing declined but after 1951 it was revived.

SCHOOLS FOR INDIAN CHILDREN

The most draconian assimilation scheme the government imposed on Native people involved the use of schools. Assimilation through white education programs was a cornerstone of British colonial policy, largely as a result of the lobbying of church groups. After Confederation, the federal government was obligated to provide education in its role as custodian of Native people. In western Canada, the numbered treaties reinforced that obligation. Native elders knew that their children would have to gain a "white man's" education to hold their own in the new economic order. Government negotiators were very aware of their thoughts on this matter and effectively held out the prospect of free education as a carrot to encourage Native groups to yield up their land. When negotiating Treaty 4, the lieutenant-governor for the North-West Territories, Alexander Morris, told the assembled nations: "The Queen wishes her red children to learn the cunning of the white man and when they are ready for it she will send schoolmasters on every Reserve and pay them." Treaty 1 made a promise to the Native people of southern Manitoba: "Her Majesty agrees to maintain a school on each reserve hereby when-ever the Native people of the reserve should desire it." All the other prairie treaties and Treaty 3 contained a similar clause. Beginning with Treaty 7, revised wording gave the government the right to decide when to comply with Indian requests for education. This treaty stipulated that "Her Majesty agrees to pay the salary of such teachers to instruct the children of said Native people as Her government of Canada may seem advisable, when the said Native people are settled on their reserves and shall desire teachers."

This movement away from the policy of granting Native people a say in deciding when instruction should begin continued in Treaty 8. In this agreement the government retained complete discretion in the matter. However, it did respond to another Native and missionary concern about education policy. When the Treaty 8 commissioners reported to Ottawa about their deliberations, they said the local Native people "seemed desirous of securing educational advantages for their children, but stipulated that in the matter of schools there should be no inter-ference with their religious beliefs." This concern was being expressed by Christianized Native people who wanted to be taught by members of the same denomination that had converted them. The treaty contained no provisions to address this matter, but the commissioners reported that "the Native people were assured that there was no need of any special stipulation, as it was the policy of the Government to provide in every part of the country, as far as circumstances would permit, for the education of Indian children, and that the law, which was as strong as a treaty, provided for non-interference with the religion of the Native people in schools maintained or assisted by the Government."

Concerned with running a frugal operation, a succession of deputy superintendent-generals of Indian Affairs sought to provide schooling as cheaply as possible. The easiest way to accomplish this was by using schools for Native chil-dren operated by the Roman Catholic, Anglican, Methodist, and Presbyterian churches. In 1879 an adviser to the Department of Indian Affairs provided another reason for turning to the missionaries. He noted that they were the best suited to root out "simple Indian mythology," a necessary first step in the "civilization" process. Needless to say, the churches were eager to participate. Federal subsidies, which ranged from $72 to $145 a student, depending on the kind of school, placed missionary operations on a sounder financial basis.

The churches developed two very different kinds of schools—residential schools and day schools. Missionaries had been operating residential elementary schools for Aboriginal children for many years. By the late nineteenth century, they had come to the conclusion that these facilities offered the best means for advancing their assimilationist agenda because children were removed from the influence of their fathers, mothers, and elders. This view was at the centre of an 1847 report on Indian affairs published by the government of Canada West. It was written by Egerton Ryerson, the strong-willed and arrogant Methodist minister who was superintendent of education. He concluded that educating Indians "must consist not merely of the training of the mind, but of a weaning from the habits and

Methodist Day School, Saddle Lake, NWT, 1901. After 1867 the education of Indian children became a federal responsibility, whereas that of Inuit and Métis children became provincial and territorial obligations. The federal government turned to religious denominations to operate its schools, especially the Anglican, Methodist, Presbyterian, and Roman Catholic churches.

feelings of their ancestors, and the acquirements of the language, arts and customs of civilized life." According to Ryerson, Native people should be kept under the control of federal rather than provincial authority, missionary efforts should be continued, the churches should operate the schools, and manual labour should be emphasized. Ryerson's recommendations became the cornerstone of the Canadian government's education policy for Native people for many years to come.

The expansion of the church-run residential-school system was one legacy of that policy. To provide education beyond the primary grades, the government encouraged the development of industrial schools for children between the ages of fourteen and eighteen years of age. These facilities for job training were situated away from the reserves. Occupational instruction for boys focused on agriculture and various trades—usually carpentry, blacksmithing, and cobbling. Girls were taught household skills. Schools of this type first appeared in Upper Canada in the 1840s. The United States began to operate similar institutions in 1869 as part of its "aggressive civilization" plan. If successful, the schools would turn out a cheap labour force, which was sorely needed in frontier areas.

The government established three industrial schools in western Canada in 1883–84, after studying the American system. The Roman Catholic Church administered the schools at Qu'Appelle and High River, and the Anglican Church managed the one at Battleford. In the beginning, the churches received a subsidy of between $110 and $145 a student to cover their costs. At the turn of the century, twenty industrial schools operated in western Canada, and the Methodists and Presbyterians had become involved.

In recent years the dark side of residential-school life has come to light as traumatized former students, and the children of those students, have recounted their experiences and passed on the stories of their parents. In his book *The Fourth World*, the Shuswap political activist George Manuel recalls his school days: "Three things stand out in my mind from my years at school: hunger; speaking English; and being called a heathen because of my grandfather." Others tell of torture, sexual abuse, and other crimes. In *Resistance and Renewal*, a very important collection of Native reactions to their residential-school experience in British Columbia, Celia Haig-Brown writes: "My father, who attended Alberni Indian Residential School for four years in the twenties, was physically tortured by his teachers for speaking Tsehaht; they pushed sewing needles through his tongue, a routine punishment for language offenders." A former student she interviewed reported: "I was first sexually abused by a student when I was six years old, and by a supervisor, an ex-Navy homosexual, when I was eight. Homosexuality was prevalent in the school. I learned how to use sexuality to my advantage, as did many other students. Sexual favours brought me protection, sweets (a rarity in the school), and even money to buy booze."

Since the public has become aware of these nefarious aspects of residential-school life, most Canadians now regard these institutions as synonymous with abuse. Some sociologists maintain that the legacy of the institutions is dysfunctional families and communities, chronic alcoholism, and a very high teenage suicide rate. On the other hand, one of the tragic ironies was that the schools probably had the opposite effect from what the government intended. Instead of stamping out Aboriginal culture, they created a new group of determined

LESSON XXXIV

1. Look! the cars are coming.
   Sâtsit! istsi-enakâs epoxapoyaw.
2. They come very fast.
   Ixka-ekkami-poxapoyaw.
3. They come from Winnipeg.
   Mikutsitartay omortsipoxapoyaw.

4. The cars are full of people.
   Matapix itortoyitsiyaw enakâsix.
5. Let us go to the depot.
   Konnê-etâpoôp istsi-enakâs-api-oyis.

A page from First Reader in the English and Blackfoot Languages, *1886.*

Native leaders by bringing children together from disparate cultural areas, by forcing them to help one another to survive, and by teaching them the ways of their oppressors.

Learning the new ways would have been painful even if the schools had had the very best of intentions, as some did. Haig-Brown's interviewees tell us, for example, that some of the children's suffering was not due simply to ill treatment by teachers and other staff. Rather, some of it was the inevitable result of culture shock. Because most Aboriginal societies did not use corporal punishment, the rigid discipline of the schools was horrifying. Making matters worse, the students faced an English-only rule the day they entered the institutions, which was inhumane because many of them spoke little, if any, English or French. In short, the children found themselves in a strange, harsh world where for years they were cut off from the solace of their parents.

In the elementary schools, academic training was minimal and Eurocentric. At the Kamloops residential school operated by the Oblates of Mary Immaculate,

The carpenter shop at the Qu'Appelle Industrial School, 1895. The federal government introduced these types of residential schools in western Canada, beginning in 1883. Boys between fourteen and eighteen years of age received training in agricultural skills and trades.

students spent the first hour of every class day studying the teachings of the Roman Catholic Church. They spent the next two hours learning reading, writing, and arithmetic. As one former elementary student said, "You learnt the three R's there, you know, the basics. You learned a little bit about history ... but there was no history about B. C.... They never taught us why Vancouver was called Vancouver or anything like that. They taught us all about Quebec and French and all the explorers. We learned a bit about South America.... We learned about King Henry the Eighth and Fifth and all those guys."

Of the many problems associated with the education that Indian children received, two stand out. First, the zeal with which most teachers sought to divorce their pupils from their cultural ancestry had the effect of undermining the children's self-confidence. They were made to feel ashamed of their heritage. And second, the Native students did not receive the same level of education as their non-Native counterparts: in the church-operated residential schools of British Columbia, barely two hours a day were devoted to scholarly activities; in the public schools, children received five hours of academic instruction.

By the turn of the century, a growing number of Aboriginal parents were opposed to sending their children to residential schools. In the beginning many

The sewing room at the Qu'Appelle Industrial School, 1895. In the industrial school, the education program for girls aged fourteen to eighteen emphasized domestic skills and provided them with less academic instruction than their male counterparts.

had allowed their children to attend, and some had even insisted. Over time, how-ever, they became justifiably resentful about not being able to see their sons and daughters for several years at a time; the department discouraged students from visiting home, fearing they would be exposed to "undesirable influences." Stories began circulating about the abuse children suffered in the institutions. Health prob-lems at the schools were another cause for alarm: poor sanitation and ventilation led to high rates of tuberculosis and other fatal diseases. Finally, most parents objected to the forced assimilation of their children. For all these reasons, parents began to resist having their children sent away to school.

Senior government officials and politicians were having second thoughts for another reason. As early as 1897 one politician summarized the prevalent thinking in Ottawa: "We are educating these Native people to compete industrially with our own people, which seems to me a very undesirable use of public money, or else we are not able to educate them to compete, in which case our money is thrown away." After looking into the matter, Clifford Sifton, the minister of the Interior and superintendent-general of Indian Affairs from 1896 to 1905, decided that the government should shift the focus of its education program so that it trained Native students in how to make a living on their reserves instead of in competition

Cree children playing in the snow at the Sturgeon Lake, Alberta, residential school, 1946. The darker side of residential school life, and other problems with the Native education system, led to increasing opposition to it. In 1972 the National Indian Brotherhood presented a policy paper calling for Native community control over schools and curriculum. Subsequently, Indian Affairs adopted this policy.

with non-Natives. The government halted the construction of new industrial schools and phased them out, beginning in 1907 when it closed the school at Metlakatla, British Columbia.

The Department of Indian Affairs now focused its attention on boarding schools and day schools. In the 1950s, Native organizations such as the Indian Association of Alberta, the Union of Saskatchewan Indians, and the Native Brotherhood of British Columbia expressed unified voices to the government against residential schools. The Native Brotherhood of B.C. campaigned most strongly for their closure. They were opposed by missionaries, especially by the Roman Catholic Oblates, who operated three-fifths of the schools at the time. Growing Native opposition to and continuing problems at residential schools eventually forced the government to close them. The last one closed its doors in 1988. Teacher recruitment was the key obstacle the department faced in operating day schools, because many of them were situated on remote reserves, and the comparatively low salary the department offered was an added barrier. In 1920 Indian Affairs also decided to force parents to send their children to school, and it persuaded Parliament to amend the Indian Act accordingly. The revised act gave the superintendent-general the authority to use truant officers and fines to track down and compel all Aboriginal children between seven and fifteen years of age to attend Indian schools.

Clearly Indian Affairs and most of the schoolteachers never envisaged that Native students would find a place in Canadian society as equals to whites. Before the wave of immigration at the turn of the century, Native youngsters were trained to be domestic and unskilled labour. As immigrants became available for these jobs, the government scrapped this meagre educational goal for Aboriginal children in favour of ghettoizing them on reserves at the peripheries of the economy.

Ever since the closing of the residential schools, Aboriginal people have sought closure to this dark chapter in Canadian history. The victims began by suing the churches that had administered the schools for their pain and suffering. It was unlikely that many of the elderly victims ever would receive compensation through this slow and expensive process. After lengthy negotiations to devise an alternative procedure for redress, the federal government, the churches, and representatives of the former students concluded the Indian Residential Schools Agreement in May 2006. It provided $2 billion in compensation, but allowed former students to opt out of the settlement and sue separately. Additionally, the agreement provided for the creation of a Truth and Reconciliation Commission that would be independent of the government and the courts and provides a safe, respectful and culturally appropriate setting where former students could share their personal experiences. The commission was established in 2007 and given a five-year mandate. It began work in the spring of 2008 with retired justice Harry LaForme serving as the chief commissioner. Unfortunately, disagreements with fellow commissioners led him to resign after six months. The others followed suit. On June 9, 2009, Indian and Northern Affairs Minister Chuck Strahl restarted the process by appointing Justice Murray Sinclair as LaForme's replacement. The minister chose Marie Wilson and Wilton Littlechild to serve as the other members of the commission. Chief Commissioner Sinclair, Manitoba's first Aboriginal justice, is Associate Chief Justice of Manitoba Provincial Court and has served as co-Commissioner of Manitoba's Aboriginal Justice Inquiry. The government gave the renewed commission a new five-year mandate. On June 11, 2008, a year and two days before the appointment of the new commissioners, Prime Minister Stephen Harper rose before the House of Commons and made a very long-awaited apology on behalf of the government of Canada for the 120 years of abuse that had taken place. Understandably, his apology provoked mixed reactions. Regardless of their feelings, however, most Aboriginal and non-Aboriginal Canadians hope that it will mark a milestone along the path to reconciliation.

CHAPTER 16

FROM BUFFALO HUNTING TO FARMING

We want cattle, tools, agricultural implements, and assistance in everything when we come to settle—our country is no longer able to support us.

—Chief Abraham Wikaskokiseyin's petition to the lieutenant-governor of the North-West Territories, April 13, 1871

I t is hard to imagine what it must have been like to give up the life of a hunter for that of a farmer. In the mid-nineteenth century, a Red River settler, Alexander Ross, thought about this challenge and wrote: "It is easier ... to hunt than to dig. The bow and arrow ... are lighter than a spade." Yet the Plains nations knew they would have to abandon their old livelihood before they shot their last buffalo. The rapid demise of the buffalo herds left them no choice and precluded the possibility of making the transformation slowly. In addition to facing the same hurdles as the white pioneers, they had to confront others that the government threw in front of them. Some groups made remarkable progress pursuing a new way of life despite overwhelming odds, and some fell by the wayside into a cycle of poverty and welfare dependence. Many of their Métis and mixed-blood cousins, who were deprived of land and most forms of government aid, fared even worse.

AN ALTERNATIVE TO STARVATION

Although the Plains nations had become the most highly specialized large-animal hunters in Aboriginal Canada by the nineteenth century, they were familiar with crop cultivation. Before contact most of them had obtained corn and some squash from the Mandan on the Missouri River, and between 1650 and the early 1800s the

A camp of Plains Cree about 1880, at a time when the collapse of the buffalo economy, low fur prices, and the difficulties they encountered learning to farm caused most Plains people to suffer acute hardships.

ancestors of the Plains Ojibwa brought horticulture from the upper Great Lakes area to the Red River valley and beyond. These Ojibwa did not abandon horticulture entirely after the merger of the Hudson's Bay Company and the North West Company in 1821, even though the new HBC paid them less for their surplus corn and squash. By the middle of the nineteenth century, declining hunting opportunities in the immediate vicinity of the Red River settlement encouraged these people to take a renewed interest in agriculture. Urging them on were the area's missionaries who advised them to take up farming at least on a part-time basis. In the 1830s the Reverend William Cockran of the Church Missionary Society established an agricultural settlement for local Ojibwa just north of Fort Garry, where he achieved modest success in teaching them to broaden their range of crops and adopt new methods.

In addition to those who worked their own fields, increasing numbers of Native people hired themselves out as seasonal farm hands and learned about farming in the process. In 1871 the Indian commissioner for Manitoba and the North-West Territories reported: "Although many years will elapse before they can be regarded as a settled population, settled in the sense of following agricultural pursuits, the Indians have already shown a disposition to provide against the vicissitudes of the chase by cultivating small patches of corn and potatoes. Moreover, in the province of Manitoba, where labour is scarce, Indians give great assistance in gathering in the crops.... [A]t Portage La Prairie, both Chippewas [Ojibwa] and Sioux, were largely employed in the grain fields, and in other parishes I saw many farmers whose employees were nearly all Indians."

Some of the part-time farmers referred to in the commissioner's report were Plains Assiniboine and Cree who lived in Saskatchewan country. By mid-century, the buffalo herds were disappearing from this region too, so a few of the bands living in the Touchwood Hills began to farm. Askenootow, a Native lay teacher from the Church Missionary Society, seems to have been instrumental in this effort. He is better known by his Christian name, Charles Pratt.

The Cree historian Winona Stevenson, a descendant of Pratt's, has studied the emergence of a Native ministry and Pratt's work within it. Stevenson notes that non-Native people have written a great deal about the failure of Christian missions; she says it is time "to determine whether Native congregations considered these efforts successful or not in an Aboriginal context. In particular, what did Indian missions do to help the people they served survive as distinct societies?" Those prairie missions that left a legacy of marginal agriculture and syncretic Christianity were considered failures by the standards set in nineteenth-century London, but is that how the Native people viewed them? Stevenson does not think so. She points out that missionaries "offered agriculture as an alternative to starvation at a very critical stage in some bands' histories. It is likely, then, that Indian peoples considered their adoption, or adaptation, of Christianity successful because it helped them to survive under trying conditions."

Pratt's story is fascinating in this context. He was born in the Qu'Appelle valley about 1816. His mother was an Assiniboine and his father was of mixed French and Native—probably Cree—parentage. The Pratt family belonged to a group of Assiniboine and Cree known as the Young Dogs. It was later led by Pratt's younger first cousin, the famous chief Piapot. Piapot's followers were among the most fiercely independent buffalo hunters of their day—a reputation they retained to the end of the buffalo-hunting era. They were also forward-looking people. When the HBC and NWC joined forces, the Young Dogs understood that the new company would be in a much stronger position. They were very aware that the HBC traders held those who were able to read and write in the highest regard, and that these skills enabled one to understand what the traders wrote in their accounts. It would be in the group's best interests, they decided, to have one of their own boys educated by white men. Pratt was selected.

The Church Missionary Society of London set up a school at Red River, under the direction of the Reverend John West, to train Native missionaries. Between 1820 and 1823, West combed the countryside looking for recruits. He had to spend a considerable amount of time persuading families to allow their children to attend his school. This was not necessary in Pratt's case; the Young Dogs sent him without being asked.

By all accounts, Pratt was a good student. He applied himself to his Bible studies, and learned to read, write, and farm. Apart from the long-established missionary tradition of equating civilization with husbandry, West had a pragmatic reason for teaching his students how to farm. His institution, which had to be as self-sufficient as possible, depended on the farm and produce its pupils grew and the country food they obtained. Significantly, most of the school's graduates went to work on local farms in the colony before they pursued other careers—mostly as servants in the HBC or in the ministry.

Askenootow (Charles Pratt), c. 1850s. As a lay teacher of the Church Missionary Society, he worked tirelessly to help his people make the transition from buffalo hunting to farming in the Touchwood Hills area of Saskatchewan.

Pratt followed a slightly different course. After spending a little more than ten years as a student, he returned to the prairies of Saskatchewan and lived as a buffalo hunter for two years. In 1835 he signed up as a bowsman on the HBC boat brigades and worked his way up to steersman over the next twelve years. In 1847 he left the company to take up hunting again—this time at the south end of Lake Manitoba. Here, he also did volunteer missionary work. The Church Missionary Society decided to retain Pratt as a lay teacher in 1850, and a year later it sent him to Fort Pelly, the HBC's district headquarters for the Swan River district. Pratt's people frequented the post at that time. His respect for and understanding of the customs of his relatives and those of other nations earned him a warm welcome. Even the medicine men, who had reason to regard his Christian message as a threat, cordially accepted him.

In 1852 and 1853 Pratt wintered at the Qu'Appelle mission among his immediate relatives. At this time he became a life-long friend of Chief George Gordon, whose family often hunted buffalo with Pratt's family. In 1858 the Gordons moved north to join Pratt and his family after the Church Missionary Society ordered him to build a new mission in the Touchwood Hills. This area was beyond the diminishing buffalo ranges, which was one of the reasons that Pratt persuaded his friends to take up farming. He was dedicated to their survival above all else and did everything he could to help them succeed. He gave them seed from his own limited supplies; he provided each convert with a young heifer, and on one occasion he butchered his only bull to feed the struggling would-be farmers.

By the 1870s Pratt had become critical of the Church Missionary Society for not offering more material assistance. He thought that the government of Canada might be more helpful and wanted his people to sign a treaty for this reason. His optimism faded rapidly after the agreement was signed. Short-sighted government policies and attitudes, adverse weather, and harsh economic times were among the chief obstacles to his group's success as farmers. "Pratt died lamenting the state of his world and the plight of his people," says Stevenson, "but he was a *Nehiyow* [one of the people], and his world was *Nehiyawishcikewin* [of them], despite his mixed ancestry. His last journal entry dated 13 July 1884 indicates that his Christian faith in the afterlife kept him, and possibly others, going through times that offered little hope."

THE PRAIRIE TREATIES

Treaties 1, 2, 4, 6, and 7 established Canada's obligation to help the Plains nations become farmers and forced the federal government to become, albeit reluctantly, a partner in the undertaking. During negotiations for Treaties 1 and 2, for instance, the Ojibwa and Swampy Cree of Manitoba refused to come to terms until the treaty commissioners verbally agreed to help their people take up farming. Although the commissioners thought they lacked the authority to make such commitments, they did attach a memorandum of what they called "outside promises" to the treaties. These promises included the pledge to provide "in lieu of a yoke of oxen for each reserve, a bull for each, and a cow for each Chief; a boar for each reserve and a sow for each Chief, and a male and female of each kind of animal raised by farmers ... when the Indians are prepared to receive them. These animals and their issue to be Government property, but to be allowed for the use of the Indians, under the superintendence and control of the Indian Commissioner." The commissioners also offered "a plough and harrow for each settler cultivating the ground." In response to pressure from Manitoba nations, the federal government made these promises formal parts of Treaties 1 and 2 in 1875.

These first two treaties set an important precedent. The nations that negotiated afterwards insisted that improvements be made to the crucial agricultural assistance clauses. In Treaty 4, the government agreed to provide any band "who are now actually cultivating the soil, or who shall hereafter settle on their reserves and commence to break up the land ..." with "two hoes, one spade, one scythe and one axe for every family so actually cultivating, and enough seed wheat, barley, oats and potatoes to plant such land as they have broken up; also one plough and two harrows for every ten families so cultivating as aforesaid, and also to each Chief for the use of his band ... one yoke of oxen, one bull, four cows, a chest of ordinary carpenter's tools, five hand saws, five augers, one cross-cut saw, one pit-saw, the necessary files and one grindstone." The treaty stipulated that this equipment, live-stock, and seed were "to be given once and for all, for the encouragement of the practice of agriculture among the Indians."

The Cree living in the fertile belt of the Saskatchewan River valley and the bordering parklands thought Treaty 4 failed to provide an adequate base to establish a farming way of life. They were particularly anxious about their future because they lived much farther away from the shrinking buffalo range than the Touchwood Hills people and other Treaty 4 groups. In 1871 Chief Wikaskokiseyin expressed the concerns of these northernmost Plains nations and asked the government to help them take up farming. Another Cree chief, Ku-ye-win (The Eagle), stated: "We never shed any white man's blood, and have always been friendly with the whites, and want workmen, carpenters and farmers to assist us when we settle." This wise chief realized that supplies and equipment alone would not suffice; his people needed to be taught how to use them. Apparently many other Cree shared his anxiety about this issue. When they submitted their official report on Treaty 6 negotiations, the government's commissioners wrote: "The Indians ... displayed a strong desire of instruction in farming, and appealed for the aid of missionaries and teachers." The commissioners reported that they told the Cree that for farming instruction they "must rely on the churches, representatives of whom were present from the Church of England, the Methodist, the Presbyterian and the Roman Catholic Church."

Although the treaty commissioner, Alexander Morris, was unwilling to provide farming instructors, Native people in the Treaty 6 region forced him to offer more liberal supply and equipment allowances. Each farming family would receive four hoes, two spades, two scythes and a whetstone, two hay forks, and two reaping hooks. Every three families were promised one plough and one harrow. And each band was entitled to one cross-cut saw, one handsaw, one pit-saw along with the required files and grindstones; enough wheat, barley, oats, and potato seed to plant their cultivated lands; and four oxen, a bull and six cows, and a boar and two sows. As in Treaty 4, the negotiators promised each chief a chest of carpenter's tools.

Negotiations with the Siksika, Piikani, Kainaiwa, Tsuu T'ina, and Chiniki (Stoney) people of what is now southern Alberta began in 1877. According to government officials, these people were "the most warlike and intelligent but intractable bands of the North-West." Treaty commissioners thought they were "unlikely to become farmers, but as the country they inhabit presents unusual facilities for that industry, they may be induced to adopt a pastoral life." Although these nations continued to be committed to the buffalo hunt, in 1876 a Catholic missionary, Father Constantine Scollen, told the government that the Siksika people had "an awful dread of the future" because they feared that the white settlers would dispossess them "without ceremony." Scollen thought they had good reason for such fears. Advancing settlement would drive away the buffalo, leaving the Siksika "the most helpless Indians in the country, and unaccustomed to anything else but hunting buffalo." When the government negotiated Treaty 7 a year later, Father Scollen helped the treaty commissioners complete their work.

Unlike other prairie treaties, Treaty 7 focused on the provision of livestock: "for every family of five persons and under, two cows; for every family of more than five persons and less than ten persons, three cows; for every family over ten persons, four cows; and every Head and Minor Chief and every Stony Chief, for the use of their Bands, one bull." The commissioners assured those who wanted to combine stock raising with crop cultivation that they would receive the kinds of equipment allotments and seed promised in the previous treaties, although the number of cows would be reduced by one a family. In 1877 Commissioner David Laird, who became lieutenant-governor of the North-West Territories four years later, said that these somewhat different provisions reflected Native demands and local conditions. He wrote: "The Stonies are the only Indians adhering to this treaty who desired agricultural implements and seed. The promises, therefore, respecting these things may be understood as merely applicable to that tribe. The Siksika and Kainaiwa asked for nothing of this kind; they preferred cattle ... the Commissioners being fully of the opinion that such were likely to be much more serviceable to them than seed and implements, encouraged them in their request."

This last concession was not costly for the government. Cattle were available at inexpensive rates at Fort McLeod (south of Calgary), and the government could have them delivered to the surrounding nations at minimal expense. Laird optimistically thought it would be cheaper for the government to supply the livestock called for in Treaty 7 than it would be to furnish the tools and seed promised in Treaties 4 and 6.

An Abortive Start

Even before the nations of present-day Alberta signed Treaty 7, serious problems had arisen in the prairies to the east as the various nations and government officials disagreed about how and when to implement the agricultural clauses of Treaty 4. Chief Gordon's band, and a few of the other bands in the Treaty 4 area, demanded that the government distribute the promised livestock, seed, and equipment immediately. However, the minister of the Interior and other officials in Ottawa had not anticipated that the nations would make this request so soon. They had thought the Plains people would hunt buffalo for a few more years before selecting their reserves and settling down. Ottawa stalled the petitioners by reminding them that the agreement explicitly stated that only those who actually were cultivating the soil or had settled on reserves were eligible for these supplies. This put the bands in an impossible situation: they could not settle on their reserves until the government surveyed them, and they could not break the ground and plant crops without draft animals, ploughs, and seed.

Some local government agents sympathized with the predicament of the Native people and lobbied on their behalf. In the summer of 1875, the Treaty 4 commissioner, W. J. Christie, a retired HBC chief factor from the Saskatchewan district, pleaded with the government to provide all treaty Indians who wanted to take up farming with the wherewithal to do so. In response, Ottawa authorized one of its land surveyors, who was working in the Touchwood Hills, to distribute equipment and livestock in that district. But he received the order too late in the autumn to act on it, and in any event, the Native people had not yet constructed the buildings needed to shelter the cattle in the winter.

The government also hesitated to fulfil its treaty obligations because it was afraid that the bands would sell any equipment they obtained to settlers at discount rates. When Angus McKay, a leading Métis from Red River, replaced Christie as government agent for Treaty 4 in 1876, he was ordered to put the letters "ID" (Indian Department) on all tools. By doing this the government claimed ownership of the equipment that rightfully belonged to the bands that had signed the treaty.

McKay, like Christie before him, was very supportive of the Native people he served. The progress some bands were making in the face of so many adversities impressed him. For example, he noted in a report that a few groups were building animal shelters and putting up hay in anticipation of receiving cattle; however, it was difficult for them to build anything without saws and work animals to haul wood. By chronicling these problems, McKay drew the suspicion of his superiors, who concluded that as a Métis he perhaps identified too strongly with his Indian clients. After one season, Indian Affairs transferred him out of the Treaty 4 area and into more remote northern Manitoba. Tensions like this often arose between civil servants in the field and those at headquarters. Unfortunately for Native people, Indian agents, fisheries officers, and other officials who sided with them in their attempts to carve out a niche for themselves were usually replaced. It also became commonplace for senior government officials to label anyone who relayed Indian complaints a troublemaker.

Of course not every problem the Native people of the western interior faced in dealing with the government was the result of bad faith or incompetence on the part of senior officials and politicians. The Canadian government had many hurdles to overcome as it struggled to create the administrative apparatus it needed to survey and govern the new territory. In particular, there was no distribution system in place to deliver the promised agricultural equipment and supplies. Eventually officials dealt with this issue by hiring the HBC and the I. G. Baker Company of Montana to deliver everything that the Department of Indian Affairs and other government departments had promised.

Late in the summer of 1875, the surveys of the Treaty 4 reserves began with the forty-eight-square-mile area the Gordon band had selected on the west side of the Little Touchwood Hills. By then, the band had twenty acres under cultivation. The surveying of other reserves in the treaty area followed, although slowly, and Allan MacDonald, the Indian agent who replaced McKay, distributed the treaty tools and equipment. MacDonald, the mixed-blood son of an HBC factor, like McKay of mixed ancestry, pointed out to Ottawa that the planting season coin-

Siksika farmers hand sowing a field. The short growing season on the prairies meant that labour-intensive farming was highly risky; it took too long to sow and harvest crops by hand.

cided with the time when the bands tended to be short of food. Low food stocks meant that the would-be farmers often had no choice but to go hunting at inopportune times. Occasionally they even had to eat their seed. MacDonald warned that unless the government provided food in the spring, or the money to buy it, the hungry Indians would not plant any seed. He noted that a clause in Treaty 6 said that "there shall be granted to the Indians included under the Chiefs adhering to the treaty at [Fort] Carlton, each spring, the sum of one thousand dollars to be expended for them by Her Majesty's Indians Agents, in the purchase of provisions for the use of such of the band as are actually settled on the reserves and are engaged in cultivating the soil, to assist them in such cultivation." MacDonald proposed that the government pay annuities on the reserves to give the Indians an incentive to settle there and devote themselves to farming.

Native leaders knew that learning husbandry was the only way to save their people from starvation, but problems continued to mount. Although Indian agents had been ordered to provide instruction in 1876, they did not have the time to do this, given their other responsibilities and the large territories that they had to oversee. The agents asked the department to hire special teachers. By 1878 the Plains nations faced disaster because of the government's failure to make significant headway in providing agricultural instruction and the rapidly declining buffalo population. The government was financially strapped, however, and lacked the will to help treaty Indians become farmers. In the spring of 1878, the minister of the Interior, David Mills, approved only token funds, and he refused to make an appropriation for food at planting time. The Treaty 6 Indians received only half the appropriation for food that they were entitled to. As a result, many Indians starved the next winter; others had to eat their horses and dogs to stay alive. The historian Sarah Carter argues in *Lost Harvests* that the government denied that food was in short supply and held Indians responsible for their own misfortune. Admitting otherwise would have tarnished the image of the West as a land of milk and honey—the picture they were promoting in immigration posters and pamphlets.

The mounting crisis in the West and the fear of Native violence finally led Ottawa to implement new policies for teaching treaty Indians how to farm. Officials decided to create a number of model "home farms" in the Treaty 4 and 6 areas. In addition to teaching, the instructors who operated these farms were supposed to produce enough food to feed the Plains bands until they became self-sustaining. The facilities were also supposed to serve as distribution centres for the agricultural supplies and equipment destined for the surrounding reserves. In the Treaty 7 region, the government created two large supply farms near Fort McLeod and Fort Calgary to produce food.

Given the tough economic climate of the times, the dual-purpose plan seemed sensible enough. Unfortunately the program got off to a bad start. The first instructors were patronage appointees. They mostly came from Ontario; they knew little, if anything, about the Indians they were supposed to teach; and a few of them were ignorant about farming. Eventually even Sir John A. Macdonald had to admit that some of the instructors knew less about farming than the Indians did! The instructors faced the additional handicap of often receiving the supplies and equipment they needed too late in the season. And frequently the supplies were substandard. When the Indians succeeded in harvesting crops or raising livestock, they often found themselves in disputes with the local teachers over ownership. The Indians understandably thought the food and animals belonged to them—they had helped in their production and owned the reserve land. On the other hand, many of the instructors thought that they had the right to sell the farm's produce.

By 1880 the government decided that it could avoid some of the problems it was experiencing by hiring more instructors from the West. It also opted to locate model farms off-reserve, and, incredibly, to operate these facilities without Native labourers. As a consequence, the reorganized farms no longer served a useful purpose and were abandoned by 1884. While the experiment ran its course, the struggling

Indian farmers continued to be hampered by inadequate supplies of food and clothing and by substandard equipment.

The attempt by Plains bands to learn large-scale grain farming was probably doomed to failure from the outset. Even Europeans and Canadians had yet to develop satisfactory farming techniques and field crops for the short, dry, and windy growing season of Canada's prairie West. Not until 1904 did government experimental farms succeed in developing the frost-resistant Marquis wheat, which was the mainstay of prairie grain farmers after it became available in 1907. When harvests did look promising, all too often plagues of locusts destroyed the crops. The sorry record of farming in the Red River colony prior to the 1880s had already shown that farming on the prairies was a very high-risk enterprise in the late nineteenth century. It is one of the tragic ironies of western Canadian history that former buffalo hunters found themselves in the vanguard of experimental farmers trying to

A Blackfoot Confederacy delegation in Ottawa, 1886. After the North-West Rebellion of 1885, most Aboriginal nations sought to address their political grievances by petitioning and sending delegations to the federal government in Ottawa or to the British government in London. Front row (left to right): North Axe (North Piikani) and One Spot (Kainaiwa); middle row: Three Bulls (Siksika), Crowfoot (Siksika), and Red Crow (Kainaiwa); back row: Father Albert Lacombe and Jean L'Heureux.

adapt an ancient humid-land agricultural system developed in the Old World to the semi-arid environment of the Canadian prairies.

Efforts to promote cattle ranching were somewhat more successful, particularly in the Treaty 7 area of present-day southern Alberta. In 1894 the government offered to exchange horses for cattle. Horses remained a symbol of wealth to the Plains nations, but some Kainaiwa leaders opted for the swap. Crop-Eared-Wolf and Red Crow took fifteen head each and the Siksika people Old Woman and Sleeps-on-Top swapped for ten each. From this core stock the Kainaiwa built up a herd numbering over fifteen hundred head of cattle by the turn of the century, thereby establishing themselves as successful ranchers in the foothills of Alberta.

Unfortunately, Hayter Reed's rise to prominence in Indian Affairs after 1885 worked against the Plains nations' attempts to become commercial crop farmers. Reed rejected the view of many of his colleagues that the Indians were trying to succeed. He believed Native people exaggerated their hardships, even though many newspaper articles and settlers' reports verified their stories. Reed argued that Indians merely wanted to avoid work while accepting the government's largess. After the North-West Rebellion of 1885, his outlook struck a very responsive chord with Ottawa politicians.

Reflecting his negative attitudes towards Native culture, Reed asserted that the traditional communal approach to economic activities prevented Indians from becoming productive farmers. Like most whites, he believed that a strong sense of individual ownership was a prerequisite for success in farming and an essential aspect of assimilation. In 1888 he introduced a program of surveying the western prairie reserves into separate parcels so that the "progressive" Indians could operate their own farms. He also pushed this scheme because he thought it would pave the way for the eventual breakup of the reserves.

The newcomers to the prairies were becoming more vocal in their objections to government efforts aimed at teaching Indians to become successful farmers. Obviously economic self-interest lay behind their protests. The market that Indian Affairs provided was important to the settlers, and many of them did not want to see the Native people become self-sufficient, much less competitors in the small regional markets. For the most part the Canadian government supported the settlers because it was trying to promote the development of the prairies and had assured immigrants that there would be markets for their produce.

Indian Affairs was eager to reduce its relief expenditures, but it had to consider the new immigrants' demands too. When Hayter Reed took over as Indian commissioner for the North-West Territories in 1888, he promptly developed a new farm policy that attempted to address both issues. Its aim was to remake Indian families into self-supporting peasant families who would not compete with whites. Besides political considerations, theories about cultural evolution shaped the commissioner's thinking. Reed claimed that buffalo hunters could not become mechanized grain farmers without first becoming yeoman farmers. They would need to make their own simple equipment and produce their food without the aid of machinery. Reed opposed the use of machinery because it encouraged Indians to pool their resources to buy it and this undermined the department's goal of promoting individualism. Also, it fostered commercial grain growing at the expense of subsistence food production.

Cree farmers at Whitefish Lake, Saskatchewan, with a steam tractor and thresher, late nineteenth century. Beginning in 1888, the yeoman-farmer scheme of the Department of Indian Affairs discouraged Native farmers from purchasing machinery.

Even in its day, this peasant-farmer plan was ludicrous and most Indian agents strongly opposed it. Nonetheless, Reed pressed forward. He used a series of amendments to the Indian Act passed by Parliament between 1880 and 1882 that prohibited Indians from selling any grain, root crop, or other produce without first obtaining a permit to do so from their local agent or farm instructor. Anyone who bought contraband produce could be prosecuted. Originally this permit system was intended to protect Indians from being taken advantage of by unscrupulous millers and others who bought their produce, but Reed used the scheme to limit Indian participation in the budding commercial economy. After 1891 merchants had to obtain a permit from Indian Affairs to trade with Indians.

Restricting the use of credit was another feature of Reed's plan. Like their white counterparts, Native farmers bought most of their machinery and a variety of goods on credit. This would not have been a new experience for these people, given their participation in the fur, buffalo, and hide trades. However, the problem Plains nations faced in this new economic climate was similar to the one Pacific Coast Indian commercial fishermen faced—the Indian Act forbade mortgaging reserve lands for any purpose. Originally, Parliament had enacted this provision with the admirable intention of protecting the Indians' stake in the land. But the lack of collateral put Indians at a disadvantage compared with white immigrants when it came to obtaining essential lines of credit. Indian farmers had no choice but to let farm-equipment dealers and merchants hold liens on the goods they bought. It was a highly risky arrangement. The merchants could, and often did, repossess what they had sold, keeping any payments their Native customers had made before they defaulted. Indian Affairs normally cited this risk, and the potential for abuse by white creditors, as the reason for tightly controlling Native access to credit, but it was no secret that promoting Reed's scheme was the true reason.

For many bands, the peasant-farmer program was a retrogressive step. On the Assiniboine reserve near the present town of Indian Head, Saskatchewan, for instance, farmers had far too many acres of grain under cultivation to harvest it by hand. The slow pace of hand harvesting also added considerably to the risk of crop failure because of the threat of hail storms and early frost. Likewise, without the use of horse-drawn mowers and rakes, the haying season was too short to yield enough feed to support sizable herds of cattle.

Reed's yeoman-farmer project was doomed to failure. Not surprisingly, Native people found ways to get around the government's restrictions. According to the economic historian Carl Beal, participation in a lively black market in farm produce and increasing involvement in livestock production were the most important avenues. Livestock production offered an entrée into the market economy for two reasons. First, horses were the private property of Indians because they had not obtained them under treaty. Second, Indian Affairs did not include cattle and other livestock in the permit system. This meant that Indians could sell livestock and the products derived from them without having to obtain the local agent's approval. Such considerations, and a rising market for Canadian beef in England, led to a substantial increase in livestock ownership, especially cattle, between 1886 and 1892. In 1892, however, the government extended the permit system to this sector of the reserve economies, which led some groups, such as the Sioux living on the Oak Lake reserve in southwestern Manitoba, to lose interest in cattle raising.

Another reason that Reed's plan was only partially successful was that it conflicted with the overriding departmental goal of keeping clothing and provisioning costs to a minimum. Agents encouraged Indians to sell hay and other commodities, to cut wood, and to work as labourers off-reserve so that they could use their earnings to buy necessities. Accordingly, agents often approved purchases of equipment that facilitated hay making, wood cutting, and freighting. In fact, agents generally approved Indian requests to buy most types of machinery. They usually withheld approval only when they thought the money was needed to purchase food and clothing. Some agents that did not apply Reed's rules stringently lost their positions for insubordination. Finally, in 1896, the newly elected Liberal administration of Wilfrid Laurier dismissed Reed when it reorganized the government ministries and made a new series of patronage appointments. Afterwards, senior Department of Indian Affairs officials did not pursue the peasant-farming program with the same zeal as before, but vestiges remained.

In the end, the yeoman-farmer policy seemed to have had its worst impact on Plains bands' crop production, especially wheat. Regrettably, this happened at the same time that large-scale commercial grain production was being established on the prairies by immigrant farmers. Most reserve farmers fell behind their non-Native counterparts at this time and were never able to catch up with them again.

TAKING AND DIVIDING RESERVE LAND

Aside from these myriad problems, the Plains bands were increasingly pressed to yield up portions of their reserves to the land-hungry immigrants. When the Laurier administration came to power, Clifford Sifton became minister of the Interior and thus Indian Affairs. By this time the Immigration Branch was also part of this ministry, and Sifton worked tirelessly to recruit settlers. As well as overhauling the federal administrative structure to make it easier for newcomers to obtain Crown land, he tried to make more land available to them by freeing up tracts that were tied up in grants to railways and to Native groups. Sifton thought he could carve up reserves by simply appropriating the desired lands by executive order. The Justice Department, however, promptly pointed out that according to the Indian Act, he could not acquire these parcels without first obtaining the consent of the bands concerned.

Although Sifton could not take unilateral action against Aboriginal land rights, the erosion of the reserves occurred anyway. Politicians and department officials offered Native groups a variety of inducements to pressure them into selling. They were told, for example, that the proceeds from land sales could relieve economic distress on the reserves, pay off old debts, or buy much-needed farm equipment. In spite of these inducements and considerations, many band councils opposed the sale of reserve lands. Their opposition led Frank Oliver, who succeeded Sifton, to amend the Indian Act in 1906 so that band members could immediately share as much as 50

Dene people cutting oats with a three-horse team in the Treaty 8 area, 1899.

per cent of the proceeds from selling reserve lands. Previously, the act limited the amount to 10 per cent. Politicians hoped that with this change in place, needy band members, and those who wanted to reap short-term gains, would readily agree to land sales. As a further encouragement, government officials came with strongboxes of cash to the meetings called by bands to consider land surrenders.

In 1911 Oliver decided to eliminate the need to obtain band-council approval for these sales by introducing two critical amendments to the Indian Act. Section 46 gave municipalities or companies the right to expropriate parts of reserves to build roads, railways, or other public facilities subject to the approval of the federal government. Section 49(a) was even more alarming to Native leaders: it gave the government the right to relocate any reserve situated near a town of eight thousand or more residents without having to obtain the prior approval of the reserve's residents. Native people and their supporters referred to this sinister amendment as the Oliver Act.

By using these various means, the Laurier government managed to acquire Native lands at an unprecedented rate. Between 1896 and 1909, the Department of Indian Affairs bought and then sold almost three-quarters of a million acres for $2,156,517. The Treaty 7 bands of southern Alberta, who held some of the largest reserves in the country, lost the most land. In 1909 Ottawa forced a vote on the

Piikani reserve, which many band members later claimed was fraudulent. It led to the sale of 28,496 acres near Calgary. Three years later the government pressured the Siksika to sell 60,771 acres and in 1918 another 55,327. Although the Siksika received nearly $2 million for these lands (about half of their reserve), they reaped little long-term benefit from the proceeds. After building a few new homes, the government used most of the remaining money to pay costs it normally incurred discharging its obligation to these people. Other prairie bands who sold land had similar experiences.

Speculation and corruption played a part in the reserve-land-sales process. The most notorious example involved the deputy superintendent-general of Indian Affairs Frank Pedley, who served from 1903 to 1913, under both Sifton and Oliver. He conducted the sale of the St Peter's reserve, near Selkirk, Manitoba, in 1907. Local politicians claimed that Pedley's department bribed band members to effect the sale to the government at a price that was only one-fifth of its true market value. A later investigation by the Manitoba government confirmed substantial "irregularities."

After the turn of the century, the number of people living on many of the western prairie reserves began to increase as the Aboriginal population started to rebound. Indian agents were still assigning parcels of land to individual band members to encourage them to discontinue communal farming. However, growing reserve populations meant that these people had to reduce the size of their operations at the very time when their successful white neighbours were expanding theirs to take advantage of improved farm machinery and new agricultural practices, particularly dry-fallowing. This technique involved letting a portion of ploughed land lie idle every year to retard weed growth, build up soil moisture, and improve fertility. Most Native farmers' plots were too small to allow them to engage in this practice, so soil fertility declined and weeds became an acute problem. The sales of reserve haying lands, in turn, forced many Native families to abandon efforts to raise livestock.

During and immediately after the First World War, Plains Native farmers fell even further behind their white counterparts as horse-and-plough farming gave way to highly mechanized agriculture. Farmers had to operate on a larger scale than ever before, and farming became increasingly capital intensive. Most reserve farmers had little choice but to practise small-scale subsistence farming. Hugh Dempsey, historian of the Treaty 7 people, observed that by the time the Great Depression struck in 1929, most of the Native nations in southern Alberta lived

Two Native cowboys from the interior of British Columbia. In British Columbia and the prairie region, especially Alberta, many Indian groups developed successful ranching operations. Native men also worked as hired hands on non-Native ranches.

such a marginal existence that they were barely aware of the larger economic crisis that gripped the country. The lot of Plains Indian farmers did not improve when good times returned during the Second World War. The consolidation of small farms into larger units continued to be a major trend in off-reserve areas, making the Native farmers' small operations ever more anachronistic. Meanwhile, the very heavy investments white farmers made in various kinds of labour-saving machinery left Native people with very few seasonal job prospects. Poverty soon became a way of life on many prairie reserves.

Today the sorry legacy of reserve land alienation, allotments, and population pressure is evident even in the Treaty 7 area of southern Alberta, where some of the country's largest reserves are located. On the Piikani reserve, for instance, most farms are too small to be economically viable. Unfortunately, few Native communities have alternative ways to make a living. Those that do, have coal or petroleum resources on their lands, or they are located near urban centres where wage labour is a possibility.

A FORGOTTEN PEOPLE

As harsh as the economic realities were for treaty Indian farmers, what most Métis and mixed-blood people endured after 1885 was even worse. According to the terms of the Dominion Lands Act of 1879, the government had the right to satisfy their title claims by making grants of land according to the terms and conditions that it considered to be expedient. No distributions of land took place before 1885. Beginning that year, a succession of "Half-breed" scrip commissions effected

Firing stubble on the Piikani reserve, 1952. The Piikani developed ranching operations in the foothills of the Rocky Mountains.

some distribution. The 1899 addition to Treaty 8 set a precedent for giving Native people of mixed ancestry the choice of taking treaty or scrip. Scrip claimants had the option of taking a $240 certificate "redeemable at its face value in the purchase of Dominion land" or one that entitled them to 240 acres of land in areas still open for homesteading.

In the end, few Métis ever took up any land. Most of them chose cash certificates or they sold their land scrip at steep discounts to speculators. There were several reasons for this. Many Métis remained committed to a nomadic life of hunting, trapping, freighting, and working as seasonal labourers on farms, survey crews, and construction gangs. They were usually encouraged by local merchants and saloon keepers to take money scrip. A story that appeared in the *Edmonton Bulletin* of the time describes the arrival of a scrip commission: "The town had flush times for four days. The stores and saloons reaped a regular harvest, horses and cattle changed hands at lightning speed and at good figures, and the spring horse race absorbed whatever money could not conveniently be blown in any other way." By the time the Treaty 5 amendments were made in northern Manitoba and Treaty 10 was concluded in northern Saskatchewan, any Métis who might have wanted to settle on Dominion lands would have had to abandon their communities and travel either to the Peace River

Cree, Siksika, and Kainaiwa coal miners, 1933. In Alberta some reserves were able to develop diversified economies based on mineral resources.

area or to the arid lands of southern Saskatchewan or Alberta—the only places where surveyed lands were still open to homesteading.

At first their loss of land did not seem threatening to the western Métis. Unoccupied land was still plentiful and people could squat generally at will—particularly on unused road allowances and at the edges of recently built towns, where they found part-time employment. Once thousands of land-hungry immigrants began arriving on the scene towards the end of the century, though, squatting became very difficult, and most Métis had become too poor to buy land and settle down. The increasing racial intolerance that became a feature of the new immigrant society further marginalized people of mixed ancestry.

During the Depression years, probably no group suffered more on the prairies than these dispossessed people. In her book *Halfbreed*, Maria Campbell poignantly tells the story of her family's struggle to survive. After the North-West Rebellion of 1885, her ancestors fled to Spring River northwest of Prince Albert, where the rolling, lake-studded countryside supported a hunting and trapping way of life until the late 1920s. In 1929 the drought began, and most of the lakes dried up and the game became scarce. Campbell's family, and many other Métis living nearby, decided to take advantage of a new homesteading program. It offered a quarter section for

$10, provided that the homesteader broke the land in three years and made other improvements. If this was not done, the government kept the title to the property. The onset of the Dirty Thirties meant that few of the Métis homesteaders—or those of other backgrounds, for that matter—could buy the equipment or hire the help they needed to meet the government's terms. Campbell says that as a result, the government reclaimed most of the Métis homesteads in her area and offered them to immigrants—mostly from Germany and Sweden. Her family, their relatives, and many of their neighbours had nowhere to go but road right-of-ways and Crown lands. These squatters came to be known as the "Road Allowance People," and they lived in abject poverty. They were not entitled to any of the meagre benefits available to Indians, nor did municipal or provincial governments provide assistance.

As with many Métis families, the Campbells' situation did not improve significantly after the Depression. As late as the 1950s they would not have survived without her father's hunting and trapping—often done illegally in national parks, or out of season. They needed the meat for food and to earn a small income from its sale to surrounding settlers. Campbell has a vivid childhood memory of the day the game wardens came to her house and tricked her into showing them her father's hidden cache of meat by offering her the rare treat of a chocolate bar. She felt terribly guilty

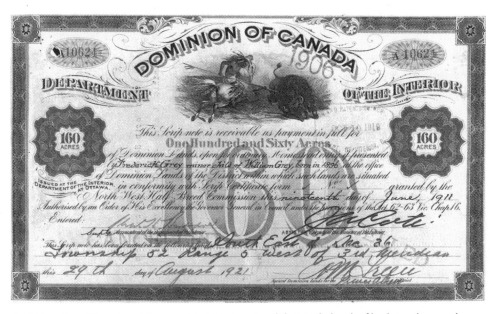

A Métis scrip certificate issued in 1911. Most Métis scrip ended up in the hands of land speculators, who bought it for cash at greatly discounted rates.

as the Mounties led her father away in handcuffs for a six-month jail term in Prince Albert: "It was a hard six months for all of us. We had no money and no meat. I had to set rabbit snares every day, and Mom and I would take the .22 and shoot partridges, ducks and whatever we could get. Mom was a terrible hunter." Like many desperate people on the prairies, they killed gophers—a plague to farmers—to receive one cent for each tail that they took to the municipal bounty officer. All Métis families lived in dread of welfare workers who could swoop in at any moment and carry off the children if they decided there was not enough food in the house.

Pairie Métis leaders decided to fight back yet again. Since the Canadian government steadfastly refused to have any responsibility for them, they turned to the provinces. In 1931 they created the Association des Métis d'Alberta et des Territoires du Nord-Ouest. It drafted and presented a petition to the legislature. Those who signed it demanded that the politicians address the issue of Métis land tenure. Because this was a time of growing unrest, the Alberta government was eager to avoid having these people galvanized into a more militant political force, so it undertook to relieve some of their problems. In 1934 it made Métis eligible to receive relief and medical care. The Métis association regarded this as only a first step and it continued to lobby hard for land settlements, registration of trap lines, welfare, and better education. The Alberta government responded by creating the Royal Commission Appointed to Investigate the Conditions of the Half-Breeds of Alberta—later dubbed the Ewing Commission after the judge who headed it—and by passing the Métis Population Betterment Act in 1938. The act, which adopted many of the commission's recommendations, led to the creation of twelve colonies in central and northern Alberta for approximately three hundred Métis families. It also provided health and social-service programs.

The long-term future of the Alberta Métis was by no means secure with the passage of the Métis Betterment Act. The province retained title to the approximately 1,235,500 acres of land the colonies encompassed. The government could, and did, amend the act at will in ways that were harmful to Métis interests. For instance, in 1940 it defined a Métis person in more restrictive terms, in 1941 it declared its right to create game reserves in the colonies, and in 1942 it broadened its taxing authority in the settlements. These problems led the Alberta Federation of Métis Settlement Associations (created in 1975) and the Métis Association of Alberta (organized in 1940 as the successor to the Association des Métis d'Alberta et des Territoires du Nord-Ouest) to press for change. Eventually the Alberta government granted the eight surviving Métis settlements title to 1,265,135 acres of land (without subsurface rights), limited self-government, and a seventeen-year financial package of $310 million. In 1987, the Métis Association of Alberta and the province concluded a framework agreement to improve services for Métis people and give them a stronger role in their delivery. In neighbouring Saskatchewan, the Métis also created an association in the 1930s to fight for their rights and to work for the improvement of their living conditions. As a result of their efforts, the province in 1940 introduced a scheme to establish a few training farms.

In the end, the failure of government agricultural-training programs, the loss of reserve lands, and the dispossession of most Métis made many descendants of the Plains nations and the Métis—two of the most powerful nineteenth-century Native groups—into paupers who scratched out a miserable existence on the edges of a land their ancestors had dominated and roamed over freely.

CHAPTER 17

THE MODERN FUR TRADE

Gone are the days of the picturesque and pompous Chief Factors. No longer do cannons roar and flags unfurl in honor of visiting potentates of the fur Trade.... The Fur Lords no longer rule the red Men.

—Philip Godsell, *Arctic Trader*, 1943

In the mid-1880s most Subarctic hunters and trappers were still experiencing hard economic times, with little hint that the best days of the industry lay just around the corner. A decade later, the rapid industrialization of northwestern Europe and eastern North America, the end of the worldwide Depression, and innovations in marketing furs created a huge market. Aboriginal trappers obtained record prices for their pelts and found themselves participating in a rapidly changing enterprise. They had to respond to the whims of fashion, renewed competition, the invasion of white trappers, resource depletion, and increasing government intervention in the name of conservation. These developments swept away the old mercantile fur trade, replacing it with an Industrial Age one that depended on railways, steamboats, the bush plane, and radio. The transformation affected the economic lives of Aboriginal groups in different ways, depending on where they lived in the North.

THE RENEWAL OF COMPETITION

Between the mid-1890s and the end of the First World War, Native trappers benefited from sharply rising fur prices and a growing demand for a wider array of furs. The spiralling prices for high-fashion furs encouraged manufacturers to devise ways of dying and treating low-priced furs—muskrat, hare, raccoon, skunk, and weasel (ermine)—to imitate more expensive ones. Often the dyed and treated furs became fashionable in their own right. Of these furs, only muskrat, which had been used as

268

A group of Inuit show a trader arctic fox at Revillon Frères' post at Cape Dufferin, Quebec, on the eve of the First World War. The strong market for this fur at the beginning of the twentieth century brought the fur trade to many areas of the Arctic for the first time.

lining material or for making cheap garments, had been highly significant in the old fur trade. During the first half of the twentieth century, mink, silver fox, and arctic fox became high-priced luxury furs. The popularity of arctic fox moved the fur trade into many central Arctic areas for the first time. Previously only the Inuit of the eastern and western Arctic had had any significant contact with whalers and fur traders, and the number of furs they traded was negligible compared with that of the Industrial Age.

The prospect of reaping easy profits brought large numbers of new traders to the north in search of Aboriginal customers. Major improvements in northern communication and transportation systems made it possible, and profitable, for them to make the journey. The telegraph, the telephone, and, after the First World War, the short-wave radio, linked northern fur-producing areas with regional, national, and world fur-marketing centres in St Louis, New York, Montreal, and London. The flow of market information reduced the financial risks fur buyers faced. In the past these risks had been considerable whenever markets moved downward because of the time it took buyers to ship their furs out of the Canadian North. Equally important, the modern communication technology meant that the Hudson's Bay Company no longer monopolized up-to-date market news. Previously this advantage had given it an edge over its competitors when setting fur prices.

Before the steam-railway era, high transportation costs barred independent traders with limited financial resources from operating in the North. The completion of the Canadian Pacific Railway began to alter the situation by opening the southern portions of the central Subarctic to small-scale fur buyers. The second era of railway construction, which ended in the early 1930s, opened old Rupert's Land to all comers. Meanwhile, the HBC and the Northern Transportation Company developed competing steamboat services in the Athabasca and Mackenzie districts between 1904 and 1926, making the western Subarctic available to large and small operators alike. Beginning in the 1920s, bush pilots using float planes visited remote areas formerly reached only by canoe and dog sled.

During the rough-and-tumble times of the early twentieth century, some of the newcomers to the Canadian fur trade built large companies that became formidable opponents of the conservative HBC. Revillon Frères of Paris was the most flamboyant and important of these concerns. The Revillons revolutionized the

Inuit hauling furs to a Revillon Frères' post on Hudson Bay in the early 1900s. Involvement in the fur trade drew many Inuit away from traditional winter hunting grounds to arctic-fox trapping areas and places where they had ready access to trading posts.

retailing of fur garments in the late nineteenth century by promoting the articles as popular fashion and by extending the market to include the burgeoning middle class. In 1899 they decided to cut costs by sidestepping fur agents and brokers and buying a substantial portion of their pelts directly from Canadian trappers. They soon operated posts throughout the Subarctic. The Revillons were particularly aggressive in the Hudson Bay–James Bay region—the traditional heartland of the HBC—and they were very active in the Arctic. By 1913 another firm, the Northern Trading Company of Edmonton, had established a network of posts throughout the Athabasca–Mackenzie region, and in 1918 the Boston-based furriers Lamson and Hubbard joined the fray in this region by creating the Lamson and Hubbard Canadian Company. By the time the First World War ended, this company operated thirty-five posts, and its sphere of operations extended as far east as Hudson Bay. All these changes meant that Native trappers found themselves in the advantageous position of being in a sellers' market. Competition for their business was more intense than it had been for their forefathers in the early nineteenth century.

Innovations in public transportation and communication systems encouraged the new competitors to introduce different business procedures. Cash fur buying was the most important of these. The risks inherent in cash purchases diminished as current price information became more accessible and buyers could get their furs to market more quickly. Aboriginal people welcomed the opportunity to sell some or all of their furs for cash because they obtained higher prices for them and they were free to buy the merchandise they wanted from the supplier offering the lowest prices. Under the old barter system, the fur buyers were also the retailers and they made handsome profits on both aspects of the transaction. The signing of treaties, especially Treaties 3, 5, and 6, had paved the way for cash merchandising. Small independent retailers had come to the central Subarctic to take part in the lively business that annuity payments generated. HBC officials complained that these newcomers followed government annuity-payment parties "like sharks after a sinking ship."

Competition for Native customers encouraged retailers to introduce new lines of merchandise—particularly "fancy dry goods" and, after the First World War, canned foods. The new railway towns offered the greatest array of goods at the most competitive prices. Aboriginal trappers who lived near the settlements often demanded cash for their furs so that they could shop in town, or buy merchandise through Eaton's mail-order catalogues. HBC post managers reported that many of their Native customers bought only groceries and other staples at the company's posts; they shopped for their "fancy goods" elsewhere.

Aboriginal trappers benefited in other ways from selling their furs for cash. During the mercantile era, traders usually bought a hunter's entire fur harvest, paying an average price for the lot. Cash fur buyers operated very differently. They paid top dollar for the highest grades of furs currently in vogue, so trappers sold their best furs to these buyers and took low-grade furs to traditional outlets such as the HBC.

These various innovations altered the character of the fur trade most profoundly in the hotly contested zones located next to transportation corridors. The HBC managers referred to these tracts as "frontier zones" and the establishments they operated within them as "line posts." Line posts were the forerunners of today's northern general stores. Typically, they were well stocked with dry goods and store foods, particularly canned goods. Cash, credit, and ready barter transactions all were commonplace at line posts. In the "remote districts," the old credit-barter fur trade continued, still featuring traditional high-priced staple goods.

Although most of these changes were beneficial to Native consumers, the emerging Industrial Age fur trade had some decidedly negative aspects as well. Slimmer profit margins and strong competition made it riskier for traders to provide credit. For this reason, senior HBC officials repeatedly tried to reduce the volume of their credit business. This was not in the best economic interests of Native trappers, however, because they still needed credit in lean times. Furthermore, many of them still held to the traditional view that the mutual obligation between trapper and trader was a cornerstone of the business. They regarded a refusal to offer credit as a breach of faith.

When war broke out in Europe in 1914, the London directors believed a worldwide collapse of fur markets would follow, making it impossible for Aboriginal people to pay back their debts. In the autumn of 1914, they ordered their men in Canada not to provide Native people with any credit. The most experienced HBC post managers knew that their clients would feel betrayed by this move and that it would hurt future business prospects. The managers devised clever schemes to circumvent the order, including keeping track of clandestine advances in unofficial accounts called "purgatory ledgers," which they hid from company inspectors and accountants. Many post managers did obey the order, however, to the dismay of their customers.

In fact, fur prices did not crash—they soared. American buyers hurried north and Native trappers eagerly welcomed them. In the Mackenzie River area, one trader reported that the North was "awash with cash" for the duration of the war. In later years HBC post managers looked back on 1914 as the "black year" in the fur

Repairing a Hudson's Bay Company birchbark canoe in northern Ontario, 1906. These craft continued to play an important role in supplying HBC outposts until bush plane services became available after the First World War.

trade. Many of them never regained the confidence of their Aboriginal customers, even though the company had resumed credit trading by the spring of 1915.

Obviously Aboriginal trappers had little economic clout when fur markets turned sour. These periodic episodes caused major shakeouts within the industry and gave the HBC opportunities to regain lost ground by taking over its financially troubled rivals. The 1920 21 recession was one notable example. It hobbled Lamson and Hubbard, enabling the HBC to buy control in 1922. The Northern Trading Company also ran into difficulties at this time. Its remaining assets were bought by the HBC during the Great Depression. Revillon Frères suffered a similar fate. By the late 1930s, only smaller operators remained in the business to oppose the HBC, but these buyers lacked the financial resources to provide extensive credit over long periods of time. This meant that many Native hunters who counted on obtaining advance outfits were forced to turn to the HBC, even though many of them no longer felt any loyalty to it.

As in previous competitive eras, the scramble for furs led to resource depletion in frontier zones and other areas, such as James Bay. The deprivation suffered by Aboriginal hunters and their families in these areas raised the question of who should provide relief on a continuing basis. Was the economic welfare of Native trappers the responsibility of fur traders or the government? HBC officials were divided on the issue. Some district managers and fur-department executives located in Winnipeg thought the company no longer had an obligation to look after the sick and destitute dependants of its clients. They argued that the Canadian government had assumed this responsibility in 1870. Most of the company men who championed this position had no Aboriginal relatives and did not have to face trappers or their families on a regular basis. One of their critics said that this made it easier for them to view the Aboriginal trapper as little more than a "fur-producing machine."

Many officers in the field—especially the post managers who had Native relatives—thought otherwise. They believed that the company could not simply abrogate its traditional responsibilities. Most Aboriginal people agreed. In 1920 a company inspector who was touring the Mackenzie River district wrote that some hunters had pointedly observed that "they were given a medal for long and faithful service, etc., but that did not help them in the least. If they were good and faithful hunters of the Company, they surely deserved some other form of recognition. The men at the posts received pensions, etc., but the hunters got only a medal, which did not prevent furs from getting scarce, or provide for them when they were ill or old."

The relief issue came to a head in the Arctic and James Bay district during the 1920s. The Arctic fur trade had been a mixed blessing to the Inuit from the outset, because the business depended almost entirely on the supplies of, and demand for, arctic fox. To trap this animal, Inuit often had to move to areas that were remote from their traditional hunting areas. Furthermore, arctic-fox populations fluctuate widely and prices were very volatile. Consequently, Inuit trappers experienced a feast-and-famine kind of existence. During downturns of the supply or price cycles, they suffered terrible economic hardship. Between the two world wars, the government of the Northwest Territories pressed the HBC to bank some of the profits it earned from the arctic-fox sales in good years to help the Inuit during the lean ones. However, the company held fast to the position that the welfare of these people was the government's responsibility.

In James Bay, the Swampy Cree frequently were not able to pay their debts and needed additional assistance to survive. Overhunting had brought fur shortages to the region, and senior HBC officials in Winnipeg repeatedly criticized the district manager for his heavy losses from bad debts. Finally, in 1924, the district manager, George Ray, had had enough of the carping. He wrote to the Winnipeg office: "If we continue as I proposed, the debt system as a means of keeping the Natives alive during the lean years, the Company may—in small measure—be reimbursed by the amounts the Natives may be persuaded to pay when the fat years shall come again.... [T]he Natives are our assets, ... we must keep them alive for future profits." The company yielded to this cold logic and decided that bad debts were to be regarded as economic aid and a normal cost of doing business.

While company officials debated these issues internally, they also pressed the federal government to shoulder a greater part of the relief burden. Rival traders and missionaries did likewise. Predictably, Indian Affairs responded very slowly and reluctantly to the appeals because of its preoccupation with keeping financial commitments and expenditures to a minimum. Government bureaucrats also feared that regular aid would discourage Aboriginal people from trying to support themselves by hunting and trapping. Finally, they balked at the idea of offering help to those groups remaining outside treaty areas. Nevertheless, government officials did provide some assistance. They arranged to have trading companies, missionaries, and the Royal Canadian Mounted Police distribute clothing and other federal relief supplies in areas not served by Indian agents. The problem with this approach was that traders and missionaries gave priority to their loyal customers or converts; and trading companies often charged the government premium prices for the goods they issued. The passage of the Family Allowance Act in 1944 alleviated some of these problems by including Indian and Inuit families under its provisions. The allowances could be paid in cash or supplies from a list of items approved by government agents.

GOVERNMENT CONSERVATION PROGRAMS

Recurrent resource-depletion problems in frontier zones can be traced to the growing number of non-Native hunters and trappers. Most of these intruders, who had ventured north as prospectors, miners, loggers, construction workers, farmers, and merchants, hunted and trapped on a part-time or cyclical basis. The income they earned from trapping grubstaked their other economic pursuits. When markets reached their cyclical peaks, these newcomers often left their jobs. This happened, for instance, just before the market crashed at the end of the First World War. For a short time, fur was more attractive than gold. Unemployed whites left the cities and headed into the bush during business recessions to eke out a living by hunting for a portion of their food and trapping to earn a meagre cash income. This happened in 1921–22 and again in the early 1930s.

Most of the white "highliners" were ruthless in pursuit of their quarry. They trespassed on the traditional hunting lands of Aboriginal bands, who called these

The trapper Isaiah Clark making out his order at Norway House, 1943. The chief clerk is the ex-Olympic Native runner Joe Keeper.

intruders "travelling trappers." Chief George Barker, who lived on the Hollow Water reserve in Manitoba, said, "These men used about 500 traps and traveled in groups of as many as eight, with good dog teams and sleds which enabled them to cover a lot of territory. They also moved each winter to new areas where fur was most plentiful." In the frontier zone of northern Ontario and in other areas, they intimidated Native trappers and sometimes drove them off their ancestral lands. Barker reported that a white trapper threatened him with a gun on his traditional muskrat-trapping area in the autumn of 1929. HBC officers stationed in the Athabasca-Mackenzie region complained that white trappers had become the scourge of the North by the end of the First World War.

Native people hoped that land treaties would provide Crown protection against the freebooters who now threatened them. In the negotiations leading up to Treaties 3 to 7, federal representatives indicated that the government would take action to safeguard fish, fur, and game resources; however, it was on the under-standing that Aboriginal people might also be subject to whatever general laws

Cree or Assiniboine Lodges in front of Rocky Mountain Fort,
April 1848, *by Paul Kane. Beginning in the late eighteenth century, fur
traders built a string of posts along the edge of the grasslands to gain access to
pemmican and other provisions that Plains buffalo hunters provided.*

Micmac Indians, 1839, *by Mary M. Chaplin. The family in this scene wear hooded
blanket coats known as* capot, *which were very popular trade items throughout Canada.*

SIR·JOS·JEBB.

Two Ottawa Chiefs who with Others Lately Came down from Michilimackinac, Lake
Huron, to Have a Talk with Their Great Father the King or His Representative, c. 1813.
*This is an important image of two Ottawa leaders at a turning-point in Native history — the War of 1812.
It accurately portrays Native dress and trade silver of the period.*

Native people dressed in potlatch attire, c. 1896. When the federal government enforced its ban against these important and colourful ceremonies during the early twentieth century, it seized the potlatch regalia of many West Coast people and shipped or sold the material to museums in eastern Canada and the United States.

Lorette, Quebec, was established for refugee Christian Huron and is one of the country's oldest reserve settlements. This watercolour by Henry William Barnard depicts the village in 1838.

The surrender of Poundmaker to Major-General Middleton at Battleford,
Saskatchewan, May 26, 1885.

This war shirt was presented by the Cree leader Sweet Grass (Wikaskokiseyin) to
Lieutenant-Governor Alexander Morris during treaty negotiations.

*A highly fanciful mid-nineteenth-century painting by Cornelius Krieghoff of a
Native hunter travelling on snowshoes in Quebec.*

Nicholas Vincent Isawahoni, a Huron Chief, holding a
Wampum Belt, 1825. *In the East, Native nations used these belts to record
treaties and other important events.*

Maydoc-game-kinungee [I hear the noise
of the deer] by Paul Kane, 1848. This Ojibwa
chief is wearing a captain's coat.

The Blackfoot leader Crowfoot addressing the Governor General of Canada, John D.
Sutherland, the Marquis of Lorne, September 10, 1881. Because of Lorne's link to Queen
Victoria through marriage to her fourth daughter, Native people thought that he was in a
special position to help them.

A collection of Hudson's Bay Company fur-trade articles, c. 1870. Blanket coats, knives, muskets — and whisky — were familiar items of the fur trade for hundreds of years.

legislators passed for that purpose. Accordingly, these treaties stipulated that Aboriginal people would still be able to hunt and fish on undeveloped surrendered lands "subject to such regulations as may from time to time be made by her [Majesty's] Government of her Dominion of Canada." At the time Native bands did not fully understand what implications this clause would have in the future. Shortly thereafter, they learned the hard way just how restrictive it could be.

In 1893 Ontario passed its first game-protection act; the federal government followed suit the next year with the Unorganized Territories Game Preservation Act. These laws established closed seasons for birds, large game, and fur-bearing animals; they banned "unsportsman like" practices such as the use of poisoned baits, hunting deer with dogs, and the use of snares to kill animals other than fur-bearing animals; and they provided game wardens for enforcement. These provisions remained corner-stones of subsequent game acts. The pioneering legislation of the 1890s did not seriously interfere with traditional Native practices because it exempted Aboriginal people from most of the restrictions in recognition of their special status.

Groups in the Athabasca River and Peace River areas expressed their worries about hunting restrictions during negotiations for Treaty 8. They had pressed the government for a treaty because news of the discovery of gold in the Klondike in 1896 triggered a stampede of gold seekers through the Athabasca, Peace River, and upper Mackenzie River areas as they made their way north from Edmonton. These reckless people poisoned Aboriginal hunting dogs in their quest for furs and caused widespread forest fires. They also destroyed Native peoples' traps and, in the Peace River country, stole their horses. Groups living in the vicinity of Fort St. John threatened to wage war against the intruders unless this mistreatment stopped and the government negotiated a treaty. During the treaty deliberations, federal negotiators repeatedly assured local leaders that the government would take measures to deal with their concerns in ways that would not seriously fetter their customary hunting practices. The local people signed the treaty in 1899, after having received these guarantees; it included essentially the same hunting- and fishing-rights clauses that were part of Treaties 3 to 7.

Just seven years later, the federal government broke its promise to Treaty 8 bands. In 1906, in an amendment to the Unorganized Territories Game Preservation Act, it imposed a temporary ban on beaver trapping by both Native and non-Native people. Beaver was an important country food, and the sale of beaver pelts provided enough income to buy necessities. It took an appeal to the courts to have this provision overturned as an infringement on the rights of Treaty 8 Aboriginal people.

An even more serious infringement occurred in 1917 when Parliament passed a new game act for the Northwest Territories. This piece of legislation, and the regulations that flowed from it in 1918, imposed closed seasons on moose, caribou, mink, muskrat, ptarmigan, wild geese, and wild ducks. It allowed resident Aboriginal people to hunt these animals out of season, but "only when such persons are actually in need of such game or eggs to prevent starvation." The local bands were furious. Commercial hunting and trapping had been well established in the region for more than one hundred years when they signed Treaty 8. Now they were being told that they would be allowed to pursue these activities only for subsistence purposes—and then only under extreme circumstances. In other words, the government would let them continue their old ways only as welfare cases.

In 1920 a large number of Tlicho, Dene, Slavey, and Yellowknife, who had assembled at Fort Resolution at treaty payment time, expressed their outrage about the restriction. Philip Godsell, an HBC trader, wrote an account of what transpired: "Pierre Mercredi, the factor [manager of the fort], told us that the Aboriginal people of whom there were about a thousand camped around, were in a most rebellious mood, determined not to take their treaty money on account of one of their number having been fined at Fort Smith that spring for killing a duck. This they said was entirely contrary to their treaty and if such was the White man's way of observing treaties they would have nothing to do with it." The local Indian agent and Mercredi took three days to persuade the disgruntled people to accept their treaty money. The assembled bands departed with the impression that they could hunt the game they needed without fear of arrest, provided that they neither wasted nor, much more important from the government's point of view, sold any of it.

Two formidable obstacles would continue to stand in the way of most Native efforts to protect their traditional hunting and fishing rights and practices, while simultaneously supporting wildlife management efforts of the state. First, Aboriginal people had to depend on Indian Affairs to represent them because of the Crown's general fiduciary obligations to protect their interests. And second, they found themselves confronted by a growing number of white pressure groups that took an active part in the formulation of government conservation policies and programs. Indian Affairs wanted to make sure that the tragedy that struck the Native buffalo-hunting economies of the prairies in the 1880s did not befall the hunting and trapping ones in the North. This type of disaster in the woodlands would leave many northern bands dependent on government financial support with little prospect of ever developing long-term alternative economic opportunities. For this reason,

Ottawa officials instructed Indian agents to counsel their clients to comply with game laws and regulations. Most agents did so, although some sympathized with the Native view that their treaty rights were being violated and encouraged Aboriginal people to press their claims and grievances. While the department promoted Native compliance, it also encouraged other government agencies, such as Fisheries, to be lenient with Aboriginal people when they enforced the acts.

The conservation movement that gained national attention in the 1910s posed serious problems for Native people because the growing number of naturalists, sports hunters, and sports fishermen who spearheaded it were keen to protect fish, game, and bird populations for their own pleasure. In general, these groups did not think that Aboriginal people deserved any preferential treatment regarding bag limits, hunting seasons, and hunting techniques. Such concessions, they believed, would interfere with "scientific" management practices. Over the years these special-interest groups lobbied very effectively for more stringent fish and game laws. Their representatives often served on the provincial advisory boards that helped draft conservation legislation. Sometimes, as happened in Saskatchewan, Native people were asked to serve on these boards, but they were unable to present their point of view effectively in the alien forums. The result was that conservation laws and regulations became ever more restrictive, protected the resources for non-Native commercial and sports uses, and made fewer accommodations for aboriginal commercial, ceremonial, and subsistence practices.

The Migratory Birds Convention Act of 1916 was one of the earliest pieces of federal legislation to reflect the interests of the new lobby groups; it dealt a cruel blow to Native culture in Canada. By the turn of the century, many North American migratory-bird populations were in sharp decline. This trend distressed gun manufacturers, sportsmen, bird-watchers, and naturalists. They lobbied Washington and Ottawa, demanding that something be done to address the problem. Jack Miner, a tireless campaigner for waterfowl conservation from Kingsville, Ontario, was a key player in this effort. He scoffed at the idea that Native people were conservationists and deserving of special consideration: "I have never heard one Indian even hint at conserving anything.... You cannot do anything for the Indians, nor have anything for the Indians, unless you control the Indians." The two governments, in response to pressure from Miner and others, worked together from 1914 to 1916 to draft a conservation agreement, which established closed seasons on a large number of birds and banned the collection of eggs of certain endangered species.

Although the Migratory Birds Convention Act did make special provisions for

Native people, it imposed restrictions that caused hardships for those groups depending heavily on waterfowl in the summer months. Some Native bands ignored the law and a few protested against it. In 1927, for example, the chiefs of the Fort Chipewyan band wrote to Duncan Campbell Scott to remind him that their treaty with the government (Treaty 8) predated the act and guaranteed their traditional hunting rights. Scott disagreed. He argued that the Migratory Birds Convention Act superseded the treaties and would have to be obeyed. His reply was predictable. Scott had helped to draft the convention as a member of the Advisory Board on Wild Life, which had been created in 1916 to formulate government conservation policy and propose legislation. Subsequently, the courts upheld Scott's view that Parliament had the power to unilaterally override Aboriginal treaty rights. Also, in Section 88 of the Indian Act, Parliament made Indians subject to all provincial laws of general application, such as large-game hunting and trapping legislation. By doing so it created a complex legal question about how to resolve situations where these laws clashed with treaty rights. When it transferred federal control of the natural resources of Manitoba, Saskatchewan, and Alberta to those provinces in 1930, it gave them the power to override the provisions of Treaties 1, 2, and 5 to 8 for the purposes of conservation. It was abuse of this sort that led Native leaders to seek and obtain constitutional protection for their existing Aboriginal and treaty rights in Section 35 (1) of the 1982 constitution.

Provincial conservation programs impinged on Aboriginal rights outside and inside treaty areas in a variety of ways. In 1925 the British Columbia government introduced a registered trapline plan. The idea was to give individual trappers a stake in conservation management by assigning them exclusive trapping rights in specific tracts of land. Some Native groups, such as those living in the southern James Bay watershed near the railway lines, proposed that the plan be introduced in their areas. These bands were aware that a similar scheme operated in parts of the United States, and hoped that the adoption of such a measure would block any further non-Native encroachment on their own hunting lands. In Manitoba George Barker and other Aboriginal leaders also lobbied for the plan. Barker, who took an interest in it after he had been threatened in his own territory, began pressing the Manitoba government for a registration program beginning in 1934; he had to wait fourteen years before the province began to experiment with the idea.

In other areas, bands opposed the registered trapline program because they regarded it as a threat to their treaty rights or Aboriginal claims. In the Peace River area of Treaty 8, for instance, many Native trappers held this view and the local

Indian agent encouraged them not to take part. These bands also knew that the proposed traplines were too small and would not yield sufficient game for their needs. In this respect, their objections recall the complaints made about the HBC's beaver-conservation program of the early nineteenth century, which gave priority to commercial rather than subsistence use of fur-bearing animals. This objection was not a major concern for most whites, or for many line-post Aboriginal bands either, because these people relied heavily on "store food." By the time many of the Peace River bands realized they had no choice but to take part in the registered trapline program, the best traplines had been awarded to whites.

In mainland British Columbia beyond the Treaty 8 area, Native groups had not signed treaties. Because they considered that the land and its resources still belonged to them, they maintained that the provincial government did not have the right to regulate their access to wildlife resources through a trapline allocation scheme, or any other conservation program, for that matter. In this way, treaty-rights issues, which emerged in the 1880s in British Columbia, became intertwined with wildlife-management concerns. Some Native groups opposed these schemes for additional reasons. The Gitxsan and Wet'suwet'en, for example, suspected that the government of British Columbia was intent on undermining their traditional communal arrangements by assigning traplines to individuals instead of to lineage groups. Eventually the Gitxsan and Wet'suwet'en houses worked around the problem by registering their traplines as companies.

Provincial and territorial governments were determined to introduce the trapline-registration program despite Native objections. British Columbia led the way in 1925, and by 1950 the prairie provinces, the Northwest Territories, Ontario, and Quebec had introduced trapline-registration schemes. Quebec was one of the last to do so, largely because it had addressed the problem of conflicting hunting and trapping interests much earlier by setting aside all the territory north of the Canadian National Railway between Sanmaur and Amos for exclusive Native use. In the end the trapline-registration systems did benefit many Aboriginal groups, whether intentionally or not, by helping to restore beaver and other fur stocks, and by keeping non-Native trappers from taking over all trapping areas. There was a high price to pay, however: trapline registration programs legitimized non-Native access to fur and game resources on undeveloped Crown land. Before this time, the Robinson treaties of 1850 and the numbered treaties that followed had given only Aboriginal people unrestricted access to these lands for traditional purposes.

Game and fur-bearing-animal preserves are a more recent manifestation of

Native trappers checking for muskrat breathing holes prior to setting traps. Even though it fetched comparatively low prices, muskrat figured prominently in many of the local Native trapping economies after Confederation.

provincial wildlife-management efforts. In the 1930s and 1940s, provincial authorities established vast beaver and muskrat preserves in the prairie provinces, northern Ontario, and Quebec. By the late 1940s, nearly all the land surrounding James Bay had been set aside. Private companies, notably the HBC, often helped to administer the refuges. In some regions, such as central Saskatchewan, Aboriginal people objected to these so-called sanctuaries, because they consisted of large tracts of undeveloped Crown land, which treaties guaranteed them access to for hunting and trapping purposes. The courts overruled such Native objections, taking the disingenuous position that preserves were, in fact, "developed" land. There is no doubt that this judicial interpretation was contrary to what the term meant to those who signed the treaties. Canadian and Aboriginal negotiators had made a distinction between "developed" and "undeveloped" land primarily on the basis of whether the land was used for agricultural, hydroelectric power generation, or mining purposes. For instance, the official government records of the discussions leading up to Treaties 3 and 4 reported that the chief representative for Canada told the nations that assembled at Fort Carlton in the summer of 1876: "You want to be at liberty to hunt as before. I told you we did not want to take that means of living from you, you have it as before, only this, if a man, whether Indian or Half-breed, had a good field of grain, you would not destroy it with your hunt...."

Some Native people did support the establishment of fur preserves, however, and sometimes helped manage the fur stocks within them. In Quebec, for instance, they acted as "tally men" who provided government officials with accurate counts of beaver populations. To address Aboriginal trappers' concerns about having their traditional trapping areas included within preserves, provincial governments across the country often granted them special harvesting privileges in fur preserves to mitigate the economic hardships they suffered when a portion of their land base was taken away.

Probably the best known of the early game parks is Wood Buffalo National Park in Alberta and the Northwest Territories. The Peace River country had teemed with wood buffalo and other game on Alexander Mackenzie's arrival there in 1792. He described the area around Vermilion Falls, near present-day Fort Vermilion, Alberta, as a place where "[o]n either side of the river, though invisible from it, are extensive plains, which abound in buffaloes, elks [wapiti], wolves, foxes, and bears.... At a considerable distance to the Westward, is an immense ridge of high land or mountains [Whitemud Hills] ... inhabited by great numbers of deer." The provision market generated by the fur trade destroyed this large-game hunters' paradise. The wood-bison herds were headed towards extinction barely one hundred years after Mackenzie visited the area.

Beginning in 1896, the herds came under the protection of the Unorganized Territories Game Preservation Act and their numbers began to increase thereafter. Word of plans to create a refuge for the expanding herds leaked out in 1921. The Dene living near Fort Smith immediately launched a protest with the local Indian agent. Afterwards he wrote: "[T]he possible creation of a large reserve west of [Fort] Smith, as reserve for the wood buffalo, caused a long and hostile discussion. The purpose of which was that from time immemorial they had made their living from this district, and that when they made treaty [8] they were solemnly assured, in the preamble to the treaty, that their former mode of life would not be interfered with except insofar as it would be in their interest, and would be necessary for the preservation of game." Sympathetic to his clients' concerns, he presented their case to Ottawa with the backing of the local Roman Catholic bishop. Although the government established the park anyway in 1922, the Treaty 8

Indians achieved a partial victory when they were "granted" the right to continue to hunt wildlife—except for wood buffalo—for subsistence purposes within the park boundaries. Local Métis, who had not signed Treaty 8, sought the same privileges, but their request was denied.

Wood Buffalo National Park proved to be a conservation success story, but its establishment caused considerable hardship among the local bands. After 1925 the buffalo population within the park increased rapidly as a result of the rigid enforcement of the hunting ban and the importation of young animals from another refuge—Wainwright Buffalo Park in Alberta. Meanwhile, the local people suffered severe deprivation because other game was too scarce to support them. Sometimes this drove the Aboriginal hunters to take buffalo illegally. If caught, they were severely penalized. A Fort Chipewyan hunter received a three-month sentence in the Fort Saskatchewan prison for shooting a buffalo. He was also banned forever from the park—a land where he had grown up and where his family and relatives still lived. While some government agents doled out this kind of tough punishment to the area's residents, other territorial officials were proposing that "large game hunters with wealth" be allowed to buy hunting permits in the interests of promoting tourism in the North!

These are but a sample of the frustrations and problems northern Aboriginal people experienced. In a sixty-year period that ended in the late 1920s, they had surrendered all the western Subarctic except for the Yukon. In doing so, they believed they had protected their cherished lifestyles through treaties with the Canadian government. For most of them, commercial fishing, hunting, and trapping had been customary ways of earning a living for a century or more before they signed the agreements. Sadly for them, senior government officials and the courts, in keeping with the theories of anthropologists of the day, equated traditional culture solely with subsistence. Accordingly, provincial and federal governments were willing to grant Aboriginal people special hunting, trapping, and fishing allowances only for subsistence purposes. However, given the long-standing interdependence of the commercial and subsistence sectors of bush economies, this approach made little sense to Native people. They used their fishing and trapping incomes to buy equipment and a growing array of staples. By arbitrarily separating subsistence use from commercial use when interpreting and implementing the crucial conservation sections of the treaties, the courts and government officials effectively denied full Aboriginal and treaty rights. Beginning in the 1980s with Regina v. Horseman, First Nations have asserted their commerical rights.

A Native woman ice fishing on Great Slave Lake, 1936. Winter fisheries, often operated by women, provided essential food supplies for Native families and trading posts.

Aboriginal people found themselves at the mercy of the local Indian agents or Royal Canadian Mounted Police officers who had the responsibility of deciding when local circumstances warranted hunting the protected wildlife. Understandably, treaty Indians felt betrayed. They fully recognized the need for conservation, which was in their interests too, but they had good reason to wonder who would benefit most from wildlife-management schemes and who would pay for them. It was beginning to look as though they were expected to make the sacrifices in return for government handouts. Today this remains a central issue in the legal battles of Aboriginal people for their economic rights.

Indian Affairs data show that in the 1920s and 1930s Native hunting and trapping incomes did not keep pace with the rising value of furs. There were several reasons for this. First, non-Native trappers increased their share of the total harvest. Second, the high prices some furs fetched encouraged the development of the fur-ranching business. By the Second World War, ranched furs accounted for almost all

Native men loading the Hudson's Bay Company's steamer Grahame *at Fort McMurray, Alberta, 1900. In the late nineteenth century, steamboats displaced York boats on the major routes. Small numbers of the displaced boat crewmen found work as longshoremen or as cutters of cordwood.*

silver-fox sales and nearly half of mink sales. This meant that an increasing portion of Aboriginal trappers' furs consisted of low-value pelts such as muskrat and hare. The populations of these animals fluctuated greatly, so in many respects a northern trapper's income was less predictable in the Industrial Age than it had been in the early contact days.

While trapping incomes became unpredictable, supplemental or alternative employment opportunities for Aboriginal people in the North diminished. The completion of railways, the expansion of steamboat service in the Athabasca and Mackenzie river districts, and the increased use of bush planes after the First World War meant that the HBC and its rivals needed far fewer Native people to haul furs and supplies. These changes had particularly devastating impacts on two of the oldest fur-trading communities in the North—York Factory and Moose Factory. In the 1860s York Factory still served as the supply depot for most of the HBC's posts in the western interior. Although the company imported most of its goods, European and mixed-blood craftsmen at the post (blacksmiths, braziers, bricklayers, carpenters, coopers, gunsmiths, and boat builders) produced an impressive array of trade goods and equipment. Depletion of the forests within one hundred miles of the post for construction materials and firewood meant that every summer armies of men had to forage for wood upriver, raft it to the post, and haul it into the storage yards. York Factory employed many local Swampy Cree during the summer as unskilled general labourers or as oarsmen on the boat brigades. These employment opportunities encouraged the Cree to establish a settlement nearby. By the 1870s, however, York Factory's overhead costs became too burdensome for the company, and it began to look for ways to curtail operations there.

Another concern of the HBC was its absolute dependence on Native labourers to operate the transportation system centred on York Factory. This workforce had become very independent minded and much more demanding in its terms. During the 1860s, for instance, York-boat-brigade crews repeatedly refused to carry the same size cargoes as formerly and intentionally travelled more slowly. At the post Native workers periodically engaged in work stoppages (referred to as "land meetings") during the summer to press for better wages. Inland, some crews went on strike in support of Riel and his followers at Red River in the summers of 1869 and 1870—costing the company dearly.

Island Lake York-boat crewmen. The strikes of some York-boat crews in support of the Métis during the summers of 1869 and 1870, and their demands for higher wages, led the Hudson's Bay Company to look for ways to lessen its dependence on Native workers.

The schooner Mink *in dry-dock in front of the "Moose Works," Moose Factory, about 1870. By the end of the century, this old fur-trading settlement had become a major shipbuilding and repairing facility for the Hudson's Bay Company. Men of mixed-blood ancestry dominated the labour force of the works.*

It is easy to understand why the company's directors looked forward to the day when railways and steamboats would enable them to disband the York-boat brigades and curtail operations at York Factory. They took their first steps in that direction in 1874 by moving the headquarters for the Northern Department from York Factory to Winnipeg. By the turn of the century, the once-great port of entry that linked the markets of Europe with the Aboriginal bands of northern Canada was nothing more than a comparatively small post. The company closed it entirely in 1957. The abandonment of the York-boat system also affected Oxford House, Norway House, and other communities whose Native residents had built York boats or worked on the brigades.

The Native community of Moose Factory was next to suffer. After 1821 this post served as the HBC's headquarters and supply base for the Southern Department, which at various times included all of present-day northern Ontario and the lands drained by rivers flowing into eastern and southeastern James Bay. Probably the most striking feature about the settlement was its large boat-building and repair facility—called the "Moose Works." By 1900 its mostly mixed-blood skilled and semi-skilled employees built schooners as large as sixty tons and a variety of smaller craft, including a steam tugboat. In addition, the HBC also employed mixed-bloods to operate a large farm, to maintain extensive warehouse facilities, to serve as long-shoremen, and to operate its "James Bay deep-sea fleet," which supplied the other bay-side posts of Rupert House, Eastmain, Great Whale River, Fort Albany, and Attawapiskat. Moose Factory, therefore, was one of the few communities with fur-trading roots where Aboriginal people of mixed ancestry learned a wide variety of skilled industrial trades. Those designated "Indians" by the company continued to be employed mostly as unskilled labour. At the turn of the century, the James Bay district manager underscored the importance of wage labour to the local residents when he observed that it was incorrect to think of Moose Factory as a fur-trading community any longer, inasmuch as nearly all the men who lived there derived most of their incomes from wage labour rather than from fur trapping or trading.

The community's glory days were nearly over, however. As early as the 1880s, local Native labourers struck for wage parity with construction and mainte-nance workers on the Canadian Pacific Railway located farther to the south. The heavy cost to the company of maintain-ing the community became more worri-some as fur-depletion problems in the James Bay region worsened. This drove the Swampy Cree out of the bush and into the community, where they turned to their employed relatives and the HBC for help. The company regarded these sick and destitute people as "hangers-on" who were a great drain on the district bal-ance sheet at a time when increasing com-petition pressed managers to economize in their operations.

Senior HBC officials decided that the best way to stop the heavy losses taking place at Moose Factory was to shut down most of the facilities. The opportunity to carry out the plan came in 1932, when the James Bay Railway

An Inuit longshorewoman at Richmond Gulf (Lac Guillaume-Delisle), Quebec, 1927. Throughout the North, Aboriginal men and women depended on summer employment to supplement their trap-ping incomes.

Ojibwa men logging reserve timber at the turn of the century. Throughout central Canada, Aboriginal people took part in the lumber industry as loggers on and off reserve lands.

reached Moosonee. The company could now import supplies by rail from the south. The dismantling of the Moose Works began almost immediately. Farming operations ceased as well. In this way the HBC severed the community's ties with its proud maritime past just as the Great Depression was taking hold. Circumstances could not have been worse for the local Aboriginal people. Lacking alternative opportunities, the skilled and semi-skilled mixed-blood workers had to turn back to the bush, where it was no longer possible to earn a livelihood. This was a particular hardship for Native people of mixed ancestry who had not obtained any economic concessions in Treaty 9.

Today many elderly local people blame the coming of the railway for the community's economic woes. One of the few resources they have left to develop is their proud heritage, which draws many tourists to their community every summer. Unfortunately, the revenues generated by tourism are not large enough to meet the needs of all the local Native community.

The loss of these trading and employment opportunities within the fur industry might have been less damaging to Native economic life if viable alternatives

Dene women dressing a moose hide in the traditional fashion near Fort Resolution, Northwest Territories, 1936.

had been available. But after 1900 such options also began to disappear. Previously Native labour had been crucial for large development projects. In northern Ontario, Aboriginal people helped build the Canadian Pacific Railway by clearing the right of way in their local areas and by furnishing railway ties as independent contractors. Similarly, they participated in the early phases of mining operations in the upper Great Lakes region as aboveground workers clearing sites, erecting buildings and mills, and constructing roads. Some worked in the logging camps and as wage labourers in the paper mills when the pulp-and-paper industry was launched in the early twentieth century. Once numbers of white immigrant workers became available at the turn of the century, however, the newcomers largely filled the labour requirements of industry. The waves of immigration pushed Aboriginal people to the margins of the economy. By mid-century, many northern Native groups were probably more dependent on hunting and trapping than they had been at any time since the late eighteenth century.

CHAPTER 18

WORKING FOR THE INDUSTRIAL FISHERY

My mother used to weave baskets and hats all winter long.... It was just like having a business. When she finished a hat she put it in a dark place and then my dad would paint a design on it.... She learned to decorate her baskets with grass [false embroidery] from a Tlingit lady in Ketchikan.... What my mother wove all winter long she sold in June when we went to the Mainland to work in the canneries.

—Florence Edenshaw Davidson, born 1896, a Haida woman of the Masset First Nation

Canada's industrial salmon fishery and fish-processing industry began by offering the West Coast people new economic opportunities. In time, however, it threatened the survival of their cultures. The industry started in 1871, when Alexander Loggie canned his first salmon at the small Annieville cannery on Lulu Island in the lower Fraser River. His factory operation was labour intensive and the work was hot, messy, and dirty. Native women cleaned, dressed, and washed the fish; cut them to the required size; and stuffed them into the squat one-pound-capacity cans. Next they placed the tins into large wooden steaming vats in a completely closed cooking room, where the workers cooked the salmon to a temperature of 230°F. Loggie's experimental operation canned enough salmon to export three thousand cases to England by sailing ship.

The infant industry expanded rapidly, and in 1883 about a dozen canneries packed approximately twenty-nine million one-pound cans of sockeye salmon—the equivalent of six million whole fish. Most of the canneries remained clustered near the outlet of the Fraser River, probably the world's greatest sockeye river, but in 1876 canneries were also built on the lower Skeena, five hundred

292

A salmon-can label featuring a romanticized image of a Native spear fisherman.

miles to the north. By the end of the century, almost fourteen thousand people found employment in the canneries, or in the fleets of sail-powered gillnet boats that supplied them with fish. Native people made up the bulk of the labour force and fishing fleets. Usually men fished while the women and children worked in the canneries.

CANNERY WORK

Because the industry grew rapidly, local Native people often had difficulty supplying enough workers for the canneries in their territories. This was especially true for the groups of the lower mainland area of southern British Columbia and the lower reaches of the Skeena River. The need to secure a large labour force, and for longer periods than Native people were able to spare from their annual rounds of economic and ceremonial activities, led cannery operators to rely increasingly on Chinese labour contractors. These persons agreed to furnish a plant with all the Chinese workers it required for a season, at a negotiated cost for each case the workers packed. They also supervised the Aboriginal plant workers, who were mostly women recruited by Native elders and chiefs. Both Chinese and Native labourers constituted the "China crew" and lived, respectively, in bunkhouses and huts provided by the cannery companies adjacent to the packing plants.

Walter Wicks, a German immigrant who grew up around the Skeena River canneries at the turn of the century, described the hustle and bustle associated with

Port Essington, British Columbia. This village at the mouth of the Skeena River was a major salmon-canning and trading centre.

the commencement of a summer's operations: "In April, White and Japanese workers arrived from the south and repaired damaged fish boats and nets, tanned sails, and checked on all gear for the short hectic season. The Chinese also came to work at can making which was done manually with hand-operated machinery." The Native families arrived later, when the fish began to run.

Cannery work attracted Native workers from a large area. The lower Skeena River workforce included people from the nearby coastal Tsimshian villages as well as villages on the Nass River near the Alaska border. Inland groups, such as the Babine from Babine Lake, descended the swift-flowing Skeena River in large cottonwood canoes. Haida sailed across the Hecate Straits from the Queen Charlotte Islands in their impressive sail-rigged dugout cedar canoes. And Tlingit from southeastern Alaska joined these other workers as they all scattered to the many canneries situated along the river.

From the first decade of the industry, the northern groups also ventured far to the south to the lower Fraser River to find cannery work. The arrival of their canoe flotillas made a lasting impression on one young boy at Steveston:

Here they come on a flood tide in the late afternoon bowling along ahead of a westerly wind. Great canoes 50 ft and over, spread to an 8 ft beam, each with 4 or 5 sails, wing and wing. Some came all the way from the Skeena and the Queen Charlottes but most were Kwakiutl [from Cape Mudge to Queen Charlotte Sound]. They came in a flotilla [of] about 12 of the big ones and an equal number of lesser ones about 40 ft or a little less. I am sure one of the big canoes would hold well up to 100 if you counted children but did not count dogs....

A few hundred yards out sails were lowered and they started singing Indian songs till they got to 5 or 6 yards from the wharf. With a final shout a sudden silence. Dead silence for about a minute. Then the biggest chief stood up and with a speaking staff in hand made a short speech. A sudden stop. A barked order, and then all hell broke loose: every paddle clawing water to sidle the canoe up to the wharf; mooring lines made fast. The lower 5 or 6 feet was under water but we had planks ready to bridge it to the first canoe & then more planks over the first and second canoe to make a cause way for the outer canoes.

Native women packing salmon in a cannery. These skilled workers were paid according to the number of trays or baskets of cans that they filled.

Native people eagerly participated in the pioneer industry for many reasons. Initially it was very compatible with their own economies. The fish packers favoured the bright red, fatty sockeye, which was the best one for the canning market, whereas most Native people traditionally depended on the leaner chum salmon, which was better suited for smoking and drying. Because the sockeye season preceded the chum season, the Native workers usually finished their fishing and plant work for the canneries at the end of the summer in time to head off to the fall chum runs for their own supply.

Native villagers could travel to and from the canneries in their own sea-going or river canoes, and at first the men also fished from these craft. The Haida, Nuu chah nulth, and Coast Salish traditionally specialized in the construction of such vessels and sold them widely to other groups. A government official said in 1884, "Masset is the shipyard of the Hydas [Haida], the best canoe makers on the continent, who supply them to the other coast tribes.... [H]ere may be seen all stages of construction of these canoes, which, when completed, are such perfect models for service and of beauty."

Salmon cannery camps also drew diverse nations together during the summer, in much the same way trading activities had done previously. Henry Assu, the subject of *Assu of Cape Mudge: Recollections of a Coastal Indian Chief*, recalled his experience: "Every year we left Cape Mudge for Rivers Inlet in Spring. I signed on first for Rivers Inlet in 1929. Our people all went off together around June twentieth on the Union Steamship that called in at Quathiaski Cove twice a week. It was like a summer holiday beginning. It must have been like that in the old days when we had this country to ourselves and our people all started off together in spring from the winter village to head out to the summer camping grounds." Native women of this era often said they looked forward to the opportunity to socialize and work with women from other villages.

The stores, which the canning companies operated for their workers, also proved to be great magnets. In the closing decades of the nineteenth century, well-stocked cannery stores on the lower Skeena River, and competing merchants in the nearby village of Port Essington, offered goods at much better rates than the Hudson's Bay Company did. Soon after these coastal retail outlets began operating, Native people hauled enough cheap goods back to the interior to seriously undermine sales at the company's inland posts. As early as 1890, the HBC manager at Hazelton protested that the Natives' cannery earnings were forcing him "to give reasonable prices for goods and full prices for furs." The construction of half a

Double-ender sail-powered gillnetters were company-owned boats, crewed mostly by Native people. They did the bulk of the fishing in northern B.C. until the 1940s. In the nineteenth century, wives usually rowed the boats while their husbands fished. The steamboat in the background towed them out to the fishing ground, where they remained for several days at a time.

dozen canneries in the preceding decade had driven the average prices for goods on the coast down by 50 per cent. In order to compete, the HBC dropped its prices to "cost-landed" rates at Hazelton.

Despite the attractive features of the infant industry, Native people had to make significant adjustments to their lives to participate in it. Canning companies liked to use Native women as workers because they were very skilled at dressing the fish and fitting it into tins for a quality-conscious export trade. But the factory environment was different from anything the women had experienced before. For twelve or more hours a day, they worked inside in racially segregated areas on canning lines. Besides cleaning the fish and filling the tins, they lacquered and labelled cans and performed various other tasks around the cannery under the eye of a Chinese boss. Although Native men had always done most of the fishing, harvesting salmon for the canners represented a major departure from traditional practices. One challenge they faced involved operating gillnet boats and gear and building up a knowledge of unfamiliar tidal fishing grounds. In pre-contact times, the majority of these people fished in the rivers and creeks, using an assortment of

Native families travelling north to work in the canneries at the turn of the century.

ingenious devices. Gillnets were rarely appropriate. The industrial fishery, on the other hand, took place in coastal waters and, after the first few years, used government-regulated gillnets followed by purse seines and trollers.

The desire to lessen their dependence on fur trading and other more established income-generating activities, such as guiding, trail blazing, freighting, and working on pack trains, provided the West Coast people with an additional incentive to meet the challenges of the industrial fishery. In many areas, other alternative employment opportunities too often proved to be both ephemeral and low paying. The economy of the Nass River and Skeena River watersheds in the late nineteenth century offers an example. Until the gold ran out, the Omineca River gold rush of the 1870s provided a small number of Native men with employment on pack trains or working for the government laying out trails in the region at the rate of $3.50 a day. Others, mostly coastal Tsimshian, briefly operated a freighting-canoe business on the Skeena River to take advantage of the increased supply traffic the gold rush generated. But local HBC men decided the Tsimshian charged too much and persuaded senior company officials to develop a steamboat service. Only a handful of Native men who lived along the steamboat route between Port Simpson and Hazelton earned small incomes by providing cordwood. The rise of the industrial fishery was timely because it coincided with the decline of several enterprises that had provided the residents with incomes outside the fur trade.

A LOOMING THREAT

Even before the early phase of the industrial fishery had passed, ominous developments were taking place that foreshadowed major problems for Native people. Cannery companies were on a constant lookout for cheap and reliable labour. Chinese and Japanese immigrants, especially the latter, provided new labour pools and the prospect of driving wages down by pitting the two groups against each other and the Native people. Most of the Japanese settled in the southern areas of the province in the new fishing communities of Steveston, on the Fraser, and Ucluelet, Tofino, and Clayoquot on the west coast of Vancouver Island. After the turn of the century, they dominated the fishery fleets and workforces of the Fraser River canneries, largely displacing Native fishermen and plant workers. Unlike the local people, they were experienced off-shore fishermen and their families would work at commercial fishing all year round.

In 1902 Indian Affairs officials were worried that their wards would soon face economic hardship and have to turn to them for aid if the Japanese were allowed to replace the 800 to 1,000 Native fishermen who still took part in the industry: "In all, including women and children, about 10,000 Indians would be affected … and if deprived … would have to be fed from the public purse." The Fisheries Department was sympathetic to its colleagues' concerns, and to anti-Asian sentiment in British Columbia, and it was usually agreed that Native people should receive priority in the industry over Japanese and Chinese immigrants. Canners, however, preferred the Japanese fishers and argued that they were more productive than Native people or whites. Certainly the Japanese were more pliant because they had less political clout than any other group except the Chinese. Also, unlike the Native groups, who incorporated their fishery work into their seasonal round of economic activities, the Japanese fishermen and cannery workers depended entirely on the industry for their livelihood. This placed them in a weak bargaining position. Given the circumstances, it is hardly surprising that the Japanese grip on the Fraser fishery tightened despite increased participation by white settlers, who fished mainly for the fresh- and frozen-fish markets. During the first waves of Japanese immigration to Canada, which began in 1885, the

Namgis from Alert Bay beach seining for salmon in the Nimpkish River, 1922. This was a very productive low-cost fishing method to obtain "Indian food fish" at their reserves.

majority of the 3,000 persons fishing for the Fraser River canneries were Native people. By 1913 the licensed fishermen included 1,088 Japanese, 832 whites, and only 430 Native workers. Japanese women were also replacing Native women in the Fraser canneries. Elsewhere, however, Native people still dominated the salmon-fishing and canning workforce and would do so until after the Second World War.

Native people did not stand idly by and watch this transformation of the fishery take place. Having seen what happened in the Fraser River area, groups living in the north decided to prevent the newcomers from displacing them on the Skeena River and other locations. In 1914 they organized the Native Fishing Society and chose the Reverend William Pierce, a Native Methodist minister working among the Tsimshian, as its leader. Headquartered in Port Essington, the society "aimed to unite all the tribes into one body for mutual protection of what they considered their natural native rights." After the First World War, the society boasted almost two thousand members from the northern coastal area and the Queen

Charlotte Islands. Pierce contended that the actions of the society helped Native fishermen to persist in the northern fishery into the 1920s. While it may have been a factor, the wartime demand for salmon, the need for women shore workers, and the federal ban against gas-powered fishing boats in the north also played a role. The latter ban favoured Aboriginal fishermen, who operated the oar- and sail-powered gillnet boats owned by the cannery companies.

In addition to trying to block any further influx of Japanese workers, Native people joined white workers in fishing and plant strikes, and organized some of their own, to pressure canning companies for better wages. They took part in the first general fishermen's strike on the Fraser in 1893. The next year Native fishermen and female cannery workers struck the Skeena; they did so again on the Nass and Skeena rivers in 1896, 1897, and 1904. The 1904 strike involved eight hundred Native fishermen and two hundred Native female cannery workers—none of whom had any union affiliations. They walked out just as the sockeye began to run. There

Native fishers in front of traditional salmon caches, late nineteenth century. The smoked salmon were stored aboveground to keep them away from predators. A dip net leans against one of the caches.

was a problem with these tactics, however; they gave the Native people a reputation for being difficult to deal with. Cannery operators thus had further incentive to hire the more compliant immigrant workers.

Declining salmon stocks posed an even greater menace than immigration to the long-term economic and cultural survival of the coastal nations. Overfishing by the industrial fishery threatened to destroy the resource that had always formed the basis of their cultures. It also led the government to attempt to prohibit Native groups from taking salmon and other fish in most of their traditional ways, and to bar them from disposing of their catches by some of their customary means. A low point in the Fraser River sockeye-spawning cycle in 1886 brought the overfishing problem to a head. The canners and white fishermen wasted no time blaming the Native people for the shortfall, claiming that their upriver fishery was the culprit. The complaints of this interest group, as well as those of sports fishermen, prompted federal Fisheries officials to take action. They soon launched a relentless assault on the Native fishery in the name of conservation, a battle that continues to this day.

The federal Fisheries Department led the attack because the conservation of marine resources is a federal obligation. In 1888, under the authority of various revisions to the Fisheries Act, it placed severe restrictions on Native fishing by defining what Aboriginal fishing rights were and by specifying the kinds of gear Native fishers could use. The regulations stated: "Indians shall, at all times, have liberty to fish for the purpose of providing food for themselves but not for sale, barter or traffic, by any means other than with drift nets [a floating net that drifts freely with the tide or current], or spearing." In her landmark history of First Nations and the law in the Pacific fisheries, *Tangled Webs of History*, Dianne Newell argues that this created the fiction of an "Indian food fishery." She adds that this was not a new idea. Since 1859 the Province of Canada had defined Aboriginal fishing rights in terms of "domestic consumption." By extending this notion to the West Coast, the government capped Native production for the benefit of the growing canning industry, as it did in eastern Canada for the sports fishery.

This government action denied coastal groups the right to continue their age-old tradition of being fish merchants. The regulations were put into effect without negotiating or concluding treaties with the various nations. Even worse, once the Fisheries Department had established the concept of a food fishery, it proceeded to define it ever more narrowly over the years. Fisheries officials came to regard the Native food fishery as a "privilege" that the government granted to the nations instead of seeing it as an inherent right. By 1915 they concluded, without any sound evidence, that Native people were taking so many "food fish" in the up-country that they were threatening the health of the canning industry. To remedy this situation, the department considered eliminating the Native food fishery.

Although the Fisheries Department did not fully achieve this goal, it came close when it issued revised fishing regulations in 1917. These required Native people to obtain federal food-fishing permits. Indian agents often decided who would get food-fish permits, if and when they were available. The permits were subject to the same types of restrictions concerning fishing areas, open seasons, and allowable gear that the Fisheries Department applied to commercial licences. Extraordinarily, the new regulations made it an offence for Native fishers to even bring freshwater salmon to the coast for their own consumption!

Well before these changes came into effect, the federal government had begun to ban certain types of traditional fishing gear. Fisheries agents focused their attention on fish weirs and traps because they thought these devices were partly to blame for the depletion of salmon stocks. The Cowichan, who lived on the southeastern shore of Vancouver Island, were one of the first groups to suffer as a result of the program. In 1897 and again in 1912, agents demolished many of their fishing stations. The government took similar actions in Nuu chah nulth and Kwakwaka'wakw territories and in the lands of the Carrier, Gitxsan, and Wet'suwet'en of the upper Fraser and Skeena rivers.

The most celebrated raids took place in the homelands of the Gitxsan and Wet'suwet'en. Here the destruction of fish barricades led to confrontations that threatened to trigger widespread revolt. The first skirmish took place in 1904, when Fisheries officers ripped out an ancient network of salmon weirs along the upper Skeena, Babine, and Bulkley rivers. In the ensuing years, the government enforced the regulations rigorously in this region because the industrial fishery had begun to undergo major changes. Most notably, in 1905 strong markets developed for pink salmon and the Native staple—chum. This led canning companies to spread into many new areas along the coast, often taking over Native fishing camps in the process. Now the processors charged that Native people were taking too many of these "new" resources. Unless the Native fishers were checked, they argued, the future of the industry would be in peril.

The federal Fisheries inspector for the northern region was convinced that the industrial and Native fishery would collectively destroy all the Skeena salmon unless stringent measures were taken. But rather than place severe limits on the expansion of the industry, the Fisheries Department decided to intensify its effort to rip out the remaining traps and weirs. Power politics dictated this choice. Cannery operators pressured their members of Parliament for action on their behalf; the Gitxsan, Wet'suwet'en, and Babine had no political representation; they could not vote. The canners and the government also knew how to use the press to their advantage. Newspapers heralded the Fisheries Department's actions with headlines that screamed "Indians wiping out sockeyes!" Follow-up stories claimed, without justification, that Native people were stealing "one of the greatest sources of the people's wealth" by depriving the industry of almost 150,000 cases of salmon a year. This kind of propaganda helped to promote the notion that Native people were not included among "the people" and that this resource, or at least the commercial benefits derived from it, belonged to newcomers and not to the original residents of the province.

Commercial-fishing licensing practices also worked to favour cannery operators at the expense of Native people. The first major effort to restrict entry to the industrial fishery began in 1890, when the federal government decided to issue only five hundred commercial licences; canning companies obtained most of them. The number any particular cannery received depended on its production capacity. Tying fishing licences to canneries in this way denied access to most individual fishermen, regardless of affiliation.

It is hardly surprising that fishermen strongly objected to the arrangement. Most Native people blatantly refused to comply by simply neglecting to take out licences. Many of them were angry about having to pay to exercise a traditional right, and beyond the lower mainland, it was extremely inconvenient to obtain a permit. White fishermen were outraged too. As far as they were concerned, it effectively transformed a "common property resource" into a privately held one. In 1892 the strong protests of white fishermen and Indian agents temporarily forced the government to modify its policy. Unlimited licences were made available, but only to British subjects, checking competition from Japanese fishers.

The canners did not look favourably on this turn of events. They liked the previous arrangement because it had given them assured access to the fish they needed. The program had also helped them obtain essential Native labour by making it possible to lure local women and their families to the plants by hiring their male relatives as fishermen. Indeed, Native fishers complained that it was increasingly difficult to find cannery work unless one could bring women. Concerned that they might lose this important economic lever, the companies persuaded the government to issue special cannery licences for Native fishermen and the female "boat pullers" who rowed for them, beginning in 1900. In 1910 the federal government banned the use of gas-powered boats in the north and brought back the practice of tying all northern-district commercial-fishing licences to specific canneries, giving each of them an allocation, and it prohibited the construction of new processing facilities.

Immediately after the First World War, the federal government re-examined its approach to conservation in the industry. In 1922, after holding a commission of inquiry, the Fisheries Department abandoned its policy of banning gas-powered boats and new canning facilities in the northern district and of limiting the number of commercial gillnet fishermen through the licensing system, with one major exception. In response to growing political pressure from white fishers, it did not extend this open-door policy to Japanese. On the contrary, the government hoped to eliminate these fishermen over time by reducing the number of licences they received. Indian Affairs and the coastal nations supported this scheme. By the late 1920s, a substantial number

Nuu chah nulth women processing halibut at Neah Bay, British Columbia. For most coastal people, halibut was the principal back-up food to salmon. Among the Haida, it exceeded salmon in importance.

of fishermen of Japanese origin had been eliminated. No further reductions took place thereafter, however, because the cannery owners and the Japanese fishermen's association used the courts to force the government to abandon this racist practice.

Shortly after the turn of the century, the southern fishing fleet began switching over from oar- and sail-powered to gasoline-powered boats. This process did not begin in the north until 1924, when the government rescinded its ban on gas-powered boats. The move towards gas power signalled the beginning of a trend to more capital-intensive fishing. Unfortunately, few Native fishermen had access to capital. They could not use reserve property as collateral for the bank loans they needed to buy boats. Furthermore, most of them could not obtain the sizable lines of credit needed to operate power boats and buy the array of gear that went with them. In the early days of conversion to gas motors, some Haida did manage to follow the trend by constructing new gillnetters. In the 1920s and 1930s, however, the industry moved towards bigger and much more costly seiners. Few Native people had any hope of owning such craft.

The handful of coastal people who managed to buy seiners were usually of high rank and were well connected to white society. James Sewid, for example, was a Kwakwaka'wakw of noble birth whose family had strong links to the Anglo-BC (ABC) Packing Company's Knight Inlet Cannery. According to his published memoir, *Guests Never Leave Hungry*, he fished for this plant as a child alongside his step-father, and later sailed with his grandfather, who skippered a gas-powered seiner owned by the company. Sewid's grandfather taught him how to operate the boat over a nine-year period. While he apprenticed, Sewid earned the trust of the cannery manager, and this enabled him to become skipper of one of the company's best seiners. During the boom times of the Second World War, he and his uncle obtained a bank loan to buy their own seiner, by obtaining the co-signature of the principal of the Alert Bay residential school and a line of credit from ABC. Eventually Sewid owned three seiners.

The onset of the Depression had brought added woes. Until that time the industry had continued to expand into new areas, and canneries dotted most of the coast. In the central and northern districts, Native women still made up the bulk of the labour force. The need to retain them remained one of the major motives for the packing companies to hire their husbands and sons to fish. When the Depression took hold, many canneries closed down, as prices for their product plummeted. Others were taken over by larger companies. As a result, an ever smaller number of plants—mostly located on the lower Fraser and Skeena rivers—

canned an ever greater portion of the catch; in turn, these plants became more mechanized and required fewer workers. Many of the Native villages that had sprung up beside the canneries (the Kwakwaka'wakw centre of Alert Bay is one of the best known) were devastated by the closures. Shore workers had to chase after fewer and fewer jobs and travel farther afield to get them. Only families with strong ties to a packing company could count on obtaining work. In short, the changes to the industry strengthened the hand of the cannery owners and reinforced the old system of company paternalism.

DEFENDING ABORIGINAL FISHING RIGHTS

Native people attempted to counteract the worst effects of the changes to the industry by organizing to protect their economic interests. They proceeded on several fronts. They campaigned for better prices for their fish and more liberal credit. The Kwakwaka'wakw led the way by creating the Pacific Coast Native Fishermen's Association in 1936. Many fishermen joined the Kwakwaka'wakw organization out of fear of losing their boats because of defaulted loan payments. The association gained some important victories for its members. It persuaded packing companies to extend all outstanding loans in the district and to accept it as the negotiating body for all local Indians. Significantly, by the outbreak of the Second World War, Native fishermen were more highly organized than white fishermen.

Native people also defended their Aboriginal fishing rights. This fight was part of their ongoing battle for a fair settlement of their outstanding land claims in British Columbia. What is important to note here is that in 1916, the Nisga'a, Coast Salish, and Interior Salish formed the Allied Tribes of British Columbia to pursue their various land claims.

Of all the traditional fisheries in the province, those of the Fraser River groups suffered the greatest damage from the salmon-canning industry and other economic development. In 1913 a rock slide, which was triggered by railway construction, killed off a massive spawning run. The resulting shortfalls of fish in the years immediately after the disaster led the Fisheries Department to ban the Native food fishery in two very important stretches of the river—at Hell's Gate, one of the best salmon-drying places, and near Mission. The department did restrict the downstream commercial fishery, however. Needless to say, Native people resented having to pay for mistakes made by others. Subsequently the government tightened restrictions on the food fishery in most upstream areas throughout the province. Native residents were to be given the "privilege" of fishing only when other sources of food were not available.

Indian Affairs made a modest effort to counteract the actions of the Fisheries Department. In 1922 the chief inspector of Indian Agencies for British Columbia, W. E. Ditchburn, told yet another commission on the fishery that the Fisheries Department policy was undermining the rights that the Douglas treaties had guaranteed to some of the southern Vancouver Island nations. He also complained that non-Native commercial fishermen were trespassing on fishing grounds that were attached to many coastal reserves, thereby making it impossible for those Native groups to exercise their rights. Finally, Ditchburn, his agents, and Native witnesses asked to have the Fisheries Department make it easier for Aboriginal people to fish for subsistence purposes. Most of these pleadings fell on deaf ears. Even when the Fraser River runs finally started to rebound in 1929, the chief federal supervisor for Fisheries made the unsubstantiated claim that the food fishery still represented an unwarranted threat to the industry and that Native people no longer needed it to survive.

By the late 1920s, it was clear to Native leaders that they could not count on Indian Affairs to defend their interests. At a 1927 parliamentary inquiry into Aboriginal affairs in British Columbia, Andrew Paull of the Allied Tribes advanced the idea that fishing territories be set aside for the exclusive commercial use of the various nations. Paull, a Squamish, was not the first Native leader to promote this idea. To some extent it reflected the thinking behind the trapline program that the province had put into effect at this time. The reaction of Fisheries officials was predictable. A former Dominion inspector of Fisheries, who also gave testimony, vigorously attacked Paull's proposal, arguing that the department did not have the power to grant anyone exclusive commercial-fishing rights in tidewater areas. When questioned closely, however, he had to concede Paull's point that previously it had been the department's practice to lease whole inlets to canning companies. Although some members of the parliamentary joint committee concluded that the Fisheries Department had the right to grant similar rights to Aboriginal people, their final report upheld the department's view. So the struggle continued.

The Second World War provided a brief respite for Native people who were involved in the fishing industry. The disgraceful removal of persons of Japanese ancestry from the coast as an emergency war measure in 1942 opened up many cannery and fishing jobs—and "surplus boats"—to Native workers. Production soared to meet wartime demand, and the general shortage of male workers at this time increased the openings for Native women everywhere. But after the war ended, most of the earlier problems resurfaced and became more serious. Technological improvements resulted in fewer and larger boats chasing a fish stock that had been greatly taxed during the war years. Centralization of packing facilities continued and together with unionization of fishers and plant workers acted as a catalyst for the move towards bigger and better-equipped fishing craft. To haul their catches ever greater distances to the processing centres—Prince Rupert and Vancouver were the main ones—boats had to be highly mobile and have the latest navigation and fish-finding devices and refrigeration equipment. Newell documents how the industry's rapidly escalating capital requirements excluded growing numbers of Native commercial fishermen from participation in it. They hung on longest in the north, but many had to use company-owned or chartered vessels to do so. Those who owned their own boats often had to sell or charter them to canning companies to make ends meet. Meanwhile, the job prospects of Native shore workers dwindled steadily, owing to the further concentration of processing plants at fewer and fewer locations and the mechanization of the remaining facilities. By the early 1960s, almost all the plants in remote areas—the Nass River, Rivers and Smith inlets, the Queen Charlotte Islands, and Johnson Strait—had been abandoned.

The salmon fishery continued to lurch from crisis to crisis, and commissions of inquiry followed one after another. Increasingly the federal government turned to resource economists for advice. Economists largely ignored Aboriginal interests in their economic models; consequently, they usually came up with recommendations intended to manage the industry for the benefit of the processors and full-time commercial fishermen. For most Native people, fishing remained one of the several economic activities that made up their seasonal round. But culture and tradition are not the stuff of economics, so the government's experts turned a blind eye to them. Operating on the advice of its economic gurus, the federal government adopted the Davis Plan in 1968; it was devastating for most fishermen, but especially for those of Native ancestry.

This licence-limitation scheme, which was named after Jack Davis, who was the minister of Fisheries at the time, called for licensing of the most productive commercial fishing boats. The idea was to create a smaller, more efficient fleet. The government began by buying back and scrapping the "obsolete" small vessels while issuing class "A" licences to large boats, those that had landed more than ten thousand pounds of fish in 1967 or 1968. For every new licence issued, an equivalent tonnage had to be retired. To maintain the quality of the class "A" boats, the government introduced a rigid inspection system.

As might be expected, the price of the boat licences, which were transferable, soared under this new scheme, and the size of the new craft increased substantially. In other words, the Davis Plan did not reduce fishing capacity, nor did it eliminate the problem of overcapitalization. It did shut out more Native fishermen and villages, however. Now, besides finding the money to build and equip a boat—approximately $200,000 by the mid-1960s—they also had to pay the going rate for the scarce "A" licences. The packing companies, on the other hand, liked the arrangement, because they could sell off their worn-out rental fleets to the government and buy modern boats. Natives had staked their livelihood on the rental fleets. Between 1968 and 1971, the size of this fleet shrank from just under five hundred boats to slightly more than two hundred. In 1971 the government made a small attempt to help Native fishermen by introducing "A-1-Indian only" licences for a token annual cost. These could be transferred among "Indians" or converted to regular "A" licences. In 1978 non-transferable band licences were issued. Yet these steps did little to stop the erosion of the Indians' position in the fishing fleet. As before, only a privileged few held their own.

Meanwhile, in spite of countless commissions and management schemes to control overfishing, the salmon stocks did not increase as planned. Uncontrolled development, particularly hydroelectric power generation and logging, was one of the reasons. Such activities destroyed spawning habitats. While federal and provincial agencies bickered about who was responsible for doing something about it, the problem got worse.

As Native people found themselves increasingly marginalized in the fishing and processing sides of the industry, they relied heavily on their food fishery. Some upriver groups, such as the Gitxsan and Wet'suwet'en, wanted to have the right to develop their own inland commercial fishery. These people were particularly upset by the Fisheries Department's inept management of the resource. They had a very good reason to feel resentful. In the 1950s the department decided that the salmon runs in the Bulkley River could be enhanced by blasting out a rock in Hagwilget Canyon near Moricetown and by installing fish ladders. The Wet'suwet'en vehemently opposed this idea because they knew it would not improve the stocks and would lead to the destruction of one of their most important traditional fishing sites. Convinced that they knew better, Fisheries experts went ahead anyway. The sockeye runs in the river immediately declined.

Pushed to the wall, Native groups across the province resorted to civil disobedience and the courts. They openly ignored fishing regulations to provoke government authorities into arresting them so they could assert their Aboriginal rights in court. In 1970, for example, one hundred Coast Salish of the Stó:lö nation staged a "fish-in" off their reserve near Chilliwack; farther upriver others followed suit. Finally Fisheries officials had had enough and arrested Chief Noll Derriksan as he led another protest. They charged him with fishing salmon for food off-reserve. In court, Derriksan's lawyer claimed that the chief had the right to do so by virtue of the Royal Proclamation of 1763. The lower courts and the Supreme Court of Canada thought otherwise, ruling that decades of Fisheries legislation to conserve the resource had effectively extinguished any rights that might derive from unextinguished Indian title.

Although the decision in the Derriksan case was very disheartening, the Native people pressed on and eventually scored a major victory in the landmark Sparrow case (1990). This case was the first to test Section 35(1) of the 1982 Constitution Act, which expressly recognizes Aboriginal people and rights. Ronald Sparrow, a senior member of the Musqueam band of Vancouver, was charged in 1984 with fishing with a drift net that was longer than his band's food-fishing licence permitted. In his defence, Sparrow's lawyers cited Section 35(1) in arguing that their client was merely exercising an existing Aboriginal right to fish and that the net-length restriction was invalid. The Crown again countered that the Fisheries Act had extinguished those rights. Predictably, the lower courts ruled against Sparrow, but this time the British Columbia Court of Appeal and the Supreme Court of Canada overruled them in a landmark decision. The Supreme Court took the position that the Musqueam had an unextinguished Aboriginal right to fish, and that legislation intended for conservation purposes has to be justified if it detracts from Aboriginal rights protected under Section 35(1). In other words, food-fishery permits were a manner of controlling the fishery, not of defining underlying rights. The Supreme Court ruled that "Indian food fishing" was, subject to conservation needs, to be given priority over the demands of other groups, and that Aboriginal "use" should be more broadly interpreted to include social and ceremonial as well as food consumption.

Further litigation will determine where this small and hard-won step will lead. Certainly it has ramifications for Aboriginal title and resource management that go far beyond the fishery. Within the fishing industry, however, it has already led the federal government to alter its position on Native fishing. In 1991 the Fisheries Department announced a national Aboriginal Fishing Co-operative Management Program, and in the autumn of 1992 the Fisheries minister, John Crosbie, announced that his department had concluded an agreement with three lower Fraser River First Nations—the Musqueam, Tsawwassen, and Stó:lö —which allowed them to sell a certain portion of their "food fish." As with the *Sparrow* decision, non-Native fishermen have greeted this development with howls of protest, issued dark warnings about the destruction of the fishery, and threatened to boycott any canners who accept fish from the three groups.

The experience of West Coast Native people in the industrial fishery parallels that of other groups in the commercial fur trade. In the beginning, both industries were in tune with ancient Native ways of life. In both, Aboriginal labour and harvesting skills were crucial to the success of the newcomers' companies. Each industry had strong paternalistic overtones throughout most of its history, which closely linked Native labourers with their white employers or trading partners. In each case, however, it was the non-Native people who amassed most of the wealth, usurping control of the resources and marginalizing the Aboriginal participants in the process. What is striking is the markedly different periods of time over which this transformation occurred in the two industries; in the fur trade it took 150 to 200 years or more, depending on the area, and in the industrial fishery on Canada's West Coast, less than a century.

CHAPTER 19

GETTING ORGANIZED

The work of creating stable and representative organizations has been one of the most difficult challenges faced by our people. It is a task that has always drawn the attention of Indian leaders in the past, and it is primarily because of their courage in attempting to meet this responsibility that things have changed for the better as much as they have.

—Harold Cardinal, a Cree from the Sucker Creek reserve, Alberta, 1969

During the summer of 1990, MLA Elijah Harper, a Cree-Ojibwa, torpedoed the Meech Lake constitutional accord in the Manitoba legislature for failing to address Native political concerns in a meaningful way. Ethel Blondin-Andrew, a Native Liberal MP representing the Western Arctic, publicly took Prime Minister Brian Mulroney to task for the same issue. Subsequently, political leaders hammered out a new constitutional agreement—the Charlottetown accord—only to have it soundly defeated two years later in a national referendum. In the run-up to the vote, Native leaders played key roles in both the Yes and No campaigns. A poll conducted by the *Globe and Mail* on the eve of the referendum revealed the striking fact that Canadians trusted Ovide Mercredi, chief of the Assembly of First Nations, more than any other prominent national politician who had fought for or against approving the new constitutional accord.

Harper's and Mercredi's achievements represented an astonishing turn of events. At the beginning of this century, Native people had little say in the conduct of their own affairs, much less those of the nation. Inuit could not vote federally until 1950; Indians could not until 1960. Since then a handful have been elected to federal and provincial parliaments. A very short while ago, most non-Native Canadians would have had difficulty naming a Canadian Native leader or parliamentarian; most certainly they would not have held them in the same regard as a prime minister or provincial premiers. Furthermore, few would have known that earlier in this century

Elijah Harper in David Neel's serigraph Just Say No, *1991.*

the federal government had effectively banned Native people from advocating many of the rights issues that Harper, Mercredi, Blondin-Andrew, and other leaders champion so effectively today. In the course of this struggle, these leaders have shifted the concept of Canada as a country founded by two immigrant peoples to one that was created by Aboriginal people and those who came later.

EARLY EFFORTS TO ORGANIZE

Canada's Native people launched a Herculean political and legal battle at the close of the nineteenth century that faced seemingly insurmountable obstacles to developing political organization and leadership. At that time, massive immigration and the ravages of foreign diseases had reduced them to a tiny minority in their ancient homeland. Collective action was absolutely essential for them, yet they had always been a culturally disparate people and their experiences after Confederation caused further divisions. The Indian Act, for instance, had defined whom the government recognized as "status" (also commonly called "registered" or "legal") Indians. Until recently, these definitions excluded people of Native heritage and their descendants who had received "Halfbreed" lands or scrip, or after 1951 had been enfranchised, or were children of marriages where the mother and the father's mother were non-status Indians, or were women who had married men who were not status Indians, or the children of these marriages. The treaty-making process further divided status Indians into two groups—treaty and non-treaty, as did the reserve system—reserve and off-reserve. Each First Nation had particular social and economic advantages and problems, making it impossible for First Nations to speak with one voice. First Nations' interests differed from those of Inuit and Métis. Missionaries also contributed to sectarian differences among Native people, and Indian residential-school programs and other off-reserve educational schemes attempted to strip Native children of their cultural identity. Finally, the First Nations and Inuit groups were physically isolated from one another. Through the pass system, which was not abolished until 1941, bans on key ceremonial activities, and prohibition on raising funds in support of a land claims case, which were not abolished until 1951, and by maintaining a tight fist on band funds, Indian Affairs often thwarted the efforts of Native leaders to unite to pursue political objectives that government officials opposed.

One of the most significant early efforts to create regional and national political organizations took place in central Canada and on the prairies. The historian Brian Titley has identified the Grand General Indian Council of Ontario and Quebec, backed mostly by Iroquois and Ojibwa communities, as one of the first of these post-Confederation associations. Its goals were modest and it rarely criticized government policies. In 1904 it even endorsed banning the potlatch and sun dances. The only time the organization objected publicly to government policies was in 1919. Its president, Henry Jackson, raised the vexatious issues of provincial violations of hunting and fishing rights and the expropriation of reserve lands at a special

Chief Thunderwater, from Cleveland, Ohio, organized the Council of Tribes during the early twentieth century. Although he gained a strong following among the Iroquois of Quebec during the First World War, he was a fraud.

meeting of the council. He could not push this or any other issue too far, however, because his organization depended on the unofficial support of Indian Affairs. To survive, the Grand Council had to co-operate with the department, not confront it.

The council did not serve the needs of growing numbers of Indians who had come to realize that the advancement of their rights demanded a more aggressive approach. They were receptive to an American who called himself Chief Thunderwater. Thunderwater organized the Council of Tribes in the United States to promote temperance, cultural revitalization, Aboriginal rights, and access to mainstream education. The Council of Tribes quickly gained a strong following in the American Midwest and among the Iroquoian groups in Ontario and Quebec. By 1916 half of the residents of Kahnawake had joined it, and two years later Thunderwater tried to incorporate a separate council for Canadian Indians. About this time, however, Duncan Campbell Scott persuaded Ottawa to block the incorporation of the council in Canada because he was afraid Thunderwater's various activities and popularity with Canadian Indians would ultimately weaken his department's control over the lives of its wards. In the end, Thunderwater proved to be an impostor—to Scott's great relief. He was an Afro-American from Cleveland, Ohio.

Although this particular organization disbanded, the time was ripe for other Indian organizations to appear. Almost four thousand Native men had just returned from serving overseas in the Canadian Expeditionary Force during the First World War. This experience had given most of them their first opportunity to meet and share experiences with Native men from other parts of the country. After having been generally well treated in Europe, the veterans were not willing to be regarded as second-class citizens at home. They understood that it would take a concerted effort to end the oppression of their people. Frederick Ogilvie Loft, a Mohawk veteran who was born on the Six Nations reserve in 1862, took the initiative by founding the League of Indians of Canada in 1918. By all accounts, Loft was physically impressive and a charismatic speaker who knew how to sway an audience and curry favour with

the press corps. But from the outset he ran into opposition from Indian Affairs, which refused to allow Indians to use their band funds to attend Loft's meetings. Loft pressed on. In speeches and circulars he advocated returning control of reserve lands to Indians and freeing bands "from the domination of officialdom."

It was among the Plains nations that Loft's league found ready acceptance in the West. The first western meeting of the organization took place in Manitoba, in June 1920, and the delegates chose the Reverend Edward Ahenakew, an Anglican minister, as their president for western Canada. By the summer of 1922, about fifteen hundred Alberta Indians attended a league meeting. Meanwhile, Loft was garnering newspaper and public support for his stand that the Department of Indian Affairs was responsible for the poor social and economic circumstances most

Frederick Ogilvie Loft, a Mohawk veteran of the First World War, organized the League of Indians of Canada in 1918. It was one of the first modern Native Canadian political organizations to promote Aboriginal rights.

Three Native veterans of the First World War. The wartime experiences of Native men heightened their political awareness and made many unwilling to accept treatment as second-class citizens at home.

Indians faced. These developments caused government officials much consternation. Scott encouraged the formation of a network of spies to monitor Loft's activities. The police, missionaries, and accommodating Indians all fed the department information, but none of it provided any solid evidence to justify taking legal action against Loft or the league.

Loft waged his campaign at a very perilous time for political radicals. In the wake of the Bolshevik revolution in Russia and the 1919 Winnipeg General Strike, Parliament amended the Criminal Code of Canada to ban meetings of organizations branded as seditious. Some of Loft's critics thought his league fell into this category. The Native leader's success in avoiding prosecution during the 1920s is a testament to his ability to navigate treacherous political waters. Not until 1931 did Loft make a move that government officials thought they could use against him. In that year he violated the Indian Act by sending out a circular asking Indians to donate money to finance a trip to London for himself and a lawyer to press the hunting-rights issue before the Judicial Committee of the Privy Council, which remained Canada's final court of appeal until 1949. Scott hoped that the government could charge Loft for trying to defraud Indians. The RCMP and Scott's network of spies, which included post-office personnel, redoubled their efforts to obtain a collection of the circulars to build a case against him. Before the government took action, the sixty-nine-year-old Loft, tired of the constant pressure, retired from the political stage without ever going to London.

The League of Indians of Canada did not disappear after Loft withdrew, however. According to Stan Cuthand, a Cree scholar and leader from Saskatchewan, Indians of the prairie provinces revitalized the western branch of the organization in 1929, when they established the League of Indians in Western Canada. Besides continuing the struggle for the preservation of hunting, trapping, and fishing rights in the 1930s, the association lobbied for an end to reserve-land surrenders, Indian control over reserve lands, and the termination of the pass/permit system. The harsh times of the Dirty Thirties forced the league to direct much of its attention to urgent economic issues. It pressed for economic aid in the form of horses, farm machinery, and seed to bolster flagging agricultural efforts, and also demanded extra rations for old people.

THE POLITICAL STRUGGLE IN BRITISH COLUMBIA

The Pacific slope was a crucible for developing Native political awareness in Canada. The First Nations of British Columbia faced most of the same problems that groups living in developed areas east of the Rocky Mountains did. But there was an important difference. With the exception of those living in the northeast covered by Treaty 8 (1899) and the small portions of southern Vancouver Island included within the boundaries of the various Douglas treaties, Native people in British Columbia had never surrendered their lands. For this reason, most Native groups were still engaged in pressuring the provincial government to recognize their Aboriginal title and to negotiate an equitable settlement with them for its surrender. The province not only refused to acknowledge the legitimacy of their claims but also adopted an increasingly stingy reserve-land policy. Not surprisingly, Native political and legal battles in British Columbia have focused on the nationally important issues of the recognition of Aboriginal title, self-government, and reserve allotments.

The political scientist Paul Tennant notes that in British Columbia the "western-style" Native political protest movement began immediately after the province joined Confederation. Various southern coastal and interior groups held rallies at that time and sent petitions to provincial and federal officials outlining their grievances about reserve sizes and other land issues. In 1881 a Nisga'a delegation went to Victoria to demand recognition of their Aboriginal title, and five years later, Tsimshian emissaries travelled to Ottawa demanding the same thing. In 1887 the two groups sent a combined party of chiefs to Victoria to demand an inquiry into title and self-government issues, and to ask provincial and federal officials to negotiate treaties. Although the province refused to take their Aboriginal-rights claims seriously, it was concerned about fighting and quarrelling in the region between Native groups and non-Native settlers. For this reason it agreed to create a two-man federal-provincial commission that would head north and hold a hearing. Negotiations, however, were not part of its mandate. The provincial attorney-general, Alex Davie, told his representative "not to give undertakings or make promises, and in particular you will be careful to discountenance, should it arise, any claim of Indian title to Provincial lands."

The Nisga'a of the Nass River region took advantage of the hearings to explain why they objected to the reserves that the province had allocated to them. At Kincolith a Native schoolteacher said, "Ever since [Indian reserve commissioner] O'Reilly was here the chiefs of Kincolith have been troubled and dissatisfied about their land. Mr. O'Reilly did not consult with them or have a talk with them about it, and he did not give them a choice about their land ... there was no wood upon it and no way of hunting.... We want the whole of Observatory Inlet and surrounding country with the streams entering it. We catch salmon in them and hunt over it all, and we get wood and berries there.... And on Portland Canal there are several streams we want secured. Each chief has always had certain places where he and his tribe always hunted and caught salmon." The commissioners grew impatient hearing similar complaints over and over again. One of them rebuked the Nisga'a at Nass Harbour, saying, "It is well for you to understand that there is no probability of your views as to the land being entertained."

Predictably, nothing positive came from the hearings. The Nisga'a and Tsimshian people gained a few additional acres of reserve land but in the process were labelled truculent and simple-minded for so steadfastly asserting their Aboriginal rights. The commissioners sent a confidential report to the government, erroneously concluding that local Methodist missionaries had convinced the two groups that they held an unextinguished Aboriginal title to the land. The commissioners' negative conclusions found ready acceptance in provincial government circles. Their findings would send the Nisga'a down a long road that would produce a major Supreme Court of Canada decision of crucial importance to Aboriginal rights in Canada.

Although there is no evidence to support claims that local Protestant missionaries implanted the notion of Aboriginal rights in the minds of the Nisga'a and Tsimshian, historians note that these proselytizers did lend strong and effective support to the campaign of the two groups. North coast groups also benefited from the fact that the federal and provincial governments had yet to establish a strong presence in the north, and the fact that white settlers were very scarce in their territories. For these two reasons, the traditional social and political structures of the Nisga'a and Tsimshian largely remained in place, and this proved to be a great advantage in their struggle.

In 1907 the Nisga'a laid the groundwork for a sustained land-claim struggle by creating the Nishga Land Committee. This committee was the first effort by British Columbia Native people to restructure themselves politically in order to deal more effectively with the government. Their idea was to create an organization that outsiders could understand. Members of the committee represented the various clans and villages, which rotated the chair annually.

In 1908 federal-provincial squabbling over the amount of land to allocate to those British Columbia Indians still waiting for reserves led Premier Richard McBride to suspend the reserve surveys. The Nisga'a felt threatened by this action because many of their reserves remained unsurveyed. Their coast Tsimshian and

Gitxsan neighbours were concerned about the construction of the Grand Trunk Pacific Railway section along the Skeena River, which began the same year. These developments prompted the Nishga Land Committee to reach out to their neighbours in the hope of speaking with a louder, united voice. They sent a combined delegation of twenty-five chiefs to Ottawa to express their concerns. The Cowichan followed their lead in 1909 by dispatching a petition of their own to the federal government. That same year they joined forces with most of the other coastal nations to form the Indian Rights Association. Meanwhile, Salish groups from the southern interior, who were very concerned about the continuing erosion of their reserves, took their first tentative steps towards co-ordinated political action. In the summer of 1909 they formed the Interior Tribes of British Columbia.

The creation of these inter-nation associations took place because nations had achieved little acting on their own. They had also learned that limiting their political actions to filing petitions and sending delegations to Victoria, Ottawa, and London achieved little. The provincial government remained steadfast in its denial of Aboriginal title and continued its miserly reserve-allotment policy. Although the federal government seemed to be more sympathetic to the province's Native people's desire for more generous reserves, it exerted only limited pressure on their behalf. The end result of the early lobbying efforts was the creation of a royal commission in 1912 to settle the differences between the federal and provincial governments respecting Indian lands and Indian affairs. Premier McBride and J. A. J. McKenna, whom the federal government had appointed to serve as special commissioner of Indian Affairs in British Columbia, signed the agreement to establish the five-member commission. It had no Native members. British Columbia's Aboriginal people regarded the intentions of the two governments with suspicion from the outset. They noted that the McKenna–McBride Commission—like the 1887 joint commission before it—had no mandate to consider the issues of Aboriginal title, self-governing rights, or the negotiation of treaties; it was authorized only to address the reserve-allotment problem. Particularly ominous was the fact that the commissioners had the power not only to increase the size of reserves where they deemed it appropriate, but also to reduce them "with the consent of the Indians, as required by the Indian Act." At the time, Native people did not believe that their right to veto reserve reductions would have any force. History would prove them correct.

The establishment of the McKenna–McBride Commission acted as a catalyst for further political activity. In 1910 Prime Minister Wilfrid Laurier met with Native leaders throughout British Columbia. When he visited Kamloops in 1910, the Interior tribes presented him with the so-called Laurier Memorial, which spelled out Aboriginal discontent with the reserve system. Laurier expressed sympathy for their cause. Nisga'a leaders recall that he told them that only a decision of the Judicial Committee of the British Privy Council in London could settle the issue of title. Apparently, Laurier even promised to help them obtain a hearing. His defeat in 1911 and the convening of the McKenna–McBride Commission prompted the Nishga Land Committee to take their case to London.

In appearing before the Judicial Committee, the Nisga'a followed in the footsteps of other British Columbia Native people who had sent delegations to London as early as 1904. Joe Capilano, who lived on the Squamish reserve in Vancouver, was one of these early petitioners. He had laid the claims of British Columbia Native people before Edward VII in 1906. However, officials in London would have nothing to do with Capilano, telling him the title issue was a "Canadian affair." Another delegation visited London in 1909, but it, too, failed. So the Nisga'a switched tactics. They retained a lawyer, Arthur O'Meara, to help them draft a formal petition. Although he was not a Native person, O'Meara strongly supported their rights struggle. He had organized the Society of Friends of the Indians of British Columbia in 1910. The society acted as a financial and political support group for Native causes.

The petition drafted by the Nishga Land Committee and O'Meara—and approved by a general assembly of the Nisga'a heavily on the Royal Proclamation of 1763 to make their claim. Previously, few of British Columbia's Native people had been aware of this document; afterwards, they routinely used it in their legal and political arsenals. When forwarding their petition to the Privy Council in London, the Nisga'a sent a covering letter to the secretary of state for the colonies, telling him, "We are not opposed to the coming of the white people into our territory, provided this be carried out justly and in accordance with the British principle embodied in the Royal Proclamation." The Nisga'a recommended the establishment of a commission, which would include Native appointees, to settle the land issue fairly.

Just as the Nisga'a were readying their petition for London, Duncan Campbell Scott assumed control of Indian Affairs. Even though the department had a fiduciary obligation to protect Aboriginal title, he did everything in his power to thwart the Nisga'a and other British Columbia groups in their search for a just resolution of their claims. Many federal and provincial politicians supported him. Scott's first move involved persuading the federal government to approve an Order in Council, during the spring of 1914, that promised it would refer British Columbia title claims to the Exchequer Court of Canada and give the Native groups the right of appeal to the Judicial Committee of the Privy Council only if they agreed to surrender through treaties any lands that either court awarded to them. Additional conditions stated that the Native people would have to accept whatever final recommendations the McKenna–McBride Commission made, and that they would have to accept legal counsel appointed by the Crown. Of course the Nishga Land Committee, the Indian Rights Association, and the Interior Tribes of British Columbia promptly rejected the government's arrangement.

In spite of Native opposition, the McKenna–McBride Commission took to the road, holding hearings between 1913 and 1916. Many nations, including the Nisga'a, boycotted its deliberations for not addressing the issue of Aboriginal title. They also feared that their very participation would jeopardize their Native claims. The Nisga'a held out until after a delegation they had sent to Ottawa returned from visits with the minister of Indian Affairs and Scott bearing promises that their involvement in the McKenna–McBride Commission hearing "would not prejudice their larger claim to Aboriginal title."

The widespread Native distrust of the McKenna–McBride Commission gave the various regional associations a strong incentive to unite politically so that they could speak with one voice. Andrew Paull and Peter Kelly were the key players in this effort. Paull was born on Chief Capilano's reserve in North Vancouver. The reserve had long been a focus of Native protests against white encroachment on reserve lands because of the threat posed by the expanding city. The pressured sales of the Songhee reserve in Victoria in 1911 and the Kitsilano reserve in Vancouver in 1913 stiffened the resolve of other Coast Salish-speaking groups to resist further losses. Paull became directly involved in the political struggles by serving as secretary to his band and as interpreter to the McKenna–McBride Commission. Kelly, a member of a noble Skidegate Haida family, graduated from the Coqualeetza residential school near Chilliwack, which the Methodists operated. He continued with his religious studies at Columbia College and became an ordained Methodist minister. Paull and Kelly both played key roles in the formation of the Allied Tribes of British Columbia in 1916.

Only days after the Allied Tribes held their first meeting, the McKenna–McBride Commission issued its report. It proved that the Indians' fears about the likely outcome of the commission had been justified. The commissioners created some new reserves and added lands to some existing ones, but also eliminated tracts of land for reserves. These came to be known as "cutoff lands." Most were located in the southern coastal and interior region and were parcels coveted by settlers and land speculators. Premier John Oliver's government delayed for two years after the report was published, then passed the Indian Affairs Settlement Act, authorizing negotiations with the federal government and the Indian nations. Oliver also asked the Allied Tribes for their reaction to the commission's report. After holding a series of meetings during the summer of 1919, the Allied Tribes presented Oliver with a six-thousand-word reply that totally rejected the recommendations of the McKenna–McBride Commission and put forward a comprehensive claim to Aboriginal title instead. It reaffirmed the intention of the Allied Tribes to take their case to the Privy Council.

The actions of the Allied Tribes infuriated Scott, who immediately began conniving to reduce reserve lands in British Columbia without first obtaining band-council approvals as required by the Indian Act. He was successful. In 1920 Parliament passed the British Columbia Indian Lands Settlement Act. It authorized the federal cabinet to implement the recommendations of the McKenna–McBride Commission "notwithstanding any provisions of the Indian Act to the contrary." Four years later, the Liberal cabinet of Mackenzie King passed an Order in Council executing the McKenna–McBride Commission's proposals over the objections of the Allied Tribes. As to the lands assigned as reserves, the province did not actually hand over title to Ottawa until 1938.

During these very dark days, a ray of hope came from London. In 1921 the Judicial Committee of the Privy Council made a ruling about unextinguished Aboriginal title in Nigeria that had implications throughout the British Empire. It ruled that Aboriginal title was a pre-existing right that continued to exist "unless the contrary is established by the context or the circumstances." If the Nisga'a or the Allied Tribes could present their case before the Judicial Committee, they might win. This prospect encouraged Paull and Kelly to press forward, while federal and provincial politicians and Scott scrambled to find ways to prevent the petition from getting to London.

In 1925 the Allied Tribes drafted a petition to Parliament asking for the establishment of a special joint committee of the House of Commons and the Senate as the first step on the road to London. Predictably, the joint committee that was formed two years later discounted the testimony of Paull, Kelly, and their lawyer on behalf of the Allied Tribes and rejected their claims. In their report the members even put forward the absurd notion that the Hudson's Bay Company had conquered the territory for the British Crown. After rejecting the claim and the need for treaties, the committee members recommended that collectively the Native groups of the province should receive an annual payment of $100,000 in place of annuities. The government subsequently implemented this policy.

The joint committee also made the sinister proposal that the government not tolerate any further claims. Scott was delighted and promptly drafted an amendment (Section 141) to the Indian Act, barring Indians from soliciting funds to hire lawyers to fight claims cases unless the government approved. Parliament quickly passed the amendment in 1927. Not only did this undemocratic measure effectively block white "agitators" from helping the Native cause in Canada, but it also barred Native organizations from forming to promote land claims.

Section 141 prompted the Allied Tribes to disband, and Kelly and Paull left the political scene temporarily. Kelly returned to his ministry work, and Paull became a sportswriter for the *Province* newspaper in Vancouver and a promoter of a wide range of Native activities. Until Section 141 was dropped from the Indian Act in 1951, the Nishga Land Committee was the only Native organization that remained openly committed to the title struggle.

The erosion of traditional fishing rights by the expanding industrial salmon fishery became a growing concern for the coastal nations. Dianne Newell's *Tangled Webs of History* shows that the actions of the various reserve commissions made matters worse. The commissioners awarded small enclaves to coastal people in the belief that these villagers did not need extensive tracts of land because of their fish-based economies. However, the expropriation of more and more salmon and other fish stocks by canning companies meant that nations on the coast and along the salmon rivers and lakes faced a bleak economic future. It was at this time that Native commercial fishermen in Alaska provided the Native people of coastal British Columbia with a way to address their predicament. The Alaskan groups had organized themselves into the Alaska Native Brotherhood to fight for a variety of political and economic rights. In 1931 Alfred Adams, a commercial fisherman from Masset and recruiter of Native labour for northern canneries, decided that the time was right to form a similar association in British Columbia. At a meeting he called at Port Simpson, leading commercial fishermen from the Haida and Tsimshian villages formed the Native Brotherhood of British Columbia, elected Adams president, and pledged to work for the recognition of Aboriginal rights in hunting, fishing, trapping, and off-reserve logging activities. In other words, they were pressing for most of the fundamental economic rights that would flow out of the recognition of Aboriginal title *without* directly pressing for land-claim settlements. In this way the Native Brotherhood skirted the limitations of Section 141. The association also fought for an end to the potlatch ban and the replacement of residential schools with ones located in Native communities.

The Native Brotherhood's structure was similar to that of the Nishga Land Committee. Various villages constituted branches within the organization, and each vice-president represented a different nation. Eventually the women's section, the Sisterhood, groomed female leaders to head the struggle for better wages and working conditions for women in the canning plants. The organizers worked hard to expand the Native Brotherhood. Prominent members provided commercial fishing boats to help them extend their outreach effort to coastal villages. Soon the Native Brotherhood gained strong support along most of the north coast. There were notable hold-outs. The Nishga Land Committee, for example, blocked any Nisga'a village from joining because the Native Brotherhood did not take an overt stand on the issue of Aboriginal title.

When the federal government decided to impose an income tax on Native commercial fishermen in 1942, it provided the Native Brotherhood with a new Aboriginal-rights issue that enabled it to expand to the south coast. Native leaders took the position that the fish belonged to their people rather than to the government, and, therefore, Native fishermen should be tax exempt. This issue drew Andrew Paull back into the fray. In 1942 he joined the Native Brotherhood and embarked on an intensive, and very successful, recruiting campaign among the Coast Salish and Kwakwaka'wakw. The Kwakwaka'wakw already had their own commercial fishing alliance, the Pacific Coast Native Fishermen's Association, but they amalgamated with the Native Brotherhood during the Second World War. Paull helped facilitate the merger.

The expanded organization not only continued to press for action on a wide range of Aboriginal-rights issues but also began to act as a union for Native fishermen. The newly formed powerful United Fishermen's and Allied Workers' Union (UFAW) pressured Native fishers and plant workers to join it. Although many Native women did, most Native fishermen took out membership in the Brotherhood. The Brotherhood signed its first contract with canning companies in 1943. It and the UFAW usually bargained jointly for subsequent contracts. About this time some north-coast hold-outs also joined the Brotherhood: the Nisga'a and the Haida from Skidegate were among them. Peter Kelly became chairman of the Native Brotherhood's newly created legislative committee, and Frank Calder, the adopted son of the founder of the Nishga Land Committee, Arthur Calder, took over the position of secretary. Although other Native political organizations existed else-where in Canada when the north-coast groups founded the Native Brotherhood, none equalled its strength, stability, and vigour. It remains an important force today.

Paull's association with the Native Brotherhood proved to be fractious and of short duration. In 1943 he travelled to Montreal for a meeting of non-treaty Native people who wanted to form a national organization for the purpose of pressuring the government to revise the Indian Act. They created the Brotherhood of Canadian Indians, renamed the next year as the North American Indian Brotherhood, and elected Paull president. The new Indian Brotherhood gave Paull a platform on the national stage and a vehicle to closely monitor the actions of Indian Affairs—something long overdue. While heading the Indian Brotherhood, Paull also devoted his considerable energy and organizational skills to organizing the interior nations of British Columbia, who had had little to do with the Native Brotherhood because of their preoccupation with coastal economic issues. The result was the Confederacy of the Interior Tribes of British Columbia, which Paull also headed. Squabbles occurred over who should represent British Columbia's Indians when Parliament convened a special joint committee in Ottawa to consider overhauling the Indian Act in 1947. The committee invited the better-known Native Brotherhood.

The revised Indian Act of 1951 that followed from these hearings eliminated the prohibitions against giveaway ceremonies and dances and cancelled the ban on claims-related activities. The latter move did not seem risky to politicians because the Supreme Court of Canada had replaced the Judicial Committee of the Privy Council as the final court of appeal in 1949. They were confident that this Canadian court would be sympathetic to the government's position. The politicians promptly discovered that the Aboriginal-title issue was alive and powerful. Native leaders in British Columbia, however, could not agree, then as now, about the strategy to adopt. Should they press forward with a single comprehensive claim, or pursue separate claims for the various nations?

The Nisga'a repeatedly refused to abandon their own claim in deference to a unified one, even though the Nishga Land Committee had long ago ceased to be an effective organization. Frank Calder, who was now an experienced and prominent Native leader, was ready to lead the renewed struggle. He had been elected to the British Columbia legislature in 1949 as a CCF representative for the northwestern riding of Atlin, where Native voters were in the majority. He was one of the first Native people to hold a seat in a Canadian legislature. The 1947 repeal of the provincial legislation prohibiting Indians from voting made his election possible. Calder believed that the Nisga'a should continue the battle for the recognition of their title through a Native lobby that was more democratic than the old Land Committee, which had been composed solely of hereditary chiefs. His efforts bore fruit. The Nishga Tribal Council, a regional political alliance of Indian bands, took shape in the late 1950s and was formally incorporated in 1963. It allowed for the representation of the hereditary chiefs of the various villages, but other people could be elected as well. The Nuu chah nulth also created a tribal council in 1958. The formation of these councils represented an important departure from the band-council structure that had been imposed by the Indian Act and fostered by Indian Affairs policy.

While these developments were taking place on the coast, a new leader emerged in the interior—George Manuel. Manuel, a Shuswap, firmly believed that his people needed to work with other Native groups on pressing matters of mutual concern, and beginning in the 1940s, he worked hard to persuade bands from the surrounding area to form a single political organization. His efforts led to the creation in 1958 of the Aboriginal Native Rights Committee of the Interior Tribes of British Columbia. It consisted largely of Coast and Interior Salish groups. In 1959 Manuel asked other provincial Native associations to meet at Kamloops. Kelly came as chief spokesperson for the Native Brotherhood, Calder arrived heading a Nishga Tribal Council delegation, and Manuel headed the Native Aboriginal Rights Committee contingent. Calder and Manuel wanted to resurrect the Aboriginal-title fight that the government had derailed thirty-two years earlier, and both wanted Native British Columbians to speak with a united voice at the 1959–61 Joint Committee of the Senate and House of Commons hearings aimed at overhauling the administration of Indian Affairs.

The assembly failed to reach a consensus about the ways and means to press their title grievances. In particular, the Native Brotherhood's representatives balked at the Nisga'a demand to pledge any new association to a renewal of the Native claims battle, knowing that the Nisga'a had decided to continue their quest through the courts. Many delegates thought the stakes were too high for such a gamble. If the courts rejected the challenge, seemingly the most likely outcome, Aboriginal claims might be jeopardized forever. When the meeting broke up, the Nisga'a headed off, determined to pursue their claim alone.

As the First Nations groups struggled to find a common voice, the federal government decided to take the initiative on the Aboriginal-title question. Among its many recommendations, the 1961 report of the joint committee had included the Native suggestion that a land-claims commission be created. When the Liberal government of Lester B. Pearson came to power in 1963, it promised to create one to settle all outstanding Indian claims and brought forward a new bill for that purpose. Native communities overwhelmingly rejected the proposed legislation. It did not acknowledge Aboriginal title as being the basis of land claims, and it did not allow Indians to file suits against the provinces for land. The lawyer for the Native Brotherhood of British Columbia, Thomas Berger, insisted that Native people had to have that right to redress their past losses. Unmoved, the government brought the bill back to the House without addressing these major objections. Most Native groups and leaders, the Nisga'a and Frank Calder among them, denounced it, and as a result, the bill died.

THE CHANGING POLITICAL CLIMATE

The political climate of the country was changing in ways that would help the Nisga'a cause and those of Native leaders nationwide who were also pushing for recognition of Native and treaty rights. In the 1960s the civil-rights movement and the war against poverty in the United States made Canadians more aware of minority groups and their plight—especially that of marginalized Native Canadians. Meanwhile, the issues of granting special status for Quebec and for the French language outside that province raised questions about the kind of political recognition that Native people should have in the country. Native leaders pointed out that if any people deserved the status of First (or founding) Nations, they did. Surely, they argued, their rights should be at least equal to those granted to people of French or English descent.

These various developments forced Indian Affairs to develop new policies that were more in tune with the times. In addition, Prime Minister Pearson's government had committed itself to developing cost-sharing programs with the provinces in the areas of health, social services, and regional economic development. Indian Affairs officials were eager to transfer many of the department's social and educational programs to the provinces because they were becoming too costly.

In 1963 the department commissioned Harry Hawthorn, an anthropologist from the University of British Columbia, to head up a research team to collect information about the social and economic circumstances of Native communities and make suggestions for future government policy. The first volume of the Hawthorn Report (1966 and 1967) showed conclusively that Native people occu-

Temporary Committee of National Indian Council of Canada, Regina, 1961. The creation of this council in 1961 was the first effort to build a modern national communication network among Aboriginal people. The leaders and members came mostly from urban areas and included status and non-status Indians. Aboriginal leaders disbanded the council in 1968 and created two new organizations: the National Indian Brotherhood (the precursor of the Assembly of First Nations), for status Indians, and the Native Council of Canada, for non-status Indians. Left to right: Telford Adams, representing Ontario; George Manuel, representing British Columbia; A. H. Brass (chair), representing Saskatchewan; Marion Meadmore (secretary-treasurer); David Knight, representing Saskatchewan; and Joe Keeper, representing Manitoba.

pied the lowest economic rung in Canada. They were "citizens minus." The researchers estimated that it would cost the government hundreds of millions of dollars to rectify the situation. They proposed that Indians be treated as "citizens plus." By this they meant that Native people should have a greater choice of lifestyles—particularly the freedom to live in or apart from their communities— while retaining their special status and privileges. For this to be a possibility, the depressed economic circumstances, inadequate housing, and poor health conditions that characterized most reserves would have to be addressed. The report also stressed that the government should abandon all forced assimilation programs and concluded that there was no legal barrier that prevented provinces from sharing part of the burden of delivering educational and social programs to Indian communities. The Hawthorn Report received considerable media attention and made the public aware of the gravity of the problems Native people faced.

Well before the Hawthorn Report's release, Indian Affairs undertook new initiatives aimed at addressing the poverty issue. The so-called community-development program—launched in 1964—was one of these. This scheme involved sending Native and non-Native development workers into Native settlements to foster self-determination and self-confidence, which would in turn encourage the communities to become less reliant on Indian agents and district superintendents. George Manuel served as a development worker among the Cowichan and the Nuu chah nulth from 1966 to 1968. The program worked so well, as he and others pointed out, that Indian agents and superintendents branded the development workers "trouble-makers" because they weakened the bureaucrats' hold on their clients. As a result, the department cancelled the program in 1968. One of its most important legacies, however, was heightened political awareness and activism in many Indian communities.

Beginning in 1965, the department established Indian advisory boards to obtain Native input at the regional and national levels for setting national goals and recommending changes to the Indian Act. Bands and Native organizations appointed members to the various regional boards and to the National Indian Advisory Board. For the most part, board members criticized Indian Affairs policies and argued that planning should begin at the community level. Once again, the department officials refused to accept meaningful Indian input and disregarded most of the board's recommendations. Ultimately, Native leaders rejected the advisory-board approach and demanded more direct involvement in the formulation of policies that affected their lives. Harold Cardinal, who was rebuilding the Alberta Indian Association at that time, was one of the leaders who attacked the tokenism of the advisory-board approach. In spite of their shortcomings, the boards did bring Native leaders from various areas together and helped some of them, notably George Manuel, who became co-chair of the National Indian Advisory Board, gain national prominence.

By the time of Pierre Elliott Trudeau's election in 1968, on the promise of a "just society" for Canadians, pressure was building on all fronts for yet another major overhaul of the Indian Act. In 1968 Indian Affairs sent the booklet *Choosing a Path* to every Indian household to stimulate discussion. It described the current act in great detail and offered government suggestions for possible revisions. Trudeau's minister of Indian Affairs, Jean Chrétien, travelled to many communities to participate in the discussions and learned that most Indians were more concerned with Native claims, treaty rights, and special status than they were with revisions to the Indian Act.

Soon the Trudeau administration grew weary of the discussions. Philosophically, the prime minister opposed awarding special treatment to different cultural groups within Canadian society and did not believe governments should redress injustices inflicted on people in the past. Even as public discussions were under way, the Prime Minister's Office and the Privy Council began drafting pro-

Harold Cardinal (standing) addresses Prime Minister Trudeau (left, with back to camera) and other cabinet members on June 4, 1970. Cardinal argued for the establishment of a "truly impartial claims commission appointed after consultation with the Indians." A delegation of about two hundred Natives also attended the meeting.

posed changes to Indian policy and revisions to the act. On June 24, 1969, the government flew Native leaders to Ottawa, and Chrétien told them that he would present a major policy paper to the House the next day but gave them no details about his impending announcement. On June 25 they listened in stunned silence from the House of Commons galleries as Chrétien delivered the now-infamous 1969 White Paper on Indian policy, in which the Trudeau government pledged to repeal the Indian Act and replace it with a land act, terminate treaties, and eliminate the Indian Affairs department in five years. Yet again the government had given the appearance of wanting Native input, then had gone in its own direction when it did not like the feedback from Native leaders.

It was no longer possible for the government to conduct Aboriginal affairs in this way, however. Native leaders spoke out forcefully against the unilateral action. Dave Courchene, leader of the Manitoba Indian Brotherhood, probably best captured their sentiments when he said, "I feel like a man who has been told he must die and am now to be consulted on the method of implementing this decision." He continued, "A hundred or more years of acceptance on the part of the Indians, of policies and programs fostered by political experts who at the same time considered themselves amateur sociologists has led us once again up the garden path of false hopes, broken promises, colossal disrespect and monumental bad faith." The National Indian Brotherhood denounced the government's denial of their Aboriginal rights. This organization had been created in 1968 largely because of the initiatives of Native political leaders in the Prairie provinces, particularly Walter Deiter, president of the Federation of Saskatchewan Indians and later the first president of the National Indian Brotherhood; Dave Courchene, president of the Manitoba Indian Brotherhood; and Harold Cardinal, president of the Indian Association of Alberta. The National Indian Brotherhood had become a powerful organization under the direction of its second president, George Manuel (1970–76), and it lobbied hard to have treaty rights included in any revised act; certainly the membership did not want them eliminated. Likewise, they were eager to have steps taken to improve living conditions for Native people, but they had never recommended transferring to the provinces the services that Indian Affairs provided, nor would they ever.

Courchene believed that the White Paper was intended to cut short the development of Native political organizations because they were beginning to be effective champions of Native-rights issues. Today most observers of Native history and political development believe that one of the most important long-term

Frank Calder, the principal plaintiff in the famous Calder case, speaks to reporters in 1973.

impacts of the release of the White Paper was that it galvanized the Native nationalist movement into a potent force—an outcome that was the opposite of what the government intended.

The best-known public statement against the White Paper is Harold Cardinal's book, *The Unjust Society*. The Alberta Indian Association, of which Cardinal was president, and the National Indian Brotherhood endorsed most of his argument in their own counterproposal, the Red Paper, which the leaders of the brotherhood ceremoniously handed to Chrétien and the full cabinet on June 4, 1970. The concept of "citizen plus" was central to this manifesto. When addressing the cabinet, Cardinal reiterated the need for the government to recognize Aboriginal and treaty rights. He proposed the establishment of an impartial claims commission whose decisions would be binding on all concerned. Faced with overwhelming Native opposition, and the public support Native leaders had garnered, the federal government withdrew the White Paper. Three years later, in 1973, the

Supreme Court of Canada's decision in the *Calder* case forced the federal government to rethink its position on Aboriginal title.

OFF TO COURT: *CALDER*

The legal battle over Aboriginal title in British Columbia, which the Nisga'a had sought for so long, unexpectedly began in the early 1960s with the shooting of six deer by Clifford White and David Bob on Vancouver Island near Nanaimo. The two men killed the animals out of season and without a licence, in contravention of provincial game laws. The defendants claimed the right to do so on the grounds that they had been hunting on unoccupied land, which Governor Douglas had purchased from their Saalequun ancestors in 1854. This treaty had guaranteed them the "liberty to hunt over the unoccupied lands, and to fish as formerly." Thomas Berger argued the case, asserting that the purchase was a valid treaty negotiated in accord with the Royal Proclamation of 1763, which protected Native and treaty rights in British Columbia. The province countered with the argument that the Douglas treaties were private agreements concluded between the nations and the HBC and that revisions to the Indian Act in 1951 extended the provisions of the provincial game acts to Indians. The British Columbia Supreme Court and the British Columbia Court of Appeal accepted the defendants' position that Douglas had concluded a treaty, which remained in force. The Supreme Court of Canada upheld the decisions of the lower courts, although it avoided addressing the Aboriginal-rights issue head-on by limiting its ruling to the question of the validity of the Douglas treaties.

Greatly heartened by the outcome in *Bob and White* (1966), the Nishga Tribal Council promptly hired Berger to prepare an Aboriginal-title case on their behalf. In the now-famous *Calder* (1973) case (*Calder et al. v. Attorney-General of British Columbia*), which went to trial in the spring of 1969, the Nisga'a asserted that their Aboriginal title had never been extinguished. The province countered that the title was not valid because the British government had never intended the Royal Proclamation of 1763 to apply to provincial territory. Even if the Nisga'a had once held title, colonial land legislation had implicitly extinguished it. The British Columbia Supreme Court supported the province, and the Court of Appeal unanimously upheld its decision. Though badly bruised, the Nisga'a advised Berger to appeal to the Supreme Court of Canada. Again, they had to go forward alone. The National Indian Brotherhood asked Calder and the Nisga'a to halt their action while discussions of various rights issues with the federal government went ahead. Understandably, Native leaders still feared that an adverse ruling from the high court would slam the door on the Aboriginal-title issue forever. As it turned out, the Nisga'a were wise to persist.

In *Calder*, six of the seven Supreme Court of Canada judges recognized that Aboriginal title did exist when European colonization of the territory began. Three of the justices agreed with British Columbia that colonial legislation had subsequently extinguished that title; three rejected this idea; and the seventh refused to rule on the matter by citing a technicality, contending that the province had not given the Nisga'a permission to bring the suit against it. One Nisga'a chief observed that this was tantamount to saying, "If someone stole your property, you had to get that person's permission, the robber …, to even go to court and sue him."

Although the Supreme Court decision discouraged the Nisga'a, they had won a major victory towards establishing the possibility that unextinguished Aboriginal rights existed in Canada. Trudeau invited the Nisga'a chiefs to Ottawa and told them that he was impressed that six judges had determined that Native people owned the land before contact. He was even more swayed by the fact that three of them—those whom he held in the highest regard—believed the Nisga'a still held their title. For Trudeau this meant that the Nisga'a and other First Nations in Canada very possibly might win future legal battles over the issue. For this reason, his government altered its course and in the mid-1970s began to lay the groundwork for claims negotiations.

CHAPTER 20

SEARCHING FOR SETTLEMENT

We know from bitter experience that others do not know what is best for us. We are engaged in a fight we will never give up, a fight to implement the policies we know will help us lift ourselves above our present problems. We hope for and welcome the support of other people in Canada in that struggle.

—Georges Erasmus, past president of the Dene Nation, past northern vice-chief of the Assembly of First Nations, appointee to the Order of Canada, 1987, and co-chair of the Royal Commission on Aboriginal Peoples, speaking in 1989

On a cold, damp December morning in 1972, several dozen Cree and Inuit hunters filed into the Palais de Justice in Montreal to challenge the right of the province of Quebec to go ahead with the largest development project in North American history. On April 30, 1971, Premier Robert Bourassa had announced that his government was launching a $5.6 billion hydroelectric generation project in the southeastern James Bay area. In preparation, the province had created the James Bay Development Corporation and the municipality of James Bay, an administrative district that included virtually all the territory to be affected by the gargantuan project. This 133,000-square-mile tract encompassed the best fishing and trapping areas of the Cree of Rupert House, Nemiscau, Waswanipi, and Mistassini. No one had bothered to consult them or their Inuit neighbours in the planning stages, or taken their rights and economic interests into consideration, so the Cree (under Billy Diamond) and Inuit had little recourse but to appeal to the courts. Initially, the Indians of Quebec Association, the neighbouring Inuit, and environmental groups backed them.

338

THE JAMES BAY AND NORTHERN QUEBEC AGREEMENT

Justice Albert-H. Malouf of the Quebec Superior Court paid close attention to the Cree and Inuit's petition to halt the project. However, in his book *Strangers Devour the Land*, the journalist Boyce Richardson says that lawyers representing the construction companies did not take the proceedings seriously at first. They did not believe that the Cree and Inuit had any Aboriginal rights in northern Quebec. Justice Malouf thought otherwise, and to everyone's great surprise, he granted a hearing.

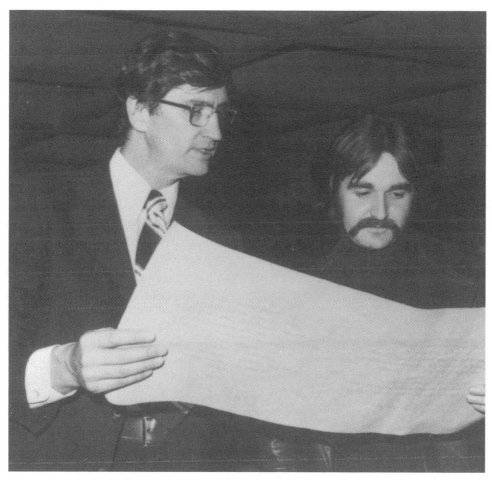

The minister of Indian and Northern Affairs, Judd Buchanan (left), and Charlie Watt, president of the Northern Quebec Inuit Association, examining the James Bay and Northern Quebec Agreement, 1975. Watt, who was one of the principal Native negotiators, also helped organize the Labrador Inuit Association. He was sworn into the Canadian Senate in 1984.

After hearing 167 witnesses during seventy-eight days of testimony, and considering 312 exhibits, Malouf took about five months to reach his decision. He granted the Cree and Inuit an interim injunction.

Malouf's ruling proved to be a temporary victory. Only six days later, the Quebec Court of Appeals suspended the injunction and the companies resumed their work. The legal warfare continued for another year until the appeal court overturned Malouf's judgment. Meanwhile, the Supreme Court of Canada had issued its ruling in *Calder*. Given the uncertainty about what the final outcome of the legal wrangling over the James Bay project and Aboriginal rights would be, the provincial government decided to negotiate with the James Bay bands, under the leadership of Billy Diamond, the elected chief of Rupert House First Nation. All the parties reached an agreement in principle on November 15, 1974. The following year the Grand Council of the Crees of Quebec (established in 1974), the Inuit, and the provincial and federal governments signed the James Bay and Northern Quebec Agreement. Diamond, a founding member of the Grand Council and chair of the Cree Regional Authority at its 1975 establishment, was the prime mover and signatory to the agreement. Subsequently, the compact was modified to include the Innu, who lived inland far to the east of the James Bay lowlands.

This was a landmark agreement, the first major settlement that Native people had concluded with the Crown since the 1929–30 amendment to Treaty 9, covering Ontario north of the Albany River. This modern "treaty" went much further than the earlier accords. The Cree and their Inuit neighbours demanded much greater compensation; they wanted their hunting and fishing rights clearly defined and protected; and they wanted to be able to conduct their own affairs. The James Bay people gained major concessions on all these issues. They are to receive $225 million in compensation, paid over a twenty-five-year period. The bands retained complete control of the lands adjacent to their communities (13,700 square kilometres [5,300 square miles]) and obtained exclusive hunting, fishing, and trapping rights to a territory of 151,600 square kilometres (58,500 square miles). In addition, they secured equal representation on a wildlife-management committee and the recognition that Native subsistence requirements had priority over the interests of others in districts where Aboriginal people did not retain exclusive hunting rights. The agreement also provided for the establishment of an income-security program for hunters and trappers; the recognition of Native languages as official languages of administration in the district; the creation of a development corporation to handle investments for the local Native people; and the creation of a Cree

Air Creebec is an example of the modern business organizations that Aboriginal people have created from the financial settlements of modern land-claim agreements.

Regional Authority to represent all Cree on local government bodies and to co-ordinate various social and economic programs.

The accord has had a major impact on the lives of the Native people of the James Bay area. Instead of the fragmented band-oriented society of the pre-1974 era, the Cree have created a coherent regional society through the Cree Regional Authority, their efforts to develop better regional transportation systems (Air Creebec being an example), Cree-oriented education programs, and improved health-care services. The Cree have also improved the local standard of living by strengthening the hunting-and-trapping sector of the economy and by expanding other employment opportunities. By the early 1980s, more Cree were full-time hunters than had been the case before the agreement, thanks largely to the hunters' income-security program. This scheme provides full-time hunters with a minimum cash income and an allowance for every day they spend in the bush. The Cree Trappers Association also helps by looking after the marketing of the trappers' furs. Unfortunately, the non-Native anti-fur-trapping movement is undermining these gains by destroying international fur markets. Most of the new jobs outside the hunting-and-trapping sector have been associated with the expansion of social services and the construction and maintenance of new houses, schools, and other government facilities.

The pressures that the James Bay Cree and Inuit faced in 1972 and 1973 leave no question that the agreement, and the advances that have come from it, represent an unprecedented accomplishment. Nonetheless, the accord has generated controversy. The Native community remains divided over whether the Cree and their neighbours received enough benefits to offset their concessions, particularly the surrender of their right to make any further Aboriginal claims. More worrisome is the concern that they may not have protected themselves sufficiently against the Quebec government's hydroelectric-generation plans. Only time will tell. The Cree have shown, however, that they are formidable foes when it comes to battling for public support to oppose such schemes. For instance, they launched a multi-media campaign against the development of Great Whale River and persuaded the utilities in New York State, one of Hydro-Québec's largest customers, not to buy power from this proposed project unless the province held proper impact-assessment hearings. In 2002, after protracted legal action, lobbying and negotiating, the Grand Council of the Cree reached a $3.4-billion agreement with the Quebec government that allowed for the development of new hydroelectric plants along the Eastman River and Rupert River subject to the completion of proper environmental reviews.

NORTH OF THE 60TH PARALLEL

It was during the course of Justice Malouf's consideration of the Cree and Inuit petition that the Trudeau government reversed its position about Aboriginal title in response to the *Calder* judgment and embraced a new comprehensive claims policy. It created the Office of Native Claims within Indian Affairs in 1974 and established procedures for dealing with submissions from Native groups. The government recognized two broad categories of claims—"comprehensive" ones, which concern unsurrendered lands, and "specific" ones, which are grievances bands and Native nations hold against federal and provincial governments for alleged failures to properly exercise their responsibilities as trustees of Aboriginal interests. The latter category concerns such matters as outstanding complaints about alleged treaty violations, forced reductions in reserves, and allegations of government mishandling of band funds. By the mid-1980s, the Office of Native Claims anticipated that Aboriginal groups ultimately would file a total of between 1,500 and 2,500 specific claims.

The settlement procedure is costly and time consuming. Bands and nations must furnish documentation to support the claims they file. However, few of them have the financial resources to pay for the necessary research. This means that the federal government has to advance claimants the funding they need as loans or "contributions." Those who are successful must repay the advances. By 1982 the federal government had provided Native groups with $116 million for research.

Ten years after the establishment of the Office of Native Claims, Aboriginal groups had filed comprehensive claims to all of Canada north of the 60th parallel and to most of British Columbia. Settlements proceeded very slowly at first, because the federal government demanded that any agreement had to include the total surrender and extinguishment of Aboriginal land rights. Ottawa insisted on these conditions both to make the agreements final and to avoid having to share royalty incomes flowing from resource development with Native groups. Understandably, the earlier history of treaty making made Aboriginal leaders nervous about "once and for all" settlements, and talks stalled nearly everywhere until after 1986, when the government modified its land-claims policy to allow for the continuation of Aboriginal title on lands set aside for Native people. Another reason for the lack of headway was that the government negotiated only six claims at a time.

To date, the biggest post-James Bay settlements have all been made in the lands north of the 60th parallel with groups whom the government had largely ignored until recently. For instance, Ottawa officials paid little attention to the Inuit during the time it was trying to subdue and forcibly assimilate Native groups in southern Canada. These Arctic people obtained little help from the government even after arctic-fox prices collapsed in the 1930s, causing severe economic hardships. Indeed, after the northerly extension of Quebec's boundaries in 1912, the federal government and the province squabbled about who was responsible for the Inuit. The matter was not settled until 1939, when the Supreme Court of Canada ruled that the Inuit were "Indians" for the purposes of the British North America Act of 1867, making them a federal responsibility. The outbreak of the Second World War forced southern politicians to pay more attention to these people. During the conflict, Canadians and Americans built and operated various airbases in the North to ferry planes and supplies to Europe. After the war ended, the military remained to monitor Canadian air space against possible Soviet air or missile attack. These personnel brought the plight of the Inuit, particularly their poor health, to public attention.

P. A. Cooper, governor of the Hudson's Bay Company, with pensioners at Moose Factory, 1934. After Native men had contributed years of service as employees or faithful traders, the company awarded medals to them. Although they were proud to receive the medals, the men believed they deserved greater compensation in areas where game was scarce and bush living difficult.

The federal government addressed the Inuit's problems in several ways. It created settlements so that it could provide medical and social services cheaply. Inuvik, in the west, and Iqaluit, in the east, were two of the earliest of these types of communities. It also set up a program to eradicate tuberculosis, which had reached epidemic proportions among the Inuit by the 1940s. Although the epidemic was arrested, the officials who conducted the program did so with remarkably little sensitivity. For instance, beginning in 1947, the RCMP Arctic patrol conducted shipboard chest X-rays. Officers quarantined on board any Inuit who tested positive and transported them to sanitoria in Toronto, Montreal, Hamilton, and Edmonton for treatment. Officials made no effort to tell the patients' kinfolk where they were sent or how their treatment was progressing. When Inuit patients were released, they were often moved to the Arctic settlement that was most accessible from the discharging sanitarium. Often these places were far from the patients' homes.

Traditional Inuit naming practices made it very difficult for outsiders to administer government programs, so bureaucrats found it nearly impossible to keep track of their Inuit clients. The Inuit did not use family names, their naming customs made no gender distinctions, and most persons received several names. Compounding these problems for outsiders, the Inuit did not alter their traditional naming practices after the arrival of Christian missionaries. Instead, they merely added Christian names to the ones they already used, without regard to gender. In an attempt to deal with this predicament, the Northwest Territorial Council approved a plan in 1941 that involved issuing a numbered disc to each person. This proved to be a poor solution to the problem, however. Understandably, the Inuit objected to being identified by a number, and people passed the discs around. In the late 1960s, the government decided to assign family names, even though this interfered with, and completely disregarded, Inuit beliefs of what constitutes a family.

The most famous instance of government callousness towards the Inuit was the way it used them as pawns in its efforts to assert sovereignty in the High Arctic by founding new settlements on remote islands. One particularly notorious case involved the forced relocation of the people of Inoucdjouac (formerly Port Harrison), Quebec, to Ellesmere Island in 1953. The government alleged that it moved the people because it feared impending food shortages would make the Inoucdjouac residents dependent on welfare. In 1990 an investigation led the

The return of some Inuit to the North in 1960 after prolonged hospitalization for tuberculosis. This disease was rampant in many Inuit communities in the 1950s and 1960s, often affecting more than half the families in a settlement. Medical evacuations to deal with this problem disrupted family life, and the patients suffered from isolation and culture shock. This insensitively administered scheme did halt the spread of the epidemic, however.

Issuing family allowances to an Inuit family in 1948. Unlike other Canadian families, Inuit families, as well as Native families living in the Northwest Territories, received their allowances in kind. By this means the government introduced many new foods into the northern diet. The government used the program to force parents to send their children to school by withholding allowances from those who did not comply.

House of Commons Aboriginal Affairs Committee to conclude otherwise. Committee members decided that the government had forcibly relocated the community to establish a Canadian presence in the High Arctic. The move inflicted great suffering and hardship on the people. Weather conditions were much more severe at their new location. In their home territory, they had depended heavily on migratory waterfowl; on Ellesmere Island, they were forced to alter their diet and hunt sea mammals and polar bears. In 1992 the Mulroney government finally agreed to apologize to the Inoucdjouac Inuit, to compensate them for the wrongs they had suffered, and to help the survivors move back home.

These various experiences made it clear to the Inuit that they needed to protect their economic interests and have more control over their own affairs. Development pressures in the Arctic, stimulated by soaring oil and gas prices in the late 1960s and early 1970s, made this need urgent. By the early 1970s the federal government had issued exploration permits covering 75,000,000 hectares (185,000,000 acres) of the Canadian Arctic. Until this time neither government officials nor the energy companies had given much thought to the impact that drilling operations or oil and gas transportation would have on the Inuit, or their southern neighbours. This changed suddenly when major deposits of oil and gas were found in the Beaufort Sea and consortiums announced various plans to move the fuel to southern markets. The Mackenzie Valley Pipeline proposal of 1971 is the best known of these early schemes.

When the pipeline was announced, the Inuit, the Dene, and environmental groups began to protest against its construction. The government responded by creating the Mackenzie Valley Pipeline Inquiry in 1974 and appointed Thomas Berger, who had become a justice on the British Columbia Supreme Court, to lead it. Over a three-year period, Berger took his commission into many remote Native communities where Dene, Inuit, and Métis told him that the project would destroy their way of life and give them little of value in return. They demanded that no work begin before the government had satisfactorily addressed their land claims. No one put their case more dramatically and forcefully than the Dene chief T'Seleie. During the August 1975 hearings at Fort Good Hope, he turned to the president of one of the oil companies and said, "You are the twentieth-century General Custer. You are coming with your troops to slaughter us and steal land that is rightfully ours. You are coming to destroy a people that have a history of thirty thousand years. Why? For twenty years of gas? Are you really that insane? The original General Custer was exactly that insane."

Chief T'Seleie's testimony and statements by other Native people and consultants convinced Berger that the project should not proceed until the government settled the outstanding land claims. He believed that new government institutions and programs, developed with input from Native people, had to be created to overcome the problems of economic and social disruption that so often accompanied large development projects. So Berger recommended a delay of at least ten years, and the federal government agreed.

While Aboriginal groups fought for their land and resources before Berger, the search for oil and gas in the North continued unabated. The Dene responded to this influx of mineral explorers in several ways. In 1973 they sought and obtained from the Northwest Territories Supreme Court an order to stop resource exploration on the homelands they claimed. Significantly, the judge who issued the ruling stated that "[n]otwithstanding the language of the two treaties (8 and 11), there is sufficient doubt that Aboriginal title was extinguished." He simply doubted that the chiefs who had signed the earlier surrenders understood the terms. Two years later, the General Assembly of the Indian Brotherhood of the Northwest Territories and the Métis Association of the Northwest Territories jointly issued the Dene Declaration, demanding autonomy and self-determination within Canada and a just settlement of their land claims. The federal government agreed to negotiate with them, believing that it would be cheaper to settle than to fight the two groups in court.

The Dene's eastern Inuit neighbours living at Baker Lake also went to court seeking protection for their economic interests. In 1979 they asked for a declaration that an area of 78,000 square kilometres (30,000 square miles) in the vicinity of the lake belonged to them. The Baker Lake people wanted to halt prospecting operations that were scaring off local caribou herds. They were also angry with wildlife officials, whom they clashed with over game-harvesting and management issues. The Northwest Territories Supreme Court decided that the Baker Lake people did hold title to the area they claimed, but it refused to order a halt to mining operations because the presiding judge concluded that such activities did not adversely affect the caribou.

During this time, the Inuvialuit of the Mackenzie River delta area moved to file a land claim to combat the adverse effects any Beaufort Sea developments might cause. After lengthy discussions, they reached an agreement in principle with federal negotiators in 1978, thereby avoiding a lengthy and costly court battle. The Inuvialuit gave their final assent to the accord in 1984. Many of the major provisions of the Inuvialuit agreement are similar to those of the James Bay Agreement, but it is more generous, considering that only twenty-five hundred Inuvialuit benefit from it. These people gave up their rights to an area of 344,000 square kilometres (133,000 square miles) in exchange for $152 million, payable over a thirteen-year period. Subsequently they have used this income to establish the Inuvialuit Development Corporation to invest in Aboriginal and non-Aboriginal businesses throughout the country. They also kept title to a tract of 90,650 square kilometres (35,000 square miles) and retained mineral rights to one-seventh of that area. The Inuvialuit retained the exclusive right to hunt fur-bearing animals and musk ox in their territory, and they secured priority hunting rights for all other wildlife, with the exception of some migratory birds. The Inuvialuit Agreement also made provisions for their people to play advisory roles in wildlife management, but it did not provide income support for hunters.

The entrenchment of Aboriginal and treaty rights in the Canadian constitution (Section 35[1]) in 1982, in response to effective First Nations lobbying, most notably the "Constitutional Express," and a more flexible federal claims policy that went into effect after 1986, made other bands and nations more willing to come to the bargaining table. The government's consent to make offshore resource rights negotiable was particularly important to the Inuit, given the importance of marine mammals and fish in their traditional economies. Three major agreements in principle followed soon afterwards. One of these, that of the Dene and Métis of the Northwest Territories, was subsequently rejected by the Dene, after the landmark *Sparrow* ruling was issued by the Supreme Court of Canada in the spring of 1990. In this non-treaty fishing-rights case, the high court determined that there was nothing in the Fisheries Act or its detailed regulations that demonstrated a clear and plain intention to extinguish the Aboriginal right to fish. Even legislation aimed at conservation must be justified if it detracts from any Aboriginal right protected under Section 31(1). Government had to consult the Aboriginal people affected, and it had to compensate them for the rights that were affected. For the Dene this decision suggested that their rights might be much more extensive than they had thought they were when they began negotiations, so they shelved the agreement. Subsequently, the Mackenzie valley Dene and Métis failed to maintain a united negotiating front.

The various groups in the Northwest Territories faced different circumstances, had different needs, and disagreed about whether to agree to extinguish their Aboriginal title as part of any settlement. Two of the more northerly groups, the Gwich'in of the Mackenzie River delta and the Sahtu tribal council of the Great Bear Lake region, came to terms with the federal government in 1992 and 1993 respectively. In exchange for the extinguishment of title to most of their territories, they retained ownership with subsurface rights to smaller tracts; extensive hunting, trapping, and fishing grounds; and various cash and mineral royalty settlements. The Deh Cho of the upper Mackenzie Valley (Great Slave Lake to Lake Chipewyan) and the Tlicho, who live north of Great Slave Lake, and the Chipewyan who live south of Lake Chipewyan continued to negotiate. In 2003, the Tlicho reached a land claim and self-government settlement. That same year, the Deh Cho signed an interim agreement with the federal government, which provided them with a share of annual federal resource royalties and the right to make interim withdrawals of land they want to protect while negotiations for final agreement continue. Meanwhile, the Chipewyan are pursuing their claims as an amendment to Treaty 8, which their ancestors had signed in 1899.

In 1990, the Council of Yukon Indians, which was established in 1973 and represents fourteen nations, ratified an umbrella political agreement with the federal and territorial governments that covered issues of land, compensation, self-government, and institutions for the management of resources. According to the terms of the compact, each member nation had the responsibility of negotiating its own final legal agreement. These settlements are to include all issues covered by the umbrella agreement and additional provisions that deal with the specific concerns of each nation. By 2002 half of the member nations had concluded their settlements. Collectively the Yukon nations will retain "settlement lands" totalling 41,000 square kilometres (15,580 square miles).

The Tungavik Federation of Nunavut, the land-settlement negotiating team of the Inuit Tapirisat of Canada, signed the final central and eastern Arctic agreement in January 1992, after eleven years of talks. The Inuit negotiators who helped draft the agreement used the James Bay and Inuvialuit agreements to guide them. Many key aspects of their accord are similar to those of the earlier settlement, except that it is somewhat less generous in its land allowance. The agreement made elaborate provisions for all aspects of resource development and wildlife management. Particularly noteworthy is the requirement that all major development projects in the future will have to obtain Inuit impact and benefit agreements before they can proceed. From the outset, the Inuit negotiators pressed to have more political control over their affairs. Eventually the federal government consented. The final agreement, which the parties signed in 1993, included a provision to create a new territory, Nunavut (our land), from the eastern portion of the Northwest Territories. The previous year the residents of the latter territory held a plebiscite to approve of divisional boundary. The Canadian Parliament assented to the *Nunavut Act* in 1999 and that same year, the first territorial elections were held. Although the Inuit had good reason to rejoice with their achievement, some Dene groups, particularly the Chipewyan, were deeply hurt by these developments. They had overlapping claims in the boreal forest-tundra transition area to the west of Hudson Bay.

SOUTH OF THE 60TH PARALLEL

After twenty years of claims negotiations, most of the country's Aboriginal people living north of the 60th parallel have come to terms with the federal government, but south of 60, many talks have achieved very little. One reason is that the provinces hold title to Crown land. The federal government holds title in the

Northwest Territories and the Yukon, which made it easier for negotiators to settle land disputes in the Far North. In the provinces many seemingly hopeless deadlocks have arisen over the issues of Aboriginal and Crown title and compensation. Frequently, it seems that the only way Native people can break the impasses is by combining political pressure, often involving civil disobedience, with litigation. Three Aboriginal groups who have used varying combinations of these methods, with uneven results, include the Lubicon Lake Cree of Alberta, the Kanesatake Mohawk near Oka, Quebec, and the Gitxsan and Wet'suwet'en of British Columbia.

THE LUBICON CREE

On October 12, 1988, the Lubicon Lake Cree of northern Alberta declared jurisdiction, ownership, and management of their traditional lands and forbade any further exploration, drilling, or extraction of oil and gas without band licences. Three days later, they demonstrated their determination by erecting a blockade on roads leading into their territory. The Lubicon Cree, led by Chief Bernard Ominayak, had taken these actions after struggling for almost fifty years to obtain a reserve in their portion of Treaty 8 territory.

The problem originated at the turn of the century, when treaty commissioners failed to visit the Lubicon Cree (and several other groups) to obtain their adherence to Treaty 8, or to assign them a reserve. In fact, no Indian Affairs official visited the Lubicon Cree until 1939. When the department finally made contact, it promised them a reserve at the site of their choice, which happened to be the settlement of Little Buffalo, at the west end of Lubicon Lake, Alberta. Accordingly, the province of Alberta set land aside there in 1940, but the federal government failed to confirm the reserve, partly because of the outbreak of the Second World War.

In the early 1950s, the federal government reconsidered the issue of the reserve and announced that it wanted to relocate the Lubicon Cree because the Little Buffalo settlement was not conveniently placed from an administrative perspective. Officials also thought that the size of the reserve originally proposed in 1939 was too large, considering that the band had diminished in size. This was because an Indian Affairs administrator had arbitrarily dropped some members from the band list in 1942, having "determined" that they were not Indians. Although two judicial inquiries ruled this action unjust, the department refused to revise the membership list. By the 1950s, Alberta was expressing a strong interest in helping to decide the size and location of a Lubicon reserve because oil and gas companies

Two Chippewa protesters man a barricade near the entrance to Ipperwash Provincial Park, September 7, 1995. The Natives claim that the park is situated over a sacred burial site. Their protest turned ugly when one man was killed by Ontario Provincial Police gunfire.

wanted to explore the area and obtain mineral leases there. The problem for the Lubicon Cree was that any subsurface rights they might hold applied only to the lands set aside for them by the province in 1940. They obviously had very good reasons to resist any attempts to relocate elsewhere.

Given the band's refusal to move, government officials decided to resort to other tactics. They tried to reduce the numbers further by arbitrarily transferring members to other bands and by encouraging others, largely unsuccessfully, to abandon their Indian status by applying for enfranchisement. The plan failed, and in the end the government reconfirmed the band's existence in 1973. But this dubious manoeuvre created lingering questions about how many people officially belonged to the modern Lubicon Cree. Meanwhile, the provincial and federal governments had not created the promised reserve.

When the province announced plans in 1971 to open the North to resource development, the Lubicon Cree joined forces with several other Native communities who had never joined Treaty 8, and together they registered a claim to a tract of land of 65,750 square kilometres (25,390 square miles). To protect this territory, they also filed for a caveat on it in 1975, to block any further development until the government dealt with their claim. While the court considered the matter, Alberta passed legislation barring anyone from filing caveats on Crown land. Because the legislature made the law retroactive to the period preceding the bands' motion, the court rejected the Lubicon Cree application.

Chief Bernard Ominayak first rose to fame when he complained to the United Nations about Canada's treatment of the Lubicon Cree. In 1989 he was again grabbing headlines when he announced that Petro Canada would have to begin paying royalties for past and current oil production on disputed land.

Now free to go ahead with its plans, the provincial government of Peter Lougheed built an all-weather road across Lubicon Cree territory and unleashed petroleum explorers who ran roughshod over the land. The Lubicon Cree claimed that these people deliberately frightened off game and fur-bearing animals and disrupted the local hunting economy. Apparently the government's strategy was to undermine the band's claim to traditional use and occupancy of the disputed lands by forcing members to discontinue traditional subsistence practices. In a ruse to have the area taken out of the category of undeveloped Crown land, on which Aboriginal hunting and trapping rights continued, the province declared the settlement of Little Buffalo to be a hamlet and offered each family a two-acre plot on-site. Officials promised those who agreed to this offer that they would be eligible for various services and public utilities. Hold-outs received tax bills as "squatters on provincial Crown land." When the federal government made a half-hearted objection to these moves, the province replied that the Lubicon Cree could not be part of any Aboriginal land claim because they now lived in a hamlet and their territory was therefore no longer officially unoccupied Crown land.

In the 1980s the saga dragged on in the courts and through negotiations. In *Last Stand of the Lubicon Cree*, the journalist John Goddard notes that the Lubicon Cree found themselves whip-sawed back and forth in a game devised by the federal government, through the federal Office of Native Claims and the Justice Department, and the province. These two levels of government alternately supported and opposed the band.

Like the James Bay Cree, Chief Ominayak and his band sought support beyond the province and the country. They asked the World Council of Churches to investigate their circumstances, and they lodged a complaint with the United Nations human-rights committee. After studying their situation carefully, the World Council of Churches wrote to Prime Minister Trudeau in support of the band, stating that the Lubicon Cree "cannot be expected to achieve a just and fair settlement of their legitimate rights and claims without help. They cannot be expected to survive as a people unless they receive immediate financial, political and legal help." The United Nations human-rights committee agreed that the band had an admissible claim to a hearing, since it seemed that they could not obtain effective political or legal redress at home. The band achieved another moral and public-relations victory during the winter Olympic Games in Calgary in 1988, when it persuaded many Native nations and museums from around the world to show their solidarity by refusing to participate in the art exhibit *The Spirit Sings*, held at the Glenbow-Alberta Institute (Glenbow Museum) as part of the event.

While fruitless discussions continued about the best way to resolve the impasse, the federal government and the province discovered new revenue-generating uses for the territory the Lubicon Cree claimed. They announced an agreement with Japan-based Daishowa Canada Ltd. to build a massive pulp-and-paper mill on the Peace River. In 1988 the federal government announced that it would provide $9.5 million for the controversial project. The province awarded Daishowa timber-cutting rights in an area of 30,000 square kilometres (12,000 square miles), which included most of the lands claimed by the Lubicon Cree. The projected cut amounted to about four million trees a year. The devastating implications that this scheme had for the essential hunting-and-trapping economy of the Lubicon were clear to everyone.

So the barricades went up on Lubicon Cree land, but only after years of government neglect, followed by decades of failed attempts to obtain redress through legal means and public pressure. Aboriginal groups from across the country lent their support in various ways. The Mohawk of Kahnawake slowed traffic for two

A ceremony marking the return of a medicine pipe bundle from the Provincial Museum of Alberta to the Tsuu T'ina. As the First Nations people regain control of their affairs, they have also reclaimed parts of their heritage that they lost to the cultural agencies of the dominant society

days on the Mercier Bridge in Montreal to distribute ten thousand flyers in support of the Lubicon. Some members of the Six Nations at Brantford held a brief blockade. Meanwhile, chiefs from other Alberta bands had gathered in Lubicon territory to express their solidarity.

Five days after the blockade began, a fifty-man force of Royal Canadian Mounted Police stormed through it to arrest twenty-seven people, while a large party of media representatives from around the world recorded the event. For a brief moment it looked as if the extremely adverse publicity that this event created for both levels of government would at last break the stalemate. The Alberta premier, Don Getty, and Chief Ominayak met at the Mile Zero Hotel on the Mackenzie Highway and came to terms. Getty announced that Alberta was prepared to grant the nearly 250-square-kilometre (100-square-mile) reserve the band had sought for so long, including mineral rights over most of this tract. Both parties avoided addressing the contentious issue of the size of the band list, and they agreed to hold further negotiations concerning environmental and wildlife-management issues.

The situation looked promising at last. There was a major catch, however: Ottawa had to ratify the arrangement and agree to provide a compensation package. The two parties gathered at the National Conference Centre in Ottawa late in the autumn of 1988. Although they readily came to tentative terms about band membership and the size of the reserve, they disagreed sharply over the issue of compensation and control over economic development. The federal government insisted that the ancestors of the band had signed Treaty 8, and it said that Canada's obligations were therefore limited to compensating the Lubicon Cree for failing to fulfil specific obligations of Treaty 8. The Lubicon Cree stuck to their position that their forebears had never signed and that they were negotiating a new agreement to share their land in ways that took into account their traditional use and occupation. The band also insisted on a land-rights agreement that offset the destruction of their traditional economy caused by petroleum exploration and extraction in their homeland.

On January 24, 1989, Ottawa presented a non-binding "final"—take it or leave it—offer that included no compensation and minimal provisions for economic development. The single aspect of the offer acceptable to Ominayak and his advisers was the one confirming the 250-square-kilometre reserve. The chief rejected the proposal and the talks collapsed. Outraged, the Mulroney administration was determined to work out separate deals with factions in the Lubicon band. Accordingly, senior Indian Affairs officials worked with unprecedented speed to register a number of local residents of Aboriginal descent as Indians, and by August 28, 1989, it had created the Woodland Cree band. Section 17 of the Indian Act made this possible, for it gave the minister of Indian Affairs the right to create new bands from existing band lists or from the Indian register. Later, Indian Affairs also created the Loon Lake band. Eventually the new bands, which included some defectors from the Lubicon Cree, approved a vastly inferior settlement than the one Getty and Ominayak had reached earlier. Goddard says the government bought the vote by falsely promising the Indians $50 each if they participated in the plebiscite and an additional $1,000 if the majority of them approved the deal. In any event, as a divided people, the Lubicon Cree no longer represented a political threat to either the federal or the provincial government. Today the Lubicon continue to search for a negotiated settlement.

OKA

The land dispute at Oka, Quebec, was another controversy that had been simmering long before it erupted in violence at the Mohawk barricades at the Kanesatake reserve near Oka on July 11, 1990. Native residents of the area had expressed concern about the status of their lands as early as the late eighteenth century and raised the issue repeatedly in the nineteenth century. Their struggle took on sectarian overtones when many of the Kanesatake residents converted to Methodism in 1868, in protest against their betrayal by the Sulpician fathers who had taken their lands. The sectarian dimension made the federal government even more unwilling to get involved on behalf of the Aboriginal people, because Ottawa traditionally was loath to antagonize the province of Quebec and its French-Catholic majority. As far as the federal government was concerned, the best solution was to relocate as many of the "troublemakers" as possible. Some of the residents moved to reserves established for them at Maniwaki on the Gatineau River, or to Gibson Township in the Muskoka district, but the land problem at Oka remained.

In 1903, while the Laurier government held office in Ottawa, federal officials decided the courts should settle the issue by defining the exact nature of Indian rights at the settlement. Eventually, the case reached the Privy Council in London, and in 1912 it ruled that the residents could not "establish an independent title to possession or control in the administration ... by Aboriginal title." The Privy Council also ruled out the parallel idea that the Sulpicians served only as trustees of the Indians' interests; instead, the Privy Council said that the order held a valid title by virtue of its original seigniorial grant and an 1841 act of the legislative council of Lower Canada, which had confirmed this grant.

Unfortunately for the Kanesatake Mohawk, however, the Sulpicians ran into financial difficulties in the 1930s and sold parcels of the land to pay their debts without ever consulting the Native people. This fragmented their settlement. Eventually the municipality of Oka received one hundred of the lots from the provincial government, which had accepted them previously as payment of a loan it had made to the order. In 1945, when the Sulpicians teetered on the verge of bankruptcy, the federal government bought the remaining mission lands on behalf of the Native residents, but only 1,556 acres remained of the original sixty-four-square-mile mission seigniory, and they consisted of scattered small plots.

In view of this history, it is understandable why the Kanesatake Mohawk were outraged when, in 1959, the municipality of Oka created a nine-hole golf course on

A media throng surrounds two Mohawk warriors and a Canadian Forces soldier at Kanesatake in September 1990.

former mission lands that the Mohawk used for wood-cutting and grazing purposes. The local white residents accomplished this by having a private member's bill passed in the Quebec Assembly without giving the Mohawk advance notice. The Mohawk subsequently asked the Diefenbaker government to disallow the bill; it refused, not willing to jeopardize its relations with a province.

During the 1961 meeting of the parliamentary Joint Committee on Indian Affairs, the Kanesatake people asked that their remaining lands be given reserve status, to protect against any further fragmentation, but the politicians ignored their request. Following the Trudeau government's announcement of its new claims policy after *Calder* in 1973, the Mohawk filed a comprehensive claim. The Office of Native Claims in Ottawa rejected their petition in 1975. Undaunted, they refiled a specific claim to their land. In 1986 the Office of Native Claims refused them yet again. The government did concede, however, that the claimants had some basis for a title and talks continued.

The town's impatience to enlarge its golf course in 1990 brought matters to a head. The white residents of Oka and local business people became fed up with the impasse between the Mohawk and the federal government, so they unilaterally decided to go ahead with their expansion scheme, which threatened to impinge on Kanesatake burial grounds. In response, Kanesatake residents, later joined by other Mohawk from nearby Kahnawake and Akwesasne reserves and the militant Warriors Society, who were armed, erected a barricade across the road into the disputed tract in March. The town and the developers responded by obtaining a court injunction on April 26, ordering the removal of the blockade. The Mohawk held firm. They also ignored a second court order issued two months later. Shortly thereafter, the frustrated mayor of Oka asked the provincial police, the Sûreté du Québec, to enforce the order, which led to a storming of the barricade by one hundred heavily armed officers on July 11. In the ensuing hail of gunfire, one police officer was killed. The siege continued with the Canadian Forces replacing the provincial police, at Premier Bourassa's request to the federal government, for the remainder of the seventy-eight-day standoff.

For a brief moment, the eyes of the world focused on Oka. In the finger pointing that followed, most people lost sight of the underlying historical causes that were responsible as they searched for scapegoats to blame for the violence. Outdated thinking, particularly the lingering colonial view that the government knows what is best for Native communities, is really to blame. Also responsible is the old notion that any rights Aboriginal people have to land they hold are strictly at the pleasure of the Crown, which could withdraw them at any time. Ultimately, the Kanesatake Mohawk had no effective way of protecting their interests against the conflicting ones of their white neighbours. The episode demonstrates, as did the James Bay Cree and Lubicon Cree sagas, just how difficult it is to resolve Aboriginal-title disputes involving different levels of government and third-party interests.

CHAPTER 21

HISTORY WARS

There was a great reluctance when we saw the history of the courts in our territories—we were always on the losing end. But in considering this situation, the Chiefs said, what other choice do we have? We knew that in order for the courts to understand what it was we were talking about, it was necessary for us to show them our histories, our laws, our practices, our customs, our obligations, our responsibilities. We had to open up our Houses and our families to people who had no understanding or respect for who we are.

—Skanu'u, Gitxsan translator and historian, *Colonialism on Trial*, 1991

When Canada's Native People took an increasingly active and effective part in the political arena beginning in the 1970s, they understood that negotiations with federal and provincial authorities to resolve their rights concerns would be fruitless unless they brought substantial bargaining chips to the table. One possible way to do this was through litigation, even though, as Gitxsan translator and historian Skanu'u observed, past efforts to have Aboriginal and treaty rights confirmed this way had not been successful. Nonetheless, they had reasons to be hopeful. A number of developments had made this avenue of redress worth pursuing. The most notable of these were the *Calder* decision of 1973, which raised the possibility that Aboriginal title still existed beyond treaty areas, and Section 35 (1 and 2) of the 1982 Canadian Constitution Act, which protected existing Aboriginal and treaty rights. Collectively, these events raised two fundamental and interrelated questions that had to be determined largely through litigation: What rights survived the colonization process; and, what were the characteristics of those rights?

The quest for answers to these questions led First Nations to take a major role in determining the research agenda in Canadian Native history. With the assistance of their experts, they presented new interpretations of cultural and historical evidence that confront many of the traditional understandings of Canadian and Native history that justified colonial dispossession and marginalization. In doing so, First Nations have turned the courts into major battlefields in Canada's Native history wars and made the public aware of how important gaining an understanding of this aspect of our country's history is for understanding key current events and issues.

DELGAMUUKW AND ITS AFTERMATH

One of the most celebrated and bruising skirmishes in the Native history wars took place in the Supreme Court of British Columbia, where the Gitxsan and Wet'suet'en filed a lawsuit for ownership and jurisdiction of their traditional homeland. Their legal action is popularly remembered as *Delgamuukw* (officially registered as *Ken Muldoe, suing on his own behalf and on behalf of all members of the House of Delgamuukw v. Her Majesty the Queen in right of the Province of British Columbia and the Attorney General of Canada*). *Delgamuukw* began in Smithers, British Columbia, in 1984, when forty-eight Gitxsan and Wet'suet'en hereditary chiefs filed their suit, which resulted in a sprawling 318-day trial that extended from 1988 to 1990. The plaintiffs, federal and provincial defendants, and witnesses for the opposing sides submitted over 50,000 pages of evidence and presented just over 23,500 pages of testimony covering key aspects of Gitxsan and Wet'suet'en, provincial, and Canadian history. This was the first time that a Canadian court had been asked to evaluate such a massive and diverse range of cultural and historical evidence. Previously, in *Calder*, anthropologist Wilson Duff made a brief appearance on behalf of the Nisga'a. Before this case, the legal community did not consider that this line of evidence was relevant to the development of Aboriginal rights law. Therefore *Delgamuukw* not only represented a huge risk for the Gitxsan and Wet'suet'en but also posed an unprecedented challenge to the courts.

The Gitxsan and Wet'suet'en took the gamble because they had exhausted every means to negotiate a comprehensive claims settlement in a reasonable time. While they did so, logging companies accelerated their operations on the 22,000 square-mile (57,000 square-kilometre) Gitxsan and Wet'suet'en homelands. The hereditary chiefs tried to halt this erosion of their people's territory by barricading existing logging roads and blocking the construction of new ones north of the Babine River.

On the rivers and lakes, they clashed with federal Fisheries officers over the use and management of local salmon stocks. Such confrontations led to the celebrated Marshmallow-Throwing War in the summer of 1986, when members of a Native blockade hurled marshmallows at about three dozen heavily armed Department of Fisheries and RCMP officers who attempted to invade a Gitxsan fishing camp. The Gitxsan and Wet'suet'en did not oppose economic development in their area or fail to appreciate the need to properly manage fish stocks for conservation purposes, but these were their ancestral homelands. They demanded their fair share of the benefits derived from any economic developments taking place on these lands, and a meaningful voice in any local resource-management schemes. It became clear, however, that civil disobedience and political protests were only stopgap measures. Taking the issue to court could jump-start the long sought negotiations; a clear declaration of their rights would strengthen their bargaining position. Also, the Gitxsan and Wet'suet'en wanted a public forum where all their elders could be heard.

In their lengthy opening statement in the small courthouse in Smithers, British Columbia, the hereditary chiefs asked the court to reject evolutionary notions of cultural history that traditionally cast their society at a lower stage of development. They asserted that their ancestors' culture was equal to those of Europeans at the time of first contact in terms of civil institutions and notions of property. In making their assertion, the chiefs noted that the "formal telling of the oral histories in the feast, together with the display of crests and the performance of the songs, witnessed and confirmed by the chiefs of other Houses, constitute not only the official history of the House, but also the evidence of its title to its territory and the legitimacy of its authority over it." Their statement stressed that the "witnessing and validation of the House's historical identity, territorial ownership and spirit power is integral to the feast. But also integral is the House's demonstration of its prosperity through a distribution of its wealth. A House's wealth is directly linked to its territory." The intimate link between territory and history were what the trial was all about. The hereditary chiefs and elders were the primary repositories of that history, and they took centre stage in court.

After the opening address to the court, these Gitxsan and Wet'suet'en leaders related the histories of their twenty-eight houses, or lineages. Traditionally, the hereditary chiefs and elders recounted their family chronicles and conventions—called *Ada'ox* by the Gitxsan, and *Kungax* by the Wet'suet'en—exclusively to fellow kinfolk. Telling them to outsiders was an act of faith, and a painful break with tradition, especially considering the adversarial setting of the courtroom, where the elders would be subjected to withering cross-examination. However, they wanted to demonstrate that their people had lived in organized societies at the time of initial contact with Europeans, to show that their ancestors exclusively occupied their traditional homeland, to show that hereditary chiefs had always managed the house

The Law vs. Ayook
Written vs. Oral History

idea:
Gertie Watson
Gitsegukla

don monet /87

Cartoon by Don Monet of Delgamuukw v. Regina *depicting the conflicting lines of evidence and views of Native history. On appeal, the Supreme Court ruled the trail judge erred in not giving adequate weight to oral history evidence.*

territories for the benefit of their kinfolk, and to make clear that their people had never acquiesced in the Crown's assertion of sovereignty over their lands.

The *Ada'ox* and *Kungax* posed a number of difficult questions for the court. Are oral histories—which are a mixture of "folklore," laws, and traditions—acceptable evidence, or should they be rejected as hearsay as they describe many events the witnesses had not observed? Could they be presented in traditional formats, which included chants and songs? We know that language structures thought and shapes people's worldview. Many of the Gitxsan and Wet'suet'en wanted to tell their *Ada'ox* and *Kungax* in their own languages partly for these reasons. To do otherwise would be to present their narratives out of context. Justice Allan McEachern reluctantly agreed to let them do so, even in song where appropriate. After a few months in the Smithers courthouse, McEachern decided to move the trial to the stunningly modern glass-and-concrete provincial law-courts building in Vancouver. Over the next two and one half years, the Gitxsan and Wet'suet'en maintained a costly vigil in Courtroom 53 and provided their people back home with updates of the proceedings.

After the hereditary chiefs and elders finished describing their traditional system of ownership and governance, numerous expert witnesses appeared and presented supporting lines of anthropological, scientific, and historical evidence. One of the most crucial of these were the journals and letters written by HBC traders, particularly William Brown, who established Fort Kilmaurs (Old Fort Babine) on Babine Lake at the edge of Gitxsan and Wet'suet'en country in 1821. Brown noted that the plaintiffs' ancestors had divided their homelands into house territories, which were controlled by hereditary chiefs, whom he called "nobles" or "men of property." Brown complained that these chiefs tightly regulated the harvesting of beaver in their house territories. He learned he could not establish a profitable trade without currying their favour.

The defensive strategy Crown counsel employed in rebuttal to the plaintiffs invoked many of the old shibboleths of British Columbia's legal and political traditions. For instance, the province asserted that the British brought civilization, order, and peace to the region. It also contended that the Royal Proclamation of 1763 created Aboriginal rights and they continued to exist only at the pleasure of the Crown. Justice McEachern estimated that the lawyers directed almost one-quarter of their argument to the issue of the Royal Proclamation. The discussion raised a number of issues, including the question of how the document should be interpreted. One viewpoint, the so-called legal positivist perspective, holds that the edict spoke once and for all and therefore applied only to the nations that were in contact with the British government when the edict came into force on October 7, 1763. An alternative interpretation is that the decree was supposed to establish basic policies for dealing with all the Aboriginal nations who were under the sovereignty of the Crown in 1763 and were taken into the realm any time thereafter. The practice of negotiating treaties in the area of former Rupert's Land lent considerable support to this interpretation. Yet another view held that Aboriginal title existed independently of the Royal Proclamation by virtue of Native occupation and use of specific tracts of land before European contact. In *Calder*, three justices of the Supreme Court of Canada had recognized the Aboriginal title of the Nisga'a on this basis rather than in terms of the Royal Proclamation.

Next, Crown counsel tried to deny the existence of Aboriginal title in the disputed land by suggesting that the Gitxsan and Wet'suet'en hereditary chiefs never had any real authority in their house territories at the time of early European contact and their territories overlapped. They argued that the people did not live in an organized society governed by customs and laws that established order and provided for the succession of title. Government counsel pursued this objective largely by dwelling on every incident of violence they could dredge up from the post-contact record left by non-Natives. This tactic did not take into account any of the disruptive post-contact forces that were at work in Gitxsan and Wet'suet'en societies, such as the alcohol trade, fur-trading rivalries, devastating European-disease epidemics that often carried away elders, and the presence of white settlers encroaching on their land. After discussing a murder that took place at the Hudson's Bay Company's Fort Connolly post in 1829, which apparently resulted from a long-simmering dispute between fort Native people and the Gitxsan, the lawyer who represented the Attorney General of Canada remarked, "That was a— is a demonstration of the ... warlike nature of the Gitxsan ... that [their] endemic violence was based on a fair degree of truculence." In other words, the ancestors of these people were inherently warlike. This certainly was an inappropriate conclusion to draw about the plaintiffs' ancestors at that time, considering that Europe and eastern North America had just been racked by far bloodier conflicts during the Napoleonic Wars.

Next, Crown counsel asserted that the feasting-house territory scheme of the Gitxsan and Wet'suet'en, which the hereditary chiefs described and reports of the HBC trader William Brown confirmed, was not of Aboriginal origin. The Crown contended that it was a by-product of the Gitxsan and Wet'suet'en participation in

Nuxalk fishers with oolichan catch on the central coast in the 1920s.

the European fur trade and, therefore, could not be cited to legitimize an Aboriginal title. For support, the Crown introduced anthropological evidence, mostly drawn from studies that employed outdated acculturation and evolutionary perspectives. Very little of this "classical" ethnographic literature had been based on fieldwork undertaken in Gitxsan and Wet'suet'en territory; also, the Crown's experts did not undertake any new work there. The Crown held that before contact, the Gitxsan and Wet'suet'en effectively occupied only a fraction of their territory, namely the village sites, burial places, fishing stations, berry and other collecting locations, and connecting trails. This conception of the traditional world of the Gitxsan and Wet'suet'en harkens back to the ideas of seventeenth-century English philosophers such as Thomas Hobbes and John Locke, who theorized that non-agricultural people did not effectively use most of their lands and lacked well-developed notions of property ownership. Colonial officials and settlers embraced these ideas because they justified seizing Aboriginal land in order to put it to more intensive use.

Besides denying that Aboriginal people ever held a valid title in British Columbia territory, Crown counsel proposed the standard argument that even if they had, the colonial government had extinguished it before British Columbia joined Confederation, when the colonial government passed various land acts to facilitate white settlement, or through the terms of Union when the province joined Confederation. Furthermore, if Aboriginal title had somehow survived Confederation, the Crown asserted that the Gitxsan and Wet'suet'en had relinquished it voluntarily by (allegedly) willingly accepting Indian reserves. (Nearly seventy years earlier, to persuade them to cooperate with the McKenna–McBride Royal Commission, the government had promised the Gitxsan and Wet'suet'en that it would never use this argument against them.) Finally, lawyers for the Crown indicated that the people no longer had a distinctly "Indian way of life" now that they lived on reserves, drove cars, received public education, had embraced Christianity, participated in the wage economy, and accepted provincial jurisdiction over hunting and trapping. This is the so-called Pizza Indian argument. Put simply, the proposition is that once Native people change in any way (eating pizza, for example), they cease to be "Indian." It recalls the days of salvage ethnography of the early twentieth century, when anthropologists searched for the remaining fragments of "authentic" Native culture before they were swept away by the tides of history. The concept also appeals to an old legal notion that Aboriginal rights are limited to the customs and practices Native people exercised before the assertion of British sovereignty. This is known in legal circles as the "frozen rights theory," and it weighed heavily on the minds of all of those who took part in the trial.

In 1991 Justice McEachern delivered his judgment. To the shock and outrage of First Nations across Canada, he quoted Hobbes to characterize life in Gitxsan and Wet'suet'en country as being "nasty, brutish, and short" before Europeans arrived. He went on to reject virtually every scrap of the oral testimony of the Gitxsan and Wet'suet'en plaintiffs—particularly their *Ada'ox* and *Kungax*—as reliable lines of evidence to establish exclusive house use and occupation of specific tracts of territory. He observed that the descriptions of house territories showed that they often overlapped one another and those of neighbouring First Nations, most notably those of the Nisga'a. McEachern further concluded that the traditional narratives had not held up under the cross-examination of provincial and federal Crown counsel. He also thought the *Ada'ox* and *Kungax* lacked sufficient detail to substantiate specific house claims. McEachern had similar reservations about most of the archaeological, biological, ethnographic, geomorphologic, genealogical, and linguistic data the Gitxsan and Wet'suet'en introduced to corroborate their oral histories. The only line of evidence that he held in any regard was the documentary record left by HBC traders. McEachern agreed with the Crown, however, that the tenure system described in these accounts was not Aboriginal; instead, it was an outgrowth of the European fur trade.

In his ruling, McEachern also decided that the Royal Proclamation had never applied to British Columbia. Accordingly, he ruled that the Imperial Crown gained title to the region after the assertion of British sovereignty sometime between 1803 and 1858 and that "Aboriginal interests did not include ownership or jurisdiction over the territory." He did allow that the Gitxsan and Wet'suet'en have the right to use undeveloped Crown land for traditional purposes, subject to the general laws of British Columbia, until the province wants this territory for other purposes. McEachern found that since Confederation the province has had "title to the soil of the province" and "the right to dispose of Crown lands unburdened by Aboriginal title."

The McEachern ruling sent a clear message to Aboriginal people: Stop wasting time and money in court, and get on with your lives. In his own words, "[T]he parties have concentrated for too long on legal and constitutional questions such as ownership, sovereignty, and 'rights.'... Important as these questions are, answers to legal questions will not solve the underlying social and economic problems which have disadvantaged Indian peoples from the earliest times.... It must be remembered, however, that it is for elected officials, not judges, to establish priorities for the amelioration of disadvantaged members of society." These remarks were incongruous at best. Throughout the post-colonial era, the Nisga'a, Gitxsan, Wet'suet'en, and other Native nations from British Columbia have pleaded with successive provincial and federal governments to negotiate a way to share the land equitably—to fulfill long-standing promises and obligations. As the legal historian Hamar Foster pointed out, the problem with what McEachern proposed is that "having governments 'do for' Native people without acknowledging their rights and title is an approach that has failed, and failed quite spectacularly."

In addition to being out of touch with the history that generated it, McEachern's judgment was out of step with developments in jurisprudence pertaining to Aboriginal rights that were taking place while the trial was unfolding. During the second year of the *Delgamuukw* trial, for example, the Supreme Court of Canada unanimously ruled that Aboriginal title amounted to more than personal occupancy and use rights. In 1990, as *Delgamuukw* drew to a close and after most of the historical evidence had been presented, the high court handed down its *Sparrow* ruling concerning Musqueam fishing rights. Of the utmost importance, it flatly rejected the notion of "frozen rights," saying traditional practices could exist in a modern form. In *Sparrow* it also enunciated the doctrine of "clear and plain intention" with respect to the extinguishment of Aboriginal rights. McEachern attempted to address this aspect of the Supreme Court of Canada's judgment by reasoning that extinguishment of Aboriginal title was a necessary implication of colonial land legislation. Legal scholars immediately pointed out, however, that the creation of statutes designed to facilitate white settlement did not necessarily revoke Aboriginal title.

Important political changes took place in British Columbia between the time McEachern issued his ruling and the commencement of the appeal hearing. By the late 1980s, public and political support for the idea of negotiating settlements of all the outstanding comprehensive claims was growing. Also, during the summer of 1990 Native communities in British Columbia put pressure on the provincial government by mounting road and railway blockades in support of the Mohawk at Oka and to heighten public awareness of their own outstanding claims. In December 1990, on the eve of a provincial election and with the decision in *Delgamuukw* pending, the provincial government agreed to the creation of the British Columbia Land Claims Task Force, which provided for the equal representation of the province, the federal government, and the Aboriginal community. The task force issued its final report in June 1991, and it recommended that the three parties seek negotiated solutions to all outstanding disputes through the offices of a tripartite treaty commission.

A newly elected provincial government led by New Democrat Mike Harcourt accepted the task force's recommendation and created a treaty commission. Harcourt's government also moved to distance itself from the McEachern ruling by abandoning the traditional assertion of the province that a blanket extinguishment of Aboriginal rights had taken place in the past. While preparing for the appeal hearing, the provincial government asked the Gitxsan and Wet'suet'en to suspend their appeal and negotiate. The tribal council refused to do so at first and pressed forward with its appeal.

On May 4, 1992, the five-judge panel of the British Columbia Court of Appeal convened to hear the petition. The Gitxsan and Wet'suet'en argued that the trial judge had erred by ruling that their rights had been extinguished by 1871. They also asserted that the judge made crucial errors in his findings of fact concerning their claim. In support of the Gitxsan and Wet'suet'en were a coalition of British

Gitxsan dancers in front of the Supreme Court of Canada building in Ottawa, performing in June 1997 as their land claim case goes before the Court.

Columbia First Nations and the National Indian Brotherhood. Influential economic interests intervened in support of the government. Among them were Alcan Aluminium Ltd., the Mining Association of British Columbia, the British Columbia and Yukon Chamber of Mines, the British Columbia Chamber of Commerce, the Council of Forest Industries, the Sports Fishing Institute of British Columbia, the Fisheries Council of British Columbia, the Pacific Fishermen's Alliance, and the British Columbia Cattlemen's Association. Clearly this was a high-stakes exercise.

The tribunal held one of the longest appeal hearings in British Columbia history before issuing its judgment on June 25, 1993. The outcome was mixed. The provincial appeal court justices agreed with the Gitxsan and Wet'suet'en that all their rights had not been extinguished by 1871. The majority of the judges ruled that the plaintiffs "have unextinguished non-exclusive Aboriginal rights, other than a right of ownership or a property right" in their homeland. The appeal court decided that in the future another trial would have to determine "the scope, content and consequences of such non-exclusive Aboriginal rights of use and occupation." Two justices dissented, and would have allowed the appeal in its entirety. Initially the Gitxsan and Wet'suet'en decided to fight on and take their case before the Supreme Court of Canada, but they also held talks with the province in their never-ending quest for a negotiated solution. In the summer of 1994, they agreed to delay further legal proceedings for a year while they tried to reach a settlement through the offices of the British Columbia Treaty Commission. By that time thirty-seven other First Nations already had their completed applications on the table. Meanwhile, the Nisga'a negotiated separately. In the spring of 1996, they finally reached an agreement with the federal and provincial governments that awarded them $200 million, 2,000 square kilometres (almost 800 square miles) of land, and extensive powers of self-government.

Despite their terrible setbacks, the Gitxsan and Wet'suet'en remained optimistic. Neil Sterritt, former president of the Gitxsan-Wet'suet'en Tribal Council, said this is their nature. He pointed out that they had already reaped some of the benefits they hoped to gain by going to court. All the elders spoke, even though a number of them died in the course of the original trial. They created a massive documentary record of their history that schools administered by the tribal council will use to keep their heritage alive for generations to come. They have also demonstrated to outsiders what their world was and is like and how they govern it. Sterritt observed that before the trial "we were a curiosity. Our histories and culture were merely interesting. A lot of non-Indian people had romantic notions about Aboriginal people's issues.... A lot of people who supported us, but really didn't know what we wanted, learned a lot."

Significant questions remained. The editor of the *Victoria Times-Colonist* asked one of them in 1875: "Shall it be written of British Columbia that she was the first province of the Dominion to oppress her natives and the last to do them justice?" More generally, the *Delgamuukw* ruling raised doubts about the possibility that the courts could move away from their English colonial roots and develop a North American law that treated the cultures and peoples who "have lived here since the world began" with the respect the Gitxsan and Wet'suet'en chiefs asked for in *Delgamuukw*. Subsequent litigation and court rulings rekindled this hope; they also raised new controversies.

On December 11, 1997, the Supreme Court of Canada brought joy back to the Gitxsan and Wet'suet'en people by unanimously overturning McEachern's hurtful ruling. Of particular pleasure to them, the high court faulted the trial judge for not giving proper weight to their oral histories. The Supreme Court acknowledged that it had not set the guidelines for the proper use of such evidence until 1996,

Herb George, spokesman for the Gitxsan of Northern B.C., talks with reporters outside the Supreme Court in Ottawa on December 11, 1997. In a landmark decision, the Supreme Court faulted the trial judge for not giving weight to oral history evidence, ordered a new trial, and defined the nature of Aboriginal title to guide future claims.

when it ruled on another Aboriginal fishing rights case in British Columbia, *Regina v. Van der Peet* (1993). The Court decreed that oral histories cannot be viewed as simply being legend and myth, having value only when they confirm other lines of documentary evidence. Rather, oral histories, such as the *Ada'ox* of the Gitxsan and the *Kungax* of the Wet'suet'en, must be given independent weight. McEachern had not done so at trial and, therefore, the Canadian high court ordered that the case be retried. The Supreme Court's instruction to give equal weight to oral evidence was a very tall order. In subsequent legal battles, especially those regarding treaty rights, litigants have devoted a great deal of attention to the relative weight that should be given to oral and other lines of evidence when they led to contradictory conclusions. It is a particularly contentious issue in treaty rights litigation because the written versions of treaties often privilege the Crown's interpretations of historic agreements, whereas oral evidence usually reinforces Aboriginal perspectives.

The controversial Treaty 8 tax exemption case *Regina v. Benoit* (2003) highlights the problems that arise when lines of evidence are in conflict, or only one of them speaks directly to the issue in dispute. Based primarily on oral evidence provided by elders, the trial judge accepted Charles Benoit's plea that he be exempt from taxes based on verbal promises that government negotiators allegedly made to

Getting the Fence Fixed *by Allen Sapp.*

The First Tourist *by Kananginak Pootoogook.*

Shaman Never Die (*centre panel*) *by Jane Ash Poitras*

Kanata by *Robert Houle*.

Scorched Earth, Clear-Cut Logging on Native Sovereign Land, Shaman Coming
to Fix *by Lawrence Paul Yuxweluptun*

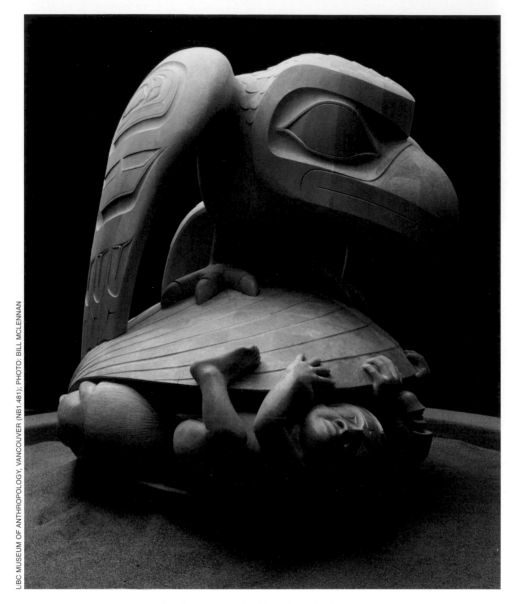

The Raven and the First Men *by Bill Reid*.

Columbus Decelebration Series: The Crucifixion *by Luke Simon.*

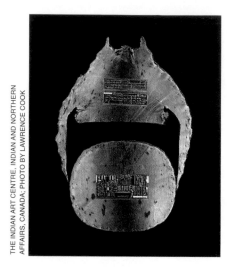

Culture in Transition
by Lance Belanger.

Elitekey *by Teresa Marshall.*

Medicine Buffalo *by Wes Brewer.*

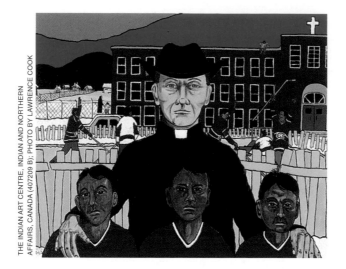

Father Image I *by Jim Logan.*

Father Image II *by Jim Logan.*

his ancestors to persuade them to sign Treaty 8 in 1899 and 1900. Subsequently, the Federal Court of Canada overturned the judge's decision on appeal. It harshly criticized the trial judge for giving native oral traditions concerning the treaty "preferential treatment." The Federal Court reached this conclusion because it decided that the trial judge had not treated oral evidence "cautiously" by considering whether it agreed with other "independent evidence." The independent evidence in this instance was the written record left by the government officials who negotiated and drafted the treaty. Except for a single brief statement in the treaty commissioner's report saying a tax promise was made, the rest of the records are silent about the tax issue. Thus, in *Benoit* the Federal Court of Canada gave more weight to the silences in the written records than it did to native oral traditions, which it treated as little more than hearsay.

In *Delgamuukw*, the high court provided guidance for any future Canadian land claims trials by clearly defining the nature of Aboriginal title for the first time. It identified two crucial rights: the right to exclusively use and occupy land and the right to decide how the land is to be used (on the condition that the ability of the land to sustain future generations of Aboriginal people is not destroyed). Thus it recognized that Aboriginal title has an inescapable economic component. The court also clarified the test First Nations had to meet to establish a title claim. It said they had to conclusively demonstrate that their ancestors occupied the land prior to the assertion of British sovereignty, which in British Columbia now is dated from the Oregon Boundary Treaty of 1846; there had to be continuity in occupation from the pre-sovereignty era to the present; and that occupation must have been exclusive. Regarding exclusivity, the court emphasized that shared use of areas was not precluded if it could be shown that the claimants or their ancestors had the intention and capacity to retain exclusive control. In making this allowance, the high court recognized that First Nations commonly granted rights of access to others and sometimes exercised joint title to lands.

It was immediately clear from the Supreme Court's *Delgamuukw* decision that Aboriginal title exists in British Columbia on land where there are no treaties and it predates Crown title, which is contrary to the provincial government's position since Confederation. Furthermore, where it survives it is protected by Section 35 (1) of the Canadian constitution. Representatives of The First Nations Summit, which represents many First Nations living in the province, led off Canada's First Nations' responses to the new opportunities for negotiation and litigation that the *Delgamuukw* judgment had created. They met with Provincial Aboriginal Affairs

Minister John Cashore and federal Minister of Indian Affairs Jane Stewart on January 31, 1998, and, according to the *Vancouver Sun* of February 2, 1998, they laid claim "to every tree, every rock, every fish and every animal in the province." In addition, they demanded a freeze on any resource development until arrangements had been made that enabled First Nations to fully participate in the economic future of the province. Also on February 2, 1998, Don Ryan, a Gitxsan hereditary chief and principal negotiator, met with British Columbia Premier Glen Clark and repeated this demand. The Gitxsan wanted to reach an accord with the province for the co-management of traditional lands. Ryan also raised the spectre of lawsuits for compensation for past resource extractions in the Gitxsan territory.

While Canada's First Nations rejoiced in the victory of the *Delgamuukw* decision, they were concerned about finding the best strategy to realize its potential benefits for them. In a stroke, the Supreme Court had taken away the cornerstone of a fundamental policy towards Aboriginal peoples in British Columbia that was rooted in the province's colonial past. For the first time, the province's First Nations found themselves in a strong position to pursue their long-standing quest for equitable settlements of their land claims. Government officials were undeterred by *Delgamuukw*, however. The province continued to issue mining and timber harvesting permits (known as tree farm licenses) on Crown lands subject to Aboriginal title claims without consulting the affected First Nations in meaningful ways. In response, the Taku River First Nation initiated legal proceedings in February 1999 to block a mining project in their traditional territory, which the province had approved. In January 2000, the Haida people launched a lawsuit to oppose three tree farming licences in their territory that the province had granted to the international lumber giant Weyerhaeuser. Both cases made their ways to the Supreme Court of Canada. In November 2004, the Court issued companion landmark decisions (*Taku River Tlingit First Nation v. British Columbia* and *Haida Nation v. British Columbia*) stating that the Crown required the government to confer with Aboriginal peoples and accommodate their interests. The court also ruled that the government "cannot cavalierly run roughshod over Aboriginal interests where claims affecting these interests are being seriously pursued" either through litigation or treaty negotiations. Nonetheless, the province continued as before. By the end of 2008, British Columbia First Nations had faced off with the government in over thirty court cases. They won the majority of them.

During the course of these struggles the political landscape of British Columbia changed, when, in 2001, the provincial Liberal Party led by Gordon

McLeod Lake Tsek'ehne inspecting land survey equipment. Apart from the Douglas Treaties of the early 1850s, colonial and provincial governments of British Columbia promoted the colonization of Aboriginal land without negotiating treaties.

Campbell came to power. This change did not bode well for the province's First Nations. Three years earlier, Campbell and Liberal MLA Jeff Plant—who had served on the Crown's legal team in *Delgamuukw*—launched an unsuccessful legal challenge to the Nisga'a Agreement. Subsequently, in the run-up to the provincial election of 2001, Campbell promised to hold a plebiscite on the British Columbia Treaty Process, in order to "jump start" the stalled talks. First Nations from across the country and their supporters strongly objected, saying that his plan was a thinly veiled attack on existing agreements between the Crown and First Nations and on court decisions concerning Native rights. After sweeping into power with a landslide election, Premier Campbell and provincial Attorney General Plant announced they would proceed in spite of the strong opposition from the First Nations. In the spring of 2003, the provincial government mailed out over two million ballots that asked voters if they supported eight negotiating positions the Liberals proposed to take to the bargaining table. After a failed attempt by

Aboriginal leaders to stop the results from being counted, the Liberals announced that they had received a mandate. It proved to be a hollow one, however; as a result of a vigorous anti-referendum campaign by First Nations and their supporters, barely one-third of voters had cast their ballots.

While these legal and political battles dragged on, treaty negotiations continued under the auspices of the British Columbia Treaty Commission all through the provincial election and the subsequent plebiscite fight. By the end of 2002, fifty-three First Nations, representing two-thirds of the province's Aboriginal people, were involved. Of these, forty-two had reached agreements-in-principle, which included the Gitxsan and Wet'suet'en. As they moved towards final settlements, many of the participants signed interim protection agreements that safeguarded First Nations interests in lands that will be involved in treaty settlements. In the summer of 2003, hereditary Chief Earl Muldoe (Delgamuukw), acting on behalf of the Gitxsan, signed one of these interim agreements. It is with the provincial Ministry of Forests and it provides for revenue sharing, a forestry licence, and consultation on forestry management issues. Although these were hopeful signs that the Gitxsan-Wet'suet'en lawsuit would yield the results they had hoped for, making it unnecessary for them to have to return to court for a retrial of their land claim, the movement from interim agreements to final settlements by these two First Nations and others has proven to be especially difficult. By 2009, only two agreements had been finalized—those of the Maa-Nulth of northern Vancouver Island and the Tsawwassen of the lower mainland.

The seemingly glacial pace of the British Columbia Treaty Commission process and the ongoing battles in the courts has been extremely costly to the government, the First Nations, and third parties. In addition, the uncertainty about unresolved Aboriginal title claims continues to plague development schemes involving crown land. To address these problems, Premier Campbell opted to try a radically new approach. In 2005 he announced that his government had negotiated a New Relationship Agreement with the three leading First Nations organizations in British Columbia—the British Columbia Assembly of First Nations (BCAFN), the First Nations Summit (FNS), and the Union of British Columbia Indian Chiefs (UBIC). The object of the accord was to "establish processes and institutions for shared decision making about the land and resources." For that purpose, in 2007 the parties created the First Nations Leadership Council, which included senior officials from the provincial government and the three Aboriginal organizations. In the spirit of the new agreement, when addressing the FNS in

Selling clams at Kitkatla. Prior to colonization, the First Nations of coastal British Columbia had vibrant trading economies. Beginning in the nineteenth century they were marginalized in the commercial and industrial fisheries by government regulations.

September 2005, Premier Campbell admitted, "We understand that our litigative strategies in the past have been offensive, and that was certainly not what our intention was. I have instructed the Attorney General and the Minister of Aboriginal Relations and Reconciliation to review our litigation strategy and to come back with a report to us as soon as possible, so that when we are in court, if we are in court, we are able to argue in court in a way that is respectful to you, to First Nations." While that promise has yet to be fulfilled, there were hopeful signs that real change was in the offing. Early in 2008, Native leaders proposed that BC formulate recognition and reconciliation legislation. Premier Campbell responded positively to their suggestion. In February 2009, the First Nations Leadership Council and the Government of British Columbia released a draft outline of proposed Recognition and Reconciliation Legislation that would have acknowledged the co-existence of Aboriginal and crown titles without requiring First Nations to prove their title in court. The proposed legislation also would have moved the province beyond the position of merely living up to its legal obligation to consult to one where it was committed to joint decision-making. The drafting of the proposed path-breaking legislation was interrupted by the provincial election in the spring, but work resumed following the re-election of the Campbell Liberals in May 2009. It seemed that landmark recognition legislation, which would have ended the age-old acrimonious nature of provincial–First Nations relations highlighted so starkly in *Delgamuukw*, was imminent. However, it was not to be. The Campbell Liberals faced a backlash from the business community, which feared that First Nations would gain a veto over land use and resource extraction. First Nations communities worried that Aboriginal title and rights would be weakened and they objected to the idea of reconstituting the two hundred or so First Nations into thirty. By the time two hundred provincial chiefs gathered in Vancouver on August 26, 2009, for a three-day BC All-Chiefs Assembly concerning the proposal, the settlement scheme had largely unravelled. When the meeting concluded, Grand Chief Ed John of the FNS announced the proposed legislation was dead. In affirmation, Grand Chief Stewart Philip of the UBIC, exclaimed "Dead, dead, dead." Faced with this reality, the assembled chiefs formed the Title Action Group to continue their struggle. So it seems that the legal and political battles over Aboriginal title and rights in BC will continue indefinitely.

While their neighbours were engaged in the British Columbia Treaty Commission process, the McLeod Lake Tsek'ehne (Sekani) opted for a radically different approach. They sued for the right to adhere to Treaty 8. They did so in the belief that they would obtain a settlement much more quickly and that the terms of the 1899 treaty were as generous as anything they could negotiate through the British Columbia treaty process. They argued that they were justified in demanding the right to join Treaty 8 because their ancestors, like the Lubicon, should have been included in the historic accord. The province denied their assertion and the McLeod Lake people prepared for a court battle. Before this happened, however, they reached an agreement with the federal and provincial governments. In April of 2000, on a table covered with a Hudson's Bay Company blanket at the site of old Fort McLeod, Chief Alec Chingee signed the adhesion on behalf of his people.

Treaty Rights: Horseman to Marshall

While the First Nations of northern Canada and British Columbia spent the past three decades in search of modern agreements and treaty settlements, those living in other parts of the country have been fighting legal battles over the rights and benefits their ancestors thought they had secured in historic treaties. Most often, harvesting rights are the key issues of treaty litigation, but a range of other concerns arise also, the most controversial being alleged federal breaches of fiduciary obligations, taxation issues, and mineral rights. In treaty rights disputes, the courts face the task of settling disagreements between First Nations and the Crown about how treaties should be interpreted.

One of the most vexing questions is whether historic treaties protect Aboriginal people's right to harvest fish and wildlife for commercial purposes. In the central and western interior of Canada, for example, the Robinson Treaties and Treaties 3 through 9 promised Indians that they would be able to continue their "usual vocations" of hunting, trapping and fishing on undeveloped Crown land. Treaties 3–9 qualified this pledge by stipulating that livelihood rights would be "subject to such regulations as may from time to time be made by the Government of the country...." Subsequently, federal and provincial governments interpreted this clause to mean that Indians were obliged to comply with conservation legislation. In practice this legislation has commonly either banned or severely restricted hunting and fishing for commercial purposes. In arguing that Aboriginal people should not be exempted, the Crown has usually asserted that commercial hunting and fishing were not typical practices of Native people.

One of the most important challenges to this interpretation to reach the Supreme Court of Canada arose in the Treaty 8 area of Alberta and involved a Cree hunter named Bert Horseman. In 1985, provincial officials charged Horseman with violating the Alberta Wildlife Act by killing a grizzly bear without a licence and selling the skin. Horseman readily admitted to these facts. He said he killed the bear in self-defence after being attacked and sold the skin a year later when he was experiencing acute financial hardship and desperately needed the money. Horseman claimed he had a right under Treaty 8 to sell the skin. The Supreme Court of Canada had set the stage for such a defence two years earlier, when in *Nowegijick v. Regina* (1983) it stated that "treaties and statutes relating to Indians should be liberally construed and doubtful expressions resolved in favour of the Indians." This marked an important shift away from earlier legal approaches to historic treaties that had treated these documents as though they were "plain of their face." The *Nowegijick* ruling and decisions that expanded on it in *Guerin v. Regina* (1984) and *Simon v. Regina* (1985) signalled to the lower courts that they had to consider treaties in their historical contexts to properly interpret them.

In light of these decisions, *Horseman* raised a very important question about Treaty 8: Could the expression "usual vocations" be construed to include commercial hunting? Horseman's legal team provided evidence that demonstrated com-

A nineteenth-century painting of a Mi'kmaq family cooking a lobster. The Marshall decision recognized that the Mi'kmaq exploited an array of marine resources for subsistence and commercial purposes.

mercial hunting was an Aboriginal practice in 1899. The defendant had shot the grizzly bear a short distance from the historic Hudson's Bay Company post of Fort Vermilion, located in the Peace River area. The accounting records of this post revealed that in the 1890s, the local Cree were selling an array of country produce, furs, and hides, including grizzly bear skins. These records also made it abundantly clear that the local Aboriginal economy was highly integrated into the commercial fur trade and it was unrealistic to separate commercial activities from subsistence ones. The Cree use of beaver was an excellent example, and was discussed at trial. They trapped the animal for meat and to sell its pelt, using the proceeds from the sale to buy the hunting and trapping equipment that was essential for them to live off of the land. This meant that denying them commercial rights threatened their ability to make a living off of the land. In light of this historical evidence, the trial judge acquitted Horseman.

After the province successfully appealed the judgment to the Court of Appeal for Alberta, Horseman took his case to the Supreme Court of Canada. The high court agreed that Treaty 8 included commercial hunting rights. The court also held, however, that the Parliament of Canada had exercised its constitutional right to unilaterally amend the treaty by passing the Natural Resource Transfer Agreement of 1930, which conveyed federal Crown lands to the Prairie provinces. This act gave Alberta the authority to regulate all Aboriginal hunting and trapping activities that were not directly associated with fishing and hunting for subsistence purposes. Although Treaty 8 First Nations were very disappointed with this ruling, the *Horseman* decision held out the prospect that commercial harvesting rights survived in other treaty areas beyond the Prairie provinces where the Transfer Agreement did not apply. This has prompted further litigation, notably in Ontario.

Undoubtedly the best-known and most controversial harvesting rights case to date involved Donald Marshall, a Mi'kmaq fisherman from Nova Scotia. Without a licence, Marshall caught 463 pounds (210 kilograms) of eels using a prohibited net during a time when the fishery was closed. Afterwards, he sold his catch. Officials promptly charged Marshall with four violations of federal fishery regulations. He responded by pleading that the eighteenth-century treaties his Mi'kmaq ancestors had signed with the British gave him the right to fish commercially and exempted him from federal regulations. Marshall's defence forced the courts to consider the complex and conflicting interpretations opposing historical experts provided regarding a series of British–Mi'kmaq treaties dating back to the period between 1725 and 1761.

During the trial in the Nova Scotia Provincial Court, the wording of a 1760 treaty between colonial Governor Charles Lawrence and Mi'kmaq leader Paul Laurent came under very close scrutiny for two reasons. First, Marshall's legal team said that it had served as the model for a series of additional agreements with other Mi'kmaq groups in 1760 and 1761. Secondly, the 1760 treaty did not specifically promise to protect Mi'kmaq commercial harvesting rights. In fact, none of the agreements that preceded and followed from it made such a promise. Nonetheless, the lawyers and experts supporting Marshall said that commercial harvesting rights could be inferred from these treaties if they were subjected to rigorous contextual and textual analyses. In important decisions that the Supreme Court of Canada made after *Horseman*, most notably *Regina v. Soui* (1990) and *Regina v. Sundown* (1999), it improved the likelihood that such approaches would be successful.

In 1760, the Mi'kmaq, who had been allies of the French before the latter's defeat, pledged to not assist or trade with enemies of the British Crown. At trial, discussion focused on the so-called Truck House clause of this accord in which Laurent promised:

for myself and my tribe that we will not either directly nor indirectly assist any of the enemies of His most sacred Majesty King George the Second, his heirs or Successors, nor hold any manner of Commerce traffick nor inter- course with them, but on the contrary will as much as may be in our power discover and make known to His Majesty's Governor, any ill designs [to] which may be formed or contrived against His Majesty's subjects. And I do further engage that we will not traffick, barter or Exchange any Commodities in any manner but with such persons or the managers of such Truck houses as shall be appointed or Established by His Majesty's Governor at Lunenbourg or Elsewhere in Nova Scotia or Accadia.

Laurent's pledge raised three crucial questions: First, did the British enter into this agreement on the assumption that the Mi'kmaq had the right to harvest resources from the land and sea for commercial purposes? Second, has this right continued to the present? Third, if this right still exists, is it limited in any way?

The historical experts supporting Marshall answered the first question posi- tively by emphasizing three important pieces of historical evidence. They noted that the British established a truck house system in response to Mi'kmaq requests, which they operated until the 1780s. They drew attention to the short-lived British-Mi'kmaq peace agreement of 1752 in which British promised: "the said Tribe of Indians shall not be hindered from, but have free liberty of Hunting and Fishing as usual and if they shall think fit a Truckhouse needful at the River Chidenaccadie, or any other place of their resort, they shall have the same built and proper Merchandize lodged therein, to be exchanged for what the Indians shall have to dispose of." Finally, the Mi'kmaq's experts provided copies of British- drafted minutes of negotiating sessions pertaining to the 1760–61 treaties. In the eyes of the court, these minutes proved to be very important because they revealed that the terms the Mi'kmaq accepted were more favourable than those contained in the treaty text. In other words, the treaty was an incomplete record of the accord. In addition to this evidence, Marshall's experts reminded the court that historians have shown that the Mi'kmaq had centuries-old trading contacts with Europeans (French and English) by the 1760s. Furthermore, they had become dependent on this trade for basic necessities, most notably firearms. So, as with Horseman and his Cree relatives, commerce was an essential component of Mi'kmaq livelihoods by the time they signed treaties.

In light of this evidence and history, the trial judge accepted the proposition

DFO boat passes by a Native man swimming to a boat for rescue, August 29, 2000. After three years of violent clashes over the Native lobster fishery on Miramichi Bay, the Burnt Church First Nation negotiated an agreement with Ottawa.

that the clause restricting the Mi'kmaq to trade with the British should be construed positively to mean that it assumed that these people had a right to commercially harvest fish and wildlife. Otherwise, he reasoned, it would have been pointless to create the truck house system. Significantly, in reaching similar conclusions on this important point, both the trial judge and the Supreme Court majority were heavily influenced by the Crown's opposing historical expert, who had stated at trial that "the truck house clause is based on the assumption that natives will have a variety of things to trade, some of which are mentioned and some not." When citing this passage, Supreme Court Justice Ian Binnie remarked: "[T]here was an unusual level of agreement amongst all of the professional historians who testified about the common intention of the participants regarding the treaty obligations entered into by the Crown." The Crown's expert later objected, saying that he was quoted out of context.

Judicial opinion was divided, however, over the crucial question of whether

Mi'kmaq commercial fishing rights survived the abandonment of the truck house system after the 1780s. The trial judge and the Nova Scotia Appeal Court concluded that the rights expired with the end of this system. In 1998, the Supreme Court disagreed and held that the commercial right had not expired. This meant it had to determine the extent of that entitlement. The court approached this issue from the perspective of the precedents for defining Aboriginal rights that it had established during the previous decade. In *Simon v. Regina* (1985), concerning Mi'kmaq hunting rights based on the 1752 treaty, the Supreme Court established the principle that treaty provisions must be interpreted flexibly to allow for "the evolution of changes in normal practice." As we have seen, in *Sparrow* (1990) the court extended this idea to Aboriginal rights, ruling that these entitlements must be "affirmed in a contemporary form rather than in their primeval simplicity and vigour." The abandonment of the older "frozen rights" approach—which had limited Aboriginal and treaty rights to the practices Native people followed when they made initial contact with Europeans, when Britain asserted its sovereignty over their territory, or when they signed a treaty—was reaffirmed on the eve of the Marshall decision in *Regina v. Sundown* (1999). In this decision the Supreme Court of Canada ruled that a Cree hunter's construction of a hunting cabin in a Saskatchewan provincial park was an aspect of the exercise of his hunting right under Treaty 6 and therefore justified.

Justice Binnie observed that one of the crucial pieces of evidence introduced at the Marshall trial for determining the scope of Mi'kmaq hunting rights was a British memorandum on treaty negotiations dated February 11, 1760. This document stated that a truck house might be established to supply the Mi'kmaq with "necessaries." From this he reasoned that the treaty did not intend to protect a general right to trade for economic gain; rather it was to sustain their livelihood. Binnie decided that the right to earn a "moderate livelihood" through trade was the modern equivalent of the practice the 1760–61 treaties aimed to protect.

The idea of a limited commercial livelihood had first arisen from case law respecting Aboriginal fishing rights in British Columbia, where a series of landmark cases forced the judiciary to address the fact that many of the coastal and interior First Nations engaged in the trade of fish and fish products well before Britain asserted sovereignty in the region in 1846. This made it clear that in B.C., Aboriginal livelihood rights had a commercial component. The problem is that they are not self-limiting in the way ceremonial and subsistence rights are. This meant that Aboriginal commercial harvesting rights threatened to leave no room for non-Natives in the fishery. The courts needed to find a way to define Native fishing rights in restrictive terms.

British Columbia Appeal Court Justice J. Lambert proposed a "history-based" solution in 1993 in his dissenting opinion in *Regina v. Van der Peet*, which addressed the Stó:lö claim to commercial salmon fishing rights. Lambert reviewed recent American case law regarding Indian rights—particularly the so-called Boldt Decision, indexed as *The State of Washington v. Washington State Commercial, Passenger, Fishing Vessel Association*, 443 U.S. 658 (1979)—and British Columbia Native history and concluded that the contemporary Aboriginal fishing rights of the Stó:lö should be broad enough to supply "sufficient salmon to provide all the people who wish to be personally engaged in the fishery, and their dependent families, when coupled with other financial resources, with a moderate livelihood." Although the Supreme Court of Canada did not support Lambert's conclusion that the Stó:lö should have a right to a commercial fishery—largely because a majority of the justices thought the Stó:lö had not demonstrated that salmon trading was of central cultural importance to them—it took up his moderate livelihood concept in *Regina v. Gladstone* (1996). This case addressed the Heiltsuk's right to sell herring roe-on-kelp. In this instance, the Supreme Court found that the evidence presented at trial had demonstrated conclusively that these people traditionally trafficked in substantial quantities of herring roe. Justice Beverley McLachlin (who later became the Chief Justice) concurred with the majority on this issue, but she interpreted the significance of this activity differently. McLachlin concluded that the Heiltsuk traditionally traded roe primarily to supply themselves with "the necessaries of life, principally other food products."

In *Regina v. Marshall*, Justice Binnie referred to the ideas of Lambert and McLachlin and concluded that the Mi'kmaq had engaged in harvesting for commercial purposes, but they did not do so to accumulate wealth. By creatively interpreting Native economic history in this manner, the Supreme Court believed it could affirm the Mi'kmaq had a treaty right to fish commercially, and simultaneously put an ill-defined limit on that right. It is based on an historical interpretation that resonates well with older romantic and evolutionary perspectives of Aboriginal people that imagined that a defining difference between them and Europeans was that they were not interested in engaging in economic production for the sake of generating wealth. This remains one of the resilient ideas of the romantic age even though there is little evidence to support it. As we have seen, Aboriginal people *were* interested in generating wealth. They differed from Europeans primarily in terms of the ways they used wealth—where Europeans amassed wealth to gain prestige and status, Native people gave it away to sustain or enhance their social position.

The court's attempt to find an acceptable compromise based on "history" failed miserably, however. The outcry of non-Native fishermen was so intense that the Supreme Court felt obliged to take the very rare step of issuing a "clarification" of its judgment two weeks later. Violent clashes took place at Burnt Church, New Brunswick, when the Mi'kmaq attempted to exercise their commercial right to harvest lobster. They also were rebuffed when they asserted that the court's decision gave them the right to log on Crown lands. In British Columbia the federal Department of Fisheries has been under increasing pressure to abandon the separate Aboriginal commercial fishery that it established in response to the Supreme Court of Canada's rulings on Native fishing rights cases.

The hostile public response to *Marshall* was not a unique event, however. Judicial rulings in the area of Aboriginal and treaty rights have increasingly come under attack. Before *Marshall*, for example, the media and the public in British Columbia vigorously assailed the Supreme Court's *Delgamuukw* decision, with those who opposed advances in Aboriginal and treaty rights accusing the courts of "judicial activism."

CHAPTER 22

THE
FORGOTTEN
PEOPLE:
THE MÉTIS

We know who we are; we know the generations of discrimination that we have endured; we don't need anybody to tell us who we are... we self-identify, just like everyone else in this country.

—Harry Daniels (1940–2004), founder and first president of the Native Council of Canada (1976–81) and president (1997–2000) of its successor, the Congress of Aboriginal People.

O f all of Canada's Native People, it is the Métis who have faced the toughest fight to establish their economic rights. The calamitous armed struggles for this goal in the prairie West and the intense discrimination that they faced in English Canada afterwards made it very difficult for them to make any headway. In many parts of the country they were driven underground. Only in Alberta and Saskatchewan did they make modest progress when they obtained some settlement lands, mostly as a result of the political activism of early-twentieth-century Métis leaders such as Jim Brady and Malcolm Norris. Prior to 1982, very little litigation of Métis issues took place apart from those related to land scrip cases, and most of this activity took place before World War I.

This situation changed dramatically in 1982, when the Métis were recognized as an Aboriginal people in Section 35 (2) of the Constitution Act. Their inclusion owes much to the tireless efforts of Harry Daniels, who, as one of the leading aboriginal leaders in national constitutional talks, negotiated with four prime ministers

The execution of Thomas Scott by the Métis provisional government provoked lasting resentment among many English-Protestant Canadians.

for constitutional protection of the rights of the Métis as Native People. Section 35 (2) set the stage for a new era of Métis rights battles, which today are taking place in courtrooms across the country. The first precedent-setting skirmish occurred in a small provincial courthouse in Sault Ste Marie, where Métis hunters Roddy and Steve Powley appeared to face charges for violating Ontario's Game and Fish Act because they had hunted moose without a licence. The Powleys did not dispute the facts, but asserted they had Aboriginal rights as Métis to hunt for subsistence purposes. Their defence raised many issues about Métis history and identity in Canada. It also raised basic questions about the way Native economies are characterized in Aboriginal harvesting rights litigation.

Lawyer and scholar Jean Teillet, the great-grandniece of Louis Riel and founding member of the Métis Nation of Ontario, headed the Powleys' defence team. When the trial began, elders and members of the Sault Ste Marie Métis community filled the courtroom. Among them was a descendant of Nebnaigoching, one of the chiefs who had signed the Robinson-Huron treaty in 1850 on behalf of the Ojibwa and Métis. Many of the men were wearing classic Métis assumption sashes, finger-woven belts made of brightly coloured wool and/or plant fibres. The trial was an extremely important event for the local community, which had endured discrimination and repression since the late nineteenth century. It gave them an opportunity to publicly recall their history, proclaim the continued existence of their community and culture, and assert their rights.

To successfully make their Aboriginal rights defence, the defendants' legal team, elders, and supporting historical experts had to prove that there was a distinctive Métis community in the Sault Ste Marie area before the British asserted effective sovereignty in the area; they had to show that this community survived to the present day and that the Powleys were members of it; and they had to demonstrate that game hunting was a defining characteristic of local Métis culture.

The Métis pose particular challenges for the courts when they assert Aboriginal rights, and the *Powley* case demonstrates this. We have seen that Canadian Aboriginal rights law, as it has been developed in the *Sparrow*, *Van der Peet* and *Sundown* cases, requires claimants to prove the existence of the communal right claimed. To qualify, the practice at issue must be a crucial or defining element of a distinctive Aboriginal society. Furthermore, the right claimed has to be based on a custom that was practised prior to European contact and is still pursued, albeit in a modern form. The problem for the Métis is, of course, that their culture is a post-contact creation that combines elements that are of Aboriginal and European origin. For this reason, the Supreme Court of Canada already had recognized in *Van der Peet* that Métis rights would not necessarily be based on pre-contact practices, but deferred dealing with the issue in depth until it received a Métis rights case. At trial in *Powley*, Justice Charles H. Vaillancourt dealt with the ambiguity by taking a flexible interpretation of the term "pre-contact." Based on the evidence presented, he decided that the rights claimed by the Powleys as members of the Sault Ste Marie Métis should be based on local cultural practices that dated to the years 1815 to 1850, or essentially the post-contact era before the British established effective control. Elders and ethnohistorical experts (I was among them) presented substantial oral and documentary evidence at trial to show that an identifiable Métis community had emerged at Sault Ste Marie well before the early nineteenth century and that it has persisted against all odds to the present day.

While the Powley litigation raised issues unique to Métis rights cases, it was similar to most Aboriginal and treaty harvesting rights cases in one important respect. It arose because the defendants had violated a specific provision of existing conservation legislation. Therefore it raised an issue that is relevant to all of these types of cases: Should Aboriginal harvesting rights be defined narrowly on a species by species basis? In this instance, when considered in the light of Métis economic history, is it realistic to focus solely on the issue of moose hunting? Or should moose hunting be regarded as one aspect of the more basic traditional practice of hunting? A great deal of trial testimony and historical evidence addressed this issue. The Powleys' defence team took the holistic approach. One reason for doing so was that I had obtained historical evidence from the HBC archives that established that moose populations had been depleted in the region by the early nineteenth century. This meant that neither the Métis nor their Ojibwa relatives hunted these animals until much later in the century, when moose populations rebounded. Also, data from the HBC archives showed that opportunism was the defining feature of the economic life of the Sault Ste Marie Métis. Similar to most historic Métis communities, they had a mixed economy that featured commercial and subsistence fishing, hunting, and trapping, part-time farming, operating as independent traders, and working for the HBC. The relative contribution that each activity made to the local Métis economy varied over time depending on fish and wildlife population cycles, commodity prices, and job opportunities. Although they did not hunt moose during the middle of the nineteenth century, they did pursue other available game, such as bear.

After a lengthy trial, Justice Vaillancourt made several important findings. He concluded that there was an historic Métis community at Sault Ste Marie that had Aboriginal harvesting rights, including the right to hunt game. He rejected the Crown's argument that hunting rights should be defined solely in terms of the species that had been hunted at any particular period in the past. Regarding the question of Métis identity, he ruled that a Métis was a person of Aboriginal ancestry who identified as a Métis and was accepted by a Métis community as a member. In reaching this conclusion, Justice Vaillancourt relied in part on the definition of a Métis that was contained in the 1996 report of the Royal Commission on Aboriginal People, which had been established in 1991 to address long-standing issues acutely highlighted by the Oka crisis and the failed *Meech Lake Accord*.

The province appealed the judge's ruling to the Ontario Superior Court of Justice and the Ontario Court of Appeal. Both courts upheld Justice Vaillancourt's decision, although they modified his definition of a Métis. The Court of Appeal for Ontario held that any person who identifies as a Métis must demonstrate a genealogical connection to the historic Métis community and be accepted by that community. In making its ruling, the Court of Appeal was sharply critical of the

Steve Powley, wearing the traditional sash, takes a break outside the Supreme Court from his landmark Métis rights case Regina v. Powley, March 17, 2003.

provincial government's treatment of the Métis. In writing the unanimous decision of the court, Justice Robert J. Sharpe stated, "I do not accept that uncertainty about identifying those entitled to assert Métis rights can be accepted as a justification for denying the right." He added that the province "led no evidence to show that it has made a serious effort to deal with the question of Métis rights. The basic position of the government seems to have been simply to deny that these rights exist, absent from the courts to the contrary." Sharpe continued, "While I do not doubt that there has been considerable uncertainty about the nature and scope of Métis rights, this is hardly a reason to deny their existence."

Powley was the first Métis rights case to reach the Supreme Court of Canada after 1982. The court upheld the lower courts' rulings. In doing so it took the opportunity to make several precedent-setting determinations that are still reverberating throughout Canada. One of these concerned the issue about the time of origin of Métis rights, which it had addressed briefly in *Van der Peet*. In *Powley*, the Supreme Court specified that the test for Aboriginal rights must take into account the post-contact ethnogenesis and evolution of the Métis. For the court this meant that attention had to be focused on the customs and practices of Métis communities before they came under the control of European laws and customs. The court also held that Métis rights were communal and were to be determined in reference to the historical customs and practices of a specific community. The Supreme Court defined the latter as "a group of Métis with a distinctive collective identity, living together in the same geographical area and sharing a common way of life."

Powley was a stunning victory for the Métis Nation of Ontario, which had sponsored the case, and a great cause for celebration throughout the Métis world. It also raised questions about the extent of that world. In the minds of most Canadians at the time, and even among some Métis, the Métis had been associated solely with the historic buffalo hunters of the west. For others, Métis were synonymous with the Métis Nation, which encompassed interrelated historical communities within an ill-defined territory reaching from Sault Ste Marie, Ontario, across the prairies to the Rocky Mountains and into the Athabasca-Mackenzie area. So, when claimants came forth from all of the provinces and the Northwest Territories in the aftermath of *Powley*, it caused confusion and rekindled the issue of Aboriginal identities. A key reason for the confusion is that in *Powley* the Supreme Court had, in effect, created a legal category of "Métis" in accordance with Section 35 of the Constitution Act (1982), which had specified that Aboriginal People included "Indian, Inuit, and Métis peoples." In *Powley*, the Supreme Court was explicit that "we should not be surprised to find that different groups of Métis exhibit their own distinctive traits and traditions. This diversity among groups of Métis may enable us to speak of Métis peoples." So, in the eyes of the law after the 1982 Constitution Act, the term Métis would include but not be limited to the historic Métis of the Upper Great Lakes and Canadian Northwest.

If the Constitution Act and *Powley* potentially expanded the number of Métis in Canada and added an element of confusion about the various legal identities that people of Aboriginal ancestry can assume, amendments and challenges to the Indian Act have added further complications. Until 1985, the Indian Act specified that Aboriginal women who married non-status Indians lost their status and their children could not register as Indians. In 1985 Parliament amended the act through Bill C-31 to address this gender-based discrimination. But problems remained. Although individuals who had one only Indian parent were able to regain their legal status as Indians, under certain circumstances they were still barred from passing it on to their children. In 1989, Sharon McIvor, who is a descendant of the

Lower Nicola Valley First Nation of British Columbia, began a long legal battle to rectify this defect in Bill C-31 on behalf of her children. Twenty years later the Court of Appeal for British Columbia decided in her favour (*McIvor v. Canada (Registrar of Indian and Northern Affairs* 2009), ruling that portions of Indian Act violated the Charter of Rights and Freedoms.

During the course of McIvor's battle, John Corbiere of the Batchewana Indian Band successfully challenged (*Corbiere v. Canada (Minister of Indian and Northern Affairs,* 1999) a section of the Indian Act that required members to be "ordinarily resident" on the reserve in order to vote in band elections. The ruling erases (in some respects) the distinction of on- or off-reserve Indians. Collectively *McIvor* and *Corbiere* may lead many "off-reserve" individuals of mixed ancestry who had previously identified

Métis Activist Harry Daniels, who played a major role in having the Métis recognized as an Aboriginal people in Section 35 (2) of the Constitution Act (1982).

as Métis to register as Indians. In these ways, revisions to the Indian Act and litigation (*Powley, McIvor* and *Corbiere*) raise afresh the identity question of who is an "Indian" or "Métis." The fluidity of legal identities is not new, however. It recalls the late nineteenth century, when Aboriginal people of western Canada made choices based on the relative economic advantages Indian or Métis status offered in terms of treaty benefits versus scrip. To paraphrase Métis activist Harry Daniels, they knew who they were regardless of how Canada's legal system pigeonholed them. What they could not foresee, however, was the long-term impact that their pragmatic choices would have for their descendants.

The *Powley* decision not only opened the floodgate for Métis rights litigation, it also raised many historical questions that lawyers and ethnohistorical experts have had to address repeatedly. Among the most problematic are the identification of historical and present-day Métis communities and the delineation of

Métis legal counsel for the fishing rights case R. v. Belhumeur *(2007) and members of the local Métis community in front of provincial court house in Ft. Qu'Appelle, Saskatchewan. The courthouse is located at the site commemorating the signing of Treaty 4 (the Ft. Qu'Appelle Treaty) in 1874. Left to right: legal counsel Clem Chartier, President, Métis Nation of Canada; Michelle LeClair-Harding; Oliver Boulette, Executive Director of the MMF and famous fiddler, who testified at trial; and members of the local Métis community. Those in the front row are Elders Joanna Potyandi and Marge Harrison.*

their territories. In *Powley,* historical evidence revealed that, on the eve of the Robinson Treaties negotiations, colonial officials knew that the Aboriginal population of the Upper Great Lakes included Métis, who they referred to as "half-breeds." These people lived at least part of the year at three fur trading places, Sault Ste Marie, Michipicoten, and Fort William. They were represented at treaty talks, which took place at Fort William and Sault Ste Marie in 1850. It was also clear from the historical record that the Métis of Sault Ste Marie exploited a large territory beyond the settlement that extended northwest along the shore of Lake Superior as far as Michipicoten, southeast to the north shore of Lake Huron, and inland. This territory overlapped that of the local Ojibwa, who were close relatives of the Sault Ste Marie Métis. This evidence led Justice Vaillancourt to determine that the Métis community's territory extended well beyond the city limits of present-day

Sault Ste Marie. The question of whether the Sault Ste Marie Métis were part of a larger community that encompassed the settlements at Michipicoten and Fort William was not of concern to the court.

It was the Supreme Court's subsequent review of Vaillancourt's decision and the appeals that led it to determine that a Métis community consisted of a group of Métis "living together in the same geographic area and sharing a common way of life." This is only a vague guideline, however. It raised a fundamental question that has dominated Métis harvesting rights litigation ever since. How extensive were Métis communities? The case of Ron Laviolette, who lives on Flying Dust Reserve located fifty miles southwest of Green Lake, Saskatchewan, was one of the first of the post-*Powley* cases to address this issue. Mr. Laviolette had fished on Green Lake with two "Indian" companions without a licence in a closed season. He was charged for doing so. Mr. Laviolette, whose legal team included Clement Chartier, president of the Métis National Council, and Ms. Teillet, claimed that he had an Aboriginal right as a Métis to do so. The province objected because Mr. Laviolette did not live in the Green Lake Métis settlement. After hearing historical evidence about Métis life in the woodlands of northwestern Saskatchewan, Provincial Court Justice E. Kalenith found in favour of Mr. Laviolette (*Regina v. Laviolette*, 2005) because the defendant had ancestral ties to a Métis community that dated back to 1820. Justice Kalenith determined that this community encompassed a vast swath of northwestern Saskatchewan and eastern Alberta bounded by the settlements of Meadow Lake, Green Lake, and Ile a la Crosse in Saskatchewan and Lac la Biche in Alberta. This included the historical HBC fur-trading districts of English River and Athabasca. Similar to Sault Ste Marie, commercial and subsistence fishing had been key aspects of Métis life in this sprawling region.

Two years later a similar case made its way to another Provincial Court of Saskatchewan. This one concerned Donald Joseph Belhumeur of Regina, Saskatchewan, who had been charged with illegally fishing on Katepwa Lake in the Qu'Appelle valley, about a half-hour drive from his hometown. Mr. Belhumeur, whose legal defence team again included Mr. Chartier, put forward the same defence as the Powleys and Mr. Laviolette. In this instance his ancestors included buffalo hunters from the old Saskatchewan and Fort Pelly Districts of the HBC. His family connections extended throughout most of the southern part of the province. The trial took place in the historic town of Fort Qu'Appelle in a small courthouse, which is located on the site where Treaty 4 had been signed a century earlier. Cultural evidence presented at trial, including Métis fiddle music, established that a distinct cultural community existed in southern Saskatchewan. I presented historical evidence at trial from the HBC archives showing that during the late nineteenth century the Métis of the Qu'Appelle valley exploited a vast territory that extended northeast to Riding Mountain, Manitoba, southeast to Moose Mountain, Saskatchewan, and south to beyond the Canada–United States border, as far as the Missouri River. After listening to a wide array of evidence, presiding Provincial Court Justice D. I. Morris, who is very active in the local historical society, concluded (*R. v. Belhumeur*, 2007) that Mr. Belhumeur was a member of a contemporary rights-bearing community, whose territory at least included Regina and the place where Mr. Belhumeur had been charged with fishing.

Shortly after the *Belhumeur* trial, the case of William Goodon, a descendant of the historic Métis leader Cuthbert Grant, came before the Provincial Court of Manitoba in Brandon, the defendant's hometown. Once again Ms. Teillet led the defence team. Mr. Goodon had been charged with illegally hunting ducks in the hilly and wooded Turtle Mountain area, about one hundred kilometres south of Brandon near the Manitoba–North Dakota boundary. Métis had hunted and trapped in these hills since the beginning of the nineteenth century. Many still live in the area, including Mr. Goodon's relatives. When commenting on the evidence presented at trial, Provincial Court Justice J. Combs observed that the historical Métis buffalo-hunting communities of the prairies were much more extensive than the fishery-oriented Sault Ste Marie community described in *Powley*. Buffalo hunters inhabited an array of permanent and seasonal sites. The key question for Justice Combs was whether the Métis of southern Manitoba comprised one sprawling community or several distinct ones. This is not a new question and the answer depends on the historical perspective adopted. If, as has been common scholarly practice, attention is focused on the agricultural/permanent settlement aspect of Métis life, it suggests that in the late nineteenth century there were several distinct Métis communities, located at Pembina, Red River, the Whitehorse Plains along the lower Assiniboine River, and St. Laurent on the southeastern shores of Lake Manitoba. On the other hand, if buffalo hunting is emphasized, which initially focused on the lands near the Turtle Mountains before shifting westward, it suggests that there was one community comprised of several components that were linked to the above places. Largely adopting the latter perspective, Justice Combs concluded that there was a large Métis community in southern Manitoba that extended west from Red River and south at least as far as the Canada–United States border. He ruled further that Mr. Goodon was a member of a contemporary rights-bearing

Métis Fishermen at Sault Ste Marie. Subsistence and commercial fishing was an important aspect of economic life for this Métis community from its inception.

community that has links to this historic community. Accordingly, Justice Combs acquitted him.

In addition to harvesting rights, Métis have pursued land rights issues arising from botched schemes to address their Aboriginal title after the Red River Uprising of 1870 and the North West Rebellion of 1885. The Manitoba Métis Federation (MMF) is seeking a court declaration that the Métis never received all of the lands to which they were entitled in Manitoba according to the terms of the *Manitoba Act* (1870) and the negotiations that led to it. The federation claims that the Métis were denied their full entitlement because of the delays in allotments and the unfair land selection procedures the federal government used after 1870. As we have seen, this is a long-standing issue. The MMF launched legal action in 1981, but was unsuccessful at the trial level in the Court of Queen's Bench in Manitoba (*Manitoba Métis Federation, Inc. et. al. v. Attorney General for Canada, et al.*, 2007). It intends to appeal the decision all the way to the Supreme Court. Farther west, the Métis Nation of Saskatchewan has filed a claim (*Morin v. Canada and Saskatchewan*) concerning the northwestern part of the province. This legal action asks once again whether the highly flawed scrip program extinguished the land title of the Métis. The Métis are convinced that it did not, and they are seeking a declaration that they still hold Aboriginal title to the land. Currently this is the only legal action that makes this claim. Presently the legal action has been halted because of procedural problems concerning pre-trial disclosures of historical evidence by the plaintiffs.

These court battles of the Métis and those of the First Nations show all too clearly that abandoning outdated ideas about the history of Aboriginal people poses major challenges. It means recognizing that the rationales that settlers, politicians, and the courts invented to justify seizing Native land and denying Aboriginal people their basic economic rights, including the notion some First Nations had no concept of commerce or systems of land and resource ownership and the idea that Aboriginal people were by nature economically conservative and unable to adjust to changing economic times, are no longer tenable. In order for First Nations to regain meaningful control over their own destinies, Canadians must respond positively to their calls for the creation of viable economic bases for their communities, often through settlement of land claims and the provision of various forms of self-government. A great deal of progress has been made already, but there is still a long and costly road ahead.

Canada's Native people have doggedly fought to survive as distinct societies in the land of their ancestors. It has been a Herculean struggle against overwhelming odds. However, they not only have endured but have forced non-Native Canadians to redefine their concept of Canada. This is probably best symbolized by the recent public acceptance of the idea that Aboriginal people were Canada's "First Nations." Their forebears are no longer seen as being part of the "wilderness" that English- and French-speaking colonists "civilized" as they built a nation in the "New" World. Also, the Métis who descended from the First Nations and newcomers are accepted as Aboriginal people after their long fight for recognition. It is now clear that Native peoples were not merely hapless victims who responded reluctantly to changes forced on them by the newcomers. Rather, they pursued goals of their own as they fought to establish a place in the new order they had helped to create.

SELECTED BIBLIOGRAPHY

Abel, Kerry. *Drum Songs: Glimpses of Dene History*. Montreal: McGill-Queen's University Press, 1993.

Adams, Howard. *Prison of Grass: Canada from a Native Point of View*. Saskatoon: Fifth House, 1989.

Ahenakew, Freda, and H. C. Wolfart, eds. *Kôhkominawak Otâcimowiniwâwa—Our Grandmothers' Lives, As Told in Their Own Words*. Saskatoon: Fifth House, 1992.

Allen, Robert S. *His Majesty's Indian Allies: British Indian Policy in the Defence of Canada, 1774–1815*. Toronto: Dundurn Press, 1992.

Assu, Harry, with Joy Inglis. *Assu of Cape Mudge: Recollections of a Coastal Indian Chief*. Vancouver: University of British Columbia Press, 1989.

Bailey, Alfred Goldsworthy. *The Conflict of European and Eastern Algonkian Cultures, 1504–1700*. Toronto: University of Toronto Press, 1969.

Barker, George. *Forty Years a Chief*. Winnipeg: Peguis Publishers, 1979.

Barman, Jean, *et al.*, eds. *Indian Education in Canada*. Vancouver: University of British Columbia Press, 1986.

Barron, F. Laurie, and James B. Waldram, eds. *1885 and After: Native Society in Transition*. Regina: Canadian Plains Research Center, University of Regina, 1986.

Bishop, Charles A. *The Northern Ojibwa and the Fur Trade: An Historical and Ecological Study*. Toronto: Holt, Rinehart and Winston, 1974.

Blackman, Margaret. *During My Time: Florence Edenshaw Davidson, A Haida Woman*. Vancouver. Douglas & McIntyre, 1982.

Boulanger, Tom. *An Indian Remembers: My Life As a Trapper in Northern Manitoba*. Winnipeg: Peguis Publishers, 1971.

Brown, Jennifer. *Strangers in Blood: Fur Trade Company Families in Indian Country*. Vancouver: University of British Columbia Press, 1980.

Bullchild, Percy. *The Sun Came Down*. Toronto: Fitzhenry and Whiteside, 1985.

Calloway, Colin G. *Crown and Calumet: British-Indian Relations, 1783–1815*. Norman: University of Oklahoma Press, 1987.

Campbell, Maria. *Halfbreed*. Toronto: McClelland & Stewart, 1973.

Cardinal, Harold. *The Unjust Society: The Tragedy of Canada's Indians.* Edmonton: Hurtig, 1969.

Carlson, Keith Thor. *A Stó:lō Coast Atlas.* Vancouver: Douglas & McIntyre, 2001.

———. *You Are Asked to Witness: The Stó:lō in Canada's Pacific Coast History.* Chilliwack: Stó:lō Heritage Trust, 1997.

Carter, Sarah. *Lost Harvests: Prairie Indian Reserve Farmers and Government Policy.* Montreal: McGill-Queen's University Press, 1990.

Charette, Guillaume. *Vanishing Spaces: Memoirs of a Prairie Métis.* Translated by Ray Ellenwood. Winnipeg: Editions Bois-Brûlés, 1980.

Clark, Ella. *Indian Legends of Canada.* Toronto: McClelland & Stewart, 1960.

Coates, Kenneth. *Best Left As Indians: Native-White Relations in the Yukon Territory, 1840–1950.* Vancouver: University of British Columbia Press, 1984.

Codere, Helen. *Fighting with Property.* Seattle: University of Washington Press, 1950.

Cole, Douglas, and Ira Chaikin. *An Iron Hand Upon the People: The Law Against the Potlatch on the Northwest Coast.* Vancouver: Douglas & McIntyre, 1990.

Cruikshank, Julie. *Life Lived Like a Story.* Vancouver: University of British Columbia Press, 1992.

———. *Reading Voices: Dän Dhá Ts'edinintth'é: Oral and Written Interpretations of the Yukon's Past.* Vancouver: Douglas & McIntyre, 1991.

Culhane, Dara. *At the Pleasure of the Crown: Anthropology, Law and First Nations.* Burnaby: Talonbooks, 1997.

Dickason, Olive Patricia. *Canada's First Nations: A History of Founding Peoples from Earliest Times.* Toronto: McClelland & Stewart, 1992.

———. *Canada's First Nations: A History of Founding Peoples From Earliest Times.* Toronto: Oxford University Press, 1996.

———. *The Myth of the Savage: and the Beginnings of French Colonialism in the Americas.* Edmonton: University of Alberta Press, 1984.

Dobbin, Murray. *The One-and-a-Half Men.* Vancouver: New Star Books, 1981.

Eckert, Allan. *A Sorrow in Our Heart: The Life of Tecumseh.* New York: Bantam Books, 1992.

Elias, Peter Douglas. *The Dakota of the Canadian Northwest: Lessons for Survival.* Winnipeg: University of Manitoba Press, 1988.

Fisher, Robin. *Contact and Conflict: Indian-European Relations in British Columbia, 1774–1890.* 2nd ed. Vancouver: University of British Columbia Press, 1992.

Flanagan, Thomas. *Louis 'David' Riel: Prophet of the New World.* Toronto: University of Toronto Press, 1979.

———. *Métis Lands in Manitoba.* Calgary: University of Calgary Press, 1991.

Francis, Daniel, and Toby Morantz. *Partners in Furs: A History of the Fur Trade in Eastern James Bay, 1600–1870.* Montreal: McGill-Queen's University Press, 1983.

Gibson, James R. *Otter Skins, Boston Ships, and China Goods: The Maritime Fur Trade of the Northwest Coast, 1785–1841.* Montreal: McGill-Queen's University Press, 1992.

Glover, Richard. *David Thompson's Narrative*. Toronto: Chaplain Society, 1962.

Goddard, John. *Last Stand of the Lubicon Cree*. Vancouver: Douglas & McIntyre, 1991.

Godsell, Philip. *Arctic Trader*. Toronto: Macmillan, 1943.

Grant, John Webster. *Moon of Wintertime: Missionaries and the Indians of Canada in Encounter since 1534*. Toronto: University of Toronto Press, 1984.

Gunther, Erna. *Indian Life on the Northwest Coast of North America, As Seen by the Early Explorers and Fur Traders during the Last Decades of the Eighteenth Century*. Chicago: University of Chicago Press, 1972.

Haig-Brown, Celia. *Resistance and Renewal: The Residential School*. Vancouver: Tillicum Library, 1988.

Hamilton, John David. *Arctic Revolution: Social Change in the Northwest Territories, 1935–1994*. Toronto: Dundurn Press, 1994.

Harring, Sidney L. *White Man's Law: Native People in Nineteenth-century Canadian Jurisprudence*. Toronto: Osgoode Society for Canadian Legal History, University of Toronto Press, 1998.

Harris, Douglas C. *Fish, Law, and Colonialism: The Legal Capture of Salmon in British Columbia*. Toronto: University of Toronto Press, 2001.

Harris, R. C., ed. *The Historical Atlas of Canada*. Vol 1. Toronto: University of Toronto Press, 1987.

———. *Making Native Space: Colonialism, Resistance, and Reserves in British Columbia*. Vancouver: University of British Columbia Press, 2002.

Heidenreich, Conrad. *Huronia: A History and Geography of the Huron Indians, 1600–1650*. Toronto: McClelland & Stewart, 1971.

Hildebrandt, Walter, Dorothy First Rider, and Sarah Carter. *The True Spirit and Original Intent of Treaty 7*. Montreal: McGill-Queen's University Press, 1996.

Huel, Raymond. *The Collected Writings of Louis Riel*. Vol. 1. Edmonton: University of Alberta Press, 1985.

Innis, Harold Adams. *The Fur Trade in Canada: An Introduction to Canadian Economic History*. Toronto: University of Toronto Press, 1962.

Jaenen, Cornelius J. *Friend and Foe*. New York: Columbia University Press, 1976.

Jenness, Diamond. *The Indians of Canada*. 7th ed. Toronto: University of Toronto Press, 1977.

Jennings, Francis. *The Ambiguous Iroquois Empire*. New York: Norton, 1984.

Johnston, Darlene. *The Taking of Indian Lands in Canada: Consent or Coercion?* Saskatoon: University of Saskatchewan Native Law Centre, 1989.

Knight, Rolf. *Indians at Work: An Informal History of Native Indian Labour in British Columbia, 1858–1930*. 2nd rev. ed. Vancouver: New Star Books, 1996.

Manuel, George, and Michael Posluns. *The Fourth World: An Indian Reality*. Toronto: Collier Macmillan, 1974.

Marshall, Daniel Patrick, *Those Who Fell From the Sky: A History of the Cowichan Peoples*. Duncan: Cultural & Education Centre, Cowichan Tribes, 1999.

Miller, J. R. *Shingwauk's Vision: History of Native Residential Schools.* Toronto: University of Toronto Press, 1996.

———. *Skyscrapers Hide the Heavens: A History of Indian-White Relations in Canada.* [3rd ed.] Toronto: University of Toronto Press, 2000.

Milloy, John Sheridan. *A National Crime: The Canadian Government and the Residential School System, 1879 to 1986.* Winnipeg: University of Manitoba Press, 1999.

———. *The Plains Cree: Trade, Diplomacy and War, 1790 to 1870.* Winnipeg: University of Manitoba Press, 1988.

Monet, Don, and Skanu'u (Ardythe Wilson). *Colonialism on Trial: Indigenous Land Rights and the Gitksan Wet'suwet'en Sovereignty Case.* Gabriola Island, B.C.: New Society Publishers, 1991.

Neel, David. *Our Chiefs and Elders.* Vancouver: University of British Columbia Press, 1992.

Newell, Dianne. *Tangled Webs of History: Indians and the Law in Canada's Pacific Coast Fisheries.* Toronto: University of Toronto Press, 1993.

Neylan, Susan. *The Heavens Are Changing: Nineteenth-century Protestant Missions and Tsimshian Christianity.* Montreal: McGill-Queen's University Press, 2003.

Pannekoek, Frits. *A Snug Little Flock: The Social Origins of the Riel Resistance of 1869–1870.* Winnipeg: Watson & Dwyer, 1991.

Peers, Laura. *The Ojibwa of Western Canada, 1780–1870.* St. Paul: Minnesota Historical Society Press, 1994.

Peterson, Jacqueline, and Jennifer S. H. Brown, eds. *The New Peoples: Being and Becoming Métis in North America.* Winnipeg: University of Manitoba Press, 1984.

Petrone, Penny, ed. *First People, First Voices.* Toronto: University of Toronto Press, 1983.

———. *Northern Voices: Inuit Writing in English.* Toronto: University of Toronto Press, 1988.

Raunet, Daniel. *Without Surrender, Without Consent.* Vancouver: Douglas & McIntyre, 1984.

Ray, Arthur J. *The Canadian Fur Trade in the Industrial Age.* Toronto: University of Toronto Press, 1990.

———. *Indians in the Fur Trade.* Toronto: University of Toronto Press, 1974.

Ray, Arthur J., and Donald B. Freeman. *Give Us Good Measure: An Economic Analysis of Relations Between the Indians and the Hudson's Bay Company before 1763.* Toronto: University of Toronto Press, 1978.

Ray, Arthur J., J. R. Miller, and Frank Tough. *Bounty and Benevolence: A History of Saskatchewan Treaties.* Montreal: McGill-Queen's University Press, 2000.

Richardson, Boyce. *Strangers Devour the Land: A Chronicle of the Assault upon the Last Coherent Hunting Culture in North America, the Cree Indians of Northern Quebec, and Their Vast Primeval Homelands.* Toronto: Macmillan, 1975.

Richardson, Boyce, ed. *Drumbeat: Anger and Renewal in Indian Country.* Toronto: Summerhill Press with the Assembly of First Nations, 1989.

Salisbury, Richard F. *A Homeland for the Cree: Regional Development in James Bay, 1971–1981.* Montreal: McGill-Queen's University Press, 1986.

Schmalz, Peter S. *The Ojibwa of Southern Ontario*. Toronto: University of Toronto Press, 1991.

Sewid, James. *Guests Never Leave Hungry: The Autobiography of James Sewid, Kwakiutl Indian*. Edited by James Spradley. New Haven: Yale University Press, 1969.

Sprague, D. N. *Canada and the Métis, 1869–1885*. Waterloo, Ont.: Wilfrid Laurier University Press, 1988.

Sprague, D. N., and R. P. Frye. *The Genealogy of the First Métis Nation*. Winnipeg: Pemmican Publications, 1983.

Sturtevant, William C., ed. *Handbook of North American Indians*. Vol. 4, 5, 6, 7, 15. Washington: Smithsonian Institution Press, 1988, 1984, 1981, 1990, 1978.

Tanner, Helen H., ed. *Atlas of Great Lakes Indian History*. Norman: Published for the Newberry Library by the University of Oklahoma Press, 1987.

Tennant, Paul. *Aboriginal Peoples and Politics: The Indian Land Question in British Columbia, 1849–1989*. Vancouver: University of British Columbia Press, 1990.

Tester, Frank, and Peter Kulchyski. *Tammarniit (Mistakes): Inuit Relocation in the Eastern Arctic, 1939–63*. Vancouver: University of British Columbia Press, 1994.

Tetso, John. *Trapping Is My Life*. Toronto: Peter Martin Associates, 1970.

Titley, E. Brian. *A Narrow Vision: Duncan Campbell Scott and the Administration of Indian Affairs in Canada*. Vancouver: University of British Columbia Press, 1986.

Tough, Frank. *"As Their Resources Fail": Native People and the Economic History of Northern Manitoba, 1870–1930*. Vancouver: University of British Columbia Press, 1996.

Trigger, Bruce G. *The Children of Aataentsic: A History of the Huron People to 1660*. Montreal: McGill-Queen's University Press, 1976.

———. *Natives and Newcomers: Canada's "Heroic Age" Reconsidered*. Montreal: McGill-Queen's University Press, 1985.

Upton, Leslie Francis Stokes. *Micmacs and Colonists: Indian–White Relations in the Maritimes, 1713–1867*. Vancouver: University of British Columbia Press, 1979.

Van Kirk, Sylvia. *Many Tender Ties: Women in Fur Trade Society in Western Canada, 1670–1870*. Winnipeg: Watson & Dwyer, 1980.

Weaver, Sally M. *Making Canadian Indian Policy: The Hidden Agenda 1968–1970*. Toronto: University of Toronto Press, 1981.

Whitehead, Ruth Holmes. *The Old Man Told Us: Excerpts from Micmac History, 1500–1950*. Halifax: Nimbus Publishing, 1991.

Wicken, William Craig. *Mi'kmaq Treaties on Trial: History, Land and Donald Marshall Junior*. Toronto: University of Toronto Press, 2002.

PICTURE SOURCES

Sources of black-and-white illustrations are as below. For reasons of space the following abbreviations have been used

AGNS: Art Gallery of Nova Scotia, Halifax
BCAR: British Columbia Archives and Records Service, Victoria
CP: Canapress Photo Service, Toronto
GAA: Glenbow Alberta Archives, Calgary
MM: McCord Museum of Canadian History, McGill University, Montreal
MTRL: Metropolitan Toronto Reference Library
NAC: National Archives of Canada, Ottawa
PAM: Provincial Archives of Manitoba
PAM/EMC: Provincial Archives of Manitoba, Edmund Morris Collection
PAM/HBC: Provincial Archives of Manitoba, Hudson's Bay Company Collection
RBCM: Royal British Columbia Museum, Victoria
ROM: Royal Ontario Museum, Toronto
VPL: Vancouver Public Library

Front Matter: Page ii: NAC (C-117917); vi: NAC (PA-122634); viii: NAC (PA-129886), photo Richard Harrington: xviii: PAM/EMC (EMN87)   **Chapter One:** Page 2: RBCM (PN#11733); 4: MM, Rare Book Collection (M11712); 7: NAC (C-142559), artist anonymous; 8: GAA (NA-1532-6); 9: NAC (PA-44223); 11: NAC (PA-112085); 12: GAA (NA-1338-111); 14: GAA (NA-667-72); 17: BCAR (C-9278).   **Chapter Two:** Page 23: NAC (C-1994); 24: PAM/EMC (EMN 498); 26: BCAR (A-6052); 28: GAA (NA-1338-98); 30: PAC/EMC (EMN 196); 31: NAC (C-142558), artist anonymous; 33: NAC (CO-9894); 34: Provincial Archives of Alberta, Ernest Brown Collection (B1004); 35: GAA (NA-667-640); 37: NAC (PA-181715), photo R. F. Waugh.   **Chapter Three:** Page 39: History Collection, Nova Scotia Museum, Halifax, photo Olive and Arthur Kelsall (NSM 59.60.3, neg. N-14, 501); 43: NAC (C-142560), artist anonymous; 44: NAC (C-94132).   **Chapter Four:** Page 47: NAC (C-17159); 49: NAC, Map Division (NMC-52408); 53: National Maritime Museum, Greenwich, London (1048), De Bray, 1602; 56: NAC (CO-16427); 59: NAC (C-5749).   **Chapter Five:** Page 61: Ontario Ministry of Tourism and Recreation, Huronia Historical Parks; 64: NAC (C-42419); 67: NAC (C-142557); 68: ROM, Archaeological Report, 1904 (NS 26988); 74: NAC (C-1225). **Chapter Six:** Page 80: NAC, Map Division (NMC-13295); 82: GAA (NA-1344-3); 83: PAM/HBC (HBCA, P-417/N8263); 87: PAM/HBC (HBCA/N11181); 91: PAM/EMC (EMN607); 92: GAA (NA-3225-2).   **Chapter Seven:** Page 94: NAC (C-35062), artist anonymous; 96: PAM/HBC (HBCA FC 3212.2 H4/N7926); 98: NAC (PA-74670); 99: GAA (NA-667-343); 101: NAC (C-1922); 105: NAC (C-2773), artist F. A. Hopkins; 109: PAM, John Kerr Collection (97460).   **Chapter Eight:** Page 113: NAC (C-70681); 114: NAC (C-38616), artist John Webber; 116: PAM/HBC, *The Beaver* magazine (June–July 1987); 117: BCAR (A-6067); 120: NAC (C-33614).   **Chapter Nine:** Page 123: NAC (C-

47435); 124: NAC (C-2035); 125: NAC (C-105765), artist Benjamin West; 132: MTRL, artist Robert Lugger (971.3.C4); 133: MTRL, artist James Peachey (971.3.C4); 137: MTRL, J. Ross Robertson Collection (T1660).   **Chapter Ten:** Page 143: NAC (C-38862), artist Henrietta Martha Hamilton; 144: NAC (C-28542), artist unknown; 145: NAC (C-28544), artist Shanawdithit; 148: NAC (C-847), artist Mary M. Chaplin; 151: NAC (C-121244), artist John Arthur Roebuck; 152: NAC (C-40312), artist John Bartlet; 154: Archives of Ontario (S-18174); 158: Archives of Ontario (S-16361). **Chapter Eleven:** Page 161: from Robert M. Ballantyne's *Hudson Bay: Or Everyday Life in the Wilds of North America;* 163: GAA (NA-1344-6), artist Lt. Robert Hood; 166: GAA (NA-1406-5), artist W. A. Rogers; 168: NAC (C-40149), artist Paul Kane; 169: GAA (NA-667-341); 170: GAA (NA-1406-47), artist W. A. Rogers; 175: PAM/HBC (HBCA B.154/Z/1 fo. 421/N3996).   **Chapter Twelve:** Page 179: PAM (N8741); 183: RBCM (PN#8247); 185: BCAR (A-01679); 188: RBCM (PN#8770); 191: BCAR (F-8291); 192: BCAR (D-692).   **Chapter Thirteen:** Page 195: GAA (NA-1406-26); 197: GAA (NA-1406-10); 198: Manitoba Museum of Man and Nature (3661); 200: GAA (NA-47-10), artist Henri Julien; 204: GAA (NA-1406-91).   **Chapter Fourteen:** Page 207: GAA (NA-4928-2); 208: GAA (NA-1406-72); 210: GAA (NA-1677-10); 214: GAA (NA-1769-1); 218: GAA (NA-1104-1); 219: GAA (NA-3432-2); 220: PAM (N9300); 221: GAA (NA-3205-11).   **Chapter Fifteen:** Page 223: NAC (PA-11216), photo W. Topley; 225: BCAR (G-210); 231: GAA (NA-1241-114); 232: NAC (C-33643); 235: GAA (NA-689-1); 237: GAA (NA-1223-7); 239: GAA (NA-5-15); 240: MTRL/Sessional Papers, Department of Indian Affairs Annual Report, 1895; 241: MTRL/Sessional Papers, Department of Indian Affairs Annual Report, 1895; 242: GAA (NA-1954-9).   **Chapter Sixteen:** Page 245: GAA (NA-1906-6); 247: photo Colin R. Pratt (1905–1983), photo in possession of Winona Stevenson; 253: GAA (NA-127-1); 255: GAA (NA-13-2); 257: GAA (NA-929-1); 260: GAA (NA-949-137); 262: BCAR (F-6822); 263: GAA (NB-44-17); 264: GAA (NA-190-1); 265: NAC (C-140133).   **Chapter Seventeen:** Page 269: GAA (NA-1338-102); 270: GAA (NA-1338-117); 273: PAM/EMC (EMN 284/N16551); 276: PAM/HBC (HBC 1987/363-T-220.1/3/N7266); 282: PAM (N7100); 285: NAC, Department of the Interior (PA-48099); 286: GAA (NA-4035-98); 287: NAC, Department of the Interior (C-73182); 288: PAM/HBC (HBC-79-107); 289: NAC, Department of Indian Affairs (PA-96687); 290: Archives of Ontario (S-4013); 291: NAC, Department of the Interior (PA-42115). **Chapter Eighteen:** Page 293: BCAR (E-6125); 294: BCAR (A-4170); 295: BCAR (D-08372); 297: VPL (2045); 298: NAC (PA-41175), photo George Menier; 300: NAC (PA-117152); 301: BCAR (C-9266); 305: NAC (C-34793).   **Chapter Nineteen:** Page 314: NAC (C-138082); 316: NAC (PA-194551); 317: Courtesy of Affa Loft Matteson, in collection of Donald B. Smith (Woodland Cultural Centre); 318: GAA (NA-5-16); 331: NAC (PA-164775); 333: CP; 335: CP.   **Chapter Twenty:** Page 339: NAC (PA-164787); 341: Courtesy of Air Creebec; 344: NAC (PA-194556); 345: NAC (PA-193047); 346: NAC (PA-167630); 352: CP, photo Moe Doiron; 353: CP, photo Ray Giguere; 355: GAA (NA-4890-5); 358: CP, photo Frank Gunn; 360: Courtesy of Sim'oogit 'Wii Muk'wilixu; 366: *Vancouver Sun,* photo Steve Bosch.   **Chapter Twenty-one:** Page 363: Courtesy of the artist; 366: BCAR (H-06862); 370: CP, photo Fred Chartrand; 372: CP, photo Tom Hanson; 375: BCAR (I-33187); 377: BCAR (HP 27037); 380: AGNS (1994–229); 384: CP, photo by Jacques Boissinot. **Chapter Twenty-two:** 388: GAA (NA-2-8); 391: CP, Tom HansonTK; 393: photo by Fred Cattroll; 394: photo by Arthur J. Ray; 397: Sault Ste Marie: Indian Fishermen [ca. 1880], Archives of Ontario, F1132-2-1-2 (ST 1226).

ACKNOWLEDGEMENTS

I am grateful to the staffs of the British Library; the British Columbia Archives and Record Service and the Royal British Columbia Museum; the Glenbow Museum and Archives, especially Andrea Garnier; the Provincial Archives of Manitoba Picture Division and the Hudson's Bay Company Archives, especially Judith Beatie, Anne Morton, and Debra Moore; the Documentary Art and Photograph Division of the National Archives of Canada, especially Irene Van Bael; the Public Record Office, Kew Gardens; the University of Edinburgh Library; and the Royal Museum of Scotland.

I would like to thank the Social Sciences and Humanities Research Council of Canada and the University of British Columbia for the generous financial support that enabled me to research various aspects of the economic history of Canada's Aboriginal people. As student research assistants over the years, Wayne Campbell, Tara Crittenden, David Dmitrisanovic, Chris Elsner, Brian Foreman, Arif Lalani, Paulette Reagan, Romana Rose, Susan Roy, Meghan Schlase, Terri Thompson, and Pam White made valuable contributions to this work. I also owe a debt of gratitude to the students of my Native history courses in the Geography Department at York University and the History Department at the University of British Columbia for their many stimulating insights and for arousing my interest in the visual dimension of this history.

I owe special debts of gratitude to Winona Stevenson for sharing her insights into Native responses to Christian missionaries in the prairie region and providing me with a photo of her ancestor, Charles Pratt; to Julie Cruikshank for her advice concerning legends, myths, and stories; to Dan Marshall and Brenda Ireland for generously providing access to their graduate research findings concerning Aboriginal people's involvement in the gold rushes and trapline-registration programs of British Columbia, respectively; to Frank Tough, for his insights into the economic history of Aboriginal people, especially the Métis, and for giving me a photograph of Métis scrip; to Louise Mandel and Stuart Rush for their advice regarding historical legal issues; and to Richard Unger for identifying the type and probable date of the European vessel depicted in the Mi'kmaq rock painting from Kejimkujik National Park, Nova Scotia. My special thanks to the editorial staffs of Lester Publishing and Key Porter Books, especially publisher Malcolm Lester for his unwavering support for this project, Barbara Hehner, Laurie Coulter, Janice Weaver, and Alison Reid for their help, and also to Stuart Daniel (Starshell Maps, Victoria) for his imaginative cartography.

While on sabbatical during the final stages of this project, I received crucial support services from the staffs of Maison du Canada, Cité Internationale Université de Paris, and the International Social Sciences Institute of the University of Edinburgh. The generous hospitality of various friends and colleagues, including Lise and Trent Appelbe, Martin Farrell, and Ged Martin, Director of the Canadian Studies Institute and Deputy Director of the International Social Sciences Institute, Edinburgh University, has been greatly appreciated.

Most of all I would like to thank Dianne Newell for making the completion of this project possible through her steady support, the sharing of her many valuable insights, and her editorial commentary on the various drafts of the manuscript. The responsibility for the contents of the book rests solely with me.

INDEX

Page numbers in italics refer to illustrations or captions.

ARTHUR J. RAY is professor emeritus at the University of British Columbia, special-
izing in the historical geography of the Native people of Canada. He is the author
of, among other books, *Indians in the Fur Trade*, and he contributed the Native history
section of the *Illustrated History of Canada*. He is a fellow of the Royal Society of
Canada and recipient of the Canada Killam Research, Bora Laskin, and Woodrow
Wilson fellowships. He has appeared as an expert in numerous Aboriginal and treaty
rights cases, including the landmark cases of *Delgamuukw*, *Horseman*, and *Powley*.